RESHAPING REGIONAL PLANNING

Reshaping Regional Planning
A Northern perspective

Edited by

FOLKE SNICKARS
Department of Infrastructure and Planning,
Royal Institute of Technology, Stockholm, Sweden

BRITA OLERUP
Department of Industrial Economics and Management,
Royal Institute of Technology, Stockholm, Sweden

LARS OLOF PERSSON
Department of Infrastructure and Planning,
Royal Institute of Technology, Stockholm, Sweden

Ashgate

Published by
Ashgate Publishing Limited
Gower House
Croft Road
Aldershot
Hampshire GU11 3HR
England

Ashgate Publishing Company
131 Main Street
Burlington, VT 05401-5600 USA

Ashgate website: http://www.ashgate.com

British Library Cataloguing in Publication Data
Reshaping regional planning. - (Urban and regional planning
        and development)
        1.Regional planning 2.Regional planning - Sweden
        I.Snickars, Folke, 1944- II.Olerup, Brita III.Persson, Lars
        Olof
        307.1'2

Library of Congress Control Number: 2001097636

ISBN 0 7546 1258 9

Printed and bound by Athenaeum Press, Ltd.,
Gateshead, Tyne & Wear.

Contents

PART V: REGIONAL EVALUATION OF POLICY PROCESSES

Contributors

Björn Alfredsson is a private consultant and author in the field of regional planning. He is based in Stockholm.

Åke E. Andersson is Professor of Infrastructure Economics at the Royal Institute of Technology. In 1995 he received the Honda Prize for his analyses of the dynamic interactions between the ecological, economic and technological systems.

Christer Anderstig is Associate Professor at the Department of Infrastructure and Planning, and Head of the Economics Division at Inregia AB, a Stockholm-based private consultancy firm. He has been in charge of developing RAPS, a regional economic and demographic model system for Sweden. Currently he is engaged in an impact evaluation project, which aims at assessing the regional development consequences of the fixed link across the Öresund strait.

Patrik Arousell is a Ph.D. student at the Department of Infrastructure and Planning and holds a Master of Science in Economics from the University of Karlstad. His main research interest is within regional economic modelling, related to input-output analysis and entropy modelling.

Eva Asplund is Senior Researcher at the Department of Infrastructure and Planning. She is currently leader of the project The Municipality and the Territory, one of four projects in the large Swedish research program The Sustainable City. Previous research has been on EIA as a tool in comprehensive planning (together with Tuija Hilding-Rydevik) and on competence in local governments to handle sustainability in comprehensive planning (together with Lars Orrskog). Eva Asplund has more than 25 years' experience of comprehensive planning at the Office of Regional Planning and Urban Transportation, Stockholm County Council.

Sten Axelsson has done extensive research on historical and contemporary processes that shape administrative and functional regions. He has a Ph.D.

in regional planning containing a dissertation about firms and regions working in networks. He currently holds a position at the Swedish National Board for Industrial and Technical Development.

Martin J. Beckmann is Professor of Applied Mathematics at the Technical University of Munich, Germany and Professor of Economics at Brown University, Providence, RI. He is the author of numerous path-breaking scientific papers and books in economics, transport analysis and optimization theory.

Göran Cars is Associate Professor and Deputy Head at the Department of Infrastructure and Planning. His professional expertise lies in issues concerning urban governance and residential and neighbourhood development. A specific focus is directed towards possibilities for upgrading deteriorating neighbourhoods. Research on this activity has included studies not only on specific housing districts but also of the interplay between neighbourhood development and municipal planning. Göran Cars has published extensively on housing and community development. His practical experience includes consulting for the Swedish Association for Municipal Housing Companies.

Vania A. Ceccato is a Ph.D. candidate at the Department of Infrastructure and Planning and Research Fellow at the Nordic Center for Spatial Development, Nordregio. A native of Brazil, Vania Ceccato's research interest is in the field of quality of life assessment with a spatial perspective. During recent years, this interest has become strongly linked with the use of tangible and less tangible indicators, using Geographic Information Systems and spatial statistics as a platform for analysis. She is presently involved in an international collaborative project analyzing the importance of less tangible indicators to explain economic performance in Swedish rural areas.

Sylvia Dovlén is a Ph.D. student at the Department of Infrastructure and Planning. She comes from an earlier education in natural science at Stockholm University. Her research interests are communicative planning theory and the practice of environmental planning.

Tigran Hasic is working as a University Lecturer at the Department of Infrastructure and Planning and pursues doctoral studies in built environment analysis. He holds degrees in architecture, urban design and planning, international space studies and environmental engineering, from

USA, former Yugoslavia and Sweden, having published several articles in the mentioned fields. He has been involved in teaching in international educational programs such as real estate management, environmental engineering and sustainable infrastructure. His expertise and current research focus concern post-conflict reconstruction of urban settlements, development of sustainable communities and project management.

Maria Håkansson is a Ph.D. student at the Department of Infrastructure and Planning. She is a land surveyor and planner, educated at the Royal Institute of Technology. Her current research interest is environmental management at local administration level, with a focus on professional performance and culture, and the dynamics in the interaction among public and private actors.

Mattias Höjer is a Ph.D. in regional planning. His main field of interest is the relation between sustainable development, information technology, transport and urban form. Working with a long-term perspective, he investigates developments that could be more desirable from a sustainable development perspective, rather than a development along current trends. He is working closely together with the Environmental Strategies Research Group, Stockholm University.

Mats Johansson is Ph.D. and Associate Professor in Economic History at Lund University as well as Research Leader at the Swedish Institute for Growth Policy Studies, Östersund. He also works as senior lecturer at the Mid-Sweden University in Östersund, and he is involved in several research projects with colleagues within the Department of Infrastructure and Planning.

Stig Knutsson holds a Ph.D. from the Department of Infrastructure and Planning. His research interest and current research deal with special transport services, rider quality, and combined transport and urban and regional planning. He is also interested in welfare, housing and home systems for elderly and disabled residents. Stig Knutsson has work experience as a social worker and worked fifteen years as Head of a Community Social Services Department in Dalarna County.

After finishing the School of Architecture at the Royal Institute of Technology, *Magnus Löfvenberg* practiced in Stockholm and Berlin. In addition he graduated from the Royal University College of Fine Arts' School of Architecture 1996. He has been engaged in research at the Royal

Institute of Technology since 1993, first at the Department of Design Theory and, since 1996, at the Department of Infrastructure and Planning in a project concerning culture, jobs and regional development. Currently he is finishing his licentiate thesis on cultural clusters and their regional context.

Brita Olerup, formerly at the Department of Infrastructure and Planning, now a Senior Researcher in the Department of Industrial Economics and Management, Royal Institute of Technology. She received her Ph.D. in Environmental and Energy Systems Studies at Lund University. Her research interests concern social science aspects of changing the present energy system towards one with sustainability. Articles of hers have been published in journals of business administration, energy policy and environmental management.

Krister Olsson is a Ph.D. candidate at the Department of Infrastructure and Planning. He holds a civil engineering degree in planning. His professional interest lies in questions concerning culture and especially the role of cultural heritage in societal development. Research on this activity has included studies not only on public heritage management but also on the interplay between public and private interests in development planning.

Lars Orrskog is Architect and Associate Professor in regional planning. He is teacher and researcher at the Department of Infrastructure and Planning, where he teaches land-use planning for sustainable development. His research is directed towards planning obstacles to sustainability in planning procedures. He specializes in planning theory.

Senior Research Fellow *Lars Olof Persson* is currently associated both with the Department of Infrastructure and Planning at the Royal Institute of Technology and the Nordic Centre for Spatial Development (Nordregio), both in Stockholm. With an academic background in human and economic geography, he has been doing research on regional development and policy issues in several positions linked to the Ministry of Industry, Stockholm. He is currently specializing in human resource management, labor mobility and policy evaluation.

Amy Rader Olsson is a Ph.D. candidate in regional planning at the Royal Institute of Technology. She also serves as a consultant on issues of sustainable transportation planning and regional development planning at Inregia AB in Stockholm. A native of the United States, Amy Olsson has been involved in regional planning and transportation issues for over ten years. Her research interests include regional governance, culture as a regional economic development factor, and urban mobility planning.

Christer Sanne, M.Sc, Ph.D. With a background in urban planning and futures studies, Sanne has written several books on work and in particular the issue of working hours which is used as a hub for analyzing the development and problems of the welfare state. At present he is concerned with sustainable consumption and how lifestyles in the rich parts of the world can be adjusted to meet ecological limits.

Folke Snickars is Professor of Regional Planning at the Royal Institute of Technology. He has been the President of the European Regional Science Association and published widely on urban and regional modelling and infrastructure policy analysis.

Jan Wiman is a Senior Architect working at the Office for Regional Planning and Urban Transportation, Stockholm County Council. He also teaches physical planning to architecture students at the Royal Institute of Technology.

Pontus Åberg has an MBA in economics and has recently finished his licentiate thesis in regional planning at the Royal Institute of Technology. His research interests cover regional economics, international and interregional trade and commuting behavior. He is also a consultant in trade analysis and regional economics at Temaplan AB, Stockholm.

Preface

Across Europe, traditional regional planning is eventually reoriented into more integrated spatial planning approaches. This volume contains twenty analyses of contemporary regional issues – predominantly those emerging in the Nordic context – and associated methods which are being developed in regional research. Altogether, these contributions reflect dominating directions of research and development in the beginning of the 21st century, as well as the need for continued reshaping of planning paradigms and practices. Hence, the volume could be seen as a bridge from an era focusing on physical planning to new regional worlds, where cultural issues and visions of sustainable communities as well as quality of life appear as equally important.

This volume is based on a longstanding process of research co-operation within the academic and professional networks of the Department of Regional Planning, Royal Institute of Technology, Stockholm. The process involves distinguished and senior scholars as well as young regional scientists. The process has been co-ordinated by Professor Folke Snickars, Senior Researcher Brita Olerup and Senior Research Fellow Lars Olof Persson, who have also edited the volume.

This volume could not have been completed successfully without the cooperation, on one hand between the editors and our stringent and patient secretary Gunvor Albihn and, on the other hand, with the equally strict and patient editorial staff at Ashgate Publishing Limited.

Folke Snickars   Brita Olerup   Lars Olof Persson

PART I
CHALLENGING THE SCOPE
OF PLANNING

Introduction

FOLKE SNICKARS
BRITA OLERUP
LARS OLOF PERSSON

The evolution of regional planning is driven by social, political and economic changes in contemporary Europe. On the one hand, there is a strong tendency towards internationalization of the economies, a deregulation in several fields of economic activity and an increasing supranational involvement in policy and planning, particularly in the fields of monetary policy, transport, social cohesion and environmental planning.

On the other hand, there is a regionalization of democratic responsibility for local issues, in line with the principle of subsidiarity. Regional planning is widening its scope from predominantly physical planning issues, to integrated planning approaches to develop each region's unique resources, to improve competitiveness in economic terms and sustainability in ecological terms.

Spatial issues as hard technical infrastructure are still core areas of regional planning, but increasingly the issues of soft infrastructure provision and environmental concern are entering the planning agenda. Regional planning thus needs to encompass the interests of several actors – public agencies, private firms, non-governmental organizations and lobbying groups – who interact with one another in negotiations when designing and implementing programs and projects.

This book provides a comprehensive analysis of issues and methods in regional planning in a northern perspective by offering twenty contributions from regional researchers active in a single research environment in Sweden. It can be seen as a specimen of current research issues pointing out directions in which regional planning needs to be reshaped. Our intention has been to establish a platform for continued and long-term knowledge creation.

Starting from a description of the evolution of the regional planning institutions in Sweden until today, the first part of the volume analyses current challenges to the planning systems. The focus is on economic-geographical, social and environmental factors, which have to be addressed in the near future.

The second part deals with specific planning issues, where each author stresses the increasing importance of integrating infrastructure development programs with social planning issues, such as human resource and quality-of-life management. In the third part, planning at the local level is reviewed and new emerging roles of planners in this new context are suggested. New issues need a different planning process, and a different planning profession, in which the informal culture of planning needs to be considered.

Mathematical as well as qualitative models are being used in both forecasting and scenario building. Examples of different model approaches in regional planning form the fourth part of the volume. The fifth part concerns problems and methods of evaluation in regional planning. The purpose is to illustrate parts of the wide range of problems which have to be subject for evaluation and the corresponding methodological problems that arise.

On the basis of these contributions, we observe and envisage further restructuring of regional planning to a more inclusive, collaborative, communicative and continuous democratic process. The recent development of the European spatial development planning illustrates that this is not a specific Nordic trajectory. It reflects the dualization of the economic, social, and political life towards both internationalization and regionalization. Spatial planning means a shift for national-level planning to international, still retaining the conflict between sectoral and comprehensive issues.

Social cohesion, culture, and human resources emerge as important targets in regional planning as infrastructure development and ecological sustainability. This calls for a need for considerable broadening of the scope and the competence of the corps of regional planners. We envisage an emerging new role of planners, where science-based analyses of regional options and threats continuously have to be debated and confronted directly with all parties concerned. Partnerships between different public sector agencies, local, regional and central governments, and private and public actors will have to be the rule rather than the exception in developing and implementing regional programs as well as projects.

Evaluation will need to be an ongoing process in regional planning, necessary to keep the information lines accessible to all parties involved and to ensure democracy as well as efficiency in any program or project. Evaluation of the planning process as such will be in high demand in this period of rapid reshaping of regional planning.

Part I: Challenging the Scope of Planning

Björn Alfredsson and *Jan Wiman* at the outset of the book outline the fundamentals of the current Swedish system for physical planning, i.e. the legislation, the main planning instruments, and the actors and authorities involved on different levels. In particular, they explain the importance of the comparatively strong position of the municipalities, incorporating both urban and rural areas, in Swedish planning.

The first part of the book contains four chapters. The authors of these describe economic, social, and environmental changes that have influenced but also will influence physical planning activities at the local and regional levels. The final solutions to these challenges remain hidden in the future, but each author makes some suggestions.

Sten Axelsson is concerned with the shaping of local authority districts in Sweden. These traits are valid in an international context, but Sweden has a comparatively strong local level and a weak regional level. He describes their evolution during the last 150 years. Geographical extents have varied over time mainly because of transportation possibilities and self-imposed duties in the form of public services in support of societal changes. The number of local authority districts is now one-tenths of what they were previously, but half of them have less than 15,000 inhabitants. However, a larger population basis and a wider geographical area will make planning regional.

In several planning areas there is now a need for a further expanded co-operation between local districts. Functional and administrative areas are once again about to be separated.

Christer Anderstig points out that strategic regional planning is shifting in focus from merely physical planning to a three-folded concept encompassing economic, social, and environmental considerations. He argues that this leads to an increased demand for analytical tools including formal models. As an example he uses the transportation situation in the Stockholm region when discussing some important issues in long-term traffic planning.

One of them is to manage conflicting interests and to identify viable compromising solutions. The focus in planning is thus changing from prescribing solutions to providing problem analyses and decision support. A neutral mediator with sharp analytical skills could then be of help so as to establish a common platform.

Christer Sanne launches the idea that the goals of planning are to keep societal change within specified limits, arguing for planning with a ceiling. According to him, the planning discourse has realized that natural resources are finite in the long term. It has, nevertheless, failed to handle the conflict with other interests, such as an expanding production aiming for a short-term economic growth. He points out that planning authorities already dispose of certain means to improve the situation, e.g. monitoring schemes, technology procurement, traffic planning, and social innovations. It would be more controversial to suggest changes in lifestyle. Planners could, however, facilitate change by their expertise in handling uncertainty. Their task is to point at inconsistent signals given by society to its citizens and to question rationality as a guiding principle.

These four chapters all delineate an increasingly complex situation that planners have to learn to manage. On the one hand, there is a need for models to systematize those values that are possible to deal with in this manner. On the other hand, there is the need to acknowledge political processes and to suggest improvements in their functioning. Each subject is dealt with further in the following parts of the book. Their common denominator is a call for multidisciplinary studies, where different experts from scientific and practical fields co-operate with one another.

Part II: Emerging Issues for Planning Actions

This part of the book addresses emerging planning problems and the need for development of new tools to be able to address them. The five contributions focus on cultural planning in a regional development context, human resource management, social cohesion and quality-of-life issues. Each of them includes empirically-based analysis of the current problems and options at hand on the Swedish arena.

Magnus Löfvenberg states that in current socio-economic change, many horizontal networks are replacing the hierarchical structures of the industrial era. In this process, cultural industries are looked upon as being some of the key generators of future economic development. Cultural production transforms the former materialistic production into a symbolic economy. The author puts the question: if the economy is increasingly revolving around the production of symbols – who are the initiators of these chains of symbols? How do these symbol-creators work? This chapter originates from a series of interviews with a creative core of members of cultural industries and with persons closely connected to these activities. The aim is to capture what circumstances these professionals have to face, with the assumption of regarding the groups as pioneers for a rising network society. With the emerging understanding of this new paradigm follows a call for the institutional structure of cultural policy to be updated.

Amy Rader Olsson states that in modern democratic societies, global markets steer development, populations are increasingly able to contribute to planning decisions, and technological change continues to offer new opportunities and problems. Governments must accept a limited capacity to directly induce change and an increased demand for direct citizen participation. Planners must now adapt to new forms of governance. In this essay, governance is defined as the process of making and implementing decisions on behalf of a group.

The author contends, however, that the overriding goal of planners to enable sound decisions by governors has not changed. Nowadays, decisions faced by regions involve constant adaptation, experimentation, and negotiation. Hence, planners must develop expertise in communicative theory, in forecasting future developments, and in recognizing social, environmental, or economic patterns which offer opportunities or threats to the region's well being. This includes the analysis and evaluation of previously implemented policies. Planners must also be communicators, offering their expertise to a variety of stakeholders and perhaps negotiating among the diverse wishes of a large group of stakeholders debating a specific policy. The author concludes that planners must have the capability to synthesize and organize information in such a way as to enable decision-makers to choose among current policy alternatives.

When markets are opened up and new technology is available, regions as well as corporations have to deal with complexity and uncertainty. Against this background, *Lars Olof Persson* discusses the importance of human resource management in regional planning. One of the most important prerequisites for economic growth and social cohesion is an efficient matching of the demand and the supply of labor at different qualification levels. Local labor market performance becomes more strategic as regional policy is gradually decentralized to the regional level.

One conclusion is that increased local production of human capital is more or less necessary in order to promote new knowledge-based industry particularly in the numerous small local labor market areas which are typical in the Nordic countries. This means that location of higher education facilities is a key factor. Another conclusion is that regional enlargement through a more extensive commuting, is more or less the only way to increase the diversity and the dynamics of the small local labor markets. However, these possibilities are limited of geographic distance reasons, especially in the sparsely populated parts of the country.

Social exclusion in the European regional context is a key concern for *Göran Cars* and *Mats Johansson*. Equality within different spheres increased during the period from the Second World War up till the 1980s, partly due to ambitious social programs. However, the latter part of the 1990s has been characterized by a rethinking of national policies. Budget constraints and reduced intervention of the public sector have resulted in increasing inequalities between social groups, neighborhoods, and regions. The two authors outline recent developments in Sweden and discuss how they have impacted on labor markets and social welfare. Swedish experiences are then related to international trends and developments. In the concluding part, current responses to stimulate growth and promote social cohesion are presented and discussed. The conclusion is that neither 'place-based' nor 'people-based' strategies are sufficient to achieve effective and substantial improvements within socially excluded neighborhoods. There is a need for strategies that combine these two approaches.

Vania Ceccato argues that quality-of-life analyses should be included in regional analysis and planning aimed at coping with issues of social exclusion. Firstly, she refers to a description of how the concept has historically been approached in Swedish urban planning. According to European Union policy, social cohesion appears to be a new way to deal with such issues.

The second part is a discussion of regional and local policies focusing on the effects of social inward cohesion. Finally, she refers to the use of quality-of-life methods for analyzing social cohesion issues in urban areas. Since studies of quality of life in the Nordic countries often have been an instrument for evaluating the efficiency of welfare state investments, there is a need to shift in planning practices. There is a growing awareness of territorial bases of inequality in society. Policies designed to ameliorate these inequalities have to regard explicit spatial dimensions. Geographical Information Systems are considered as a useful tool for spatial studies of which social analysis seems to be a potential research field.

Each of the five contributions argue for a widening of the scope of regional planning, particularly by focusing more on social and human resource issues linked to infrastructure development. The tools for regional analysis are eventually getting refined, partly by the advent of new statistics and information systems. The demand is recognized for comparative analyses in regional planning and for analysis at different geographical levels, from the scale of the functional local labor market area to the scale of the housing district.

The diversity of the Nordic settlement system provides a specific challenge to regional planning. On the one hand, the few city regions are facing economic and social problems and options very similar to those found in core areas of the European Union. On the other hand, the numerous rural areas and small towns have particular problems in developing attractive living conditions for the new generation and in stabilizing dynamic labor markets.

Part III: Professional Cultures

The three chapters in this part of the book are all concerned with the integration of environmental aspects in planning activities at the local level. Since the integration rarely is successful so far, there is a need for new approaches. Each author departs from the political reality and suggests how environmental planners could improve the process. Their suggestions are based on an understanding of different professional cultures and their interactions.

Eva Asplund questions the capacity at the local level to tackle the problem of sustainable development in planning and strategic action. She focuses on human perspectives in processes operating within the local administration. She claims that a different approach in planning is now essential to improve the balance of exchange between urban and rural areas. First of all there is a need to understand the mechanisms behind the interactions of professionals with different kinds of competencies. Complex problems need a cross-sector co-operation, but there are problems of competition among different departments struggling for power as well as differences in language use and thus problem understanding. An important issue would be to explicitly verbalize the different perspectives and make them transparent to all those taking part in the process. Planners could then function as co-ordinators provided that they realize that they, too, are biased within their profession.

Sylvia Dovlén and *Maria Håkansson* focus on professional performance as a complement to theories on communicative planning, taking the starting point in the sociological theory of professions. They are interested in processes taking place inside the local government. In particular, they study what happens when various planning professions interact with other departments in a municipality and try to integrate their interests. The two professions elucidated are an environmental and health inspector and a local ecologist. In spite of a growing awareness in favor of environmental issues, such professional issues are often neglected in practice. It is then important to understand that any new topic in demand of attention threatens to dethrone not only existing problems but also existing experts. Time and an instinctive feeling for the rules of the game are necessary prerequisites to gain in respect. Successful planning is hence a question of communication.

Lars Orrskog argues that physical planning at the sustained local level with comprehensive ambitions is more or less out of date in Sweden. The dream of a rational planning and building process has remained a dream. He suggests instead an approach originating in a planning-theoretic conception of society in accordance with current economic and social conditions. Such a discourse analysis is based on speeches, texts, and opinions rather than realities. Planning is a suitable application for discourse analyses, since it is an arena built on talk. Consequently, planning in the future would come closer to politics and be less of calculation. He uses the sustainable city as an illustration.

All three chapters suggest that the role of planning should be changed from problem analysis and decision support into a more explicitly political task. However, this could pose a threat to those who in their profession deal with political issues. Political boards and corporate management tend to prefer making their planners into calculators, whereas the planners themselves would prefer a more strategic role. This divergence in perspective will also need to be addressed in the research area. The societal values of planning does not only consist in the preparation for taking the right action but also in the provision of a form for strategic public conversation.

Part IV: Reshaping the Tools for Regional Planning

Mathematical models, computer models and verbal models are used supplementary or in competition analysis, forecasting and scenario building at regional and interregional level. In this part of the book, five examples of different model approaches in regional planning are developed and to some extent evaluated. All of them deal with aspects of local, regional or interregional transportation planning. They provide examples of new tools to address reformed planning matters in a context when market speculations tend to dominate over top-down planning.

Martin Beckmann and Åke E. Andersson state that transportation planning for major urban areas is ultimately an economic decision problem. Political support is needed, no matter how the economic optimum is calculated. They argue that meaningful and operational economic criteria are centered around the so-called consumers' surplus. But they also put forward other objectives for transportation planning, for instance the fiscal goal of maximizing state revenue. Their major concern, however, is the enumeration and valuation of benefits from transportation. The case of Stockholm is discussed where a ring-road of tunnels is an obvious environmental or economical option. Hence, the concluding section of the chapter discusses the long-term consequences of alternatives to new central highways in tunnels. The recommendation is that although some qualitative conclusions can be drawn, quantitative conclusions are needed in order to base decisions on correct estimations of benefits and costs. In such a quantitative evaluation the key factor in determining long-term benefits including external economies will be reflected in increases in land values in areas experiencing increased accessibility.

According to *Patrik Arousell*, the growing importance in the use of quantitative models in regional planning has to do with the globalization of the economy. Reduction of trade barriers between nations means that the national level becomes less relevant for the analysis of economic issues. Instead, the performance of the regional economy would be a more appropriate starting point for analyzing the national economy. He reviews flow distribution models used in regional forecasting, the gravity model, the entropy model and the minimum information model. The theory behind each of the models is presented and recent applications are reviewed. A gravity model has been formulated for the analysis of how reduction of trade barriers between countries affects the regional level. An entropy type model is used to forecast labor demand and supply in a region within a multiregional context. The third model gives an example of how a national input-output model could be partially regionalized with the use of the minimum information model. The ensuing model could be used in estimating the trade coefficients within a multiregional input-output model. The strength of using the minimum information model, is that regionalization can be done in an input-output framework without the costly estimation of trade coefficients. This is particularly important in Sweden, since interregional input-output data are still not regularly available.

Pontus Åberg's chapter aims at evaluating a method of modeling trade, focusing on its ability to predict future trade flows and future transport demand. A method is developed which begins with a trade model in value terms with a following model that estimates commodity values per ton. A combination of these models allows for calculating trade measured in tons. The work is applied on the Baltic Sea region towards the year 2015. The first purpose of the chapter is to analyze whether the concept of commodity value is a good method to forecast trade. As many scholars in transport and regional economics have realized, there is a huge discrepancy in statistics about trade in value terms and trade in tons. There are a number of methods and models to estimate trade between countries measured in value terms. It is also more understandable to find a correlation between for instance trade in value terms and gross regional product. The study includes quantitative results in the growth of trade across the Baltic Sea as a consequence of a future EU membership. Finally, the author discusses how this may affect the future need of infrastructure investments and requirements on the transportation system in the Baltic Sea region.

Mattias Höjer states that a classical task for research on land-use and transport interaction has been to investigate how commuting can be reduced in a city while high access to the labor market is maintained. The chapter deals with this issue, but from a partly new angle. In the first part, literature on the connection between transport demand and urban form is combined with literature on the possible influence from the development of information technology on work organization. This combination displays some new knowledge opportunities. In the second part of the paper, some of these opportunities are exposed in a telecommunication scenario. Working teams are then organized around individuals connected with telecommunications, whereas work mates are found at office hotels where the ordinary work place is situated. Consequently, work mates do not need to be colleagues. This new organizational form suggested by the author facilitates an urban structure organized around a network of nodes for work, telecommunications and public transport.

Tigran Hasic addresses the major challenge to regional planning raised by the fact that during the war, Bosnia and Herzegovina suffered an almost complete destruction of its social systems, physical infrastructure, environment and economy. In the aftermath of this and other man-made disasters, two tasks emerge, the repatriation and resettlement of temporarily homeless persons or internally displaced persons and refugees, and the reconstruction of the basic infrastructure and the economy of the disaster zone. Hence, the key elements that Hasic considers are community, sustainability and post-conflict reconstruction. Sustainability is defined as integrating human patterns and natural systems into habitats which promote stability and placemaking. Within this context the author launches visions of and proposes a model for sustainable urban communities in post-conflict zones. The suggested model differs from conventional thinking as it is based on the principle that it is not solely economic and political factors that matter in a successful policy initiative. It argues that in a complex arena of human settlements arising from crisis situations, no one aspect by itself can result in the success of an initiative. What is required is an approach that integrates and facilitates cooperation among various relevant fields to deliver effective and successful results.

There is an increasing need for both quantitative and qualitative models at the regional level to estimate the regional impact of suggested policy changes and to forecast regional and interregional flows. National data and models are becoming less useful for regional policy analysis. One reason is the globalization of the economy, which makes regions more directly linked to the world markets. These five chapters of the book all deal with the problem of how to overcome lacking information in modeling change at the regional level. In the first paper principles for the selection of baskets of transport investment projects are discussed. In the second case, methods for overcoming the lack of information of interregional input-output data are discussed. In the third case the problems of discrepancy between trade in value and trade in volume are analyzed. In the fourth, focus is on the potential impact of information technology on urban form. All authors suggest and discuss combinations of methods in order to manage the problem of missing relevant information.

Part V: Regional Evaluation of Policy Processes

Several regional planners argue that *ex ante* together with *ex post* evaluations are at the very core of or even synonymous with regional planning. However, this very broad evaluation concept is not used in this concluding part of the book. The three contributions deal with different situations of evaluation. Each of them departs from theories of policy valuation. They emphasize project evaluation rather than program evaluation in regional development.

Krister Olsson is concerned with a model on how to evaluate the preservation of the built heritage. Cultural as well as natural tangible and intangible values in the environment are important for local people as carriers of meaning and identity. At the same time there is a need to develop areas for residences or work places. Local planners thus have to co-ordinate conflicting interests, but there are no guidelines on how to weight different interests against one another. He uses two case studies from the city of Umeå in Sweden to illustrate different interests of the actors involved, suggesting a taxonomy for the cultural built heritage with respect to rivalry and excludability in consumption, direct and indirect use value, option value, and existence value. Public heritage management must draw on the actors' incentives for preservation, and hence their valuation of the built environment as a whole. Knowledge about all actors' preferences are critical in the planning process, not only those of experts.

Stig Knutsson's contribution is oriented towards the situation for the handicapped and elderly in transport planning. He wants to evaluate rider quality in public transport. His model is based on a basic logit model formulation. An index of Rider Quality (IRQ) of Swedish Special Transport Services is provided as a platform for the calculations based on data from the Stockholm region. He compares the Swedish values of five key quality attributes. In addition and as a consequence of the findings a customer profile is presented of low and high willingness to pay for the Special Transport Services.

Finally, a cost-benefit approach is introduced and examined against the empirical results in a consequence scheme. This is done in the light of some actual rationalization strategies in Swedish Special Transport Services in Sweden.

Folke Snickars contributes a paper on the importance of culture for job creation and regional development to the current volume. The research presented is a result of a long-term research program at the Department of Infrastructure and Planning in creating new knowledge about the working of the culture sector in the regional economy. Cultural production is to a large extent a public good with benefits spilling over to most other sectors of the economy. The culture industry thus creates values beyond what is reflected in the market.

An open cultural landscape is as important for the urban economy as an open agricultural landscape for the rural economy. The paper presents empirical results for ongoing investigations of cultural firms seen as innovation carriers in the extended Stockholm region. The aim is to provide new perspectives useful in formulating a role for culture in consumption or production oriented policy strategies for urban and regional development. The chapter adds to the body of literature on policy evaluation through empirical analysis at the establishment level in manufacturing and service industries and among R&D institutions.

The conclusions from these three contributions are that there is a wide field of future regional planning research in developing methods and principles in for evaluation of alternative modes of action. There seems to be a consensus that there has to be developed alternative evaluation methods, which could be used independently or at different planning stages.

The primary importance of articulating the interests of all actors is stressed by all three authors. Hence, evaluation in regional planning means – more than anything else – methods to facilitate the exchange of information between different levels of the public domain, the business environment and the individual sphere.

1 Planning in Sweden

BJÖRN ALFREDSSON
JAN WIMAN[1]

In principle, there is a municipal planning monopoly in Sweden, and the planning system is therefore basically designed for the municipalities. All municipalities must have a comprehensive plan that covers their entire area of responsibility. Although the plan is not binding, it must be kept up to date. The detailed development plan is a legally binding, executive planning instrument – a legal agreement between the municipality, the public and landowners – that makes it possible for the intentions of the comprehensive plan to be implemented. Special area regulations are also binding, and this form of planning is used within limited areas to guarantee compliance with certain comprehensive plan goals. A property regulation plan may be used to facilitate implementation of the detailed development plan. For the planning of matters that are of mutual interest to several municipalities, the national government may appoint a regional planning body with the task of monitoring regional questions and providing basic planning data for municipalities and Government authorities.

In the environmental field, environmental impact assessments are compulsory in certain cases. In order to obtain a permit for implementing measures that affect the environment, public health or the conservation of natural resources to a significant extent, an assessment must be enclosed with the detailed development plan. Consideration will also be given to other environmental and risk factors, in conjunction with comprehensive planning, in order to strengthen the connection with detailed development planning.

Central Concepts in Planning Legislation

'To safeguard the right to employment, housing and education and to promote social care and security, a good living environment' may be said to be the platform for Swedish planning legislation with the Act on

15

Management of Natural Resources (NRL) and the Planning and Building Act (PBL) in the center.

The Act on Management of Natural Resources serves as an umbrella for the Planning and Building Act as well as other special legislation connected with the physical environment. Work is currently in progress on combining the Act on Management of Natural Resources and a number of special acts in the Swedish legal statutes into a so-called environmental code.

The Act on Management of Natural Resources and these special acts focus on four items for protection: public health, the physical environment, the biological diversity and the conservation of natural resources. The acts also highlight geographical areas that are particularly worthy of protection. They also clarify situations in which the national government must make decisions on planning issues, namely in connection with granting permits for major industrial and power generation plants. In these cases, where national interests are felt to weigh more heavily than local interests, a Government permit is required. However, the municipalities can oppose siting decisions since legislation gives them the opportunity to lodge a municipal veto.

The Planning and Building Act provides the practical framework for physical planning. Activities that require permission permits in order to build new structures, demolish or excavate or fill etc. –are subject to certain requirements. The municipalities are to examine whether the activities meet the requirements and, in order to facilitate a review, present the demands in the form of plans. The compulsory comprehensive plan is used to promote public interests. It must be considered in connection with action-oriented planning. Detailed development plans and special area regulations have the character of implementation tools. These plans are both a way of rationalizing permit review and at the same time an instrument of municipal politics for controlling urban development. In the Social Services Act the connection is forged between the physical environment and the well-being of the people. By observing people's living conditions and placing them in relation to their surroundings and the environment, it should be possible to add important knowledge to the planning process. With the participation of social services in planning, a preventive feature is introduced.

Divisions of Responsibility

Detailed development plans and special area regulations become binding when they are adopted by the municipal council. This is accompanied by both rights and obligations on the part of the municipality and individual inhabitants. But the decision has not thereby achieved legal force, because anyone affected by the planned measure, and who is not satisfied with the plan, can appeal it. However, a basic precondition for this is that, when the planning proposal was exhibited for public review, a resident expressed his or her concerns in writing, but these concerns were not taken into account further on in the planning process.

Via the county administrative board, such a matter can be finally settled by the national Government. In conjunction with the adoption of the plan, the county administrative board can review the municipality's decision if it is suspected that national or inter-municipal interests were not satisfied or that public health and safety were jeopardized. Unless an appeal has been made against the decision, or unless the county administrative board reviewed it on its own initiative, the municipal adoption of a plan becomes legal after three weeks.

Decisions concerning comprehensive or regional plans can also be appealed. This is the right of every municipal resident. But it is only the formal administration, or the fact that the municipal council has exceeded its authority, that can serve as the basis for the appeal. The fact that a person is dissatisfied with the content of the plan does not constitute grounds for an appeal, since these plans only serve as a form of guidance and are not binding.

Special Legislation

As for the County of Stockholm, special legislation exists which regulates the implementation of regional planning. The responsibility for this rests with the Stockholm County Council, as the law appoints it as the permanent regional planning body.

Legal Interpretation

As society becomes increasingly complex and the planning tasks have increased, the laws have undergone a general change in character. In the past, laws were to a large extent normative and contained a large number of material stipulations. In time, however, the laws have become more politically goal-oriented at the expense of specific stipulations or so-called framework laws. These laws provide greater latitude for different interpretations. At an administrative level the framework is filled with new codes and the final implementation of the laws are determined by practice.

Framework laws make it possible to change the content and make adaptations relative to prevailing social and political conditions.

In the long term, this means that the interpretations of different laws, which were originally standardized, will in time lead to contradictions. This is a tangible problem within planning legislation, which by nature is based on many laws.

Emphasis on Local Government

In Sweden, there is in principle a municipal planning monopoly, or in other words it is primarily the task of the municipality to plan the use of land and water. The monopoly is granted, however, under certain restrictions The municipalities must give due consideration to the interests of the State. The monopoly is regulated by formal legislative procedures, for example the liability for consultation.

In other areas too, the municipalities have the ultimate responsibility. This applies, for example, to social welfare, the care of children and the elderly, and education up to and including the upper secondary-school level. The municipalities must provide both the social services and the physical preconditions to conduct these services.

There are basically two planning instruments which the municipalities use for their planning tasks, namely the comprehensive plan and the detailed development plan. These planning tools are intended for the planning of the municipalitys' land and water. In planning practice, it is often difficult to distinguish between the planning of activities and the physical preconditions for conducting the activities. This means that the planning processes for both the comprehensive plan and the detailed development plan are in practice supplemented with different types of investigations and analyses, and several authorities and organizations are requested to participate. There are a number of public opinion groups that can almost be regarded as institutions, as planning proposals are regularly submitted to them for their review. These groups stem from older, idealistic associations that grew from one particular issue, for example the Swedish Environmental Protection Association.

Comprehensive Plans

As the name suggests, it is the task of the comprehensive plan to describe, in general, how the municipality's land and water are to be used. It must be comprehensive with respect to the area of the municipality, and should also be comprehensive with respect to the activities that are conducted within and by the municipality.

Comprehensive plans are to an increasing extent taking on the form of municipal development programs in which housing, employment, and the environment play leading roles. Land use proposals are increasingly being weighed against social welfare goals.

Detailed Development Plans

The detailed development plan is the municipality's implementation instrument. It is legally binding and gives the municipality the opportunity to assess land use impacts. Most of the measures prescribed in the detailed development plan are implemented by others outside the municipality.

Local Agenda 21

Municipal planning has been inspired by work in connection with the local Agenda 21. Despite the lack of legislation, a democratic and active planning process has been initiated. The work has given insight into the preconditions for sustainable development and the need for closed ecocycles.

Welfare and Infrastructure

The overriding objectives, as they are expressed in planning legislation, provide indicators of where planning resources are to be concentrated. At the beginning of the Act on Management of Natural Resources, it is stated that 'Land, water and the physical environment in general shall be used in a manner that encourages good long-term management from ecological, social and economic viewpoints'.

The Planning and Building Act is introduced in the following way: 'With due consideration to the freedom of the individual, the regulations aim at promoting social development with equal and good social living conditions for people living in today's society and for coming generations'.

Ultimately, the objectives involve developing social welfare within those limits dictated by the environment, and creating living conditions that make it possible for everyone to participate in the process. It is not merely a task for 'here and now'. The long-term perspective that welfare must also be available for coming generations is becoming increasingly apparent.

The basic precondition is that people have jobs, that they can create material value, which in turn provides resources for medical care, other types of social services, education and culture. If we discount the public sector, business development and employment are not something than can be planned and controlled directly by public planning instruments. Planning is implemented via indirect means. It is a question of creating favorable conditions for productive forces. Land for industrial sites, the service sector and offices is reserved in the land-use plans. Simplifying the regulatory system for business activities is an important task. Another important localization factor for the business community is a sound environment.

A significant task, which is extremely important for the development of the economy and employment, and over which society largely has full control from the planning stage to implementation, concerns regional transportation and communication systems. Other important tasks concern the supply and construction of housing. Through the financing system, society has, more or less, total control over all new housing construction and conversion.

Where housing is planned, service is also necessary. The planning of education and medical care facilities and other forms of social services is closely related to housing planning. The influence on society is also considerable. In the case of commercial services, the potential for direct control is not particularly strong. Even though these services are necessary, there are no social planning requirements.

Regional Issues

From a regional point of view, there are two questions that are becoming increasingly important in connection with planning: the environment at large and infrastructure. Both these issues are of a comprehensive nature. It is not normally possible to isolate environmental problems in one individual municipality. Admittedly, it may be possible for a particular source of pollution to be pinpointed to one municipality or place, but the pollution itself does not simply stop at the municipal boundary.

The same applies to infrastructure. In the case of rail and road developments, it is clear that planning must be carried out through cooperation between the municipalities or through a joint body.

Government Superstructure

There is another group of actors that belong to the planning process superstructure. Parliament, the body responsible for instituting laws, belongs to this category, as does the national government, which has the highest responsibility in certain planning matters, and the county administrative boards, which serve as regional advisory and bodies of appeal.

On the regional level, the county administrative board is the highest civil government administrative unit and comes directly under the national government. The county administrative board has a number of important tasks in connection with planning. It coordinates the national government county-based authorities and their interest in planning issues. It must ensure that national goals are implemented at the county level, and it has control and consultative functions in conjunction with regional and municipal planning. The county administrative board is also the first level of appeal for planning and development cases.

The county administrative board co-operates extensively with the government administrative units that include planning functions. The board has experts connected with the central administrative units, a county architect, a director of planning, a director of environmental protection, the county antiquarian, veterinary officer, etc.

Because certain regional issues are also of national interest, it would be unreasonable to expect regions inspected to be solely responsible for their resolution. A typical example of this is transportation and communications investments, as they are used by, and for the benefit of, far more people than a region's own residents. Roads and railways are to a large extent financed by the State. As far as national roads are concerned, the State is responsible for their entire cost. Municipalities are not responsible for regional roads that also serve national interests, as the State provides subsidies for both them and the municipal road network.

Note

1 Reprint from Guinchard, C.G. (ed.) (1997), *Swedish Planning: Towards Sustainable Development*, The Swedish Society for Town and Country Planning, Stockholm, with permission from the authors.

2 The Shaping of Local Authority Districts: A Historical and Ongoing Process

STEN AXELSSON

Introduction

In almost every society there is some kind of local authority such as municipalities, town districts or rural districts. The most important role for these politically governed organizations is to organize public services. Local authorities appear to reflect a geographical level far removed from nations and supranational systems; it is the most provincial type of government. But this does not mean that it is isolated from the outside world. The evolution of local authorities in Europe was a part of an international movement and is an illustration of how local authorities reflect changes in the outside world.

A few decades after the French revolution local governments were given legal status in many European countries. European society was in a state of upheaval from the end of seventeenth century to the middle of the nineteenth century. The era is above all associated with the industrial revolution and the economic change it brought to society. But many political and administrative systems such as local authorities, which still exist, were also formed during this period.

Even if the legal base of these systems appeared to have much in common, the outcome of the reforms in different countries varied. In some countries the local level became the most important political level after the central government.

Another feature of this group is that the regional level has relatively little importance and influence. Sweden definitely belongs to this group, in which the regional level has few administrative tasks and compared to the local authority is politically insignificant. In contemporary Europe local authorities continue to exercise an important role. Within the European

Union it is postulated that political decisions should be made and carried out at the lowest political and geographical level when possible.

An important question throughout the history of local authorities has dealt with the issue of geographical size. What is the optimal geographical size for local government? The obvious answer to such a question is that there is no such thing as an optimal size. The geographical extent of local authority districts has varied over time. There are two factors that are especially important. Every era has been dominated by a mode of transportation that shaped local authority districts.

It is clear that the hinterland will be different if most transportation is carried out by horse and carriage or if it is based on motor traffic on modern roads. Another element that will determine the geographical size of local authority districts concerns the question of what local authorities are supposed to do. How much public service should be carried out at the local level? The more political authority that is placed locally, the greater the hinterland needs to be; increasing ambitions in this field will in most cases create larger municipalities.

This chapter presents a broad picture of how local government has evolved in Sweden, but the focus is mainly on the last 150 years. Within a few years in the mid-nineteenth century, several laws were passed in Sweden that regulated the scope of power and geographical size of local authorities. These laws have been changed on several occasions since then, but it is in the nature of modification and not complete change.

The history that is recounted in this chapter has in part unique national traits, but many of the features are international in the sense that they could be found in any other country. Many of the factors that shaped the size and scope of authority of Swedish local government are valid in an international context.

The perspective taken in this chapter is historical, and the aim is to understand the elements that influenced local authorities brought about. However the process is ongoing; history never ends. There are probably as many changes in contemporary society as there were when the modern local authority was born in Europe more than 150 years ago. Transformation of the economy and technology will inevitably alter the size and scope of future local authorities.

Today we do not know what the effects will be. But by looking back we can gain a better understanding of the processes that shaped the past and that will also strongly influence the future.

How it Started

Descriptions of Swedish local self-government customarily begin by stating that it has ancient roots. There is a long history of the village and its moot presided over by the alderman. When Sweden converted to Christianity in about the year 1000 and the first churches were built, the natural systematizing principle was for several villages to form a parish. There is much to suggest that these districts existed as natural tracts of the country prior to this period. When church-building was intensified during medieval times, churches were frequently established on the same spots that had been the venues of the ancient moot and cult. These ancient points of the landscape were situated in high places to emphasize their prominence, on land which dried out early in the spring but was unsuitable for cultivation. Prehistoric place-names and rune-stones are further signs of the bygone importance of these places. The extent of the parishes was determined by the distance that could be covered on foot in one day. They were also shaped by the natural routes of travel. The routes followed ridges or other easily negotiable terrain, and in the winter they traversed frozen lakes and watercourses. But the size of parishes was also determined by the population that could live off the soil of the district. A certain number of people were needed in order to form a parish – perhaps not more than a mere handful of families. Districts with many people built many churches, especially in the fertile plainlands, while sparsely populated forested tracts formed parishes that were large in area (Lindqvist, 1981). The center of the parish was wherever the church was, but this was not a population center in today's sense. At most it would be a church hamlet consisting of a few buildings: a parsonage, church stables, a parish hall, a poorhouse – seldom more, usually less.

While the course of events underlying the geographical distribution of parishes may be reconstructed, it is more difficult to know anything about the significance of self-government in olden times. The parish was first and foremost an ecclesiastical unit, but in those days there was no clear distinction between ecclesiastical and secular issues. The moot discussed the routing of roads, fencing of livestock or utilization of common land along with questions concerning the religious lives of the parish's inhabitants. The parson was the obvious head of the parish and participation in the parish moot was confined to freeholders. It was certainly a form of local self-government, but it would probably be misleading to imagine these organizations to have been true forerunners of the civic assemblies called *kommuner* (from the Latin *communis* = common) which were established in the second half of the nineteenth century. There was no legislation enabling them to function as independent local authority districts (the term we shall use in this article) in the modern sense. The transition in the 1530s from a Catholic to a Protestant church subject to control by the state brought a stronger central influence to bear in the parishes. Their position can best be summarized as one of spontaneously emergent units standing without legal protection under the direction of the state, i.e. the church and its priests (Johansson, 1937).

European Movement Toward a Local Authority

It was not until the late eighteenth and early nineteenth centuries that the currents of modern ideas on local self-government appeared in Europe. This was the time when liberal ideologies were developing which advocated greater independence on the local plane. These ideologies were derived from the influence of 'natural rights', which implied that there was an original and naturally given right of local self-government. At the same time a movement towards local government was under way in Europe. It began with the Prussian municipal reform of 1808, which asserted the principle of local self-government based on civic influence. Several decades later Austria introduced a local government statute proclaiming that, in accordance with the 'natural rights' spirit of the age, local independence was also the prerequisite for a free national life. The first Swedish local government ordinance came in 1817 and was supplemented in 1843 (Sörndal, 1941). Broadly speaking, it was a codification of an already-existing situation. The parish became legally empowered to administer civic affairs. Management of the parish was still a purely ecclesiastical matter. Local self-government also remained limited, since the central government was empowered to test not merely the legality of local decisions but also their appropriateness for their purposes. The Swedish statute still fell far short of contemporary currents of opinion and reforms compared with the rest of Europe (Wallentheim, 1950).

In practice, it was reforms other than those concerned purely with the legal status of local government organs that sped up the process on the issue of the legally established right of local civic authorities to govern themselves. After 1842 every parish was obliged to provide schooling, while requirements for relief for the poor were also increasing, making the issue more acute. What were really needed were a larger population base – and therefore more taxpayers – than small rural parishes provided.

After the local government ordinance of 1843, however, it became possible for parishes under the same incumbency to amalgamate to form a joint parish administration. But the cooperation which ensued was very sluggish in practice. A number of enquiries were instituted to prepare a new scheme of division into local authority districts. The (generally rural) district known as the *härad* had existed since Viking times as a jurisdictional and administrative unit. There was a proposal to use this as the basis of division into local authority districts, but it was abandoned because it lacked the sense of local solidarity that prevailed in the parishes (Kaijser 1959; Widberg, 1979).

It is true that the parishes of the rural areas had too small a population base, but they had already been given local authority status in the ordinances of 1817 and 1843, which in practice proved to be the decisive factor for the reform of 1862. The small authorities were at the same time counterbalanced by the county councils (*landsting*). They were established at the same time and covered territories largely corresponding to those of the central government's regional division into the administrative provinces known as *län*, which were formed in 1634 and administered by the central government's regional organ in the counties, the county administrative boards (*länsstyrelserna*). The county councils (*landsting*) constituted an 'upper tier' of local authority but with rather unclear political responsibilities. After approximately ten years they were assigned the care of the sick as their primary task. By the mid-nineteenth century it was obvious that political power besides the central government had its focus on the local authority and not on the regional level. This development gave Sweden its administrative characteristics, which are still present, consisting of a relatively strong central government and a politically powerful local authority with the right to collect taxes from its inhabitants. This is an important pillar in the Swedish local government system, which from the beginning had important implications.

The modern local authority district as a civic unit was born on January 1, 1863, but the basis of demarcation consists of the medieval parish boundaries. Towns and cities stood out as self-evident units by virtue of their populations, but they were also the objects of special legislation which gave them a place apart. The smaller urban centers known as *köpingar* were regulated in a similar way to towns. 'Village communities' (*municipalsamhällen*) were still smaller built-up centers which were included in rural local authority districts but to which some parts of the legislation pertaining to towns were applied. There was a hierarchy among the forms of local authority districts. A rural district (*landskommun*) could become a village community (*municipalsamhälle*), then an urban district (*köping*) and finally a borough. Sweden consisted at the time of the reform of about 2,500 local authority districts, 89 of which were boroughs, 8 urban districts and 10 village communities (Den lantkommunala författningens historia, 1944; Andersson, 1993).

The reform involved a separation between ecclesiastical and civic affairs. The word *socken* disappeared as the term for a parish and was replaced by *församling* (still translated as 'parish', however) for ecclesiastical business and *kommun* (local authority district) for civic affairs. An elected chairman at local council meetings replaced the parish priest, who had presided *ex officio* at parish meetings.

Not until after the enactment of the local government statutes of 1862 did it become possible to speak of local self-government comparable to that of today. Viewed in this light, Swedish local self-government can hardly be described as ancient. The local government reform reflected the society existing in the mid-nineteenth century. Many of its features may seem old-fashioned today. Local democratic representative forms did not exist for local authority districts comprising fewer than 3,000 inhabitants: instead, all inhabitants were entitled to take part at meetings. This created practical problems, of course, in finding venues capable of accommodating the entire adult population of a local authority district or borough. Rapidly rising populations soon caused the boroughs to abandon this system. In the case of the small rural districts, it was not until 1918 that it became obligatory to have elected councilors (Palme, 1962).

The franchise was still restricted even though enlargements were made towards the end of the nineteenth century. At this time the right to vote was still conditional on the possession of land and income. Not until after the introduction of universal suffrage in about 1920 did equality emerge as a feature of modern democratic local government. Outside the major towns there were no paid staff to administer local government business. Instead, the duties of keeping the books or checking that taxes were paid were carried out by honorary office-holders. At most, they might receive a modest honorarium for their services. Later on, the value of such voluntary service was to have a large role in the debate over the size of local government districts. The issue provided arguments to both opponents and advocates of new local government boundaries. The latter remembered the earlier period as one of arbitrariness and submission to the ruling class. The former looked back to an era of devoted sacrifice for the public weal.

Evolving Local Authority Districts Mirror a Society in Upheaval

It is no exaggeration to say that the structure introduced by the local government reform was out of date before it was implemented. Great changes were in progress in Swedish society, as well in many European countries, in the second half of the nineteenth century. These began in agriculture, which was losing its self-evident role as the leader of the economy. Up to the end of the eighteenth century, broadly speaking, a degree of balance had prevailed between the population and the demand for agricultural labor. The population barely increased and subsistence was the norm for the majority. By this time mortality was declining, more children were surviving into adulthood and the population was increasing. Despite intensive land reclamation, which brought land with ever-poorer yields into production, more and more people found themselves being marginalized. They swelled the growing ranks of the agrarian landless, who dreamed of having land of their own but had to be content with an inadequate plot of ground at best, or with work as an employee (Montgomery, 1951). Emigration to the United States became another way of escaping these somber prospects.

The pace of change was stimulated by the metamorphosis, almost unnoticed, of the craft trades into small-scale industries (Heckscher, 1941). The liberation of commerce enacted in 1864 was another contributory factor. Prior to this time it had been illegal to establish a commercial enterprise within 30 kilometers of a city. Regulated trade had direct links with the various local government bodies. Only certain towns were authorized to trade with foreign countries, and markets could be held only in boroughs and market towns. These distinctions disappeared when the freedom of commerce was established, and this favored a number of smaller centers. Small places which had consisted at best of a cluster of houses began to grow. The church villages, which had been the old centers of rural parishes, consisting perhaps of a hundred or so families, now found themselves in competition with new population centers which, despite being small, began to attract more inhabitants.

Industrialization proceeded faster in the countryside than in the towns. In this early period of vigorous growth, which started around 1870, the majority of industry was located in rural areas. As late as around 1900, three fifths of industry was still to be found in rural locations. The expansion gave birth to groups of merchants and manufacturers with perspectives different from those of the freeholding peasantry of the church villages. The new groups had no obvious connection to the soil but saw their future as bound up with the expanding industries and trade of the populated centers. Rural local authority districts, which had been designed to conform to agrarian concentrations of people, were beginning to creak at the joints. The new industrial and *bruk* communities (the latter being a patriarchal and distinctively Swedish blend of ironmaking and rural pursuits based on the manorial system) drew people into growing population centers. In the eyes of the new groups in the small but growing population centers of the countryside, local government policy was something which took far too little account of their most pressing concerns. The only solution in the long run was to break free from the rural local authority district and form a district of one's own.

The road from subordinate status to that of independent district was often long and tortuous for the new industrialized communities. The evolution from rural district (*landskommun*) to urban district (*köping*) or from urban district to borough was regarded as external proof of a successful policy on the part of its local government. The smaller places were seeking a collective identity to match the growing self-confidence and prosperity of artisans, manufacturers and merchants. A contest began to be played out which in large part represented a battle between industries and lifestyles. The local government assemblies dominated by countryfolk resisted every attempt to subdivide local authority districts: in the name of ancient parish solidarity, these districts were not in favor of demolition. Official letters were written to the central government spelling out the disadvantages which would ensue from subdivision. The correspondence has survived in the archives and its protracted course can be followed in detail. A negative decision handed down from the highest level laid the issue of subdivision to rest for decades before a new generation of local government leaders in the populated centers took up the cause again.

There could only be one end to the story in the long run: the rural local authorities had to relinquish their rights and the growing communities were allowed to establish their own local authority districts, perhaps becoming urban districts, a great event when the New Year was ushered in. Local newspapers reported the event as a fateful moment. This was how one eye-witness began his report of the transition from village community to urban district at the turn of the year 1913/14: it was a cold, sparkling New Year's Eve with the snow plowed up into heaps in the square. The windows of the lower wooden houses cast their rays of light. Snowy crystals captured some of it, beaming it here, there and back again. The square and its buildings may easily be described: straight ahead the Grand Hotel, one story higher and crowned by a balustrade; beside it the ironmonger's; to the left the grain merchant's office and to the right the watchmaker's shop in its leaky building. Having thus completed a revolution about the axis, there was little more for the onlooker to see. If there is little to be said about the square, that leaves all the more to say about the place of which it is a part. It was an ambitious place without rights which now, at the stroke of twelve, was to be transformed into an urban district. When the hour arrived, the chairman of the council mounted a primitive rostrum and made a speech containing most of the items a public address ought to contain, then proclaimed the motto for the future: 'Assiduous labor and communal harmony' (Gärme, 1970).

During the half-century following the reform of 1862, the rural districts relinquished large tracts to the urban districts and boroughs, thus also losing a significant portion of their tax base. Up to the First World War the number of local authority districts increased somewhat. But this increase took place as a result of more local authorities being created in population centers. In 1863 there had been 89 boroughs, 8 urban districts and 10 village communities. By 1914 the number of boroughs had risen to 100, urban districts to 33 and village communities to 170. Of the nation's five and a half million inhabitants, nearly four million lived in rural areas at this time.

Decreasing Population

The 1919 local government statute provided increased opportunities for changing the boundaries of local authority districts. There was no longer to be the same scope for preventing districts from being incorporated as boroughs or urban districts from hiving off from the rural parishes. During the period 1910–1919, 75,000 inhabitants were transferred to boroughs in this way. Development accelerated between 1920 and 1951, and the redrawing of local authority boundaries caused rural parishes to lose 600,000 people to boroughs and urban districts. Considerable tracts of land were sliced away from the rural parishes, a total of 20,000 square kilometers being thus added to boroughs and urban districts – an area equivalent to half the land surface of Switzerland (Kaijser, 1959). Rural districts, which had already been alarmingly small in 1862 for purposes of school provision and relief for the poor, were now being nibbled away at their margins by boroughs and urban districts and at the same time were losing inhabitants through migration to the population centers. The number of boroughs and urban districts increased substantially during the period 1914–1951. By 1951 the number of boroughs had risen to 133, urban districts to 84 and village communities to 198. Over one hundred rural districts had vanished during the same period, and those which were left were getting smaller; see Table 2.1. These developments were part of the urbanization process going on in Sweden. Around the middle of the century the country had seven and a half million inhabitants, of whom three million lived in towns, two and a half million in other population centers and two million outside the population centers.

Table 2.1 Number of local authorities of different sizes

Population	Number of local authorities	
	1910	1940
Under 500	388	523
500–999	673	648
1.000–1.999	733	659
2.000–2.999	313	272
3.000 and above	302	304
Total	2.409	2.406

Source: Principer för en ny kommunindelning, Statens offentliga utredningar 1961:9.

Conditions in the very small local authority districts are described in contemporary reports and books dealing with the issues. The very smallest district, with its 78 inhabitants, became well known. The literature documenting the debate cited drastic examples of the way in which the care needs of a single individual could occasion a dramatic increase in local taxes (Wallentheim, 1950). We are told in anecdotal form of the small local authority that almost halved its local tax bill from one year to the next. The central authorities in Stockholm wrote to the local authority inquiring what had happened. The reply was brief and to the point: 'The village idiot died last year.'

The existence of the small local authorities was now threatened by a third quarter. The central government was requiring increased involvement of local authorities in such matters as school provision, children's welfare, youth services and health care. Central government grants were made to local authorities, and by the turn of the century they already accounted for 15 per cent of the latter's income.

By the 1940s they had increased to about 20 per cent of local authority revenues. What was more disquieting was that rural district authorities were becoming increasingly dependent on these grants, which on average represented 35 per cent of their income. This meant that there were some local authorities in rural areas, which received more than half of their income directly from the central government.

Personal Responsibility or Professional Organization

Avenues for cooperation had long existed via *Kommunalförbundet*, the Association of Local Authorities. But this route had been found to be slow and impracticable in many respects in achieving any broadening of the local authority base. The first attempts dated from the middle of the nineteenth century and were concerned with relief for the poor; the results were meager. The same applied to schooling; a mere 66 joint school districts were in existence as late as 1944. Only in one field – the police service – had any significant results been achieved. In this field a total of 1,325 local authorities were united in 400 police districts. But this was because cooperation had been actively urged by the central government's regional organ in the counties, viz the county administrative boards (*länsstyrelserna*).

Sweden had become a true industrial society during the period extending from the close of the nineteenth century to after the First World War, but it was not until the 1940s that the numbers employed in industry and craft trades exceeded those in agriculture and its subsidiary occupations. Whereas the growing population centers of the mid-nineteenth century had been clusters of wooden houses, many of them during the first half of the twentieth century became both small market towns and centers of industry. Buildings in stone had also begun to appear here as in the towns. But these usually covered no more than one or two blocks, bearing witness today to the ambition and faith in the future that prevailed in that era. There were many places where craft trades and small-scale industries grew into large-scale industries employing several hundred people. There were energetic factory owners and a body of workers organized into trade unions. In a way these industrial communities presented a picture of the history of the 'Swedish model': a long period of wage negotiations against a background of mutual understanding between industrialists and trade unions.

In the thick of the Second World War a committee was appointed to formulate proposals for a revision of local government boundaries (Betänkande med förslag till riktlinjer för en revision av rikets indelning i borgerliga primärkommuner, 1945). Wide-ranging inquiries were instituted in furtherance of the task. An important element of the studies undertaken concerned the question of how local authority services should be deployed. Opponents and advocates of the local government reform saw two different kinds of threat. The former visualized the end of an era of personal responsibility in local politics. Personal knowledge and the personal responsibility that went with it would disappear. For example, the chairman of the temperance board of a major local authority would lack sufficient personal knowledge to take action in good time. Moreover, a chairman who was an honorary office-holder would be better inspired to perform the duty than would the anonymous official who would replace him after the reform.

The advocates of reform for their part contended that the bonds of friendship in small local authority districts made it difficult to take action against an alcohol abuser. The disgrace occasioned by such action in a small community, where everyone knew everyone else, meant that all measures were postponed until it was too late. The enquiries made, which were based chiefly on the reports of government inspectors, gave prominence to the advantages of the anonymity of salaried officials. And it was only in the larger local authority districts that it was possible to administer care and welfare services on a scale that would allow anonymity and therefore impartiality (Bilagor till kommunindelningskommitténs betänkande, 1945).

The detailed descriptions recount the unsatisfactory state of affairs prevailing for example in the fields of children's and young people's welfare in rural areas in Sweden in the 1940s. The consistent theme of the narratives is one of deficiencies in local authority welfare services. There are tales of totally passive child welfare committees, which allow problems to fester rather than take action, sometimes out of fear of making inroads upon the district's budget but most commonly from ignorance of the existence of a law applicable to the case. We hear of old people's homes run by managers with no training, in which half the patients are mentally unstable. Examples are even cited of gross evils reminiscent of the nineteenth-century treatment of paupers. One mentally deficient man was boarded out to a farmer and fared very badly in the outbuilding in which he had to live. The district public assistance committee was well acquainted with the case but dared not take action for fear of upsetting neighborly relations.

There was also a glaring shortage of honorary office-holders in the small local authority districts. There were instances of chairmen of child welfare committees being appointed against their will and sometimes without their knowledge. In one case the post had been handed down through three generations since the end of the nineteenth century. The majority of honorary office-holders possessed no detailed knowledge of such matters as the special statutes relating to child welfare – if indeed they were even aware of their existence.

The overall picture formed by all the cases recounted in the appendices to the report is clear-cut: it is only in exceptional instances that the personal element is of any benefit; otherwise it is arbitrary factors that determine the measures taken by local authorities. In many cases no action is taken when to do so would in fact be justified. The inspectors' findings disclose a clear connection between unsatisfactory situations and local authority size. Only in those instances where local authorities have cooperated with one another have they succeeded in arranging proper care of the elderly. Most of the bodies whose comments on proposed measures were sought believed that a revision of local government boundaries would improve local authority services. Many of the small local authorities were dubious, however. Their replies show there were apprehensions concerning increasing distances from local authority services, and also of higher taxes and rising administrative costs.

None of the reports submitted in preparation for the revision of local government boundaries in 1952 went very far in discussing the question of the size of local authorities. The smallest authorities were to have 3,000 inhabitants and only in exceptional cases could a lower limit of 2,000 be accepted. The limit was set by means of a rough estimate of the population numbers required in order to meet the demands for local services. At this time the parish still had a large role in the rural district authorities. For the local government reform of 1862 had in practice not actually involved anything more than the break-up of the historical parish (*socken*) into the new parish (*församling*) and the civic local authority districts. The further reform of boundaries implemented on January 1, 1952 reduced the number of local authority districts from 2,281 to 1,037. The very small districts had been merged so that only 4 had fewer than 1,000 inhabitants. Nearly one third, or 326 districts, fell below the recommended lower limit of 3,000 inhabitants. The reform is redolent of some spirit of caution and gives the impression of constituting one step along the road. Much heed is paid in the report to parish sentiment, for example with regard to the question of names; districts which were merged were allowed to retain both names in hyphenated form (Anvisningar till kommunindelningsreformens genom-förande, 1949). The fact that seven years later a new commission was appointed to report on local government boundaries yet again suggests that the reform of 1952 hardly matched the needs of the time.

A More Scientific Approach

The 1952 local government reform took reports on the state of local government services as its main starting point. The commission posed the question: are people receiving from their local authorities the services and care which it is reasonable to expect in the Sweden of the 1940s? To the extent that the answer was in the negative, measures were suggested for overcoming these problems, which involved merging the small local authorities into larger units to provide a better base for local services. In this respect the new commission, which submitted its report in 1961, adopted a different stance. In the course of its work it had called in experts whose approach was quite different. These were based on theoretical positions, incorporating new quantitative methods and comprehensive statistics aimed at tackling the question of local government boundaries scientifically. Part of the basic data consisted of a population forecast for different types of settlements, showing a continued decrease in the rural population up to the forecast year of 1975. It also pointed out a clear link between the size of the local authority district and population change. Small districts were losing population, which in time would make their situation even more parlous. By 1975, more than 40 per cent of local authority districts would have a population of less than the target figure which had been set prior to the 1952 reform, i. e. fewer than 3,000 inhabitants. Possibilities were accordingly seen here for creating a better regional balance by uniting districts of declining populations with districts of expanding ones (Principer för ny kommunindelning, 1961).

The term 'social engineering' has sometimes been applied to the sort of political and social planning which asserts that improved social conditions can be planned by making use of scientific methods. These ideas first cropped up in the industrialized world around the 1930s. An important ingredient of them is the close influence of and collaboration with the emergent social sciences. During the 1930s they constituted a part of the reforming endeavors of the age aimed at better housing and living conditions. Social engineering has changed with time, assimilating new elements and assuming new forms. During its early period there was a strong influence from the behavioral sciences, but later on inspiration was taken from other social sciences, chiefly economics.

The new reform of local government boundaries accorded with the spirit of social engineering. The preliminary work leaned towards theories and arguments borrowed from academic studies. A considerable proportion of the basic data came from ethnogeography. Geographical models developed in Germany around the 1930s played a particularly large role (Christaller, 1933). The most important one was the theory of centrality, which describes a hierarchy of place. The population of a place determines its position in this hierarchy. The higher up in the hierarchy, the more advanced the services the place can support.

Studies of the flows of bus travelers were utilized in order to determine the trading area of a place (Godlund, 1954). Areas with intensive bus traffic within their confines ought also to constitute their own local authority district. Such areas also corresponded to the trading areas for skilled services (e g visits to the doctor or dentist), thus reinforcing the argument that the right size for local authority districts had been found. The study of bus traffic was made about 1950, i.e. immediately prior to the real motoring revolution in Sweden. Despite this, it shows a high degree of correspondence with the local government boundaries which were to be introduced in the early 1970s and which, with minor adjustments, gave Sweden the local authority districts still existing today.

Another point of departure for the commission was concerned with what had constituted the determinants of administrative boundaries in the historical sense. It was mainly law that defined the farm, the local authority district, the county or the national boundaries. The landscape contains other territories without boundaries that were actually more important. This applied to business establishments, which constituted an assembly point that created a trading area and maintained its own spontaneous boundaries. In preindustrial society the administrative and functional area coincided. The traditional parish (*socken*) in its early days was the area within which relief for the poor and schooling were administered in the church village in a fairly natural way. Changes in society had loosened the ties between administrative and functional areas. Transportation facilities had played a large role in this development. The successor parishes (*församlingar*) were a result of the era of horse transportation. After that, the railway had reshaped the trading areas. But above all motor traffic had totally transformed the situation as regards boundaries. What were needed now were a restoration of harmony between the administrative and the spontaneous boundaries.

With these considerations as a foundation, a test study was launched with two alternatives. In the one case the local authority districts would have at least 6,500 inhabitants and in the other 10,000. No shortfall in these population targets was to be permitted for the next fifteen years. Every local authority district was to have a center that would be large enough to create a natural trading area. There was to be a uniform type of local authority, and boroughs, urban districts and rural districts would thus disappear. No contact would be made with local authorities during the test study, the purpose of this being to avoid any influence from factors, which the commission called irrational and incapable of being weighed in concrete terms. In addition to the population targets the investigatory work consisted of determining the centrality of the population centers, i. e. finding out how large a trading area was serviced by the commerce of the population centers. Known local changes in industry were also to be taken into account. Another objective was to create local authorities with an all-round balance of different industries and businesses. The outcome of the test study was a recommendation that local authority districts should have at least 8,000 inhabitants by 1975.

Towards Large-Scale Local Authorities

At the same time as the new scheme of local government boundaries was being prepared, many other factors were in the process of undergoing change. The growth of the economy had been more or less uninterrupted for a number of decades. But signs had begun to appear suggesting that many small industrial centers in particular had passed their zenith. The blockade during the Second World War had favored home-market industries. But increasing international competition had begun to make itself felt. Industry was flourishing and employees shared in its prosperity in the form of higher wages, which helped to make foreign competition still more severe. The industrial transformation was in many ways simpler in the larger towns, where labor- and capital-intensive industries were being displaced by more knowledge-based industries. Moreover, expansive service industries outside the public sector were creating new job opportunities. Nothing of this kind was happening in the small industrial centers. All that came here were older industrial establishments with little capacity for surviving very long. Many of the industries on which the smaller local authority districts depended – they usually lived off a mere one or two firms – closed down. New industries did come, but things were never the same as they had been during the palmy days. Instead it was the public sector – i.e. the activities of the local authorities themselves – that became an increasingly important employer and therefore a job lifeline. In many small local authority districts, the shutting down of the largest industrial firm meant in practice that the public sector expanded almost immediately to become the greatest source of jobs.

Resolutions on new local government boundaries were adopted by the Riksdag in 1962. The boundary reform was based on voluntary cooperation. The county administrations were charged with the task of dividing the county into local authority districts. The drawing of boundaries for the new districts, termed 'local authority blocs', was adapted to the existing districts as far as possible. 'Cooperation committees' were established to facilitate the transition to 'local authority blocs'. Their most important task was to prepare the amalgamation of local authority districts. How the work of clearing up was effected varied greatly, of course. In certain cases a good deal of investigation and lengthy negotiations were required. In other cases it was a simple administrative process (Fröjd, 1961, 1962; Larsson and Hedfors, 1961; Åström, 1961).

The pace of amalgamation increased after the reform, especially in the case of rural district authorities, which fell in number almost immediately from 821 to 675. For the rest, the amalgamation into 'local authority blocs' proceeded slowly. By 1969 only a minor proportion of the planned local authority mergers had been implemented. The central government decided to make them compulsory in order to speed the process. According to the plan, the reform was to be completed at the end of 1973. For most local authorities, enquiries and negotiations were under way with a view to amalgamation in January 1971. In the meantime a step had also been taken in the direction of a uniform type of local authority, and in 1971 the distinction between boroughs, urban districts and other local authorities was wholly abolished. Thus vanished the town charters that had existed for hundreds of years but had long been virtually meaningless (Enhetlig kommuntyp, 1961). The local authority amalgamations came into effect on January 1, 1974 and Sweden then consisted of 278 uniform local authority districts. Thus a drastic reduction in the number of local authorities had been accomplished in just over ten years; see Table 2.2. The main thrust of it had been the reduction in the number of smaller authorities.

Table 2.2 Number of local authorities of different sizes

| | Number of local authorities | | | |
Population	1.960	1.970	1.975	1.999
Under 5.000	722	182	4	12
5.000–9.999	198	106	63	59
10.000–14.999	43	62	66	70
15.000 and over	68	114	145	149
Total	1.031	464	278	290

Source: Statistics Sweden.

Swedish society changed enormously between the local government reforms of 1952 and 1971. About 1950, agriculture and its subsidiary occupations still accounted for about one fifth of the labor force. Industry was still on an upward path in terms of employment. It was not until the 1960s that the process peaked. Service industries grew slowly during the

1950s. During the period 1960–1975 a vigorous expansion of public sector services started. From having accounted for 20 per cent of the labor force at the beginning of the period, the figure rose to 34 per cent by its end.

Attitudes to local self-government underwent a fundamental change during the period. The principle of paying high deference to local opinion, which had governed the reform of 1952, had changed by the time of the next boundary reform to that of ignoring 'irrational factors incapable of being weighed in concrete terms'. The trend towards large-scale production was one of the most palpable features of the age. In agriculture, small farms were going out of production and fields were reverting to forest or being assimilated into what were called rational cultivation units. Large industrial firms were accounting for an increasing proportion of the nation's industrial employment. Big business was not only getting bigger inside Sweden but was also growing vigorously on the other side of the national borders via foreign subsidiary companies. Retail trade too was becoming concentrated into larger units, and shopping centers were beginning to develop.

Bearing in mind the spirit of the age, it is not surprising that local self-government too should be organized in accordance with the same large-scale recipe. The small local authorities, whether obsolete or not, had little defense against the forces thus set in motion. Moreover, local authority services were in the throes of vigorous expansion in such areas as child welfare, care of the elderly and administration. On top of this there was the recent introduction of 9-year compulsory basic schooling, which, though admittedly financed by the central government, was administered by the local authorities. In 1950, local authority services accounted for six per cent of the gross national product calculated at current prices; by 1970 the figure had risen to 13 per cent and ten years later to 22 per cent. This meant that local authority services became an increasingly important base for employment. From a modest one per cent around 1960, employment rose by 1970 to about five per cent, and by 1980 it was nine per cent. In the smallest districts the provision of local authority services became an increasingly important substitute as industry receded, and in one third of small local authority districts it is now the most important source of jobs.

The reform of 1971 also brought about an upheaval in local government politics (Gidlund 1983; Strömberg and Westerståhl 1983). Prior to 1951 there were 40,000 local politicians; the corresponding figure in 1974 was 13,000. Furthermore there were fewer functions per politician – the days of multiple office holding in local politics were over. Local administration in rural district authorities was still conducted on a voluntary basis in the 1950s, at modest remuneration. Staff employees started to become more common at this time, even in the small local authority districts. After the latest redrawing of district boundaries the proportion of full-time officials grew substantially. But professionalization did not stop there: leading local politicians became full-time employees as well.

Future Development

For over 150 years, Sweden's development has been intimately bound up with the rise of its modern local government authorities. It is a story which goes back to the local government statutes of 1862, which in turn can be traced back to arguments concerning the natural right to self-government. After the adoption of this historic reform, a battle to reduce the number of local authority districts was fought over a period of more than one hundred years. Today there are less than one tenth of the total in 1862. All through this period, echoes can be heard from the first half of the nineteenth century: how large must local authorities be in order to provide a base for local services? In all probability the issue will continue to be a live one in future.

At the same time there has been a contest between town and country. In this contest the country has been victorious despite its positions having been undermined over many years. The church village as a unit of division lived on in many places until 1971, i.e. long after it had lost its *raison d'être*. Not until after the most recent boundary reform does there again appear to be conformity between the 'trading area' for local government services and the size of local authority districts. Or is there? Few give any thought to the fact that local authority boundaries are determined by the same trading areas as were measured out in the 1950s – by criteria based on slow country buses plying between small communities at low speed and with many stops. As history has demonstrated, the boundaries are stable and an area once having attained the status of local authority district has had a great capacity for survival. The stability can also be explained by local identity. This is an active force to keep small local authorities as independent units. Local identity is in this sense a restraint but at the same time it is the base for a functional local democracy.

There are two especially important variables in history for shaping local authority districts, population size and population density. The historical struggle for larger local authority districts has focused on expanding the hinterland to generate the population numbers required in order to meet the demands for local services. In every epoch the size of the local authority district has also been determined by different transportation facilities. With the increased reach of a transportation system, it has been possible to compensate for low population density. Despite this development half of the local districts in Sweden today have fewer than 15,000 inhabitants. When planning demands a larger population base and a wider geographical area, planning becomes regional. This means that regional planning deals with issues that call for collaboration between two or more local authority districts. In several sectors of planning there is a need for expanded cooperation among the districts. At the same time local authority services are now being organized on a scale and in forms which were probably inconceivable 25 years ago. This has also meant that a number of forms of service which were previously regarded as needing to be headed by someone with a broader territorial perspective – that of the county council (*landsting*), covering approximately the same area as the *län* – have been transferred to the districts.

But the economic progress and spirit of the age which formed the driving force behind the last boundary revision have now been superseded by new developmental features. We who are living through these times are unable to discern the contours with the same clarity as the future historian. Some of the signs are clear, however. Industry's share of employment is continuing to decline. The public sector is grappling with the problem of how to finance its activities. The new situation has posed a number of new problems as to what the future holds for those local authority districts in which the public sector is the most important source of jobs – most of them in the provision of local authority services. These districts seem still to be living in the industrial society. Traditional industries have not been replaced properly by more knowledge-oriented manufactures. It is true that many industrial firms are making good profits but the question is whether they can survive price competition from abroad in the long run. Another sign that these districts have placed themselves on the margins of the knowledge-based society is the low average educational level. Those who pursue an education can hardly count on finding a job in their home districts. Higher education leads to emigration in the vast majority of cases.

Today much has changed as regards the role of the local authorities. They have quite different responsibilities compared with 30–40 years ago, and the change since the reform of 1952 has been revolutionary. Local authority services have also been organized in a fashion permitting smaller units. Since 1974, 12 local authorities have been permitted to break free and many more have tried. In all cases local identity has played an important role as a force in forming a new local authority. The spirit of the age which preceded the last reform and embraced large elements of large-scale thinking has been superseded by a greater faith in the possibilities offered by smallness of scale. We have a fairly good picture of how the role of local authorities has changed during the post-war period; we know much less about other types of changes. What has happened to mobility and range during the half-century which will soon have elapsed since the 'trading area' was determined by bus traffic and the supply of professional public services? In what way have new mobility patterns affected local identity? The local authority districts were created 20–25 years ago with the idea that the areas they comprised should be both functional and administrative. More time has now elapsed since the reforms of 1951 and 1974. Has there again been a loosening of the ties between administrative and functional areas? Has the same process recommenced which once upon a time made the traditional parish with its church village obsolete as a unit of local government? Are we living in a time of upheaval on the same scale as occurred in the era of the reforms of 1862, 1952 or 1971?

References

Andersson, P. (1993), *Sveriges kommunindelning 1863–1993*, Draking, Mjölby.
Anvisningar till kommunindelningsreformens genomförande. (1949), *Inrikesdepartementet*, Stockholm.
Betänkande med förslag till riktlinjer för en revision av rikets indelning i borgerliga primärkommuner (1945), Statens offentliga utredningar, SOU 1945:38.
Bilagor till kommunindelningskommitténs betänkande med förslag till riktlinjer för en revision av rikets indelning i borgerliga primärkommuner (1945), Statens offentliga utredningar, SOU 1945:3.
Christaller, W. (1933), *Die Zentralen Orte in Süddeutschland : eine ökonomischgeographische Untersuchung über die Gesetzmässigheit der Verbreitung und Entwicklung der Siedlungen mit städtischen Funktionend*, Gustav Fischer, Jena.
Den lantkommunala författningsregleringens historia. En översikt med särskilt avseende å landsbygdens primärkommuner (1944), Statens offentliga utredningar, SOU 1944:37.
Fröjd, A. (1961), 'Principer för en ny kommunindelning', *Svenska stadsförbundets tidskrift*, 1961:2.
Fröjd, A. (1962), *Kommunindelningsfrågan*, Brevskolan, Stockholm.
Gärme, E. (1970), Bondebygd och bruksbygd, Ringarums socken genom tiderna, Söderköping.
Gidlund, J. (1983), *Kommunal självstyrelse i förvandling*, Publica, Stockholm.
Godlund, S. (1954), *Busstrafikens framväxt och funktion i de urbana influensfälten*, Lunds Universitet Geografiska institutionen, Lund.
Heckscher, E. (1941), *Svenskt arbete och liv*, Bonnier, Stockholm.
Johansson, K.H. (1937), *Svensk sockensjälvstyrelse 1686–1862, Studier med särskild hänsyn till Linköpings stift*, Gleerup, Lund.
Kaijser, F. (1959), *Kommunallagarna 1*, Svenska kommunförbundet, Stockholm.
Larsson, Å. and Hedfors, N. (1961), *Kommunindelning och självstyrelse*, Tiden, Stockholm.
Lindqvist, S.-O. (1981), *Sockenbildningen på Gotland – en kronologisk studie*, Gotländskt arkiv 1981, Visby.

Montgomery, A. (1951), *Svensk socialpolitik under 1800-talet*, Kooperativa förbundets bokförlag, Stockholm.

Palme, S.U. (1962), *Hundra år under kommunalförfattningarna*, Svenska Kommunförbundet, Stockholm.

Principer för ny kommunindelning (1961), Statens offentliga utredningar, SOU 1961:9.

Strömberg, E. and Westerståhl, J. (eds) (1983), *De nya kommunerna – en sammanfattning av den kommunaldemokratiska forskningsgruppens undersökningar*, Liber, Stockholm.

Sörndal, O. (1941), '1817 års förordning angående sockenstämmor och kyrkoråd', *Statsvetenskaplig tidskrift 1941*.

Wallentheim, A. (1950), *Ny kommunindelning – varför?*, Tiden, Stockholm.

Widberg, J. (1979), *Från socken till kommunblock*, Departementsserien Kommundepartementet, Ds Kn 1979:14.

Åström, T. (1961), *Kommunsammanslagningsfrågan*, Gävleborgs läns bildningsförbund, Söderhamn.

3 Strategic Regional Planning – Issues in Long Term Traffic Planning in Stockholm

CHRISTER ANDERSTIG

Introduction

Strategic planning is currently a central concept in the Stockholm region planning context. 'Towards a Sustainable Stockholm Region in an Uncertain Future' serves as a guiding principle for the present regional planning process, where three Sector Strategies have been defined by the Office of Regional Planning and Urban Transportation (1999):

> The long term objective is a high level of wealth and prosperity for the inhabitants of the region, both today and in the years to come. It is necessary to create an economic growth within the frameworks set by nature and with a fair distribution of the resources that are created by the growth. Against this background, the emphasis is being shifted from physical planning to questions of economic development, social conditions and the environment.
>
> Three areas – economy, environment and social conditions – have been specially studied with the aim of trying to establish a common approach to the long term goals and to the efforts that are required in order to steer development in their direction.

The *economic strategy* means that the 'productive climate' is to be improved. Regional planning must create the preconditions needed, but at the same time promote economic growth through renewal. The traditional tasks of regional planning – land use and infrastructure – will be used for this purpose. Other resources, for example for education and research, must also be strengthened.

The *social strategy* aims at creating equal and sound living conditions in the region and focusing on work, education, living and health. Solutions within these four areas have the greatest impact on living conditions.

The *environmental strategy* takes up the environment both as a resource and as a limitation. The starting point is sustainability in its broadest sense. A number of ecocycles can be recreated. The individual municipalities require support and guidance in order to adapt the local measures into a more overall strategy.

Eventually, as these strategies are being established, conflicting goals will be imminent. Among the relatively few planning instruments for promoting economic growth, developing the regional transportation system is both viable and weighty. Traffic planning has, however, become an activity constrained by environmental considerations. During the last ten years 'sustainability' has more or less become the bedrock for regional planning.

From this perspective transportation is, above all, accountable for an increasing share of total emissions, in particular with respect to CO_2, NOX and CH. It thus seems very straightforward to place the focus on transportation, when discussing measures to attain given environmental goals, disregarding possible conflicts with other goals.

The reluctance to see and discuss possible goal conflicts in this field is typical, as exemplified by a report on sustainable cities from the European Commission (1996). The report concludes that implementing several of the measures suggested means that it is necessary that cities move towards a state of 'closed' systems, to have the power to manage resource and financial flows. But it is difficult to create a sustainable city with an open economy. Therefore, '...These issues may require some reconsideration of other policy goals such as free trade', a recommendation in direct contravention of the main EU principle about free mobility of goods etc.

In connection to environmental concerns and conflicting goals, the purpose of this chapter is to discuss some issues in long-term traffic planning in the Stockholm region. More specifically, the chapter pleads for adequate planning tools and sensible decision processes.

Planning in Perspective – Persistent Infrastructure Projects

Central Stockholm is founded on a number of islands. The northern part of the region is separated from the southern part by the waters of Lake Mälaren. This geographical location limits the potential solutions that can be adopted to improve the traffic situation.

In brief, the shape of the Stockholm region resembles an hour-glass. It is therefore natural, for environmental reasons and because of the constraints on land, that a large portion of the new roads and railway tracks are planned to be located in tunnels and new bridges in eastern and western locations.

Not surprisingly, ring roads and outer bypass routes have been on the agenda in the Stockholm region for a long time – in fact since the beginning of regional planning activities in Stockholm. The ideas were first presented in the Regional Plan in 1958 more than forty years ago, and have reappeared in several plans since then. In 1958 the plan for additional transportation capacity was designed on the assumption that the population would increase by around 400,000 to 1990, a forecast that proved to come very close to actual growth. Since 1990 the population has increased by an additional 130,000. Thus, it is merely indecision in the past that has made traffic problems in the region in urgent need of a solution.

In addition to this, in the emerging knowledge and network economy, the quality of the metropolitan transportation system is a matter of growing importance.

One important matter concerns the attractiveness of metropolitan areas as a place of residence. Access to labor with a higher education has an increasing influence on the location of knowledge–oriented firms, (Giuliano, 1989), and if the metropolitan regions cannot offer attractive residential areas they run the risk of losing their role as centers of knowledge production and innovation.

One prerequisite of a diversified labor market and a highly specialized labor supply is a transportation and communications infrastructure that makes the metropolitan area function as a whole. However, the low investment in transportation in Stockholm has resulted in the deteriorating quality of the transportation system, with congestion becoming prevalent as traffic volumes increase. Without any special steps being taken, much of the increased travel threatens to be dominated by car trips, which would worsen the environmental situation, especially in the inner parts of the metropolitan area.

Further, when companies plan to move from Stockholm, it is more often the case of moving to London, or other metropolitan regions in Europe. The reasons stated for the move are very frequently 'larger market', 'access to market' – reasons which basically concern reduced geographic transaction costs. That is, the reason reflects accessibility to customers, specialized labor, professionals, suppliers etc.

In sum, the quality and capacity of the transportation infrastructure is of greatest importance if the Stockholm region is to be integrated into a major metropolitan region, able to attract global companies in competition with other European metropolitan regions, and provide sufficient market potential to give equal growth opportunities.

It is thus obvious that the *economic strategy* for the Stockholm region should be fundamentally based on improvements of the transportation system. It is likewise obvious that the transportation system plays a crucial role in the *environmental strategy*. However, what has been paid less attention to is the integrating and uniting role of the transportation system with respect to the third, *social strategy*. This role can be demonstrated by analyzing how the location of households and firms depends on accessibility in different parts of the region.

Preliminary studies support the hypothesis that the transportation system has an influence on the choice of residential area for households with different educational levels, as well as on the choice of location of firms with different education profiles. During the period 1985–1995 the education gap between the northern (higher education) and southern part (lower education) of the region became wider, both with respect to location of households and firms. This development could partially be influenced by investments in the transportation system. By improved north–south links differences in the education structure between the northern and the southern part of the region would probably decrease.

Against this background it was with great anticipation that a political agreement on an overall solution for traffic in the County of Stockholm was finally reached in 1992, the so-called Dennis Agreement. According to a directive from Parliament and the Government, the aim of the Agreement is 'by means of measures taken in connection with the overall traffic system, to improve the environment, increase accessibility and create greater potential for regional development'. Coincidental or not, the threefold focus on economic development, the environment and accessibility seems to be well adapted to the three Sector Strategies, formulated as a basis for regional planning.

As for the content of this Agreement, it may be worthwhile to examine an extract from official documents:

The improvement in public transportation is an important part of the Dennis Agreement. For bus services in the inner part of the city, a trunk route network served by environmentally adapted buses is planned – a form of underground railway system but located on the surface. The buses will not have to compete with other traffic in the street environment and journey times can be cut by up to 35 percent.

In order for the trunk routes to function properly, there must be a reduction in the volume of traffic on the streets in central Stockholm. The measures adopted to achieve this are an orbital route, referred to as the Stockholm Ring Road, and the Outer Bypass Route.

The trunk route network reflects the idea behind the Dennis Agreement and represents a comprehensive approach. Each part of the Agreement can be described as a piece of a jigsaw puzzle, and all the parts are needed in order to create an overall solution.

According to estimates made in 1995, the investments in the Dennis Agreement amount to more than SEK 40 billion, for the period 1992 to 2006, with figures calculated at the January 1992 price level. In 1996, however, the Agreement was broken and the jigsaw puzzle is now very incomplete. Some parts have been carried out; others will be later. But, as for components like the Stockholm Ring and the Western Link – a strategic part of the Outer Bypass Route – these projects have, again, been indefinitely postponed.

Without going into details as to the reasons why the Dennis Agreement failed, two specific comments could be given, concerning methods used for decision support.

First, the highway appraisal exercise approved (Cost Benefit Analysis, CBA) provides a very narrow model. In the Netherlands, like Sweden a country with strong planning traditions, CBA is seen as a necessary but not sufficient tool in appraising large transportation projects, and therefore also other factors also have to be included, for example land use effects.

Second, CBA (and its national parameters) is not adapted to the specific setting in the Stockholm region. Evidently, a large and strategic investment, like the Western Link, which will obviously influence conditions for the future development of the Stockholm region, cannot be evaluated using the same set of assumptions and tools assessing the effects of a minor road in some sparsely populated region elsewhere in the country.

This kind of methodological argument is discussed further in the two concluding sections of the chapter.

The Need for Adequate Land Use and Transportation Planning Tools

In some respects there has been a renaissance in large-scale urban models – perhaps somewhat unexpectedly. There are many reasons for this, both on the supply and the demand side. A brief retrospection could help to bring this into perspective (Anderstig and Mattsson, 1998).

When large-scale urban and regional models emerged on the scene in the sixties, a lot of expectations were raised about a paradigmatic change in planning practice, from an intuitive style to one based on scientific principles. A decade later a common view was that these efforts had essentially ended in failure (Lee, 1973; see also Lee, 1994). The models were accused of being too data hungry, non-transparent, and in need of extensive and costly computer hardware, just to mention a few points of criticism. Lee also argued that the traditional planning process, as well as the land-use models that were developed, fitted into a top-down or command-and-control approach that supported centralized planning aimed at a detailed specification of land uses and behavior.

Large-scale urban land use modeling did not die, however; it survived and developed as an academic activity rather than as a regular instrument in comprehensive urban and regional planning. As a matter of fact, the following period turned out to be quite successful from an academic point of view, as rapid progress was made in many areas of importance to building land use models.

Firstly, advances in random utility theory, discrete choice modeling, entropy maximization, and network equilibrium theory have been of importance for the present understanding and sometimes also for the unification of different modeling approaches. Secondly, sophisticated applications of optimization principles have become standard ingredients in formulating models consistent with rational behavior, in solving different kinds of equilibrium problems and in estimating model parameters efficiently. Thirdly, more recently, concepts from the theory of dynamic systems have enriched the repertoire.

On the whole this progress has been helpful in combating the black box syndrome and should in the long run increase the transparency of applied urban and regional models. Furthermore, computer speed has continued to increase as if there is no limit. It is less known that many computational algorithms have been improved at approximately the same rate. This has facilitated the application of large-scale models. Today data availability rather than computer capacity is the main restriction.

The environment in which urban and regional planning takes place has also changed. Now it is neither acceptable nor possible for planning authorities to dictate land uses in detailed plans. No one believes that planning can be a strictly scientific activity, even if planners can become better in making use of scientific findings, methods, and tools. The focus of planning has changed from prescribing solutions to providing problem analyses and decision support. Often the planners have the role of finding good compromises among different conflicting interests. Negotiation planning has become an established form of planning.

These changes in planning practice do not imply that computer-based modeling instruments will be less important. On the contrary the demand for detailed forecasts, precision and flexibility will increase, as it becomes established practice to support decision-makers and the public with broad impact analyses. This is now increasingly the case in the field of large-scale infrastructure investment. These new demands often go in the direction of more detailed analyses, which may require more elaborate and perhaps also more complicated models, and may counteract the endeavor to make transparent and simple models.

The criticism of the command-and-control character of planning, and of urban and regional models, has sometimes taken the form of an attack on the rational mode of planning. Here a swing back can be noticed. Environmental issues, which are now so urgent, call for more rationalism, not less. Consider for example the issue of promoting economic development without sacrificing the opportunities of future generations, i.e. the aim of sustainable urban development. Coping with such problems necessitates a comprehensive understanding of the urban system, and this is what operational urban and regional models attempt to provide.

Proposals of large infrastructure investment raise the question of the interaction between the transportation system, the land use structure, and the environment. To what extent do new roads and improved public transportation systems contribute to excessive urban commuting? Will such investments lead to a more dispersed land use pattern, and hence further impair the market for public transportation? Can various planning measures counteract such tendencies? What restrictions can sustainable urban and regional development place on the freedom of mobility?

To investigate such strategic long-term issues, carefully designed operational land use and transportation models could be very useful. The models could help planners to convince decision-makers that the (often unpleasant) recommendations they propose will have the stated consequences. In many situations, when practical experiments are too costly or would take too long a time before reliable conclusions could be drawn, they are perhaps the only realistic alternatives (Harris, 1994). To be useful such strategic models must be built on a systems view of the urban economy, reflecting a comprehensive understanding of the driving mechanisms. They must be able to simulate the urban housing, labor, and transportation markets realistically, to give useful evaluations of cost changes, different investment strategies, regulation policies and economic incentives, preferably within a common framework.

The impacts of major infrastructure projects in metropolitan areas are discussed intensely in Sweden today, as in many other countries. Better tools for analyzing long-range impacts on the settlement structure have been explicitly demanded (Governmental Bill, 1994). Yet such analyses do not have the same legislative support as in the US, where the Clean Air Act Amendments of 1990 and the Intermodal Surface Transportation Efficiency Act of 1991 explicitly require such analyses (Lakshmanan, 1998). However, in the Swedish follow-up of Agenda 21 of the 1992 UN conference in Rio de Janeiro, the municipalities were ordered to investigate the long-term relationship between the transportation system, the land use structure, and the environment. In particular they were supposed to consider to what extent a sensible regional planning policy would be capable of linking long-term development in compliance with sustainable development.

These and similar observations in other countries indicate that we may very well be on the threshold of a breakthrough in the application of operational urban and regional models. For this to succeed it will be necessary to pay close attention to the problems and needs of the planning organizations, for which the models are meant to be useful. Closer interaction, co-operation and the exchange of ideas between academic researchers and urban planners would definitely be necessary, and could also stimulate new research. Perhaps the final step from academic journals to user-friendly computer systems (and one should not underestimate the investment needed) is best performed in privatized forms, as has been the case with the fortunate market penetration of some urban transportation planning software packages.

Towards Sensible Decision Processes – As an Alternative to Indecisive Cost Benefit Analysis

As hinted above, the traditional tool for decision support in transportation planning and cost benefit analysis, has obvious shortcomings when it comes to application in a metropolitan setting – where land use effects necessarily have to complement traditional components in the CBA calculus, i.e. effects on generalized costs and environmental effects, evaluated at some price per kg of a specific emission, agreed on often in political negotiations.

Other shortcomings come even more into focus especially in the inner parts and, from the point of view of the transportation system, narrower parts of a metropolitan city, like Stockholm, – mainly due to the clearly manifest conflicting interests.

This point may be illustrated by the recent, or rather renewed, proposal about analyzing the conditions for added capacity for rail and public transportation in central Stockholm. The Government has assigned to the

National Rail Administration, together with the National Road Administration, and in co-operation with the municipality of Stockholm, the task of analyzing the consequences of building a third rail in 'surface position' and bury the Central Bridge in a tunnel.

This is about the narrowest part in the Stockholm transportation system, considering the capacity in relation to the amount of traffic flows – by car and public transportation, and local, regional and national trains. A large number of analyses have already been carried out over the years. Most of these reports have resulted in strongly stated feelings and lively debates. These debates do not seem to increase the willingness for compromise, or allow progress toward a solution to the problem. On the contrary, it seems as if the strong feelings have made the positions even more fixed. Given this fact it may seem reasonable to believe that an objective analysis of benefits and costs for society (CBA) could contribute to canceling the deadlocks and creating unity for a solution to the problem.

As far as we know, a cost benefit analysis has not been applied to the so-called Central Tunnel. The benefits of the tunnel have, however, been thoroughly discussed in a report from the Riddarholmen Commission, called 'Spår, Miljö och stadsbild i centrala Stockholm' (SOU 1996:121). As for the other part of the proposed capacity addition, the so-called Third Rail, a cost benefit analysis is given in 'New Rails through Stockholm', from the National Rail Administration.

Some other, more qualitative discussions about the benefits and costs of the proposal have also been produced.

One reason why CBA has not been applied to the Central Tunnel may be that its positive effects are difficult, first, to identify and, second, to evaluate. It may of course be easy to agree that the tunnel does not produce any significant timesaving for car drivers, in comparison to the existing bridge. Further, the effect of noise reduction may not be very difficult to estimate, or even evaluate. But, it is much more difficult to assess the economic benefit of more attractive scenery and the effect of improved environmental quality in a historically sensitive district.

Given these difficulties it is natural to ask whether it is worthwhile to try to perform a traditional cost benefit analysis. There are many actors involved, representing partly conflicting interests. In addition it is easy to imagine that the many uncertain factors involved would mean that the results would be called into question by some actors. Thus it cannot be taken for granted that the result of a traditional cost benefit analysis would imply that the question about the Third Rail would come closer to a solution.

On the other hand it can be argued that a decision about added public transportation capacity in central Stockholm by necessity is associated with a large number of very difficult judgements and assessments. It could also be argued that all participating interests must demonstrate that their arguments are based on a balance between social benefits and costs, if the arguments are to be taken seriously. They must, for instance, pay attention to the traffic consequences if there is no added capacity. It could also be claimed that interested parties try to see the expected effects of realizing alternative solutions. With such a common knowledge base, it would probably be feasible to agree on a sensible solution.

The discussion seems to end in a logical dilemma. It can be expected that the results of a cost benefit analysis would be strongly questioned, and not unite the different interests around a common view. On the other hand it seems as if a judicious and sensible decision would make judgments and assessments of the very same kind as those included in the cost benefit analysis.

The logical dilemma is, however, just illusory. The key to a solution is accepting that various interested parties are involved, and that they legitimately represent partly conflicting interests. Accepting this, a decision process could be shaped, a process which with the support of a neutral mediator would make it possible to establish a common platform, give each party additional knowledge concerning the interests of the other parties, and finally produce a solution. The mediator/conciliator must have resources to establish the platform, and reasonable resources to give the parties involved the kind of information and knowledge required during the process.

The common platform should initially include a description of the background and definition of the problem, agreed on by all parties.

Once the process starts, the role of the mediator is to successfully help the parties to identify and describe the effects generated by the different alternatives, and describe the magnitude of the economic values associated with the respective effects. Finally, the social benefits are then compared to social costs and an attempt is made to agree on a solution.

The kind of decision process outlined has been applied with increasing frequency in the last ten years. As seen from the recent NSF conference, 'Alternatives to Traditional CV in Environmental Valuation', variants of the process are used increasingly in environmental contexts in the US. In Sweden researchers at the Department of Infrastructure and Planning, Royal Institute of Technology, have developed this approach for real applications. They have also acted as mediators in real decision processes, among others in the field of urban housing renewal.

References

Anderstig, C. and Mattsson, L.-G. (1998), 'Modelling Land-Use and Transport Interaction: Policy Analyses Using the IMREL Model ', in L. Lundqvist, L–G. Mattsson and T. J. Kim (eds), *Network Infrastructure and the Urban Environment*, Springer-Verlag, Berlin, pp. 308–28.

European Commission (1996), *European Sustainable Cities*, Report by the Expert Group on the Urban Environment, DG XI, Brussels.

Giuliano, G. (1989), 'New directions for understanding transportation and land use', *Environment and Planning*, vol. 21A, pp.145–59.

Governmental Bill (1994), 'Finansiering av vissa väginvesteringar i Stockholms län m. m.' ('Financing of some road investments in the county of Stockholm etc.'), Regeringens proposition 1993/94:86.

Harris, B. (1994), 'The real issues concerning Lee's 'Requiem'', *Journal of the American Planning Association*, vol. 60, pp. 31–4.

Lakshmanan, T.R. (1998), 'The Changing Context of Transportation Modeling: Implications of the New Economy, Intermodalism and the Drive for Environmental Quality', in L. Lundqvist, L–G. Mattsson and T. J. Kim (eds), *Network Infrastructure and the Urban Environment*, Springer-Verlag, Berlin, pp. 53–71.

Lee, D.B. (1973), 'Requiem for large-scale models', *Journal of the American Institute of Planners*, vol. 39, pp. 163–78.

Lee, D.B. (1994), 'Retrospective on large-scale models', *Journal of the American Planning Association*, vol. 60, pp. 35–40.

Office of Regional Planning and Urban Transportation (1999), *Stockholmsregionens framtid* (The Stockholm Region in the Future), Stockholm.

4 Planning with a Ceiling

CHRISTER SANNE

Introduction

Regional planning has traditionally been concerned with land use and with infrastructure(s) and buildings of great longevity. A long time horizon is natural. Ecological issues and natural resources management, which also demand a long time horizon, have now come into focus at all levels of society, including the regional level. The term sustainable development is a reminder that we live in a finite world.

But even if the planning discourse has taken limits of natural resources on board, it has by and large failed to problematize how this conflicts with the notions of expanding production and the economy. Today's planning, including at the regional level, normally aims at satisfying demands – sometimes referred to as 'needs' – expressed or defined in society. Such demands are principally unbounded and the notion of (unlimited) economic growth is an integral part of most planning exercises.

In contrast, this chapter proposes 'planning with a ceiling' where the ceiling is set by nature's biophysical limits for resource exploitation and pollution. We argue that this means a veritable paradigm shift compared to the present projective type of planning and that this shift is unavoidable in order to achieve sustainability. Like the idea of back-casting it proceeds from a specific future state of society and seeks a path connecting now and then although the concern here is limits rather than desirability.

Regional planning is taken as the activity of preparing for a future state of a region – itself a vague term implying a geographical area usually corresponding to an administrative unit with some planning authority. The focus here is on the content of the planning – the description of external conditions, analyses and action proposals – rather than the process of arriving at these: the institutions, the rules; the 'what' rather than the 'how'.

Planning is assumed to be a task of the administration according to guidelines handed down from political assemblies. Thus planners are assumed to represent the general will rather than act as the mediators in a power game between private and public interests. This is not to deny that the plans and the processes we see today are thoroughly permeated with the interests of business.

Given the dominant role of economics and its growth paradigm in regional planning – and the stated claim that this perspective is untenable in the long run – most of this chapter is devoted to the issues of limits to growth and sustainability.

The discussion follows a recognized pattern in the ecological discourse and should be useful to planners at large. The chapter continues with a section on sustainable development in relation to conventional planning while the last section discusses the possible role and structure of regional planning with regard to sustainability.

Limits to Growth – Original and New Interpretations

The use of natural resources cannot expand forever in a finite world. This has been a message for a generation now, since the Club of Rome document 'Limits to Growth' (Meadows et al., 1972). At the time of publication, it met with a very strong public response, because of its common sensical character but also because people could themselves observe the adverse environmental effects of growing industrial production. Books like 'The Silent Spring' (Carson, 1963), which disclosed the extinction of species with pesticides and industrial pollution, were very timely.

But several objections were raised to this notion of limits to growth (Cole, 1973, Freeman and Jahoda, 1978). The modeling was claimed to be crude and even deceptive. The concept of growth also needed clarification. Economic growth was seen as boundless because it concerned a valuation of goods and services, which is not conditioned on the resources employed. It was also held, against the notion of limited natural resources, that the production system, which the economy describes, would adapt. Scarce resources would be substituted if the prices signaled that they were becoming scarce.

All the same, the outcome of this alarm was a certain adaptation to environmental conditions. Research institutions and public agencies became concerned with the protection of nature (mainly from pollution, less from exhaustion of natural resources). But this never kept governments from pursuing a policy of economic growth. As time went by, and especially with the financial problems of the 1970s and 1980s, the environmental issues became embedded in the normal administrative order and were rarely allowed to interfere with the growth policy.

In the 1990s a new generation of limits-to-growth analyses have appeared which are more planning-oriented. In several European countries, reports have set the conditions for sustainable development. 'Sustainable Netherlands/ Germany/ Norway/ Britain' provide examples. The reports vary in character from NGO documents to semi-official or official reports.[1]

These reports reopen the issue of the physical limits of the earth. The concern has shifted from the lack of natural resources to issues of (mainly) global pollution. 'Sinks' more than 'sources' are assumed to constitute the gravest problem. Few argue that we are running out of essential minerals. Renewable and non-renewable resources are treated separately. But there is a broad scientific consensus about a 'greenhouse effect' due to human activities with great threats of adverse future effects. 'The ozone hole' is another adequate metaphor describing the global, long-lasting environmental damage caused by certain chemicals released into the atmosphere.

Beyond that – but less in public focus today – is a growing concern about future food supplies. In many parts of the world land and water are used unsustainably. Urbanization and industries infringe upon productive soils. Erosion and salinization reduce the available areas or limit the yields. Meanwhile the demand for grain grows rapidly with rising living standards in newly industrialized countries like China. In a few years time, world trade in grains may change dramatically with severe consequences for people worldwide with low purchasing power.

To remedy the problems, all reports suggest concerted action to reduce the flows of raw materials and cut energy use. To this end, it is suggested that many activities be restructured, i. e. agriculture and transports. A number of toxic substances should be banned in industrial use. Some reports also foresee or propose rather far-reaching changes in lifestyles.

The emerging discipline of 'ecological economics' is based on a parallel tenet: we have outgrown the planet. Human action – in the technosphere – is no longer insignificant compared to the size of the surrounding natural system, the eco- or biosphere. Boulding (1966) long ago expressed this as the switch from a 'cowboy economy' to a 'spaceship economy'. Daly (1991) calls it a fallacy of the discipline of economics to acknowledge that it has three dimensions which must all be considered. Traditionally, economics has been occupied with *efficiency* in the allocation of resources. A secondary issue is the social *distribution* of goods (and bads). But until now economics has largely neglected the *scale* of human activities. Today this has become crucial in relation to the capacity of the environment. This is also the idea of a ceiling in planning.

Economics, Environment and Sustainability

The new generation of limits-to-growth books hovers around the concept sustainability, introduced to politics and planning by the Brundtland report (World Commission on Environment and Development, 1987) and at the Rio conference in 1992. As a much used term, it is also much disputed. Basically it is concerned with the maintenance of the biophysical stocks and flows and the capacity of the biosphere to provide essential environmental services. The standard definition (taken from the report) also emphasizes intergenerational justice. The needs of future generations must not be curtailed by our use of natural resources (or our polluting of the sinks; sinks and sources are matches).

The discipline of economics has also accepted the challenge posed by the environmental threats and the opinions of economists are in the midst of the debate. Three points will be discussed: pricing, sustainability and economic growth.

Pricing

The principal reaction of the economic discipline to the problems of pollution and overuse of natural resources is that they represent 'market failures'. A suitably designed economic system with 'correct prices' is assumed to be able to handle the situation satisfactorily. In this view, the crucial point is that polluting emissions are now discharged freely into the 'commons' – such as the atmosphere or rivers – without compensation for those harmed, i. e. in the case of the atmosphere all humans. If the emissions were priced, the discharges could be 'internalized' into the economy as a cost levied on production. Principally this can follow two lines. A hypothetical market may be created with prices based on individual preferences as revealed by 'willingness to pay' (WTP) analyses and operated by public bodies. Or property rights may be defined for what is now the commons, thereby creating a real market (although this is unlikely in cases like the atmosphere). The understanding is that with correct prices – including reimbursements for the harm caused – actors in the market would also make decisions which would optimize welfare in society.

These thoughts have led to a lively discussion about 'green taxes' and similar duties. But the political penetration is slow. There are carbon dioxide taxes in some countries. A system of tradable permits for sulphur dioxide emissions has been quite successful (in terms of increased cost efficiency) in the US. But the inertia is very great for various reasons. As long as levies do not affect all producers, they are liable to distort competition and will be vigorously opposed. In the case of gaseous emissions – which spread in the atmosphere, to which nobody can claim ownership – levies must be agreed upon by the international community in order to be efficient and avoid free-riding. This is obviously a slow process (although the CFC-abatement procedure against the ozone hole may be quoted as a fairly rapid one).

Sustainability

In economic parlance the concept of sustainability is often transformed into a requirement to bequeath sufficient capital to future generations. Capital is regarded as the stock of resources which is capable of providing a flow of benefits. Various views are possible between 'weak' and 'strong' sustainability. In the weak variant it is considered satisfactory to leave a constant total volume of various types of capital behind. This means that natural resources may be consumed if other types of resources are created. Strong sustainability requires that each kind of natural and man-made capital remain (at least) intact in size. This is based on the claim that they complement each other; a favorite example from ecological economics is trees and sawmills.

No matter how many industries we may construct, the inputs from nature will still be essential. If categories like human capital –knowledge and skills in a population – are included as an asset, the claim for sustainability with constant total capital appears all the weaker since humans perish with their talents.

Some analysts even claim that only the strong variant, which explicitly safeguards nature, merits the name sustainable. Likewise it should be noted that correct prices, as discussed above, do not imply sustainability. There is no reason to suppose that what people individually express as a willingness to pay will limit the material flows sufficiently (Jacobs, 1997).

Sustainability as concerns the relation between present and future generations is handled in economics by discounting.[2] Costs and benefits occurring at different points in time are referred to a common instant according to the rules of cost-benefit analysis (which is also a standard tool for planners). But calculations applying a discount rate comparable to normal financial practices (as suggested by e. g. Nordhaus, 1994) tend to obliterate the interests of future generations weighed on a discounting scale.

One example: by using a discount rate of 6 percent over a period of 400 years – which is a fair definition of 'sustainable' – the discounted utility of the final 250 years amounted to as much as the first three (3) years! This is clearly not reasonable. Most people would hold that coming generations have inviolable rights and that other ways of describing this are necessary; see also Jacobs (1994).

Economic Growth

The third and perhaps most controversial issue is the feasibility of continued economic growth. Growth has become an integral part of the Western understanding of progress – growth, progress and efficiency form a unit of thought. Full employment is a major welfare goal and a common assumption is that this requires economic growth. This explains the present concordance between the political system and business to maintain economic expansion. The business interest in larger turnover – for larger profits – coincides with government's interest in more jobs. By and large, economic growth remains unquestioned in the political discussion. In economic theory, it is justified by the assumption that growth promotes people's welfare.[3]

This is economic growth in a rather abstract mode. The goals of the early welfare state were mostly expressed in tangible advances like better housing, schools or medical care. Today's growth is measured in percentage growth over last year's gross domestic product. A constant rate of growth thus means an acceleration in real terms. Even moderate growth rates will result in sizeable increases in the economy over the periods of time discussed in regional planning.

Historically, economic growth has always been accompanied by large increases in activities and consumption, causing a heavier environmental load. And economic modelers prescribe what economic policy to pursue in order to make the wheels move faster, often with little regard to the ecological or social consequences.

Favored proposals include not only higher education and vocational (re)training and improved transport facilities but also tax cuts, subsidies to business, encouraging household consumption and relaxation of environmental restrictions. All of this is evidently contradictory to a prudent environmental line.[4]

It is intriguing that several 'top-down' economic analyses (quoted by Kågesson, 1997) claim that repressing carbon dioxide down to a very low level – down 60–80 percent which merits the label sustainable – can be achieved with very marginal consequences for economic growth – down in the order of 0.1–0.2 percent annually.

One way to explain this is that these changes reflect an economy based on totally different prices. The goods and services we are used to demand a higher price – because of their environmental adjustment – in such a way that there is apparent growth, but higher incomes do not allow increased consumption or a higher level of activities (of resource-demanding kinds).[5]

In Defense of Business-as-usual

Thus economic growth is vigorously defended. But on a closer look, this defense is very much an appeal for – literally – business-as-usual, i.e. the upholding of the economic structure much as we know it today. Four kinds or arguments are used to refute the environmentalists' – or the ecologists' – demand for a change of direction in society. Since this is of vital importance for planning, we will spell them out, each with accompanying counterclaims:

- *'We do not know for sure'*: The claim for change of direction, or even for prudence, is set aside by pointing at the scientific uncertainty. The topical case is global warming. This is an extremely complex issue and an arena for conflicting and resourceful interests groups. Skeptics within the scientific community may feel encouraged to voice their views and they will readily find listeners. Economists have claimed that protective measures would be so costly – in terms of forgone economic growth – that it is better to suspend any action until more knowledge has been gained (Nordhaus, 1994). The large and very cautious IPCC panel of scientists has, however, concluded that there is indeed a human-induced climate change and the objections to cost-benefit analysis apply in full to the economists' work. Waiting for scientific unity is senseless; this issue rather calls for application of the precautionary principle in one or another interpretation.
- *'We do not get the signals'*: Many economists have pointed out that the notion of resource shortage is not supported by the rising prices of fossil fuels or minerals and conclude that there is no problem at hand.[6] The conclusion may however be premature, an unreasonable trust in the efficiency of the market. Lacking price signals in these cases is probably more due to the political aims and conditions than to satisfactory supplies. Each of the petroleum exporting countries is not in a position to set its prices in such a way that it guarantees the supply of future generations. The unbalanced power relations in the global

trade also force poor and indebted countries to sell their produce cheaply. Likewise, the lack (by and large) of proper pricing of harmful emissions (due to the lack of appropriate global agreements as discussed above) gives the wrong signals to the actors.

- *'We are underway towards a sustainable society'*: The economies of advanced countries are undergoing a change. Demand gradually turns to services, which make up an increasing portion of the economy. These services are presumably less resource demanding and less environmentally harmful. This leads to a 'dematerialization theory' of the economy. Decreasing material intensity for some important materials in Western countries supports the theory – less is used per unit of GDP. But in most cases, this effect is nullified by the growth in the economy; there is a 'relative delinking' from growth but not an 'absolute' one because volumes still rise. This does not lead to a sustainable state.[7]

- *'We have the means'*: This fact, that production in the most developed countries is turning more material/energy efficient and less ecologically harmful per unit of output, creates the eco-efficiency claim: we can do better because there are technical fixes to the problems. We just have to apply them. This is expressed in the topical 'factor-exercise' which claims that 4- or even 10-fold efficiency increases are 'possible' or even 'likely'. The noted book 'Faktor Vier' from the Wuppertal Institute in Germany (Lovins et al., 1995) provides a list of illustrating cases and the idea has gained a great political following. But the authors never claim that a factor 4 is generally technically possible, much less a factor 10. It is more correct to say that 4- or 10-fold reductions in resources are *required* in the north to achieve sustainability.

Sustainable Development and Planning

Although the term sustainability in modern usage evidently stems from ecology, it has been widely adopted in the planning discourse, especially as 'sustainable development'. In this process, various interests tend to transform the term in ways that favor them.

One interpretation which is clearly at odds with the basic idea is to regard the present development as what should be sustained in the sense that it should be continued (as in the term sustainable (economic) growth – in most quarters regarded as an oxymoron).

A related interpretation is to broaden the meaning to include the triple notions of ecological, economic and social sustainability (sometimes cultural as well). This seems to imply the safeguarding of what one considers valuable within each sector (and in the economic sector it need not be growth but might indicate stability). But such a usage of a trinity of sustainabilities can be ambiguous. It seems to suggest that one can put the three on par or make a trade-off between them – just as contemporary planning often involves a deliberate balancing of interests. But it goes almost without saying that nature's services are, and will always remain, a prerequisite for human culture, i. e. for the economy (the production and valuation system) and the social system. Ecological sustainability remains the base because we are infinitely complicated beings and cannot survive in a world of artefacts only.[8]

This said, the cards can still be turned to illustrate another and very relevant relationship between the three. A malfunctioning economic or social system threatens nature, the ecological system. An extreme breakdown of the social system is warfare; a topic example is the burning oilfields in the wake of the Gulf war in 1991, which caused extensive smoke pollution over large regions. Another case is environmental damage from hillside or slash-and-burn agriculture and mismanagement of forests (as described in several parts of the world). If the economic system affords no other way, people may – in order to survive – destroy the productive capacity of their own environment.

These examples illustrate a mutual dependency. Nature's services are prerequisites for human economic and social systems. But these human systems must also function well in order to maintain ecological sustainability. But if planning is constituted as a process of negotiation – as is proposed and practiced in much of contemporary planning – nature cannot play the role of an interested party. Nature can only punish a society that does not respect the conditions for ecological sustainability, the ceiling that applies to human planning. But due to the resilience of nature – which often enables it to buffer damages up to a point – nature's arguments may be overlooked and neglected.

An ingenious way of expressing the ecological limits of sustainability – in the political discourse as well as in everyday speech – is the concept of environmental space (Vereniging Milieudefensie, 1994). The concept is derived from the idea that the earth has a certain carrying capacity and implies that each individual is entitled to a space as the right to use a certain amount of land and raw materials or the right to emit a certain amount of waste products (like carbon dioxide).

The total allowable space is determined by the scientific knowledge about resources and the environment. By division, each person's allotted share can be calculated – including future generations whose opportunities must not be narrowed by our actions.

The value of the concept is that it is simple and commonsensical and manages to link the global issues with local individual ones – daily activities can be regarded in the light of a long term development. This transparency also gives the concept a readily understandable ethical content (including the aspect of distribution).[9]

A related concept is the ecological footprint which expresses the amount of land required to cater for a human being – or the whole population of a region – at a given level of consumption. The footprints cover the areas needed for production as well as for taking care of pollution. This makes the concept very relevant to regional planning: it gives a ready answer to the question whether a region can manage with its inhabitants within its physical borders or whether it draws on the resources of other regions.

Neither of these concepts sets a fixed limit to the goods and services rendered to humans. That will at any time depend on the technology available to transform raw materials, energy or land to human use with the concomitant pollution. But the concepts set the ceiling based on today's scientific evidence about the geophysical world and available technology. Higher efficiency in material or energy or reduced emissions would allow material growth in useful output within the same environmental space. Thus the concepts do not imply zero-economic growth, neither by definition nor in practice.

All the same, the present global production system, the global economy, is by almost every account unsustainable. This point was made already in the first generation of limits-to-growth reports and is repeated by each new one.[10]

Whatever measure is chosen, rich Western countries like Sweden would have to change their production and consumption patterns radically to safeguard the needs of future generations. The environmental space should be reduced by at least a factor of 4; our ecological footprints are more than three times the permissible ones (Wackernagel and Rees, 1996; Sånnek, 1998).

In addition to this global overdraft, there is the glaring – and still growing – gap between rich and poor countries. The production systems in less developed countries may be less efficient in environmental terms but the richest 20 percent of the world still consume 80 percent of the resources. It is mainly here that reductions are due.

Regional Planning with a Ceiling

In the long run, it is inevitable that planning with a ceiling for a continuous expansion will be substituted for the current system in the rich parts of the world. But there is little today to indicate such a change of course, nor are the forces to achieve it very obvious. Nonetheless, it is important to discuss the possible role of regional planning: the scope for intervention, the dominating versus emerging trends and the role of planners.

Evidently any spatial or regional planning occupies an intermediate position between national policies (which could be, but seldom are called national planning) and the deliberations individuals make on their activities, their personal plans. At either level, we can envision how a ceiling is applied.

The nation is an established arena for discussing long term developments such as the conditions for future generations or the defense of the territory (including the land's productive capacity) – in short the destiny of the nation's people and culture. Furthermore only nations possess the appropriate legislative capacity and the monopoly of use of physical force. Sometimes the nation also has the exclusive right to levy taxes.

Individuals, for their part, have the freedom to choose lifestyle. If convinced to do so, they may establish personal norms of sufficiency. This is the main key to change. Technology continuously increases the efficiency of production. But we have seen that the growing efficiency must not be used to increase the volumes, the material throughput, in the economy. In a sustainable world, efficiency must be matched with a corresponding norm expressing that what has been achieved is enough – sufficiency. This would be a commitment, based on a personal conviction and ethic, to conduct one's life with a ceiling. Individuals would assume a responsibility as consumers but also as citizens by instructing their legislators to pass laws which help curb the growth in volume.

Regions occupy a position in between. A trend in the capitalist world is that regions, rather than nations as a whole, become the nodes of economic development. Regions strive to attract investments with international capital employing their competitive advantages such as an efficient infrastructure, cultural attractions, a well developed (and possibly docile) labor force. Thus regional planning is very much concerned with the competition between regions. Mainstream regional planning takes on the task of analyzing the conditions and prescribing the appropriate means to achieve optimal (economic) development. Economic growth is an integral part of the suggested future. Most plans describe an expansion – more travel, larger housing and higher consumption per capita – which contradicts goals of (ecological) sustainability. There is little in this planning to indicate the costs of this policy to the hinterland – in other words, the ecological footprints caused by the chosen policies; see also Harvey (1982) and Harvey (1985).[11]

But regions also have a significant quality, which points in the opposite direction. A region forms a local arena where the effects of economic and environmental policy can be quite tangible. The feedback from the growth of activities to pollution, traffic congestion and other daily concerns is obvious to all. People react to this and being in the local arena can join in action from their experience. This is the opposite of distancing – the tendency that the globalized economy inhibits any concrete and effective action.[12]

There are presently signals of a reversal in the omnipresent tendencies of globalizing the economy where all regions are competing on a single market. The drawbacks of fierce international competition have become evident. There is a loss of local influence and loss of – or insecurity about – job opportunities and intense underbidding to attract investors. In the environmental field, international corporations are set on externalizing as many effects and costs as possible while locals in the region demand that these be internalized.

The signals have been weak and divided but many observers at the recent WTO meeting in Seattle – the 'Battle of Seattle' – regarded it as a turnabout in the attitude to the globalize economy, towards more local empowerment. Measures are being taken in many places to re-regionalize the economy – to shield at least parts of it from the ravages of the global economy. 'Taking the economy back home again' may for instance mean to favor local banks, which in turn lend to local enterprises; this is a call often heard in the US. It may also mean working for local self-sufficiency in various respects, e.g. by contract with farmers in the surrounding districts; see Douthwaite (1996).

Such actions squarely contradict the economic dictum of efficient allocation, which is also a cornerstone of mainstream regional planning. The economic textbooks claim that it means reduced growth, i.e. a staggering welfare increase. But if inhabitants of the region are concerned with job security they may prefer local firms, as more stable, to outsiders. If they believe that local enterprises will care more for the environment, they may favor them, regardless of what economic theory claims, all the more so if they expect local firms to offer a fairer distribution of benefits than outsiders.

This prompts a closer look at the role of regional planning and the planner. Planning, as does the discipline of economics, claims to be based on rational analysis. But planning is never a politically neutral activity. Just as the camp of environmentalists is divided in light and dark greens, planners belong to various factions and may take sides with one or the other social group.

The agenda-setting groups in the political debate tend to accept and even lean on the conventional rules of the economic game in a conviction that the exposure to the global economy is a win-win situation which in the long run will be beneficial to all. But large groups in the population are currently concerned with how to cope with the fast changes in the labor market and the conditions of work. At the same time, they can observe that the present policies tend to widen the gaps in incomes and living standards. The distrust that follows causes serious strains in society.

Issues of sustainability display a similar divide. Most planning has adopted a measure of environmental concern. Many planners also work hard to achieve more efficient structures and this has often been quite successful within the intended frame of thinking. Evidently planning bodies have some means at their disposal:

- They can develop monitoring systems expressed in welfare terms to encourage analyses of a more relevant type than economic monitoring. Such systems would not only include safety and health and social integration but what Amartya Sen calls the 'fulfillment of human capabilities': how people fare in terms of activity and creativity.[13]
- They can demand and promote more stringent efficiency requirements for new construction. Some recent ambitious housing developments in Stockholm and London feature a reduction in domestic heating on the order of a factor of 2.[14]
- They can organize for less polluting and resource-demanding transport; this is traditional traffic planning with the well-known problems of promoting public over private transport.
- They can foster social innovations – such as leasing, sharing and other ways of making do with less – to complement lean production and the design of durable, long-lived and reparable products which are needed for a reduced resource use.

Such measures are rather uncontroversial tools in the planner's kit. But planners today cannot, without risking their authority, suggest a reduction in per capita consumption. Even if this is a logical condition for obtaining a factor 4 (or more) reduction, such suggestions are truly wild words.[15] To cut out half the mileage or half the housing area per capita – which may still be required – is certain to raise vehement objections in a world used to continuous expansion. Even the limits-to-growth reports on sustainability mentioned above dodge here. Some set their hope on technological development. Others refer to the need for a value change without elaborating how this is to come true. This is, in essence, also what is said above about the need for a sense of sufficiency. In any democratic setting, the individual is the key to change.

It has been argued that the Achilles' heel of the green movement is to be found here (Dobson 1995). The greens demand far-reaching changes in attitude and lifestyle. But they still assume that these changes can be accomplished within the present parliamentary framework. Information about the situation will suffice to make people accept the necessary changes.

Even if this seems unlikely, there is no other way at hand and the planner at work has an important role as a facilitator of change. Planners as professionals have a distinctive faculty for forward-looking analyses. Referring to the cited defense for business-as-usual above, a few final comments on planning method are warranted:

- *Uncertainty*: Planners are used to discussing decisions under uncertainty. This should give them an excellent position to deal with the situation of scientific dispute over ecological demands and to muddle through in a process where societal goals may be trailing behind, rather than guiding, a change in practice.
- *Signals*: There is a trend in planning to be less directly prescriptive, relying more on signals to independent actors. This makes it imperative that the signals of society are consistent with social goals. It calls for a clear policy to avoid rebound effects: that higher efficiency leads to lower prices which lift the demand. Planning with a ceiling demands means to delink this demand to ensure that more fuel efficient cars or cheaper electricity will not lead to more driving or higher consumption of electric power; see also Greening et al. (1998).
- *'We are underway'*: The tendencies built into this rebound effect and, even more importantly, the notion that growth is a solution to society's problems and thus desirable must be exposed and questioned. The understanding of limits means a reorientation in the planners' work. Planning in the golden years was very concerned with setting aside appropriate spatial reserves for future expansion and planning infrastructure investments. A topical planning issue tomorrow would instead be to scrutinize the relevance of reserves (which always carry a

cost) or investments in higher capacity. The planner may even have to learn and exercise the art of orderly contraction in an oversized infrastructure.

• *'The means are available'*: This is partly true. A clear step towards planning with a ceiling would be to substitute the principle of rationing for the principle of satisfying demands. An obvious first case – and one which has been debated for 30 years – is the idea of road pricing instead of increasing the capacity of the road system.

In conclusion, regional planning may not be the most obvious subject for our adjustment to a sustainable future. But it does contain sufficient opportunities to merit a further discussion on how to arrive at a policy of sufficiency and planning with a ceiling.

Notes

1 (Vereniging Milieudefensie, 1994). A similar report about Sweden, 'Ställ om', was published by Miljöförbundet Jordens Vänner (1997).

2 Discounting also enters the procedure when presumably it is adopted by real or assumed owners of natural resources to guide them to the most profitable rate of exploitation.

3 Several attempts have been made to measure society's progress in terms other than economic growth. Green GDP accounts for the depletion or destruction of natural capital by deducting it from the value of production. Another measure is the Index of Sustainable Economic Welfare (ISEW) which includes the value of non-marketed production and deducts defensive consumption which is compelled by the circumstances, such as long commuting trips to work. Time series of this index show that GDP and ISEW tended to develop in parallel until the early 1970s in most countries. But from that time, GDP continues to grow whereas ISEW levels out or declines (Daly and Cobb, 1994, Jackson and Stymne, 1996).

4 It is telling that the common principal demand to apply BAT (= Best Available Technology) is in practice often softened by the modification (BAT)NEET (= Not Entailing Excessive Costs); see Turner et al. (1994).

5 Kågeson (1997) takes on the question of whether there is a trade-off between growth and the environment. His somewhat diffuse answer is no (at least in the OECD). He arrives at this by making partial analyses of the kind described above with a number of qualifications about changes that are possible, technically and costwise, although not practiced at present. But he never claims that this would include global sustainability. We give growth a more pragmatic meaning as the current practice of business approved by the political system. There is a cloudy zone in between these views. The clouds can only lift with further analyses.

6 This argument was strongly emphasized by Herbert Simon in a public dispute with Paul Ehrlich. Also see Simon (1981), which is an extreme argument for unending supplies of natural resources.

7 It is noteworthy that there is a relative decline of steel and cement but total consumption remains more or less constant. There is increased intensity of aluminum, electricity. It is

also important to observe that a structural relocation of heavy and polluting industry from the West to developing countries may explain part of the statistical effect of dematerialization.

8 Ecological economists have attempted to calculate the value of nature's services (as the term goes) and have compared its money value with the value (at market prices) of human production. The pros and cons of this enterprise are discussed by a number of authors in Ecological Economics, vol. 25, No 1. It is obvious that the authors of the original paper have only managed to make very superficial calculations. It must be noted that they by no means claim that humans could do without or replace nature's services, regardless of the valuation made.

9 Environmental space does not contradict international trade as such but implies shadow areas for producing goods which are exported to be included in the environmental space of the country of destination: coffee, cotton and tropical fruits consumed in the north use many resources in tropical countries.

10 The follow-up of the original 'Limits to Growth' from 1972 is called 'Beyond the Limits' (Meadows et al., 1992). In spite of the title, the new volume attempts to describe a way out for the next century.

11 The case for more sustainable consumption was raised to the international level at the Rio Conference in 1992 and is now a recurrent topic at UN meetings. The approach here, as well as the one at the national level, is cautious. Increasing efficiency is welcome but it is rarely matched by any notion of limiting volumes.

12 Princen (1997) argues: how can a consumer in the North possibly improve the living conditions of overseas fruit growers by any local action at the point of sale?

13 See Sen (1987) and the UNDP Human Development Report UNDP (1998).

14 Hammarby Sjöstad and Millennium Village. The evaluation of the plans, however, shows that no other resource parameter is as favorable; car mileage, for instance, is expected to be virtually unchanged.

15 Confer J.M. Keynes: 'Words ought to be a little wild, for they are the assault of thoughts on the unthinking.'

References

Boulding, K. (ed.) (1966), *The Economics of the Coming Spaceship Earth*, Environmental Quality in a Growing Economy, John Hopkins University Press, Baltimore.
Carson, R. (1963), *Silent Spring*, Hamilton, London.
Cole, S. (ed.) (1973), *Models of Doom – a Critique of the Limits to Growth*, Universe Books, New York.
Daly, H. (1991), *Steady-State Society*, 2nd ed., Island Press, Washington DC.
Daly, H. and Cobb, J. (1994), *For the Common Good: Redirecting the Economy Towards Community, the Environment, and a Sustainable Future*, Boston Beacon Press, Boston.
Dobson, A. (1995), *Green Political Thought*, Routledge, London/New York.
Douthwaite, R. (1996), *Short Circuit: Strengthening Local Economies for Security in an Unstable World*, Lilliput Press, Dublin.
Freeman, C. and Jahoda, M. (1978), *The World Future – the Great Debate*, Martin Robertson, London.
Greening, L., Greene, D. and DiFiglio, C. (1998), The Rebound: Potential Responses to Improvements in the Technical Efficiency of Energy Consumption (unpublished).
Harvey, D. (1982), *The Limits to Capital*, Blackwell, Oxford.

Harvey, D. (1985), *The Urbanization of Capital*, Blackwell, Oxford.

Jackson, T. and Stymne, S. (1996), *Sustainable Economic Welfare in Sweden. A Pilot Index 1950–1992*, Stockholm Environment Institute, Stockholm.

Jacobs, M. (1994), 'The Limits to Neoclassicism. Towards an Institutional Environmental Economics', in M. Redclift and T. Benton (eds), *Social Theory and the Global Environment*, Routledge, London/New York.

Jacobs, M. (1997), 'Sustainability and markets: on the neoclassical model of environmental economics', *New Political Economy*, vol. 2.

Kågeson, P. (1997), *Growth versus the Environment – Is There a Trade-off?*, Dept. of Environmental and Energy Systems Studies (Inst. för miljö- och energisystem), Lund.

Lovins, A., Lovins, L. and Weizsäcker, E. (1995), *Faktor Vier*, Droemer Knaur, München.

Meadows, D., Meadows, D. and Randers, J. (1972), *The Limits to Growth: a Report for the Club of Rome's Project on the Predicament of Mankind*, Universe Books, New York.

Meadows, D., Meadows, D. and Randers, J. (1992), *Beyond the Limits: Confronting Global Collapse and Envisioning a Sustainable Future*, Chelsea Green Publishing Company, White River Junction, Vermont.

Miljöförbundet Jordens Vänner (1997), *Ställ om för rättvist miljöutrymme. Hur ser ett hållbart Sverige ut?*, Miljöförbundet Jordens Vänner, Göteborg.

Nordhaus, W. (1994), *Managing the Global Commons. The Economics of Climate Change*, The MIT Press, Cambridge.

Princen, T. (1997), 'The shading and distancing of commerce: When internalization is not enough', *Ecological Economics*, vol. 20, pp. 235–53.

Sen, A. (1987), *On Ethics and Economics*, Basil Blackwell, Oxford.

Simon, H. (1981), *The Ultimate Resource*, Princeton University Press, Princeton, New Jersey.

Sånnek, R. (1998), *Ekologiska fotavtryck – metodansats och tillämpning i samhälls-planeringen*, Department of Infrastructure and Planning, KTH Rapport 98-79, Examensarbete.

Turner, R., Pearce, D. and Bateman, I. (1994), *Environmental Economics. An Elementary Introduction*, Harvester/Wheatsheaf, New York.

UNDP (1998), *Human Development Report 1998*, Oxford University Press, New York.

Vereniging Milieudefensie (1994), *Sustainable Netherlands*, Vereniging Milieudefensie, Amsterdam.

Wackernagel, M. and Rees, W. (1996), *Our Ecological Footprint. Reducing Human Impact on the Earth*, New Society Publishers, Gabriola Island, British Columbia.

World Commission on Environment and Development (1987), *Our Common Future*, Oxford University Press, Oxford.

PART II
EMERGING ISSUES FOR
PLANNING ACTIONS

5 Catalyzing Culture

MAGNUS LÖFVENBERG

Introduction

Many urban planners claim that the socio-economic change we are facing today is of another character, a new order, where the hierarchical structures of the industrial era are being replaced by many horizontal networks (Castells, 1996). This shift in paradigm evokes apprehensions about social exclusion and loss of democracy where the beginning of a one-fifth society (Simai, 1994; Martin & Schumann, 1997) might arise. Social polarization is furthermore being followed by a decrease in institutional power (Sassen, 1994). Along with this, cultural industries are looked upon as some of the key generators of future economic development. Where traditional industrial production declines, cultural production transforms the former materialistic production into a symbolic economy (Zukin, 1995).

So, if the economy is increasingly revolving around the production of symbols, who are the initiators of these chains of symbols? How do these symbol creators work? And if the paradigmatical shift is concerned with horizontal structures – does it not resemble the informal networks artists have always striven to function within?

The treatment of symbols is a communicative process aimed at formulating new experiences such as the global village. It is obvious that multinational companies are forerunners in trying to find a global community of values. One has only to look at the prices of jeans to exemplify to what extent people pay for a leisure non-status lifestyle compared to the actual production costs. The brand is launched to depict more than the actual goods. The trademark can also function as a crossover to neighboring fields, as in the case of McDonald's, which has expanded from being just a fast-food chain to becoming an organizer of children's birthday parties, orchestrating joint launches with the film industry and contributing to children's hospitals. Together, these functions form an umbrella-like constellation for a generalized childhood. Europe's biggest construction site, Potsdamer Platz in Berlin, the most prestigious spot in a united Germany, has neighborhoods named after multinational companies –

one from the old industrial era – Mercedes Benz – and the other from the new – Sony. Another example of how the entertainment industry has placed its trademark in the cityscape is the Disney company's purchase of areas lining Times Square in New York. They have cleaned the place of its notorious elements and established a museum. Yet, are they gaining from the thrills of the former rundown district as an important part of the growing city tourism – 'Cities have become exotica' (Sassen, 1997)? Thus substantial efforts are being made to establish a global set of urban symbols.

But the cultural sector also plays an important role on other geographical levels (Heinze, 1995). The regional and local levels in particular gain from what the cultural sector produces (Bianchini and Parkinson, 1993; Wynne et al, 1992; Wynne and O'Connor, 1996; Hall, 1997). It has been shown that the contribution of cultural industries to urban and regional development is substantial in many respects (Benkert, 1995; Gnad, 1998; Olsson and Karlström, 1997; Söderlind, 1997). But we would even use the broadest definition of culture to highlight that culture is of course crucial on the individual level. Culture, in all its forms, is the very meaning-bearing grid to which symbols apply in formulating all mental landscapes – from the individual to the urban to the evolving global level.

This chapter originates from a series of interviews with a creative core of members of cultural industries and with persons closely connected to these activities. The aim is to capture what circumstances these professionals have to face, with the assumption of regarding these groups as pioneers in a rising network society. With a better understanding of this new paradigm there follows a call for an update of the institutional structure of cultural policy.

Theory and Method

We argue in this chapter that the smallest units of the cultural sector, the self-employed artists, are important to study for two reasons:

- They have already lived for generations under circumstances that resemble what other categories are now facing in the new economy. This means that the individual level is emphasized and short-term projects are structurally linked as networks.
- They contribute more to economic development than has been recognized traditionally. Since art and culture productions create pre-products and pre-services, they are important upstream requisites and a

strong location factor for the cultural industry as a whole. Their products are regarded as supplying a basic need for non-superfluous end consumption and are extremely dependent on intense innovation activity.

The chapter has its starting point in a series of interviews with professionals in the cultural industry in the Stockholm region. The aim of the interviews was to survey as many different categories of occupations in the cultural industry field as possible with an emphasis on what may be called the creative core. Of course, all professions in general have a content of creativity, but in this case the distinction roughly follows the classical art forms. Furthermore, there are interviews with some neighboring occupations, that is, those who use the first category's products as raw material. The division of the cultural industry into a creative core and an outer shell, called cultural industry here, was a primary assumption of the model.

Creative core		Cultural industry
Author	Architect	Publisher/ Graphic designer, two persons
Comedian	Scriptwriter	Journalist/TV producer
Mime/Performer	Musician/Composer	Journalist, Assistant editor-in-chief
Actor	Artist	Translator
Magician	Furniture designer	Cultural Travel Agent, two persons
		Buyer, TV programs

Figure 5.1 Interviewees in a preliminary round of cultural catalysts

In the last few years the economic debate has focused on small firms and the new establishment of firms. This is in line with government policies and there is a consensus for this among most political parties. Despite this there are still many circumstances hampering professions in this category. This applies even more to cultural entrepreneurs, who suffer from outdated legislation and obsolete conceptions of culture's role in society. We believe there is great potential that can be catalyzed in the cultural field. The term catalyst is meant here in two senses:

- How the cultural creative core catalyzes economic development as innovators of symbols in immaterial production.
- How cultural entrepreneurs need intermediate professions that catalyze contacts between them and the market.

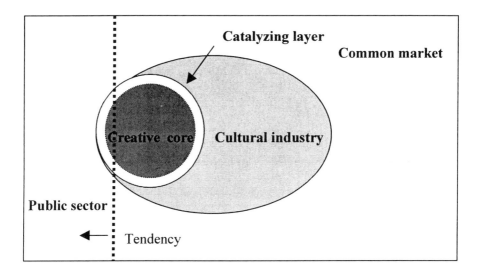

Figure 5.2   **Relations of the cultural sector and proposed role for a catalyzing layer**

To meet the demand of comparability, the persons interviewed were all in the same age bracket (30–45 years) and all professionally active. This means that they have all survived the first struggling career years and reached a similar phase in their careers. They were established and still in full professional progress. Eight of the 18 interviewees were women.

The methodological approach is qualitative and follows an ethnographic strategy (Morse and Field, 1996). The limited number of interviews implies that the results must be regarded as preliminary.

We used a questionnaire which was drawn up for cultural industry firms. It has a strategic economic perspective aimed at investigating the production technology of cultural firms, their markets and suppliers, their labor use and their location factors. It was sent prior to the interviews with the caveat that it was just a skeleton for the coming discussion. The purpose of this procedure was to encourage the interviewees to formulate both their specific work situation and the entrepreneurial side of it. In most cases it worked, so that the interviewees expounded their views on individual conditions and initiatives. When that was done, answers that more or less fit the formalized questionnaire could be put forward.

The interview sessions were taped and lasted two hours on average. With the exception of two cases, the interviews were held in Swedish.

The Existential Dimension

Early capitalism fostered an individualistic lifestyle called 'the new frontier' (Riesman, 1950). It was the dismantling of the feudal basis of valuation that encouraged hard-working Puritan individuals to form their own destiny. When industrialism matured into large-scale capitalism and the escalated division of labor necessitated elaborate organization, another character emerged. Now it was time for smooth leadership and compromises. The colorful loner had been replaced by a caste of grey eminents managing the epoch of mass production and rational planning.

However, if those personal features correlate to an industrialized society, what can be said of the identity of capitalism during post-Fordism?

The relation between individuals and working life constitutes one of the strongest factors providing social norms and in extension edifying character. A corrosive mechanism (Sennett, 1998) in post-modern identity springs from the loss of stable relations in the labor market. While working conditions increasingly deal with projects and networking, there is more focus on utility on short-term and direct production of value. The entrepreneurial person lives in the tension between the sped-up new economy and the rigid social relations among relatives and friends. It is obvious that there are many common attributes among this rising personality and the 'new frontier' of the 19th century in their quest for consensus in a restless and troubled world. They both face a shift in paradigm. But the contemporary person languishes without reliance on a harsh and obsolete moral.

The 'new frontier' personality was an individual governed by forces from within who formed the hierarchical structures of early industrialism while the post-modern personality is fading in the horizontal networks. The interviewees in this investigation combine the inner drive of the early industrialist with the networking of the early post-industrialist. Cultural networking is not just a strategy for survival but also a method for identifying mutual artistic goals. It is through this extensive interaction that they can keep a focus on their life projects as promoting individual growth.

Most interviewees were initially offended by the questions. They protested against the simplistic attitude in the questionnaire and claimed it was economically biased, thus missing the point of their work. A hidden suspicion that the investigation was based on a mistake of categories prevailed at the beginning of the interviews. Yet this highlights the first characterization of interviewees – the existential dimension of their professions.

'It is impossible to go bankrupt', claimed the author, 'it does not matter whether we sell any books or not, we will never stop writing.' It is distressingly obvious that the choice of profession was not made for economic reasons. Many claimed that there had not been a choice at all. It had been clear from early childhood what they preferred. In short, it was the urge to express themselves and the creative drive that overruled all other considerations in choosing existential pathways.

One way of describing this phenomenon is that ever since the 19th century, art has been driven by criticism of society. The role to question established society and to see the artist as an outsider was mentioned in most of the interviews. One example is the furniture designer when he claimed that the reading of newspapers functions as a major creative input. The importance of being informed about society, getting a broader view than from trade publications, serves as a source of criticism. As a consequence he has been forced to choose to be more or less outside the main market of the furniture business. His aim to create good quality for as many people as possible could have materialized when he contributed as part of a special group of designers to the major multinational manufacturer in the market. But he found out that, despite what was said in the beginning of the project, they would never produce 'good quality furniture in modern design for laymen'. Nothing was right when it came to material and detailing. He saw it as a swindle that relies on most people's lack of money. Therefore he simply refuses to be part of this consumerism.

In addition to raising one's voice, there is the urge to be independent, which the interviewees share with other entrepreneurs. A good example of this are the publishers, who are both architects but recently decided to start their own business because of their disappointment with the architectural situation in Sweden. By publishing they can both be independent and have an outlet for their designing skills. In addition it should be emphasized that both are women who indicate that after working for many years under male dominance, they can now define their own situation, at least in their own office. The founders of the cultural tourist travel agency had the same motive. Today they have two employees on a part time basis, both women.

To have as much of one's life in one's own hands was expressed as being a strong driving force by the actor who claimed that 'the most giving and clean way of performing is the street theater. You gather the audience by yourself, meet them on the same stage that they are standing on and get paid to the extent with what they are willing to give. You are never that close to your actual value under other circumstances'. Given the enticement in this market place situation, with the absence of the institutions of industrialized society, they have a double benefit in being more direct towards their audience and yet more of an outsider towards the established theaters.

It was no surprise that very soon in the interviews all interviewees turned out to be skilled entrepreneurs. They had strategies, well-developed networks of contacts, an awareness of prices, an openness towards possible solutions and so on. But without the existential dimension, there is no understanding of the cultural entrepreneurs whatsoever.

Flexibility – Vocationally and in Space

Another concept that is bound to be elusive is flexibility. And the persons in the investigation were indeed stunning examples of working-lives in flux, especially considering the constant change in vocation and location. A statement often heard was that education is the key to the future. Yesterday's school taught for life, tomorrow's educational system is more like a continuous process. Gradually learning is continually seeking to meet an ever-changing demand. Another generalization is that location factors are keeping pace with the changing conditions in society as a whole. Industrialized society was organized around the supply of raw materials whereas the key in the growing network society (see Castells, 1996) is in the nodes of global flows. The importance of mobility thus seems to increase over time.

The general connection between socio-economic background and higher education is clear in this investigation. Eleven of the eighteen interviewees come from academic families and in four cases the interviewees pursued one of their parent's occupation in the cultural sphere. On the other hand, in at least four cases the choice of occupation was against family wishes. However, what seems to be the most striking finding is that no one regarded their graduation as a certificate for their profession. At first sight this seems to be contradictory given the fact that 13 graduated and three trained in special education abroad. Three of them even have two academic degrees. Most of the interviewed people explained this by giving examples of colleagues who did not receive any established education and yet found their way into a professional career. A closer look shows a more diverse picture.

'The university years' as the magician puts it, were for him as well as for the other person in the investigation without a degree, the first time of struggle. They did not have any opportunity to get an education for the very simple reason that no education existed for those professions at that time. But this also goes with the choice of lifestyle. The rock musician and composer has now reached the level of professional credibility where he can choose among people who want to play with him. He collaborates very seldom with academically educated musicians.

Education could function as an indirect prerequisite. For the author there was a desire for knowledge in her family, but there was no classic middle-class cultural heritage. In her case it was therefore important to study at the university to learn a canon, the tradition and different styles. The mime stated that because of her studies in Paris she gained the confidence to perform, that she 'had the right to stand in front of people with the right to say something'.

Almost everyone else criticized their school. In many cases education felt incomplete or obsolete. The architect, both publishers, the artist, the furniture designer or those working in more traditional forms of companies complained that there was no preparation in their education for running one's own business. There was a hidden assumption that everybody should begin to work at existing firms or in the public sector as employees. At the same time the actor spoke for most of them, mentioning that the importance of drama schools can not be overestimated. It was the connections one made during one's learning years that turned out to be fruitful.

Some of the schools have tried to modernize their educational programs with varying results. In the case of the furniture designer the main benefit was taken away when the administrative procedures changed. From being a single open, experimental workshop, it was transformed into splintered parts protecting the different departments' budgets. For the scriptwriter as well, school was a disappointment. The education at the journalist school (JMH) seems to be better, especially given the new opportunity for graduates from other disciplines to complete their education with a year at JMH. This indicates a shift towards a more academic approach to the profession in their training.

The overall tendency is clearly that the connection to higher and specialized education and cultural professions is strong. Generally the most important result of education was the first connections made along with the training. The ambition to attain professionalism could only later be fulfilled. Therefore, education has to be reformulated to meet the professional situation.

The overlapping of professions over time shown in Figure 5.3 indicates that the first categorization of a definable core and its outer shell must be modified. In reality there is substantial crossover between the professions studied. One illustration is the artist, who studied for 12 years, becoming both an architect and artist, but who now works with set design, layout and illustrations. He is also attending the academy of music and is working on a PhD thesis in design theory.

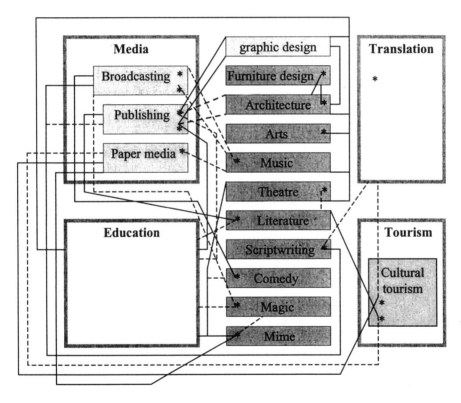

*   Denotes person professionally active within demarcated category
—   Professional or side activities last year
----- Professional or side activities previous years

■ Creative core   ▨ Cultural industry   ▢ Platform/cultural industry

Figure 5.3   Interviewee's professional activities according to network model

Flexibility is to be seen as well in the fusing of different art forms. The magician/performer states:

> (I have also worked) as an actor, director, teacher, I have done many multiple kinds of productions. I have done anything from Shakespeare to avant-garde, underground like smashing television sets against the wall, anything you want.
>   What I am working on now is mostly magic. Magic is the base. But it should not be separated from other categories. It is magic but it is also dance, text, mime, music, sounds, ambience, installation. It is not reality.

The very point of Figure 5.3 is to show the complex but not chaotic pattern of the informal networks. There is no clear simplicity visible, but a network needs its nodes to build up stability and permanence, which in our case are seen as platforms. These platforms differ substantially from one another but share very important stations during a person's professional career. They mostly offer short-term employment or part time work, which is project based. For the cultural professionals this has a double advantage in providing payment and contacts in their own field and also time over for creating their own work.

After graduation many schools function as professional starting points for a considerable number of the interviewees. The cultural field is strongly characterized by continuous reformulating practice and therefore it is seen as an asset to be young and involved at the heart of the development of events. What now can be recognized in computer science, where pupils sometimes are more up to date than their teachers, has been the case for many years in the cultural field. A clear example from the investigation of school as a platform is the two publishers. They met for the first time at architectural school while one was a doctoral student and the other was a teacher. They became involved in editing a publication on the school's profile which presented selected works by students and essays by the teachers. That collaboration proved to be fruitful and they felt ready to use it as a take-off to form a publishing company of their own. This also means that a platform does not necessarily facilitate development strictly within its field. More ordinary circumstances can be seen in how the mime and actor occasionally teach at different schools. Most frequently they conduct workshops at a high school in their hometown which specializes in drama. During their youth there was no such education there and it is fair to say that they are a part of making that happen. So, apart from the needed income, it is also a continuation of their efforts to establish a drama scene in their hometown.

The media cluster is also a very important platform. With its fast tempo and demand for up-to-date contributions, it serves as an excellent opportunity for cultural entrepreneurs to express themselves as well as gain economic support. Except for the editor-in-chief, who works full time, the printed media serve as a valuable source of side income for four of the interviewees. The scriptwriter writes film reviews and articles. The author has written columns and articles in previous years, as has one of the travel agents, who also did illustrations. The other travel agent freelances as a design reporter and translates articles from Italian to Swedish. As far as translation is concerned, it is not surprising that at least three of the interviewees have some earnings from that field. By traveling extensively they possess good knowledge in languages. The market for translation increased dramatically in the beginning of the nineties when the broadcasting monopoly disappeared. Together with the general internationalization process, this field may be of increasing importance for the cultural core as well.

The cultural travel agency can itself serve as a platform. They arrange special trips to Tuscany tailored to the customers' wishes, which are to be fulfilled by subcontracted members in the cultural core. Since tourism as a whole is growing and there is a clear tendency for specialized demand, such as cultural-related traveling, this should result in enhanced demand for cultural services.

If anyone in the investigation has succeeded with a flying start in their career, it must be the author. Her first book was chosen to become the book of the month of the leading book club in Sweden. She wrote it while she was pursuing doctoral studies in literature. At the same time she also worked part time as a reader for a small publishing company. In other words, she used two of the platforms mentioned above simultaneously (here called platform 1 in Figure 5.4). Despite her prosperous debut, the payment from her publishing company was about one month of pay for an industrial worker. A comparison with the first half of the last century shows how authors of that time could live for a couple of years for the same type of compensation. However, her rapid establishment opened doors for writing columns, articles, reviews and short stories for newspapers and magazines. As mentioned above, she was also invited to give readings at libraries and schools around Sweden. She had even changed publishing companies, working half time as an editor (these two platforms, called platform 2 in Figure 5.4). It should be noted that she did not regard her editing work as inhibiting her creative writing. On the contrary she benefited from the day-to-day stability and above all the fact that it was in her field. When her editing work was finished, so was her second novel. It proved to be a best-seller and attracted interest from international publishing companies. Her books are now translated into the major European languages. For the first time she is able to live entirely from the income of her books. One way of describing this process is to focus on the driving force.

As mentioned above, most interviewees strive for independence, which is an important parameter in the existential dimension. In the author's case, she managed to use existing platforms to provide space for both her creative work and to develop her informal network. By acting strategically, she reached a level at which she was independent of other decision-makers. She does not even have to rely on her platforms anymore and has now emigrated from Sweden (see below under Mobility).

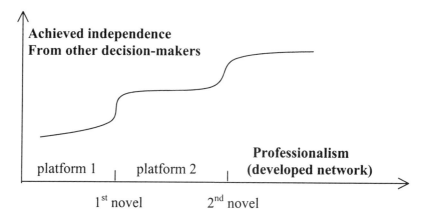

Figure 5.4 Author's career according to platform model

Finally the actor can describe an interesting platform of private–public partnership. He is connected with a theater company, which is essentially subsidized, but also has substantial income from work-shops he conducts in the private sector. The theater is located in an abandoned cinema whose rent is paid by the municipality. The company produces its own material and has developed an unconventional dramatic form of expression. They collaborate with theaters in Poland, where they have also toured. Their activities also include giving courses for youngsters and developing projects involving unemployed immigrant actors. Furthermore they offer therapeutic methods for treating interpersonal conflicts. He mentioned in particular a group of personnel managers whose position between the staff and the company management often made them suffer from too much stress. The method is very practical and direct. By role-playing under the guidance of the actors, the participants are given a chance to loosen up stiff conceptions. The participants were surprised at how effective the method was after trying different managing courses, psychological meetings and likewise. On the other hand, the actors were astonished at how much their customers were willing to pay. This serves as an example of a potential being directly utilized by the creative core and the private sector.

Mobility

As many as 14 of the 18 participants in the investigation had lived abroad for at least six months and eight of those have lived in other countries with different languages. Of the four who have not lived abroad, at least two traveled for longer periods as back-packers. This suggests a chosen lifestyle where insight into other cultures, knowledge of languages and the crucial role of being connected to different networks are emphasized.

A majority of the interviewees had moved to Stockholm in their early twenties, mostly to get an education. Together with the Stockholmers, most of them now consider Stockholm as the only possible place to function in their profession, at least in Sweden that is, because many claimed Stockholm to be lacking in many respects. The alternative would then be another city in another country. The only exception was the buyer, whose wife and children live 500 km away from Stockholm. He saw an opportunity in teleworking, where the need to visit the office in Stockholm would most likely be at two-week intervals.

The importance of the city as a strong location factor can be seen when the mime artist, the composer and the magician formed a group together in the mid-eighties with two musicians, one from Stockholm and the other from New York. They rented a farmhouse 20 minutes from a medium-sized town in the south of Sweden, sharing lives as well as work. The main benefits were the low rent and space for rehearsals. The supply of technical equipment was also advantageous since a most benevolent music shopkeeper lived nearby. But the Stockholmer spent most of his time in Stockholm, where there were the most opportunities to give concerts that united them. The factors that united them slowly dissolved and when the New Yorker finally found the situation too isolated, the entire group split up. The magician went on with his nomadic existence, and the composer and mime artist moved back to Stockholm to start solo careers. It is important to emphasize, however, that all of them have continued to cooperate occasionally since the split. The group became a core in an innovative cluster.

The most explicit example of mobility is the magician, who has worked all over the Western world. With his profession, he can reach his audience globally, or as he puts it: 'Magic is a universal art form; it means something to anybody, it exists everywhere. And always has.' He sees himself as 'an eclectic global person, expatriate, I have no identity related to any specific culture. So that makes me perfect for the job.' He sums up:

> Born in Bristol. Became professional when I was 17. Worked basically around England. Moved to London when I was 19–20. Stayed there maybe 1 ½ years, then I moved to France and worked there four or five years. And I traveled within that time also. I went to Asia and everything, Ika (the mime artist) and I moved here for about four years, and then I went to the States and traveled around northern America for about two years. Then moved back to Paris for about two years. Then I moved to Montreal and have been living there seven years.

He explains why he has settled in Montreal:

> Montreal is a very cosmopolitan city. Even though Montreal is not the capital of anywhere. 2/3 of the population is French-Canadian and there are also a lot of Latinos. It's a multilingual city. You can get your phone bill in one of 25 different languages. So it is the only Nordic Latin city. Basically it's mixed up with Irish, Scottish. But it's run down, third world, not as clean as Stockholm. Poorer. But things like micro engineering, software it's huge there. McGill is supposed to be number four in Northern America. It is a very good place to have as a base. Easy access to New York, the East and West coast of America, to the prairies and the central part of the continent, Europe ...everywhere. Global node. It's kind of a cool society, it's like here where you can walk around safely the streets. It is easy to feel comfortable there. It's not hard to get by.

In trying to find a contrast among the interviewees, it is a cliché to say that an author works in splendid isolation, withdrawn from hectic life. But the author in this investigation has to be mobile, giving readings around Sweden at libraries, schools and bookshops. Even longer trips are essential for two reasons, collecting facts for her books and developing her contacts with friends and colleagues in other cultures. By visiting the Middle East for example she gains insight into her own culture as well as the one she visits. She finds this of utmost importance.

After the series of interviews was completed, the buyer managed to arrange his working conditions to work partly in Stockholm and the rest of the time at his home 500 km away from Stockholm. The scriptwriter left Stockholm for the same lifestyle reasons for London and has recently moved again to Berlin. The same reasons made the author move first to London since – 'Stockholm is a beautiful place, but London can offer so many more different life forms, a richer context to dwell in' – and later to a smaller town in Brittany. Instead of regarding this as contradictory to the overall tendency of cultural clustering in cities, we see this as achieving independence. Her contacts with the market are stable and economically she does not have to work part time in the publishing company anymore. So when a new opportunity arrives in her private life, she has reached that level of freedom to choose a lifestyle outside a city for the first time in her life. She does not have to spend time marketing herself. In short, the market seeks her out instead of the opposite.

The interviewed group can serve as a good example of employment conditions for cultural workers. Their spatial flexibility is not just because of where the jobs happen to be found but also depends on a constant need for mental inputs crucial for personal development.

Networks and Cultural Infrastructure

This group roughly follows development in general, where the cult of the genius during the 19th century was analogous to the self-made entrepreneur. The genius served as an exception, the one who could criticize society from the level of the avant-garde. The era of organization saw culture as a common good for the welfare state to distribute. This should not be regarded as meaning that culture merged into society but more as a reflection of a benevolent and patriarchal attitude from the authorities to foster and cultivate the common man.

Culture was still seen as something untouched by simple commercialism. It was first in the sixties that post-modernism evolved with its deconstruction of art itself, and the pretensions of an ideally exclusive position was abandoned. Art moved towards public relations and the previous differences between different art forms were blurred. We believe that the genius was replaced by the cultural cluster and thus serves as a pioneering group of post-modernity.

The public sector has traditionally had a hold on cultural financing in Sweden. Sponsorship is fairly new and the monopoly of the broadcasting systems was abolished just a few years ago. So now even the old institutions are adapting to the small, flexible structures around them. This chapter can show two examples.

The Swedish public television company has been forced to cut costs and increase efficiency for more than a decade now. Each department has its own budget, which means for example that studios can be hired by companies other than 'in-house departments'. The number of employees has been reduced by approximately 400 persons in ten years and the process continues. The buyer has worked at his company department for ten years. He is still the last person hired. The same economic pressure has hit Sweden's second biggest morning newspaper. The editorial staff is collaborating with freelance writers, with the assistant editor-in-chief working as a spider in a net of more or less closely associated collaborators. The newspaper is situated in a high-rise building, whereas the entire production used to be under the same roof. One could say that the idea of the industrialized era is reflected here, but now its obsolescence is clearer and clearer every day. For example a whole category of professions has disappeared and the printing is located elsewhere. The interviewee made a remark that perhaps in the future there will be a newspaper whose different editorial offices are spread throughout the city. He looked forward to working in an ordinary apartment in the city together with a few employees and in continuous contact with collaborators around the nation electronically.

But there are advantages with large organizations. Both the buyer and the assistant editor were trained at their organization. There are too few buyers of TV programs in Sweden to support any formal education program. Even in the case of the assistant editor, his skills had to be learned in-house, since he is a key person who decides the layout of the paper. It takes a number of years to grasp such an abstract yet dynamic concept as a newspaper's profile.

The translator works in an intermediate form in the gap between employment and freelancing. In his case it means that both public authorities and the employer interpret his terms of employment to his disadvantage. He is excluded from the unemployment fund but in practice works as an employee.

The author can exemplify how well-established interest organizations can meet and catalyze different organizational structures. The two largest cultural networks in Sweden are the schools and the libraries. The Authors' Association mediates between the individual author and the informal systems established by the authors themselves. This is in contrast to commercially driven structures, where the musician/composer is in the process of building up a personal network of venues around the country. He was disappointed with the existing booking offices run by the international record companies.

With regard to people who are self-employed, we can let the comedian exemplify the entrepreneurial spirit of this category:

My real background for comedy is from market trading. My father was a sales pitcher, (he) put me through the market, I have done lots and lots of selling (...) I look at my network as the whole world. I just have to know what it is I want to contact people about. I learned that in public relations, which I worked with for a year in New York (...) So if I want to make a CD, go to the Internet to see who is making them, ring some person to get some basic information, phone another one to let them know what I got so far and get more from them, speak to friends, then to people who are like colleagues working the studio. I still do not know much about computers but I know kind of what I need now. Then I can start to talk about the price with these people and play the price game, so no matter what you are looking for, buying and selling is always the same thing. I have a certain technique of formula (...) When you have no money, you have to be versatile. You can not say you could not do what you wanted because you did not have cash in the bank.

Among the self-employed and small firms, many indicate that laws and regulations are written with larger companies in mind. They correspond badly with the circumstances for actors. Even a biased decision process that promotes larger firms is at stake in existing structures developed to mediate between inventors and financiers. The designer could provide an account of a depressingly high number of shortcomings, stolen ideas and rigidity amongst established institutions.

Most interviewees mentioned complicated legislation and insufficient comprehension of the circumstances.

The Importance of a Third Party

The overall tendency of a declining role for the public sector indicates an enhanced commercialization process. Where subsidies and established cultural infrastructure are replaced, a certain need arises for professional help, for example in marketing (see Figure 5.2). In the investigation only four persons worked in a larger organization that took care of the administrative machinery. The rest were engaged more or less enthusiastically with their tasks. A need for a good producer, an impresario, a manager or an agent was voiced by many of the people interviewed. Or as the magician put it:

It depends on the person. We need a manager on our show, we do not have one, but we really need to find a brilliant impresario. This is essential, we do not have time! We have so much to do, it is a big thing, it is somebody else's job. We wanna be a teamwork, using delegation.

I had my first agent when I was 15 years old, and I had many agents, most of them have helped me, some not. But the idea is OK, but it is individual. People like Diagheliev are very, very important in culture.

On the other hand the author points out that in comparison with England and the United States, where the system of agents is the rule, the direct contact with the publisher is lost. According to what was said by the interviewees, this contact is of great importance. The publisher is a valuable combination of an unbiased professional dimension and very personal contact whose task is to be interested in what the author has done so far:

When I have written something, it is done from my innermost part and therefore a sense of security can emerge when this person is only a single individual (...) The question is whether one can have the same relation to an agent, but the economic incentive is probably predominant.

The actor claimed that he did not have the time to contact all the people he could benefit from. He did not have a system of agents in Sweden. Although the monopoly to mediate for unemployed people disappeared in 1995, it still functions in practice as a prohibition. That is because it is seen as the actor employing the agent.

Therefore the set-up is to be regarded as one with a company without the security of an unemployment fund. Another example of a third party can be seen in how the concept of design manager is about to be introduced in Sweden. Such a person could facilitate the connections with the producers of furniture by giving the right arguments and above all formulating a design profile for other companies. This person links designers to contribute to the project.

With the removal of institutional and mental factors that hamper activity, there still seems to be potential to be fulfilled in Sweden. A comparison with circumstances abroad shows a wider variation of professions supporting the creative core.

Considering the present structural shift to an informational society, a stronger policy focus on the cultural industry could be justified. With its growing significance in the service sector, the cultural sphere may work to absorb redundant industrial labor. This might be described as a more lenient transformation since culture is a preferred choice of vocation among young people. Last but not least, a developed cultural sector has direct societal importance in its task to express this paradigmatic shift for society as a whole.

Conclusions

The interviewees constitute a very heterogeneous group, yet some general conclusions can be made about their working conditions. These individuals in creative and artistic professions are driven by a strong existential urge which is easily seen in the difficulty to distinguish their life-project from their work. The initial assumption of a creative core as a more or less distinct category in the cultural sector had to be abandoned. Some participants act in both categories at the same time, while others move between categories when necessary or preferred. This mobility is not just between professions but also works spatially. Many depend on being mobile over time, such as performing on concert tours, or devoting time to specific educational opportunities. Education is important for this sector but it is even more important to develop training platforms and recognize their importance in the grooming of beginning networks for students. Many find themselves squeezed between time-consuming creative and productive activities and the duties of managing their own companies. This paper argues for the importance of supporting expertise. This suggests a new strategy for the Swedish public sector: playing a more active role in using these catalysts of cultural life instead of continuing the attitude of subsidizing cultural consumption.

We are facing an epoch of increased conflicts, structural transformations and institutional change. Castells (1996) uses the dichotomy nature-culture to describe this paradigm shift. Where the first phase in human history was marked by the struggle for survival against a merciless nature, the second characterizes how nature was conquered. Now we seem to have emerged in a phase where nature has become one cultural form among others, which can be seen in the environmental movement. Culture refers to itself without having to engage nature as a counterpart. We have entered the era of the super-reflexive. If so, it might be a good idea to further study those who have been doing this ever since cultural professions arose.

References

Benkert, W., Gnad, F., Ebert, R., Kunzman, K.R., Söndermann, M. and Wiesand, A.J. (1995), *Kultur- und Medienwirtschaft in der RegionenNordrhein-Westfalens*, Ministerium für Wirtschaft, Mittelstand und Technologie des Landes Nordrhein-Westfalens, Düsseldorf.

Bianchini, F. and Parkinson, M. (eds) (1993), *Cultural Policy and Urban Regeneration. The West European Experience*, Manchester University Press, Manchester.

Castells, M. (1996), *The Rise of the Network Society*, Blackwell, Oxford.

Gnad, F. (1998), 'The Contribution of Culture Industries to Urban and Regional Development', Paper presented at the Conference *City and Culture*, Stockholm, May 1998.

Hall, S. (ed.) (1997), *Cultural Representation and Signifying Practices*, Sage, London.

Heinze, T. (ed.) (1995), *Kultur und Wirtschaft*, Westdeutscher Verlag, Opladen.

Martin, H-P. and Schumann, H. (1997), *The Globalization Trap*, Brutus Östlings Förlag, Symposion, Eslöv.

Morse, J.M. and Field, P.A. (1996), *Nursing Research. The application of qualitative approaches*, Chapman & Hall, London.

O'Connor, J. and Wynne, D. (eds) (1996), *From the Margins to the Centre*, Ashgate, Aldershot.

Olsson, K. and Karlström A. (1997), *Kultur som strategi i lokalt och regionalt utvecklingsarbete*, Nutek, Stockholm.

Riesman, D. (1950), *The Lonely Crowd: A Study of the Changing American Character*, Yale University Press, New Haven, Connecticut.

Sassen, S. (1994), *Cities in a World Economy*, Pine Forge Press, Thousand Oaks, California.

Sassen, S. (1997), Personal communication.

Sennett, R. (1998), *The Corrosion of Character: The Personal Consequences of Work in the New Capitalism*, W.W. Norton, New York.

Simai, M. (1994), *The Future of Global Governance. Managing Risk and Change in the International System*, United States Institute of Peace, Washington, DC.

Söderlind, J. (1997), *Konstnärerna – stadens nomader och nybyggare*, Kungliga Tekniska Högkolan, Stockholm.

Wynne, D. (ed.) (1992), *The Culture Industry*, Avebury, Aldershot.

Zukin, S. (1995), *The Cultures of Cities*, Blackwell, Oxford.

6 Governance and Planning for a New Age

AMY RADER OLSSON

Introduction: the Goals of Governance and Planning

Most planning practitioners are so immersed in issues of planning methods and cases that they have never gone through the exercise of rationalizing the participation of the public sector in regional planning. Why ought the public sector be involved in planning, bearing its costs with public resources? What is the actual output of planning, and why should the private sector not produce plans?

This is not simply a rhetorical issue, but rather one that has real implications for the future of planning and governance, especially at the regional level. Some political leaders and private sector actors challenge the need for a regional level of governance charged with regional planning at all, claiming that regional planning should be left to the businesses who drive the economy and govern municipalities. A regional level strategy, they claim, is a costly activity with few benefits and indeed significant negative effects.

A starting point for the discussion of this issue could be the assertion that planning does not exist for its own sake; rather, planning works as a tool of governance. Therefore, in order to identify a rationale for planning, we must first examine the role of regional governance in society and how it has evolved in recent decades.

Planning, Governors, and Governance

That the discipline of planning and the nature of governance are undergoing tumultuous change is evidenced by the amount of effort expended by texts in defining the terms *planning* and *governance*. Part of the confusion is semantic. One might expect to be able to claim that planning is simply 'what planners do' and that governance is 'what governors or governments do'. However, these definitions, while not inaccurate, are also not

95

sufficient. Planning has been described as a style of governance, and governance almost always includes planning.

In order to discuss the changing roles for planners in a new era of governance, it is important to define what we mean by these concepts within the scope of this chapter.

What is Governance?

The definition of *governance* is perhaps most problematic. The Webster Revised Unabridged Dictionary defines *governance* as 'exercising authority'. However, this definition seems insufficient as it does not help explain to what end authority is exercised. Lefèvre (1994) provides an overview of definitions of governance as it is used within various disciplines. Management sciences, including business economics, uses the term to describe how transaction costs are managed among companies using various structures and hierarchies. In spatial economics, governance is used to describe forms of regulation which organize communication and interaction among actors within local economic arenas. Political science uses the term governance when describing power relationships among players and the process of coordinating public action (Lefèvre, 1994). Healy (1997) argues that governance encompasses not just the actions of a set of formal institutions called government, but the entire 'process through which collective affairs are managed'.

In this chapter, governance is defined as the process of making and implementing decisions on behalf of a group. The breadth of possible forms of governance and their effectiveness is not discussed here.

What is Planning?

Detailed definitions of planning are offered by various scholars. Alexander (1995) offers a review of definitions of planning. These range from very broad, as Miller's definition of planning as a component of all human behavior, to definitions emphasizing planning as forethought in formulating future activities (Ozbekhan and others, in Alexander, 1995), to Wildavsky's definition of planning as the control of future actions. Finally, Alexander offers his own definition of planning, 'the deliberate social or organizational activity of developing an optimal strategy of future action to achieve a desired set of goals, for solving novel problems in complex contexts, and attended by the power and intention to commit resources and act as necessary to implement the chosen activity'.

This long definition seeks to include several aspects of planning: its nature as an organizer of future activity, its aim to produce a certain future despite its admittedly limited capacity to do so, and its subsequent need to constantly adapt to changing situations. This definition also defines planning as both the act of making plans and as the implementing of plans.

The definitions of *regional* planning are also evolving. Friedmann (in Wannop, 1995) defines regional planning as 'the process of formulating and clarifying social objectives in the ordering of activities in supra-urban space – that is, in any area which is larger than a single city'. In practice, this is a process which at one time was fairly narrowly defined as the determination of land use for various purposes: housing, commercial development, industry, recreation, and so forth.

Today, regional planning practitioners wrestle with issues as broad as social, environmental, and economic planning, development and implementation of physical and institutional infrastructure, and strategies for competing with other regions and other government levels. Hall (1992) notes another evolution in what we mean by planning, from the production of a 'master plan' which is implemented to a continual process of attempting to shape the future: '(away from) the old idea of planning as the production of blueprints for the future desired state of the area, and towards the new idea of planning as a continuous series of controls over the development of the area, aided by devices which seek to model or simulate the process of development so that this control can be applied.'

In general, definitions of planning have come to emphasize the role of plans in providing a facilitating framework in which society can flourish. Rather than pretending that a regional plan can determine the future course of a region, planners attempt to forecast future developments, identify their determinants, and produce strategic plans which will enable an alternative, more desired scenario. In crafting this strategy, planners must review the strengths and weaknesses of the region from various perspectives, and the opportunities to change these conditions.

Planning and plans are often used by all forms of government as an aid in making decisions. Therefore, we can define planning as input to the decisions made by those who govern. This is essentially a restatement of Sager's more complex definition of planning as 'technique and communication aiming at organizing knowledge to provide a basis for decision-making on future collective action'.

This may seem self-evident, but is important to underscore as we seek to rationalize planning, as certain forms of planning may be effective in serving certain institutional structures for regional governance but not others.

Planners and Governors

What do governors do, if not simply govern? What do planners do, if not simply plan? The answer is the focus of this chapter. The identity and role of governors is changing, as is the role for those employed in public service as planners. For the purposes of this chapter, governors are those who take decisions and planners exist to aid the decision-making process. As will become evident, this basic division of roles has not changed. However, the definition and scope of *decision-making* has.

Regions: an Arena for Planning and Governance

What is a Region?

Regions, as defined by most regional planners, are not simply geographical designations but functional areas delimiting labor markets, commuting patterns, cultural and social networks.

Perhaps it is useful to think of regions as arenas in which a society operates. These arenas may be physical, as a political border or a water drainage basin, or immaterial, the traditions and informal rules which affect the interaction among individuals in a region.

Political regions may be simply administrative borders representing a certain population size, especially regional offices of national entities. Administrative regions may also represent agreements among municipalities to cooperate on certain issues, such as a park or education district. Or they may be more 'organically' defined regions, political borders which mirror historical patterns of housing, work, and travel. A cultural region could describe an area with a common history, tradition, language, or values, and may be informally accepted, as the Appalachian region of the United States, or formally recognized, as Flanders and Wallonia in Belgium. Environmental regions may be air or water basins, flood plains, or represent the borders of a unique ecosystem.

One person may be under the jurisdiction of several regions simultaneously – associations of local municipalities, counties, EU-defined regions, cultural regions, school districts, water districts, air quality districts, park districts, etc.

Wannop (1995) defines regions as homogeneous – 'effectively constant in some principal characteristics (population, physical character, etc)' or nodal, a string of labor and housing markets, communications centers, etc. Regions are often defined at the whim of higher or lower authorities, to suit a specific purpose, or they may be ad hoc associations of local municipalities cooperating on select issues. Regions may cross national borders and may even include physically separated land parcels, especially in the case of a region comprised of several small communities that share a common language.

For the purposes of this chapter, regions are defined as a type of arena for coordinating activities among local governments, or between local and national governments. These may be general governmental bodies (such as county councils) or sector-specific organizations.

Immaterial Infrastructure – The Rules of the Game

One important role of regional governance is a manipulation of the formal and informal rules that govern interaction. Let us take as an example the decision of an individual of how to commute to work.

A few of the formal decisions that affect his decision are driving license regulations, vehicle and fuel taxes, public transport ticket prices, and availability of parking. The individual is also affected by the rules of the market economy, which in large part determine the price of owning a vehicle or bicycle. Finally, the individual may be affected by cultural rules, such as the tradition at his workplace of cycling, or a workplace rule that allows him to work at home.

Table 6.1 Immaterial infrastructure in regions

Rules of the Game	Regional Actors	External Actors
Cultural rules (traditions)	Society at large; ethnic groups, families	Cultural rules of other societies with which the region may interact
Regulations	Regional politicians, local politicians and regulators	National and international politicians and regulators
Market rules	Local and regional businesses	Supraregional markets, other regions

These are just a few of the formal and informal rules that come into play even when making an 'independent' decision. Structures of governance in the region, together with external factors, determine the rules of the game, and planning can both analyze the effectiveness of the current rules and propose modifications that appear to be more effective. We have defined immaterial infrastructure as including both formal and informal institutions. Healy (1997) makes a distinction between a 'hard infrastructure of institutional arrangements legal rules and resource flows' and a 'soft infrastructure of institutional capacity building among firms and citizens'.

Material Infrastructure

Regional governments are commonly responsible for producing physical infrastructure; the board upon which the game will be played. Common examples of material infrastructure may include roads, bridges, sewage systems, hospitals, and schools. Planning is both the process of determining that material infrastructure is needed, what could be provided and when. Planning theories may be relevant in determining priorities for investment, by formalizing selection criteria or elucidating goals for the region. Regional politicians (governors) then have responsibility for making decisions and allocating public investment funds for infrastructure. Decisions concerning material infrastructure may also be affected by the 'rules of the game' described earlier; land use regulations limiting or encouraging various types of development being the most obvious example of this.

Summary: What is Regional Planning?

In sum, the region is the arena, the field upon which a variety of actors play. The interaction of individuals is governed by a complex set of formal and informal rules and regulations. Planning may address the effects of formal and informal 'rules of the game' by implementing new regulations or policies – effectively rules themselves. Rules encourage, discourage, or enable behavior, but rarely control it. Similarly, planners use rules to enable behavior considered desirable, but can rarely be guaranteed of the effect of their actions. This is discussed in more detail below.

Goals of Governance and Governments

The question of why we should govern has been debated for thousands of years, and will not be resolved in this short paper. All forms of governance seek to order a society for the benefit of all. Why then have human societies persisted in according at least some responsibility for governance to governments? With the exception of tyranny, governments, even monarchies, have had public welfare as an overriding goal. The form of government which will best provide public welfare is determined by societal preferences, ethics, and political theories.

Almost all human societies establish some set of formal institutions which could be termed *government* and which are given some responsibility to govern. The process of governance includes a range of actors and incorporate a variety of decision-making forms. Moreover, it can change.

As Healy (1997) reminds us, the degree of governing responsibility accorded to formal institutions of government is 'not fixed but rather negotiated over time'.

As noted, regions are arenas for the interaction among local governments as well as the interaction between local and national governments. Regional governments may be established to provide a framework for this interaction. Another common motivation for the establishment of regional governments or authorities is the desire to coordinate the production of goods and services among municipalities, to take advantage of scale economies.

Below, the governance of regions is used as an example of changing roles for government. As discussed below, the possible roles for governments in a society depend on the decision-making capabilities of the populace, its relationship to other regions and nations, and its resources.

Relationship to other Regions and Nations

Most regions are highly dependent upon surrounding regions and highly affected by them. Regional governments are often concerned with creating or preserving the comparative advantages of the region relative to other regions, determining strategies for competition and cooperation with other regions.

The scope of responsibility that societies choose for their government may also be affected by the relationship of the region to areas exogenous to it. For instance, a society in isolation may accord to its government the independent task of planning and constructing roads. A society that sees itself as part of a network of communities, on the other hand, may decide to plan a road infrastructure together with other regions, or even create a supra-regional level of government to decide these issues. The access of the region to other areas, and the access of other areas to a region, also affects the ability of a government to control what happens inside it. In a modern metropolitan region, the local and regional government is only one actor in a group including multi-regional or multinational corporations, other regional and national governments, and even other peoples. Its citizens behavior may be affected by contact with and travel to other regions. Moreover, the natural environment upon which all societies depend for their survival does not respect political borders.

As recently as a few hundred years ago, many regions lived in relative isolation. Even in Sweden, united under various monarchies, the king had relatively little control over the day to day workings of regions under his authority. Modern regions, however defined, are connected to the 'outside world' by roads, bridges, planes, boats, telephones, televisions, economic systems, family ties, and most recently, the Internet. This restricts the ability of regional and local governments to control the actions and behavior of its populace.

What are the Region's Resources?

The goals of regional governance, and the resulting role defined for regional government, take into account the resources available to the region. These may include both natural, human, and economic resources. Traditionally, the ability of a region to sustain a society was entirely due to its location, or rather, the resource and accessibility assets of a particular location. Fertile land was necessary for food production, or a body of water to supply fish and drinking water. Mountains sheltered villages from weather or from competing tribes. Later, mineral resources in the immediate vicinity allowed men to fashion tools. Finally, tribes could trade with each other, with mutual benefit. This made locations with good access to other tribes even more attractive. Most areas recognized today as regions were built up as trading centers or areas of rich natural resources permitting industrial production.

Today, locational resources are not critical to the ability of a region to sustain a society of people. Natural resources are as important as ever, but technological advances have allowed societies to distance themselves from the source of natural resources. Energy, water, minerals, and food can be transported long distances via air, sea, rail, road, and wire. Economies once dependent on industrial production have become commercial service centers, creating value through the production and manipulation of information. This is not to say that a community's location is unimportant, rather that it is not critical in the same sense as it was only one hundred years ago. Human resources and the communications technology to optimize human intellectual potential are of increasing importance to vibrant regions.

Can the People Decide?

The question of whether or not individuals are capable of participating in a democratic society has been debated since Plato. On the one hand, direct governance by individuals has the highest probability of producing decisions that most closely reflect the preferences of the people in the region, unless they are all identical. On the other hand, it is often highly inefficient to poll individuals on every topic of collective interest; nor do all individuals have the skills and capacity to participate in all decisions.

Debate focuses on two issues: the complexity of the decision at hand, and the capacity of the individual to make the decision. Individual capacity is a function both of intellect and of an ability to synthesize needed information. The latter is itself a function of both access to information and methodological tools to use that information as a basis for decisions. Governments attempt to provide a balance between direct and representative governance that provides an efficient division of governance responsibility and reflects individual preferences within the region to the greatest extent possible. When applied to an actual political situation these determinations can be quite subjective.

In essence, forms of government are the political theoretical expression of a trade-off between two basic roles of government: helping increase the capacity of citizens to make decisions, and making decisions. Almost all forms of government attempt to achieve some balance between these two activities. A pure 'direct democracy', in which all decisions are taken by citizens through consensus or referendum, indicates a primary role for government in preparing citizens for making decisions and a small role in making decisions themselves (which may include the administration of the referendum process, for example). An autocracy (assuming it is benevolent) is mainly concerned with making decisions; its activities in helping citizens make decisions are primarily designed to help gain popular support for the autocrat's decisions. Representative government entails a strong role for government both in increasing citizen capacity to make decisions (needed to elect representatives) and in making decisions once representatives are elected.

Despite regional variances, two things are true of regions and their citizens in modern developed societies: issues facing the region are more complex, and citizens are better educated. Moreover, our access to information has increased exponentially, in no small part due to advances in information technology. Finally, decision-making methodologies, including political theories, modeling, economics, and natural science, may increase the capacity of both governments and individuals to make decisions.

Remembering the overriding goal of governance, to improve the welfare of the governed, it is interesting to note current research into the relationship between 'direct democracy' and social welfare. While definitions of social welfare are many, few would argue that the happiness of citizens must be a critical element of welfare, if not its exclusive measurement. A recent study of Frey and Stutzer (1999) attempts to isolate the effects of the extent of direct democracy on citizens' happiness. Direct democracy, here chiefly in the form of decisions made through public referenda in Switzerland, appears to increase the self-reported happiness of citizens in systematic and statistically significant way. Moreover, cantons with a high index of direct democracy appear to positively affect the well-being even of foreign-born residents, who cannot participate in referenda. These findings support an increased role for governors in allocating more authority for governance to citizens. Note that this does not necessarily change the scope of decisions that the society has decided should be collectively determined, but rather may represent a move along the 'frontier' representing the scope of governance towards more direct decision-making by citizens.

Changing Roles for Governments

The issues regions face are more complex, its citizens better educated. Regions are integrated into national and global structures of culture, commerce, and information. The locational basis for a region's existence is less critical. What does this mean for the role of governance? The basic role of governments has not changed; governments exist to improve the welfare of citizens. However, the evolution of societies described above has caused governments to rethink the ways in which they should act in order to provide welfare.

As regions grow both in area and population, and as the issues affecting them have become increasingly complex, the scope of responsibility for governance will likely change. There are more issues affecting a multi-centered, globally-connected modern region than for a small isolated set of villages. But it is not necessarily efficient to make formal collective decisions on all of these new issues. Regions must re-evaluate which issues should be decided formally through a structure of governance (rather than being left to market or other forces). It is probable that both the number and type of decisions that we determine should be decided formally will change. We may decide that responsibility for some decisions previously accorded to governments should be accorded to the private sector, or to another government level. This decision is extremely complex, and many contributing factors exist that are not described herein.

However, one factor that could affect this determination of scope for governance responsibility is a second issue: how to balance responsibility for resolving new issues between individuals and governments. A better educated citizenry, with better access to information, may demand a more direct role in decision-making. They can argue that it is now more efficient to decide certain issues directly, and that this will lead to decisions which better reflect individual preferences within the region. However, both the scope and complexity of decisions facing a region, in part due to its contact with regions and nations outside its borders, makes it inefficient or even impossible to poll citizens on every issue.

Regions are thus expected both to decide more issues directly, and to decide more issues in new regional governance bodies. This could encourage a widening of the appropriate scope of governance responsibility, making the set of decisions we take formally in regions ever larger. This recognizes an increased role for direct decision-making by citizens while assigning governments responsibility for addressing new, and increasingly complex, issues as representatives of the people.

This is, however, only one theory, which should be more closely analyzed. There are those that argue that in as much as regions have a decreasing ability to control or even influence what happens inside their borders, they ought to be decreasing rather than increasing their scope of authority. Not surprisingly, many regions face simultaneous calls for more authority to governments and calls to decrease the scope of regional governance, even banish it altogether. It would be fascinating to track the *scope* of governance responsibility in relation to the *balance in decision-making responsibility* among governments and citizens, to better understand this relationship.

Goals of Planning

One important input of planning to decision-making is to analyze decisions that may be in conflict with each other. Planning cannot prioritize among society's goals, but can help decision-makers to understand the consequences of various decisions, anticipate change, and even suggest policy.

Modern planning is rooted in late 19th century philosophies that have guided the growth of cities through the industrial revolution. Three philosophical streams identified by Alexander (1995) as defining planning goals are scientific efficiency, civic beauty, and social equity.

Scientific efficiency, the theory that there are systems and technologies which can increase production or output of a region under the same resource constraints, is echoed in many modern infrastructure plans for sewerage, rail, roads, water supply, etc. It is also a prevalent goal in plans for public administration and even spatial plans which seek to design the physical location of housing and services which promotes the most efficient movement and interaction of people and goods.

Civic beauty, a philosophy institutionalized in the 19th century City Beautiful movement in the United States, is seldom the stated goal of modern plans but continues to affect plans nevertheless. Recreational spaces, cultural and heritage planning, and the planning of public spaces are in part produced because planners seek to create beautiful spaces. However, in recent decades the priority of this goal relative to other planning goals seems to have diminished, so plans to beautify cities are often rationalized as helping to attract new business or tourists (city marketing) or promoting positive social interaction.

Social equity goals, rooted in utopian ideals that were translated into social programs from the late 19th century, are the basis for much social welfare, housing, and public health planning programs. Calls for public participation in planning may also be related to this philosophy (Andersson and Sylwan, 1997).

Just as models of governance must adapt to a transition from an industrial to a post industrial society, so too is planning adapting to modern regional challenges. The industrial revolution brought about the construction of large, efficient industrial complexes and regional infrastructure, housing, and social programs to support them. Planning supported industrial production. Post industrial, information-based systems of flexible, networked producers and consumers crave planning systems that are equally flexible and facilitate the creation of new networks within and among regions. Therefore, while the basic goals of planning have not changed significantly since the beginning of the industrial revolution, the process of planning in realization of these goals has changed significantly in response to changes in the structure of society. The creation of master plans for regions includes an underlying assumption that is possible to construct a medium-term plan that simultaneously serves efficiency, equity, and aesthetic goals. In order for this to be true, society must be fairly stable, goals must be well defined, and exogenous trends affecting the society must be limited. In the post industrial society, it is less the interaction than the interplay of goals which is desired. The post industrial society assumes that anything, anyone is potentially related, if only remotely, if only for a brief period. Planners operating in a society with this assumption focus on the dynamic interplay of various goal areas as new areas of conflict and cooperation emerge and others disappear.

Table 6.2 Assumptions of planning and plans

Industrial planning	Post-industrial planning
Isolated, fixed 'closed loop' systems	Global, ad hoc, simultaneous networks
One optimal solution	Several solutions
Static	Dynamic

The response of regional planners to this structural development in society has yet to be fully developed. In the industrial society, a planner could work towards the creation of an optimally designed master plan. In the post-industrial society, planners must instead design processes which facilitate dynamic interaction across boundaries of space, scale, and time. Traditional master planning methods are not necessarily useful in this new context. In addition, with the creation of global networks, and the increasing interdependency of regions and nations comes a reduced ability of planners to predict the effects of a plan. A regional plan today affects numerous other regions, and a region's future is affected by numerous internal and external forces beyond the planner's control to forecast, much less manipulate (for further discussion of the reduced role of government in modern society see Andersson and Sylvan, 1997).

Planning and the Market Economy

An Economic Rationale for Planning

In order for it to be reasonable to engage in planning, we must believe that there is a benefit to planning: that planning improves the efficiency, equity, or attractiveness of regions. In economic terms, we could define these benefits as elements of social welfare, and argue that planning provides the basis for decisions that improve social welfare in a region.

Depending on the state of the region, effective planning may do one of several things. It may correct a regional situation in which the region's economy is not operating to its maximum potential. Or, it may act as an additional resource to the region, increasing the total potential output of the region. Finally, because planning involves an attempt to manipulate a certain expected future, we can think of planning as improving the regional situation in future periods, again allowing for a higher total level of social welfare.

Planning/Market Dynamics

There are several conditions and situations in which economic markets fail to produce a situation considered socially desirable. Some have to do with the fact that markets actors generally seek to maximize profits as a first priority. Society may have other important priorities (such as equal access to income) which are not goals of the market economy. There are also a number of market situations that will not produce an economically efficient result.

Markets in regions are not unlike biological systems. A functioning market is the aggregated expression of businesses and individuals responding to signals and making decisions that maximize individual welfare. Similarly, individuals and species within an ecosystem respond to environmental signals, adapting in order to ensure the survival of themselves and their progeny.

An ecological system is characterized by natural cycles of growth and decay of plant and animal populations. These may be affected, as noted above, by various long- and short-term exogenous factors: climate, natural disaster, pollution or air quality degradation, for example. These external factors can affect the ecological system both positively or negatively, and invariably disrupt the balance between various species until the system settles to a new equilibrium.

Often, man will intervene in an ecological system to correct a crisis situation, like a drought. By irrigating a drought-blighted area, for example, man is changing the 'rules of the game' in the ecological system, changing the environmental signals to which species of plant and animal respond. Whether or not the drought was caused by endogenous or exogenous factors, man has in this case made a decision to manipulate the conditions for growth in that ecological system. Similarly, planning is often used to counteract market conditions that have failed to produce a socially desired result. The similarities between the activities of a natural resource manager and a regional planner may be exploited to demonstrate the various alternative responses planners suggest to improve regional conditions.

Let us say that the ultimate goal of a natural resource manager is the preservation of a certain species of deer. The deer population is normally kept in check by its one predator, the wolf. However, a severe drought threatens to eliminate the remaining deer population. The planner is attempting to help governors respond to high unemployment in the textile industry, which has been an important employer in the region.

In both cases, the natural resource manager and the regional planner may offer one or several alternatives. We assume that both have determined that some type of action is preferable to no action. They can either change the signals to the market or ecological environment, which will trigger certain responses, or change the rules of the game, the regulatory structure which guides interaction among market or ecological actors. One special type of rule that may significantly affect the market is a shift in production from the private to the public sector.

Signals to the market or ecological system may be short or long term, sustainable or not. The natural resource manager may decide to simply transport massive quantities of water to the drought-blighted area, or temporarily re-route a nearby stream to provide emergency water for the deer. Or he could choose a more sustainable solution, planting a type of tree which stores water so that deer can obtain water in drought conditions by nibbling its leaves. The regional planner can also choose a short term solution – low interest loans which support technological advances which may make the textile industry more profitable – or job retraining programs for unemployed textile workers, so that they may find work in emerging industries.

The resource manager and planner may also recommend that governors change the 'rules of the game' which guide the environment and the region. The natural resource manager may decide for example that instead of trying to battle the drought, he can remove the deer's other predator, the wolf. He may therefore kill a large number of wolves, shifting the ecological balance between species. Similarly, the planner can argue for the removal of the 'predators' to the textile industry, mandating government purchase of domestic textiles, even blocking imports of foreign textiles.

Finally, the natural resource manager may decide to actually remove remaining deer from the ecosystem and instead breed them in zoos. Effectively, this is a decision by the ecologist to produce deer himself, rather than letting the ecological system produce and sustain deer. The regional planner can effectively do the same, by suggesting state-owned textile factories with a protected production monopoly.

Table 6.3 A comparison of ecological and regional planning responses to unfavourable conditions

Type of response	Natural resource management example – deer population threatened with extinction by drought	Planning example – unemployment within the textile industry
Change signals – short term	Provide water through emergency assistance	Low interest loans to textile industry Make-work programs for unemployed textile workers
Change signals – long term	Plant water-saving trees	Job retraining programs for unemployed textile workers
Change regulatory structure	Kill predators to endangered species	National policy that all government textile purchases be from domestic factories
Change public private balance	Breed threatened species in zoos	Establish state-subsidized textile industry

Although planners attempt to correct market failures, they are not always successful. It is therefore important to note that markets also respond to planning failures. For example, markets adapt when planning fails to create sufficient incentives or infrastructure for development, or actually create incentives that dampen development. One example is the army of privately-run minibuses which serve Jakarta, Indonesia. Jakarta has a public bus system, which although practically free is of such poor quality that it is virtually useless for trips outside of a few major nodes. However, walk to the edge of almost any major street and a minibus will slow, the driver asking where you want to go. Routes are flexible, determined by passenger needs, and prices are competitive with bus fares and far cheaper than taxis. However, there are drawbacks to this solution – hundreds of minibuses making unscheduled stops at unmarked streetsides contributes to an already severe traffic safety problem. Also, in order to maximize profits, these minibuses serve major streets and densely populated areas, leaving more remote neighborhoods without service. As will be discussed in more detail below, a market solution which contributes to economic development in the short term may also have detrimental effects on public health, safety, social equality, or other socially desired benefits. The most effective way to meet social goals may involve both planning solutions and market solutions, or a negotiated combination of the two. It is the role of regional governance to negotiate this balance, within the scope of authority accorded it. As noted above, planning may suggest that a market operate without intervention, may suggest incentives to act in certain socially beneficial ways, or may suggest that market activities, such as the production of certain goods and services, be taken over by government. In practice, the response of regional governments to such issues may involve negotiation among market actors, citizen groups, other government levels, and other regions.

Negotiation is the process of reaching consensus among actors with differing views and goals. In this way, the operation of the market is itself is a sort of negotiation. Planning-led decisions act to manipulate the market, which responds in a certain way. Planners react to this response, and so on until the region meets some sort of equilibrium – a negotiated new condition. However, this process is linear – acting and reacting. Negotiation may also occur as a bargaining process in which market, government, and social actors offer and demand certain conditions and eventually arrive at a consensus acceptable to all. This raises the issue of how regional governors, planners, and market actors will interact. Is the planner the 'right hand man' of the governor, together representing a united public interest voice to meet the market in negotiation? Or are planners themselves the negotiators between political and market forces? What is the accountability of the planner to citizens? Authors envision various roles for the planner in the context of new roles for government; these are discussed below.

New Roles for Planners

Both the scope and role of regional governance are called into question by the changing 'rules of the game' in the post-industrial society. Regions are involved in ever more complex issues, both within the region and as a representative to other regions and levels of government. Simultaneously, citizens are better able to participate in direct decision-making, and appear to benefit from doing so. The relationship between governance and market forces is a subject of constant debate, in part because of the inextricable ties of the region's economy to a global market.

What is the planner's role in a society undergoing such tumultuous change? This chapter began with the contention that planning is the basis for the decisions of governors. How then should planners best serve governors, considering both the limited ability of governors to effect change within the region and increased calls for individual citizens to accept a greater role as governors?

The Planner as Expert Advisor to Politicians

A traditional role for the planner is as a sort of expert advisor to politicians. Planners survey the society, gather statistical and qualitative information as to its status, identify potential patterns of development, and formulate alternative strategies for a future course of action. Politicians then review the work of planners and prioritize among suggested alternative strategies.

The classic theorist of this role for planners in Scandinavia is Leif Johansen, who provides a basic model for the interaction between expert planners and politicians in his *Lectures on Macroeconomic Planning* (1979). His basic model argues for planners as fairly autonomous and isolated experts, free from political and social pressures to produce alternatives not fully grounded in the scientific method. Politicians, the representatives of the people, then choose among presented alternatives based on political ideology and available resources.

This planning paradigm seemed appropriate to the principles of social engineering popular in the Scandinavian political ideology of the Social Democratic movement that developed after the Second World War. (Wirén, 1998). The implication of this model is that planners are insulated both from citizens and from politicians. Citizens express their political will in the election of their representatives, and politicians choose among alternatives but do not seek to alter them, accepting their legitimacy as optimal alternatives in a range of areas.

The Planner as Right Hand Man

Though not written for planners serving the public interest, Mintzberg's *Rise and Fall of Strategic Planning* (1994) offers an alternative role for planners which could be applied to regional planners. Describing planning and strategy-making in the corporate world, Mintzberg argues that the isolation of 'strategic planners' from both the reality of activity in the firm, and from the pragmatic decisions of the firm's director, leads to plans and strategies that are of little benefit to the future development of the firm. He argues that 'strategic planning' is in itself an oxymoron; planning formation and strategy formation are related processes but are not the same process. Strategy formation is described as a 'black box' to which planning acts as an input (to the strategy formation process), as support for the process, and as analysts of the process' output. Mintzberg prefers the term 'strategic programming' to 'strategic planning' because it underscores one important role of the planner, that of programatizing defined strategies. Planning according to Mintzberg is not strategy formation, but effective planning is critical to the formation of effective strategies. Planning is analysis, and strategy is synthesis; 'because analysis is not synthesis, strategic planning is not strategy formation'.

This theory presupposes a strong communicative relationship between planners (of various types, providing the various types of program and analysis input described above) and managers, who are responsible for strategy formation. However, even Mintzberg articulates a role for planners in 'recognizing patterns' which ultimately become the basis for strategies. Effective planners seem therefore to mimic the intuitive process, organizing information in such a way that managers can quickly determine both strategic and tactical options. Once strategies have been adopted, planners analyze current and predicted effects and help take into account emerging strategies. The key difference between Mintzberg's vision and that of Johansen is that it is the firm's director (or the politician) who ultimately devises strategy, based on planning input, rather than prioritizing among planning-generated strategic alternatives. Mintzberg also implies an iterative, interactive relationship between politicians and planners; the planner as 'right hand man' to the governors. Note that Mintzberg does not raise the issue of self-governance, other than to note the importance to planners of observing and collecting information from 'the factory floor'.

The Planner as Communicator and Arbiter

Two recent theorists imply a very different role for the planner, that of communicative link among all actors in the decision-making process. Sager (1994) outlines a complex taxonomy for the various ways in which planners can guide communication among actors in addressing a given issue. Sager notes that not all such communication has the goal of reaching a decision; planning may simply have the goal of organizing the sharing of information among affected parties. In all cases, Sager sees a critical role for the planner in acting as a link among those public and private parties affected by a decision. Healy (1997) agrees, planning approaches which seeks to respond to democratic demands should seek to 'transform these demands into inclusionary styles of argumentation'. She argues for a shift in emphasis for planners, from supporting the 'hard' infrastructure of formal institutional arrangements, to recognizing the importance of the 'soft' infrastructure of institutional capacity building to support inclusionary governance.

Flyvbjerg's (1998) cynical description of the planning process for a large transportation package in Aalborg notes the inability of the carefully designed 'technical plan' to be approved and produced in the face of a complex power relationship among other actors, chiefly political leaders and the local Chamber of Commerce. Planners in the Johansen ideal spend years perfecting a comprehensive, integrated transportation package, only to see it systematically decimated by interest groups and shortsighted political negotiation.

A key role is played by the local newspaper, which despite its appearance as an objective reporter of information related to the transport planning process essentially acts as the mouthpiece of the business community. Flyvbjerg ends his treatise with a call to planners to serve those actors who are underrepresented in such a power play, namely small interest groups and individual citizens. Planners can systematically organize information and present it directly to citizens in such a way as to help people formulate and express opinions.

In direct contrast to the theories of Mintzberg and Johansen, Flyvbjerg sees an educative and empowering role for planners in helping increase the capacity of citizens to take a more active role in governance (Flyvbjerg, 1998). Hall echoes this idea in his description of the current evolution of the planner as 'aim(ing) to help communities think clearly and logically about resolving their problems…it should aim to provide a resource for democratic and informed decision-making' (Hall, 1992).

The Planner as Systems Analyst

Peter Hall (1992) addresses the issue of an ideal role for planners in an increasingly integrated society subject to external forces beyond the governance control accorded to regions. He traces the evolution of planning from a process basically involved in the creation of master plans to an emphasis on the planning of flexible systems which can enable society to meet stated goals.

The evolution of the definition of planning from master planning to 'systems planning' reflects an admission by planning practitioners that master planning may not be possible in modern democratic societies. When an autocrat had complete control over an uneducated population, with little contact with other countries, and a fairly slow pace of technological change, it was fairly easy to design and implement master plans. However, this condition has not existed for several centuries, and there are those that argue that it never existed at all; we have never had certainty about the future state of the world, for example. Instead, Hall notes the attempt of modern planners to systematically analyze the complex interaction of processes and actors that affects the state of the region, and the importance in understanding the operation of the system as a whole in order to effectively control it.

The role of the planner as systems analyst has found wide acceptance in Scandinavia, perhaps due to its similarities to the traditional role for the planner as expert. Admittedly, processes are more complex, and actors more numerous, but this theory still legitimizes the need for planners who posses unique capabilities to contribute to regional decisions. This model envisions less of a role for planners as communicators, but does stress the need for planners to identify communicative patterns that affect system operation.

Hall notes the controversial nature of this cybernetics-based approach to planning on both practical and ethical grounds. Andersson's contribution to this volume provides an explicit example of the impracticality of planning a comprehensive, non-linear network. As noted earlier, regions are increasingly dependent not only on road and rail networks but on the non-linear networks of the type examined by Andersson, such as telecommunication. In this context, planners would not seek to model efficient systems that would be implemented, but rather would seek to guide and facilitate the growth of self-organizing networks. This could be applied both to 'physical' communications networks such as the internet but also to the facilitating of communication networks among individuals, for example through the provision of public spaces or grants to study circles.

Summary: The Planner as Enabler

In modern democratic societies, global markets steer development, populations are increasingly able to contribute to planning decisions, and technological change continues to offer new opportunities and problems. Governance must accept a limited capacity to directly induce change and an increased demand for direct citizen participation. Planners, having acted in the diverse capacities described above, must now adapt to new forms of governance. As more open, more educated societies begin to demand a more broadly based form of government, planners draw upon their various and varied competencies to support the process.

If we return to the original contention of this chapter, that planners should provide a sound basis for decision-making by governors, we see that this basic role has not changed. Rather, the definition of what constitutes a decision has changed, and the identity of the governors may well shift to accept an increased role for direct governance by citizens.

Decisions faced by regions today involve constant adaptation, experimentation, and negotiation. Decisions are not static, master plans but rather flexible, iterative activities adapted to a current understanding of the operation of a complex regional system. Governors may be a both representative politicians and individual citizens. Actors involved in the communicative process of arriving at decisions include a host of interest groups as well as the business community, at the local, regional, and international levels.

What then is the role of the planner in this complex and flexible system of governance? Some synthesis of the roles presented above seems possible. Planners seek to provide the basis for decision-making. In this capacity they must strive for expertise in understanding an increasingly complex interactive system affecting the society; this may take the form of expertise in communicative theory, in forecasting future developments, and in recognizing social, environmental, or economic patterns which offer opportunities or threats to the region's well being. This includes the analysis and evaluation of previously implemented policies. Planners must also be communicators, communicating their expertise to a variety of 'governors' and perhaps negotiating among the diverse wishes of a large group of stakeholders debating a specific policy. Finally, planners must have the capability to synthesize and organize information in such a way as to enable governors to choose among current policy alternatives.

In this role it may be argued that the summary description provided above entails that planners be everything to everyone. It is true that that current development in society and subsequent evolutions in forms of governance imply an extremely diverse and flexible role for planners. However, Healy (1997) warns against making generalizations of what style of planning will evolve in specific circumstances – criteria-driven (hard infrastructure-policy measures), or entrepreneurial (consensus building, focus on soft infrastructure) since actual practices evolve out of specific conditions. However, the overriding goal of planners remains the enabling of sound decisions by governors. Paradoxically, in this age of increasingly complex, confusing forces interacting in the regional arena, directed by diverse group of actors, planners have a greater chance than ever before to achieve this goal.

References

Alexander, E.R. (1995), *Approaches to Planning: Introducing Current Planning Theories, Concepts and Issues* (second ed.), Gordon and Breach Science Publishers SA, Luxembourg.

Andersson, Å.E. and Sylwan, P (1997), *Framtidens Arbete och Liv*, Natur och Kultur, Stockholm.

Flyvbjerg, B. (1998), *Rationality and Power – Democracy in Practice*, University of Chicago Press, Chicago.

Frey, B. and Stutzer, A. (1999), 'Happiness, Economy, and Institutions', Preliminary paper (unpublished), University of Zurich.

Hall, P. (1992), *Urban and Regional Planning*, Routledge, London.

Healy, P. (1997), *Collaborative Planning: Shaping Places in Fragmented Societies*, Macmillan Press Ltd, London.

Johansen, L. (1979), *Lectures on Macroeconomic Planning*, North Holland, Amsterdam.

Lefèvre, C. (1994), *Urban Governance in OECD Countries*, Division des Affaires Urbaines, OCDE, Paris.

Mintzberg, H. (1994), *The Rise and Fall of Strategic Planning: Reconceiving Roles for Planning, Plans, and Planners*, The Free Press, New York.

Sager, T. (1994), *Communicative Planning Theory*, Avebury, Aldershot.

Wannop, U.A. (1995), *The Regional Imperative: Regional Planning and Governance in Britain, Europe, and the United States*, Jessica Kingsley Publishers, London.

Wirén, E. (1998), *Planering för säkerhets skull*, Studentlitteratur, Lund.

7 Local Labor Market Performance in the Knowledge Economy

LARS OLOF PERSSON

Introduction

Full employment and basic service provision have for a long time been prioritized in Swedish regional policy, mainly oriented towards sparsely populated regions with a lagging industrial structure. It seems that equal stress is now put on stimulating economic growth in all regions. The central government has through its Ministry of Industry invited all regions (counties) to design programs for regional economic growth, which will be negotiated for co-financing at the central level (Prop. 1997/98:62). The idea behind these growth accords was to obtain better co-operation between various actors that are instrumental in creating growth. An important point in this new policy is to increase the region's influence over how resources are used.

One reason for this shift in policy is that in the early 1990s, Sweden was found to have a comparatively weak position in the race for economic growth, at least in the European arena. Only a few regions stood out as being more successful than others, in particular the county of Stockholm, which is also the largest urban region in the country. These most competitive regions are also characterized by a relatively high level of education in the labor force and by an expanding knowledge-based industry.

In the course of the 1990s, Stockholm and a few other urban regions were the only regions in the country with a positive net gain in migration, particularly of young people with a university education.

In this emerging regional industrial policy, the efficient matching of the demand and supply of labor at different qualification levels is considered to be one of the most important prerequisites both for economic growth and social cohesion. Increasingly, regional development programs are designed to improve the performance of functional local labor markets. Strategic planning and the implementation of regional policy are gradually decentralized to the regional level.

Hence, analysis of regional labor market processes is an increasingly important task for regional planners. This includes analyses of structural change, labor mobility, the location of higher education institutions and transportation systems. This development also reflects the need for closer planning co-operation between clusters of neighboring municipalities, since the functional local labor market area usually comprises several municipalities.

Annual gross stream labor statistics, which are available in several countries, provide useful tools in this analysis. These data allow for a multidimensional analysis of labor market mobility, that is, in geographical terms as well as between industries and according to the level of qualification of the labor force. Based on this emerging knowledge of the structure and function of labor mobility, we envisage human resource management to be integrated in strategic regional planning.

The increasing emphasis on human capital in regional development planning is a result of the fact that, as markets open up and new technology is available more frequently, regions and corporations increasingly have to deal with complexity and uncertainty. Business firms try to cope with this by developing an integrated business strategy and recruiting labor with both specialized and general skills. Usually such strategies include the increased quality of products and new products, marketing and different ways to control the uncertainty (Fonda and Hayes, 1988).

Productivity is generally expected to increase as a result of training – on the job, and through recruitment of labor with a fresh degree or professional experience. In all industrial branches the improvement of product and especially service quality can usually only be achieved with the use of qualified labor.

A climate for innovations often requires repeated creative meetings of people with quite different skills. Hence, it is not surprising that many comparative analyses of competitiveness between corporations and regions underline the importance of labor and, specifically, the heterogeneity of labor.

It is not only a matter of human resource management and recruitment strategy at the level of the corporate firms but also obvious at the macro level, that is, involving the strategies of industries and regions trying to cope with changing markets and technologies (van der Laan and Ruesca, 1998).

The Knowledge Concept

The qualification of the labor force is a complex concept. Economists stress the role of four less tangible factors related to the qualifications of the labor force in maintaining the competitive strengths of business firms. The first is management skills, which include consistent incentives within the firm and suitable organization. The second is knowledge, that is, in order to ensure innovation and increased productivity and high product quality. The third is co-operation both within the business firm, but also with suppliers and customers. The fourth is flexibility, which entails the ability to adapt rapidly to internal or external changes, particularly concerning the markets (OECD, 1998).

These less tangible factors are different from the more tangible resources such as raw materials, equipment and labor, which are described as a homogenous category, since most of them are effective only as they are embodied in motivated people. The human capital is useful for the firm as a part of the competitive strategy only as it is activated, that is, as the knowledge of the staff is initiates action.

The difference between the concept of knowledge and human capital according to Machlup (1984) – is that human capital is active, while knowledge can sometimes be passive. Machlup distinguishes three types of knowledge and accordingly three potential categories of human capital:

1. Knowledge embodied in individuals, who are trained in specific skills.
2. Knowledge embodied in machines and tools specially developed in research and development.
3. Non-embodied knowledge created and disseminated at a cost but not inseparably embodied in any particular knowledge carriers (type 1) or any particular products (type 2).

All these kinds of knowledge are important in order to improve the competitive strength of a firm, an industrial sector or a region. In this chapter, we focus on the importance of activating knowledge of the first category. As we take an empirical approach in describing and analyzing the impact of knowledge and human capital input on a regional economy, we need an operational definition of the knowledge embodied in labor. Hence, in the empirical analysis based on official register data, we are left with a definition based on the level of formal education of each individual.

This is motivated by the fact that the less tangible nature of knowledge does not mean that assessment and validation of knowledge is not practiced. In fact, this is one of the important tasks of universities and professional associations in certifying certain professions or skills. However, we are aware that it is not a simple task for an employer to determine what skills people possess, especially what ability they have to activate formally acquired knowledge as it appears on their diplomas.

In the Fordist society, the task of recruiting and allocating suitable labor was probably simpler. If each task in the production line was simplified and routinized, it was also simpler to match the task and the worker. Education policy at that time was also aimed more than today at providing the labor market with labor with a uniform standardized education.

In post-Fordist society, the challenge is to recruit relevant staff to businesses which continuously have to adapt to changing markets and new technologies. In all industries and in most positions in firms, there is a demand for labor which is able to take responsibility and act accordingly in unanticipated circumstances.

As Miller (1996) puts it: 'In order to compete on quality, timing and price the competitive producer will need to add even more knowledge. They will have to innovate, diffuse ideas, adapt technology, scan the competition and generally transform a vast amount of information into the knowledge that not only distinguishes them from the competition but also generates an acceptable return on the investment'.

Project- or task-based knowledge work is now common in several industries, both in goods and in service production. As Bridges (1994) points out: 'our organizational world is no longer a pattern of jobs, the way the honeycomb is a pattern of those little hexagonal pockets of honey. In place of jobs, there are part-time and temporary work situations. That change is symptomatic of a deeper change that is subtler but more profound. The deeper change is this: Today's organization is rapidly being transformed from a structure built out of jobs into work needed to be done. Jobs are artificial units superimposed in this field. They are patches of responsibility that, together, are supposed to cover the work that needs to be done.'

The focus of our analysis is the differing performance and competitiveness of local labor markets in terms of the rate of activation of labor with a high level of education. As Storper (1994) suggests '... the logic of the most advanced forms of economic competition – those capable of generating high-wage employment – can best be described as that of learning. Those firms, sectors, regions and nations that can learn faster or better (higher quality or cheaper for a given quality) become competitive because their knowledge is scarce and therefore cannot be immediately imitated by new entrants or transferred, via codified and formal channels, to competitor firms, regions and nations'.

To sum up so far, strategies developed by corporations and regional partnerships need to be based more on activation of knowledge and competence. Less tangible factors are increasingly being recognized as important for economic growth. It is important to have not just knowledge of the production process, but also on the entire production system, logistics, market knowledge and the organization. More attention is now given to the dynamics of the production environment in regions. The mobility within the local labor market and its institutions, including facilities for education and training, are important elements in this production environment.

Classifying Regional Potential in the Knowledge Economy

The production environment is largely synonymous with the functional local labor market area. The way Sweden is split administratively into municipalities and counties rarely coincides with functional regions, which are created by the various choices and decisions of individual people and business firms. A useful division is functionally coherent local labor markets. They are the areas in which the businesses concerned have to recruit most of their labor force. The quality of the functional regions has a strong influence on both productivity and prosperity. In the knowledge economy, efficient and instant matching of the demand and supply of competent labor in the local labor market is one of the most important elements in territorial competitiveness.

The local labor market (LLM) regions, which are based on current registered commuting connections between municipalities, change according to the trend in employment, settlement patterns, the infrastructure and communications, as well as the willingness of the population to commute. Using the same criteria for linking municipalities to each other according to dominating commuting flows, the number of 'independent' LLM regions in Sweden decreased from 187 in 1970 to 109 in 1997 (Kullenberg and Persson, 1997). This should be compared to the currently 288 municipalities in the country. The labor market regions for men are greater than for women and people with a high level of education travel to work within larger labor market regions than those with a low level.

It is conceivable that this process of 'regional enlargement' will continue with the rapid regional rail systems being built around the country. Shorter journey times combined with the greater use of IT to allow teleworking a few days a week will make longer commuting distances acceptable and thus lead to further enlargement of the regions.

The local market is especially important to small enterprises and businesses in the service sector. Because the importance of such enterprises is growing, in terms of employment, this suggests that the size of the local market will assume an ever-more important role in future development. This is also evident from an analysis of the breadth of the industry structure. There is a strong correlation between the number of industries present in and the size of the local labor market area. Stockholm LLM, which is by far the largest in the country, contains almost 600 different industries (5 digit level).

A typical regional center with a university has approximately 250 industries present, while each of the numerous small town-based LLMs typically has fewer than 100 industries present. Already these figures indicate that regional enlargement – that is, more extensive commuting – is more or less the only way to increase the diversity and the dynamics of the many small local labor markets in Sweden. It should however be remembered that these possibilities are also limited for distance reasons, especially in the sparsely populated parts of the country.

Production conditions in the regions differ widely within Sweden. What we refer to here as the regional production environment includes, for example, the size of the LLM region, supply of human capital, the dynamics of trade and industry, various aspects of accessibility and communications etc. Other factors, such as the quality of life, the climate for industry, the spirit of entrepreneurship and culture, may also be attributed to regional production conditions.

The Swedish LLM areas are classified according to more tangible production conditions (NUTEK, 1997). The purpose is to identify similarities in the fundamental production conditions that prevail, focusing on the supply of human capital. This leads to an analysis of the reasons regions within one and the same regional category perform at different levels. The LLM regions are analyzed and weighted on the basis of five fundamental production conditions. Both the selection of variables and their weighting were based on qualitative assessments. The focus on the importance of human capital activation is reflected in the first two production factors:

- Human capital: Proportion of population with post secondary education – weighting 25 percent.
- Access to a locality with a university or other institute of higher education – weighting 10 percent.
- Size of labor force: population aged 16–64 years – weighting 30 percent.

- Dynamics: Number of entrepreneurs/population aged 16–64 years – weighting 25 percent.
- Access to a municipal center – weighting 10 percent.

This procedure resulted in the following regional categories. Sweden's three main *conurbations:*

1. Stockholm (1 LLM).
2. Gothenburg (1 LLM).
3. Malmö (1 LLM).

Regional category 4 is made up of LLM *regions with a full university*, as well as a number of large regions with an institute of higher education of another kind (8 LLM).

Regional category 5 comprises the *medium-sized regional centers*, these too including a regional institute of higher education (12 LLM).

Regional category 6 consists of *medium-sized industrial regions*, some of which are characterized by small scale industry, while others are dominated by a large corporation (16 LLM).

Regional category 7 includes certain *regional service centers* (11 LLM).

Regional category 8 is made up mainly of *smaller, manufacturing industry-biased regions* (30 LLM).

Regional category 9 includes 29 smaller LLM regions, mostly with a high proportion of employees in the *public sector*.

The classification into regional categories enables us to compare the production capacity of the regions and the performance of the labor market within each 'category' in a more accurate way. The purpose is not only to describe how differences exist between the groups. More importantly, this offers a method that helps us understand what lies behind these differences. In theoretical terms, it may be argued that if the production conditions on which the classification was based were to explain all the differences in production results, then the LLM regions in each regional category should be closely gathered around a common point.

As we will show, this is not the case; we have to search for other explanations. This benchmark analysis may serve as a starting-point for a discussion of why certain regions perform better than others with similar conditions do.

An underlying hypothesis is that certain less tangible factors play an important role.

Differing Arenas for Labor Market Careers

In this new and more flexible labor market situation, there is a need to develop methods for both describing and managing the stocks and flows of human capital. We use available annual statistics for describing careers in terms of the labor market status for each individual. In total we distinguish between nine alternative careers:

From: one of the three statuses employed, unemployed or student year t,

To: one of these three statuses year t+1.

In the empirical analysis we use data on each individual 16 – 64 years of age. By this 'career approach' we are able to describe to what extent and where labor at different levels of education is *activated* by the following three modes: a) continuation of employment in the same industry next year, b) change to another branch or c) recruitment to a local labor market.

Labor market performance is defined here as a *dynamic* concept: the ability of the local labor markets both:

- to adapt to and facilitate structural change in the local economy by activating all segments of labor
- to increase the input of as well as return on human capital investments.

The segmented structure of the labor markets by level of formal education will be inherent in the analysis. Each individual in the local labor force (16 – 64 years) is classified according to the highest level of formal education: Primary; Secondary and Post secondary. Each individual is also classified in terms of careers to employment status year t+1 from either of the following statuses year t: Employed, Unemployed and Student. In migration, careers leading to employment is related to gross in-migration (Table 7.1).

Hence, the Labor Market Performance Index is a description of the *rate of activation of ten pools* of the labor force in the LLMs in comparison to the corresponding activation rate in the country as a whole. In the aggregate index – that is, the sum of the activation rate for ten careers – each element is given the same weight, following definition (1) of labor market performance, that is, the *equal importance* of activating all segments of the labor force.

Table 7.1   Composition of Local Labor Market Performance Index. Rate of activation of ten pools of the labor force

Status year t	Status year t+1: Employed		
	Education: Primary	Secondary	Postsecondary
Employed in same LLM	*JobJobPRIM*	*JobJobSEC*	*JobJobPOSTSEC*
Unemployed in same LLM	*UnemplJobPRIM*	*UnemplJobSEC*	*UnemplJobPOSTSEC*
Student in same LLM	*StudJobPRIM*	*StudJobSEC*	*StudJobPOSTSEC*
Any status in other LLM – in-migrant	*InMigJobALL*		

The results at the aggregate level in 1996–97 are plotted in Figure 7.1. The Stockholm LLMs performs better than the national average, but there are a small number of medium sized and small LLMs in other regional categories performing even better in activating all segments of labor in that particular year. The LLMs of Gnosjö in regional category 6 (medium industrial) stands out with its extraordinary performance, in contrast to Eskilstuna in the same category.

A closer look on the components of the Index reveals that Gnosjö performs better than the national average in all segments (Figure 7.2). The deviances are however small concerning the ability to keep people in employment (Job-to-Job careers). With one exception (the career Unemployed-to-Job with Post-secondary Education) there is a tendency for Gnosjö LLMs to perform better at offering careers for labor with a low level of education than labor with a higher level. Eskilstuna's poor performance is mainly due to its difficulties in offering jobs to new entrants – Student and Unemployment careers and Immigrant statuses.

Local labor performance varies widely from the national average in most regional categories, particularly within the smallest categories containing several LLMs. We interpret this wide variation within groups of LLMs with similar production conditions as a reflection of differences in less tangible production factors. For instance, from other regional studies we know that the Gnosjö Region is well known for its 'entrepreneurial spirit' (Gummesson, 1997).

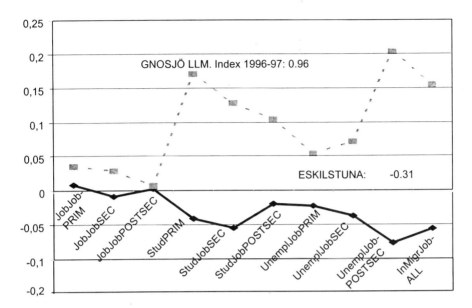

Figure 7.1 Performance index of labor force activation in the 'best' and 'worst' performing LLMs within regional category 6, Medium Industrial. 1996–97

In concluding this analysis of labor market performance, we suggest that the fairly ambitious Swedish labor market policy, in combination with a still strong dependence on employment in public services in most municipalities – particularly for individuals with a university education, contributes to reducing the effects of the initially large differences in production conditions, which form the basis for the classification of regional categories.

Evidently, several small, remote local labor markets with a low level of education in the labor force, are also able to perform quite well as arenas for labor market careers for most segments of the labor force.

Human Capital Input and Regional Economic Performance

However, regional economic performance in terms of Gross Income per capita, shows a different picture (Figure 7.2). Very few of the labor market areas within regional categories 5 – 9 (medium and small LLMs with a relatively low level of education in the labor force) perform better than the national average.

Already from the two examples, we find that there is not a close correlation between the aggregate labor activation rate and economic performance: Gnosjö has a lower income per capita than Eskilstuna. One of the most important factors behind regional economic performance is instead the educational level of the labor force.

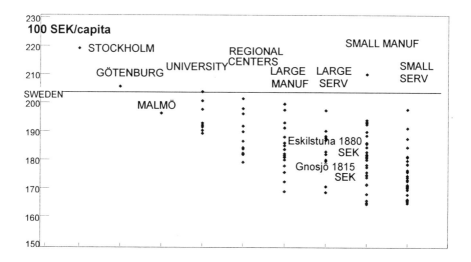

Figure 7.2 Income per capita in LLM areas within nine regional categories 1997 (100 SEK)

Here, regional economic performance will be analyzed as the result of careers in local labor markets for individuals with long formal training. The four sources of such human capital in a region are (Figure 7.3):

- Employed both year t and year t+1, with post secondary education (EmplPOSTSEC).
- Activated by In migration to Job, with post secondary education (InMigrPOSTSEC).
- Cross Industry Mobile Labor, with post secondary education (CrossIndustryPOSTSEC).
- Recruitment from Local Pool of not economically active with post secondary education (LocRecPOSTSEC).

Figure 7.3 shows the relative importance of these four careers for people with post secondary education for regional economic performance in regional categories. In metropolitan regions the permanently employed with higher education typically contribute 30–37 percent of gross regional income; in smaller LLM regions the figure is much less or 20–25 percent.

Cross industry mobility of human capital is quite an important source of regional income especially in the metropolitan regions; in Stockholm it contributes to as much as 4.8 percent of total income. Local recruitment is on whole twice as high in metropolitan regions as in the smallest categories of LLMs. The contribution to regional income of one year's local recruitment is 1.6 percent in Stockholm but only 0.8 percent in small towns. In-migration labor with post secondary education contribute 0.6–0.7 percent of total region income in all types of regions. This means that small regions depend as much on in-migrating human capital as they do on the activation of 'fresh' local human resources.

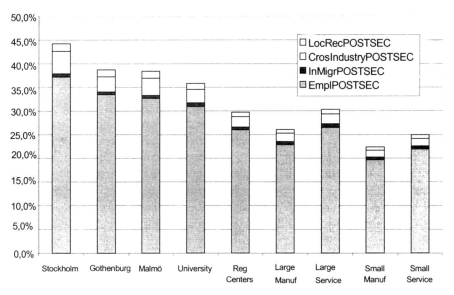

Figure 7.3 Contribution (%) to gross regional income year t+1 by four modes of activation of human capital in nine regional categories 1994–97

In conclusion, the major differences in the performance of local labor markets in activating human capital between larger city regions and smaller regions are that (1) larger regions already employ proportionally more well-paid labor with a higher education, (2) cross industry mobility is much more frequent in larger regions, and (3) local gross recruitment is roughly twice as high in larger regions. The dependence on activation of in-migrating labor with a high education is the same in all types of regions and small compared to other sources.

The return on higher education – measured as income change per annum – is substantially higher in labor market careers in Stockholm than in most other regional categories (Figure 7.4). This is most evident for in-migrants to Stockholm. In all other regional categories, it is 'more profitable' to migrate out than in. The dual character of the emerging knowledge economy in Sweden in geographical terms is very much reflected in these results (cf Axelsson et al 1994).

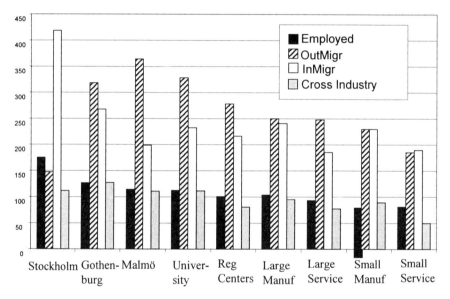

Figure 7.4   Return on higher education.   Annual income change 1994-97, SEK 100.   Four careers in nine regional categories

The question is still open as to whether the large gap between the very few 'knowledge-based' regions and the numerous regions still left in the Industrial Society and the public service-dominated labor market will ever be closed. The question is also open as to whether the emerging regional industrial policy aimed at growth in each region will more than marginally affect the persisting large differences in economic performance both between regional categories and between local labor markets within each category.

Concluding Remarks

The differing performance – in terms of contributions to both economic growth and to employment – of local labor markets is becoming the focus of regional policy and planning in Sweden. The shift is from a policy of national support mainly for lagging and sparsely populated regions to one promoting industrial growth in all regions in the country. The regional growth agreements derived from SWOT analyses in each region mean a shift to more negotiational planning between regional partnerships and the central government.

There is also a need to shift the territorial unit subject to planning. The functional region is largely synonymous with the local labor market area. This calls for closer partnership between politicians and planners at the municipal and the county level. In a country like Sweden, with its sharp contrast between sparse settlements and the limited number of metropolitan regions, there are large differences between the roughly one hundred local labor markets as environments for production. In the emerging knowledge economy only a few city regions have proved to have developed a modern industrial structure activating substantial input of human capital. The size of the current gap between the largest metropolitan region and the smallest local labor markets is illustrated by the fact that highly educated labor contributes almost 50 percent of gross income in the first region, but less than 25 percent in the second.

The need to activate human resources is the focus of this analysis. The focus on human capital in regional development planning is attributable to the fact that regions and corporations increasingly have to deal with complexity and uncertainty, as new markets and new technologies are introduced. Operationally, our analysis of the differing performance and competitiveness of local labor markets is made in terms of the rate of the activation of labor with a high education. Annual statistics describing the labor market career for each individual constitute the basis.

The Swedish LLM areas are first classified according to more tangible production conditions, before focusing on the supply of highly educated people and the access to a university education. The purpose is to identify similarities in the fundamental production conditions that prevail. This then leads to an analysis of the reasons why regions within one and the same regional category perform at different levels.

Labor market performance is defined here as the ability of the local labor market both to adapt to and facilitate structural change in the local economy and to increase the input of as well as return on human capital investments.

LLMs are found to vary considerably in performance according to this index, first of all between the regional categories, but also within each category. We suggest that this 'benchmark' analysis serve as a starting-point for a discussion – preferably in the regions concerned – of why certain regions perform better or worse than others with similar conditions. An underlying hypothesis is that certain less tangible factors play an important role, factors such as the quality of life, the climate for industry, the spirit of entrepreneurship and culture. It may well be that the informal qualifications or competence of labor is also an important factor.

The results show that the activation of local sources of human capital is most important in larger regions. There, the frequent exchange of labor with a high level of education between industries contributes a great deal to gross regional income. The main reason for this is the much wider range of industries represented in metropolitan regions. Smaller regions are relatively more dependent on interregional migration of human capital. However, the low rate of all modes of activation of human capital in smaller regions cannot narrow the gap between small and large local labor markets. One conclusion is that increased local production of human capital – in practice the location of decentralized university courses – is more or less necessary in order to introduce new knowledge industries in these small LLM regions.

Our conclusion is also that 'regional enlargement' – that is, more extensive commuting – is more or less the only way to increase the diversity and the dynamics of the many small local labor markets in Sweden. However, these possibilities are limited for distance reasons, especially in the sparsely populated parts of the country. The return on higher education – measured as income change – is substantially higher in labor market careers in Stockholm than in most other regional categories. This is most evident for in-migrants to Stockholm. There are several university towns in the country which in practice serve as producers and exporters of human capital in order to match the demand in Stockholm's labor market.

Again, analysis of regional labor market processes is an increasingly important task for regional planners. This includes analyses of structural change, labor mobility, the location of higher education institutions and transportation systems. This development also indicates the need for closer planning co-operation between clusters of neighboring municipalities, since the functional local labor market area usually comprises several local administrative regions.

Labor statistics based on gross stream data provide tools in this analysis. These data allow for a multidimensional analysis of labor market mobility, in geographical terms as well as between industries and according to the formal qualification of the labor force. Based on this emerging knowledge of the structure and function of labor mobility, we envisage that human resource management will be integrated in strategic regional planning. However, the tangible factors which can be measured by official statistics are not sufficient in fully explaining differing local labor market performance and regional economic growth. Hence, the statistical analyses suggested have to be supplemented with qualitative analyses of cultural and historical conditions in each region.

References

Axelsson, S., Berglund, S. and Persson, L.O. (1994), *Det tudelade kunskapssamhället*, ERU-rapport 81, Fritzes, Stockholm.

Bridges, W. (1994), 'End of the job', *Fortune*.

Fonda, N. and Hayes, C. (1988), 'Education, training and business performance', *Oxford Review of Economic Policy*, 4–3.

Gummesson, O. (1997), *Därför lyckas Gnosjö: bygden som har blivit ett begrepp*, Ekerlid, Stockholm.

Kullenberg, J. and Persson, L.O. (1997*), Tänjbara räckvidder. Lokala arbetsmarknader i förändring*, Institutet för regionalforskning, Rapport 101, 1997.

Machlup, F. (1984), 'Knowledge: its creation, distribution and economic significance', *Economics of Information and Human Capital*, vol. 3, Princeton University Press.

Miller, R. (1996*), Meaning what People Know. Human Capital Accounting for the Knowledge Economy*, OECD, Paris.

NUTEK (1997), *Regioner på väg mot år 2015: Förutsättningar, fakta och tendenser*, Närings- och teknikutvecklingsverket, R1997:10, Stockholm.

OECD (1998), 'Territorial development and human capital in the knowledge economy', *Towards a Policy Framework. Leed Notebook No 23*, OECD, Paris 1996.

Prop. 1997/98:62, 'Regional tillväxt – för arbete och välfärd', Government Bill.

Storper, M. (1994), 'Institutions of the Learning Economy', paper presented at the *Conference on Employment and Growth of the Knowledge-Based Economy*, November 1994, Copenhagen.

van der Laan, L. and Ruesga, S.M. (eds), (1998), *Institutions and Regional Labour Markets in Europe*, Ashgate, Aldershot.

8 Social Exclusion in Post-Fordist Sweden

GÖRAN CARS
MATS JOHANSSON

Introduction

For a long period of time Swedes were regarded as having a high standard of living. For many years, from the end of the 1970s, the annual OECD reports used to put Sweden at the very top. Sweden has also had an international reputation of having not only a high GDP but also an even distribution of welfare among its population. Equality within different spheres increased during the period from the Second World War up until the 1980s, because of ambitious social programs.

Guided by the concepts of 'The People's Home' (Folkhemmet) and 'The Strong Society' (Det starka samhället) the Swedish welfare state was created after the Second World War.[1] A characteristic feature of the development of the Swedish welfare state was the very central position given to social welfare goals. Social well-being was not a concern to be addressed merely by social policy. Instead, the entire focus of public policy was aimed at improving social conditions and the social well-being of citizens. Issues concerning work and employment were given priority and powerful efforts were launched to create full employment. To a large extent, these efforts were successful. In the 1960s and 1970s Swedish planning was in its heyday. Housing production and improvements to the existing housing stock led to an average housing standard that was hard to find elsewhere in Europe. Radical improvements were made in the provision of public services and cultural and recreational activities. Unemployment was reduced to a marginal problem, basically seen as temporary friction in the restructuring of the labor market.

However, this picture has changed. The 1990–1993 period saw an unprecedented deterioration in public finance, leaving Sweden with the largest deficit in the OECD area. The growing deficit was accompanied by a large decline in aggregate output and an increase in unemployment to levels that had been unthinkable since the 1930s. The severe economic problems facing Sweden reflected both the recession in the economy, experienced by most countries within the OECD, but also structural problems in the Swedish economy. The public sector had become too large and it was doubtful whether institutional arrangements and incentive structures could bring about the much needed expansion of employment opportunities in the private sector.

The latter part of the 1990s has been characterized by a rethinking of national policies. The core of the debate has been focused on the concepts of growth, employment, and welfare. In this paper we outline recent developments in Sweden and discuss how they have impacted the labor market and social welfare. In this discussion Swedish experiences are related to international trends and developments. In the concluding part of the paper, current responses to stimulate growth and promote social cohesion are presented and discussed. The argument we would like to put forward is that recent structural change in society calls for a parallel refocusing of regional planning. The rapidly growing gap between different groups in the population, the emergence of a 'two-speed' society and social exclusion must constitute a starting-point for this reformulation. The challenge facing regional planning lies in developing strategies that are effective as engines for economic growth and competitiveness and at the same time adequately address issues regarding social welfare and social cohesion.

Fordism to Post-Fordism and the Labor Market

During the past few decades, the world economy has experienced substantial and structural changes. Globalization is a concept often used to summarize these changes. Globalization has had different implications for various countries depending on their previous role in the world economy and also depending on their potentials for developing competitive strategies to meet the emerging demands of the global markets. For the member countries of the European Union – like Sweden – the process of globalization has brought about substantial changes within the labor market, changes that in turn have affected their welfare systems, and raised the issues of social integration and social exclusion.

Patterns of rapid economic growth have as a rule been associated with the movement of resources between different firms, branches, industries, and regions. These structural changes were an important growth factor in the Swedish economy, for instance, during the post-war years and especially during the 1960s. The rapid growth and the structural transformation of the economy also resulted in extensive geographical mobility. The latter was especially pronounced during the 1960s, which was characterized in Sweden by high growth, rapid structural transformation, and a shortage of labor in expanding regions. The industrial society stood at its zenith. This decade was perhaps also the last in the Fordist era – a time characterized by mass production and mass consumption, assembly lines, Taylorism and 'scientific management', hierarchical and pyramidal structures in the organization of the working process, and standardized competence. The Fordist era was also a period of de-skilling the labor force (see e.g. Rifkin, 1996).[2]

Deindustrialization, Post-Fordism and the Spatial Division of Labor

Deindustrialization is intimately bound up with the structural transformation of the economy. However, friction-free economic transformations are not the rule – instead, disharmonies arise by virtue of the fact that resources are not shifted out of stagnating activities into expanding ones. Reindustrialization and deindustrialization occurs simultaneously.

New industries are replacing old ones has always been both a central and a natural element of the process of economic transformation and change. Reindustrialization, like deindustrialization, is not a cyclical but a structural phenomenon. However, the term reindustrialization obtains an extra dimension when coupled with deindustrialization and the rise of the service society. Much of what is growing in the borderlands between manufacturing industry and service production – industry-related service production – is a significant feature of the reindustrialization process.

Another problem is, however, that the processes of deindustrialization and reindustrialization – in most cases – do not coincide spatially. Reindustrialization usually occurs in regions other than the traditional industrial centers (see e.g. Cheshire and Hay, 1989; CEC, 1993). In the deindustrialized regions the economy is characterized by economic stagnation or retardation. Particularly hard hit are traditional industrial regions with one-sided labor markets. In these regions, there is often a surplus of labor, but the 'wrong' type of labor from the employer's point of view. The workers in these areas have found it very difficult to find new jobs resulting in long-term unemployment as one outcome and – for the older workers – early retirement as another. The result has thus been a withdrawal from the labor force of older people in these old manufacturing regions both in Europe and in Sweden (Dunford, 1996). In the reindustrialized regions the development pattern is different. The economy is growing and there is a shortage of labor with qualifications matching the skills required for the new jobs that are emerging.

This also ties in with the changed alignment of investment. In the old traditional industrial regions, expansion and well-being were to a large extent associated with investments in material assets such as buildings and machinery. Today and tomorrow, it is the non-material investments – R & D, product development, training and marketing – that form the foundation for expansion and dynamics (Johansson, 1996). This process is a central ingredient in the transformation of society from Fordism to post-Fordism – a transformation that has consequences for both employment and the organization of working life.

Thus, the post-Fordist localization patterns differ from the Fordist ones. The new suburbs were indeed a Fordist phenomenon, a result of the improved means of transportation, but the investment pattern was almost the same. The natural resources and the markets were the dominant factors behind the localization of the factories and workplaces. In the post-Fordist era, these location patterns have changed. In the post-industrial society, the settlement pattern of the labor force – especially the highly educated – is an important factor in decision-making concerning spatial location for investments (see e.g. Andersson, 1985; Anderstig and Hårsman, 1986; Claval, 1990; Hall, 1990, 1991; Massey, 1995; Johansson, 1996). Different regions have differently composed capital and labor markets, which implies that the development possibilities are not equal regarding the choices of technology available for adoption. Since there is a mutual dependence between the labor force's competence structure and the introduction of new technology, a lack of competence is a restriction to innovative activities and technology renewal. With the rise of the post-industrial society, companies have increasingly been inclined to locate operations where there is skilled and highly educated labor. A location shift from traditional industrial areas in decline to innovative and creative ones is visible. This feature is especially noticeable with respect to knowledge-intensive activities, which are characterized by capital that is easily moved. Attractive living conditions appeal to well-educated people, who thereby drag the companies along with them. In Europe, this is one of the factors behind the growth of the dynamic arc from northern Italy through southern France and down to north-western Spain.

With regard to labor market development, the social polarization processes are thus not only an interregional or an urban-rural problem. Social exclusion is perhaps even more pronounced within regions and especially in big cities. In many respects, social interaction and social integration are more pronounced in rural areas and small towns, compared to larger cities. The social network is more developed and even if there are a lot of problems related to age, education, and gender structures, social exclusion seems not to be of the same magnitude as in urban areas. In urban areas, segregation is much more pronounced – also in the spatial sense – with concentrated pockets of poverty and deprivation as only one illustration. The social structure is much more homogenous in rural areas and small towns than in metropolitan areas with a lot of in-migrants, where the lower labor force exclusion seems to be more obvious as illustrated by drug problems and dependence on social benefits.[3] The social structure in the rural regions and municipalities has more the form of a pyramid – in the urban areas the social pyramid has been replaced by an hourglass. The income distribution in the post-Fordist society not only looks like an hourglass, but the metaphor also describes an economic mechanism. 'If, under Fordism, one could argue that 'the rich lived off the expenditure of the poor', i.e. wage workers' expenditure accounted for the turnover of entrepreneurs, in the case of the hour-glass society 'the poor live off what trickles down from the expenditure of the rich' (Lipietz, 1998). The heterogeneity of the labor force in the big city areas seems to be a precondition for economic and social transformation and development (see e.g. Andersson, 1985) at the same time as it is seem to be a hampering factor with regard to social integration.

Labor Market Segmentation in the Post-Fordist Era

During the Fordist era the division into primary and secondary labor market segments was developed and accentuated as a result of the organization of the working process, which was characterized by mass production. The primary labor segment was characterized by high wages, good working conditions, chances of advancement and employment stability. The primary labor market segment was also in many ways an internal labor market where on-the-job training and workplace-related knowledge were central ingredients. The secondary segment – on the other hand – was characterized by low wages, poor working conditions, little chance of advancement and a high turnover among the labor force. There were more or less sharp dividing lines between the two segments.[4]

The industrial society, organized according to Fordist principles, changed during the 1960s and 1970s with the introduction of 'lean' production that 'combines the advantage of craft production and mass production, while avoiding the high cost of the former and the rigidity of the latter' (Womack, Jones and Roos, 1990, quoted in Rifkin, 1996). For many of the old products the markets were saturated and niche production was the new prestigious word. Once again, flexibility, teamwork, and multi-skilled workers were back on the factory floor. This post-Fordist organization of the work process does not, however, mean that the segmentation of the labor market disappeared. Instead, it took other directions since the mismatch in the labor market increased. Hand in hand with 'jobless growth', there has been the development of long-term unemployment, declining unionism and higher labor force participation rate of women, and thus more part-time and casual work as well in the EU (Samers and Woods, 1998). The fragmentation of the labor market has resulted not only in increasing uncertainty about job opportunities – it has also resulted in increasing uncertainty about future income (George, 1996).

Thus one element of the transformation process from Fordism to post-Fordism is an increased segmentation of the labor market. In the industrial society, labor and capital were interchangeable to a large extent. Today the picture is different. The introduction of new technology requires labor with certain qualifications and thus also a certain degree of training, at the same time as flexibility has become increasingly important – labor, as a factor of production has become increasingly heterogeneous. The increased labor market segmentation thus hampers the transfer of unemployed industrial workers from traditional blue-collar jobs to new jobs in knowledge-intensive activities in the manufacturing industry as well as in the dynamic parts of the service sector.

Similar problems have existed in the labor market since the beginning of the industrial period. In Europe, at least until the 1970s, laborers that moved from rural areas generally had no problem finding work in rapidly growing industries in the expanding urban areas. During the Fordist period, manufacturing required a lot of labor with 'standardized competence', that is, labor which could be placed directly in simple, repetitive tasks. Today, one of the problems in the post-Fordist labor market is the existence of both shortages and surpluses of labor within the same companies, industries, and commuting regions. The reason is that the labor market has become increasingly segmented and fragmented with respect to competence levels. A segmented labor market consists of a number of sub-markets, which are more or less separated from one another by various obstacles, resulting in a heterogeneous and unsubstitutable labor force. These sub-markets have their own supply and demand situations, their own wage structures and their own surpluses or shortages of labor. Investment in intangible capital has replaced investment in tangible capital in importance in the development process. The result of these processes is a further segmentation and polarization of the labor force and consequently changing working life conditions in which the trade unions' minor role is a weakening factor in the social cohesion at the working place level. [5]

Thus, structural changes in the labor market have in most Western countries led to a deindustrialization process with a rapid decline in employment in the manufacturing industries. Blue-collar jobs within these sectors of industry have declined as a consequence of increased competition from other countries and the subsequent closure of plants, or because of improvements in efficiency and a subsequent reduced need for labor. This development is drastic in itself as it has led to the loss of millions of blue-collar jobs in particular and subsequently to substantially increased levels of – predominantly structural and long-term – unemployment. However besides this direct and immediate effect, the decline of the traditional industrial sectors has also – as in the case of Sweden in the 1990s – led to the successive erosion of the foundations of national welfare systems with reductions in employment in the public sector.

The transformation of society in a post-industrial direction is confirmed by the fact that, despite the upswing of the European economy over the last few years, the 'old industrial jobs' are permanently gone. Instead the expansion of work opportunities lies in other sectors of the labor market. Schematically, the new jobs can be found in two fields of the economy. First there is the rapid growth in jobs relating to modern technologies, e.g. information technology, education and the media. Second there is an increased demand for labor within the basic service sectors. The change in the composition of work opportunities has social impacts in various ways. It is obvious that there is a 'mismatch' between the skills required for many of the 'new and qualified' jobs and the skills normally held by people who are unemployed. Thus, at the same time as there is a lack of labor and bottlenecks in some business sectors, there is vast unemployment. There is also a shortage of work opportunities in the relatively unqualified service sector, where there are problems in matching the skills of traditional blue-collar-workers with the demands of the labor market. An additional problem in the expanding unqualified service sectors is that wages are often low. This in turn has led to welfare considerations as households relying on incomes from this sector often face various kinds of economic and social hardships.

The regional maladjustment or the mismatches in the labor market thus seem to have been accentuated over the past few decades.[6] Different regions have differently composed labor markets. The labor required by the expanding urban labor market in the post-industrial society is also different from that of the old industrial areas. The division of labor has increasingly been a regional division with an accentuated regional polarization as one result (Massey, 1995, Johansson, 1996). The result of these processes is – as mentioned above – a further segmentation and polarization of the labor force and consequently changing working life conditions between as well as within regions and cities according to competence levels, age structure, income development, and employment opportunities.

During the 1990s, the connection between labor market conditions and long-distance migration in Sweden disappeared. Most of the migratory movements during the 1990s had no connections with the labor market in the sense that the majority of the movers are people that are not looking for jobs. Only one third of the migrants in 'active' ages seem to be job-seekers. The increase in the propensity to migrate during the 1990s compared to the 1960s and early 1970s is instead a consequence of higher migration intensities among those aged 19–26.

Most of the young people today migrate as a result of studies and other non-job related reasons. These migratory movements have been very asymmetrical in the sense that the flows have been directed to metropolitan areas and larger university towns, which have accentuated the skewed age structure in these areas as well as in the out-migration areas. Even if the young movers in many cases are not highly educated, the result will in any case be a form of brain drain as many of these youngsters will be highly educated after the move and very seldom go back to their home regions. Instead, there are signs – at least during the crisis years in 1990s – that there is a positive correlation between the unemployment level in the in-migration region and the percentage of people unemployed among the in-migrants (Johansson and Persson, 1999).[7]

Another factor that has reduced the impact of labor market conditions during the 1990s in Sweden is the internal migration of foreigners and refugees. In this case, there has been a flow of foreigners from almost every part of Sweden to big city areas. This phenomenon results, however, in an over-estimation of the internal long-distance migration. The foreigners are registered as immigrants from abroad in the first phase and then as in-migrants from other parts of Sweden to the metropolitan regions in the next phase. It should, however, be noted that this phenomenon contributes only a small part of the rise in internal migration and its impact was most accentuated in the middle of the 1990s. These migratory movements have nothing to do with labor markets conditions in differing parts of the country – either in the crisis regions or the expanding ones. Instead, it is the agglomeration of relatives and other foreigners that is the pull-factor. The result will in any case be accentuated segregation both on the interregional and intraregional level.

Fordism, Post-Fordism and the Quality of Working Life

Compared to the Fordist era the organization of the working process has changed. Assembly lines and standardization have declined in importance and flexibility has become the new key concept in the organization of work. In terms of the quality of working life, mechanization and automation have reduced much of the physical pain of hard manual work but the psychological strains of jobs – often white-collar – have increased. However, recent studies show that people with blue-collar jobs still are less satisfied with their jobs than people with white-collar jobs (Vogel, 1997).

It is not only the organization of the working process that has changed during the transition from Fordism to post-Fordism –the employment and unemployment structures have also changed. Security of employment and the risk of unemployment are important ingredients in the quality of working life conditions. During the Fordist era unemployment was as a rule the result of ordinary variations in the business cycles. People who were unemployed in various homogenous segments returned to their 'old' jobs when the economy entered an up-swing. In the post-Fordist era the significance of the structural transformation has increased. 'Deficient-demand' unemployment has been replaced by structural unemployment. The structure of the economy in the post-Fordist era has changed the matching process with regard to different 'vintages' or segments of labor on the workplace, local, and regional level.

One of the indications that the mismatch in the labor market has been accentuated is the increase in long-term unemployment both in absolute and relative terms. This phenomenon is most pronounced in depopulating areas where both young people with a low education and – especially – older workers are overrepresented. Long-term unemployment has been relatively higher even in the more dynamic and expanding metropolitan regions during the past few decades. In these areas, the crisis of the 1990s has hit refugees and foreigners from outside the Western world very hard in Sweden as well as in other EU countries.

Unemployment – especially long-term unemployment – is one of the most obvious causes of social exclusion. Unemployment differs between various regions but also within regions, where there are significant differences in unemployment according to age, gender, education, domestic and foreign workers, and competence. The increased segmentation or dualization of the labor market has accentuated the unemployment problem and a substantial segment of the population has lost a foothold in the labor market with social exclusion as a result. The compulsory early retirement has an effect of course on the income situation of the individual and a financial impact on the municipalities where these people live. Long-term unemployment and compulsory early retirement, however, also have social implications.

The increased complementarity between new technology and a highly educated labor force – often younger people – often results in a belief that the person is useless and unproductive and thus in a loss of self-respect, stigmatization and decreased social status (George, 1996). This stigmatization problem has been growing in the past few decades even among younger people with the 'wrong' competence as a consequence of the rapid transformation of the economy (Walker, Alber and Guillemard, 1993).

Open unemployment, however, is not the only a problem with regard to the quality of working life. 'Hidden' unemployment between and within different regions and local areas as well as between different groups in the labor force constitutes a large and growing problem. This also has an urban-rural dimension – traditionally hidden unemployment has been higher in rural areas as a consequence of the economic structure, with its possibilities of self-supportive activities, and perhaps also because of the more developed social networks that hamper the risk of social exclusion.

Further more, trade unions play a role in respect to the conditions of working life. Trade unions are more frequent in areas dominated by large-scale industry than in areas where the private service sector, agriculture and small-scale industry are overrepresented. The influence of the trade unions on working conditions has eroded during the post-Fordist era and subsequently so has their ability to hamper the social effects of unemployment. In addition the existence of a 'grey working sector' can be observed in metropolitan areas, frequently occupied by 'marginalized' people, where self-employment is the rule, which probably accentuates alienation and social exclusion. Many of the potential jobs will, however, be found in the lower segments of the private service sector and many of the migrants will be self-employed in these kinds of jobs or unemployed (Ekberg, 1993; Scott, 1999). This process will accentuate social exclusion and hamper social cohesion and integration, especially in urban areas and big cities.

In conclusion, it can be noted that some groups in society have been hit hard by the structural changes in the economy. A substantial group is unemployed; others rely on casual work or low-income jobs. For people who are unemployed or working only casually, life is normally not only characterized by economic hardship, unemployment or casual work but also often has other social impacts. Participation in the labor market can be a gateway to other social arenas. The workplace has often been the base for building social relations. It can be observed that this social aspect of employment has been of special importance for immigrants. The work place has been the arena for learning the language and for becoming familiar with the culture and traditions of their new country (Madanipour, Allen and Cars, 1998).

Fordism, Post-Fordism and the Quality of Social Life

The structural changes in the labor market have yielded substantial social consequences. Many countries, like Sweden, have seen rapid changes in social conditions. Thus structural changes in the labor market have accentuated both spatial segregation and social exclusion during the past few decades. As long as people moved into new dwellings in the areas surrounding the metropolitan areas as a response to the shortage of labor, social and spatial segregation was held to be a minor problem. In Sweden, for instance, 'the million homes program' – in which one million dwellings were built from the second half of the 1960s to the first half of the 1970s – was a production program following Fordist principles in housing and construction. The issue of segregation was addressed, but relative to the advantages of the concept of massive new suburban construction it was considered to be a minor problem. The large-scale housing schemes provided high-standard flats, with affordable rents. Parallel investments in public transportation and roads made workplaces relatively accessible. Segregation was also combated by schemes aimed at the improvement of everyday life for people living in these areas, e.g. substantial investments in education, health care, culture, and leisure activities.

The structural changes within the labor market have successively altered the conditions in these areas. Previously, residents were predominately poor working class with largely common values and interests. Informal networking to improve life conditions was a significant feature of many of these neighborhoods. Today the situation is different. The unemployment numbers are significant. Further, the homogeneity which previously characterized these neighborhoods is long gone. Rather than homogeneity the neighborhoods are characterized by diversity. These diversities can be based on age and conflicts between generations, between 'old' residents and 'newcomers' or on tensions between residents of different ethnic backgrounds. Issues of employment, gender and culture also contribute to the diversity of the neighborhoods. The fact that the economic base, in terms of employment, is lost for many households, combined with the fact that the composition of the neighborhood is becoming increasingly diversified, has resulted in weakened local solidarities. The 'working class identity' has eroded and diversification has made it more difficult to establish networks for collaborative efforts to improve the situation of individuals and the neighborhood (Madanipour, Allen and Cars, 1998).

This development has taken many of these neighborhoods into a vicious circle of decline, and today many of them are characterized by marginalization and stigmatization. Households with resources have moved out of the estates, replaced by households with fewer resources and opportunities in the housing market. Low-income housing areas are also unstable with respect to the level of mobility. The result is negative selection and accentuated segregation both between and within neighborhoods. The consequences of this urban planning program can be matched to 'social housing' in other parts of Europe in terms of segregation and social exclusion (SOU 1989:67; Lindén, 1989; Lindén and Lindberg, 1991; Johansson, 1993).

There is increasing policy concern about the processes of social exclusion within the European Union in general. An increasing social and economic gap is emerging between various population groups. While some groups are benefiting from the increasing economic and cultural integration within the European Union, others face increasing difficulties. For substantial groups of citizens the last few years can be described as a vicious circle that is gradually taking them into poverty. The consequences of poverty, marginalization and increased polarization are understood by EU member governments as a problem given top priority on the national agendas. On the European level there is recognition of the dangers of increasing social divisions and social polarization and the necessity for measures to increase social cohesion and to reintegrate excluded groups: 'The starting point for future urban development must be to recognize the role of the cities as motors for regional, national and European economic progress.

At the same time, it also has to be taken into account that urban areas, especially the depressed districts of medium-sized and larger cities, have borne many of the social costs of past changes in terms of industrial adjustment and dereliction, inadequate housing, long-term unemployment, crime, and social exclusion. The twin challenge facing European urban policy is therefore one of maintaining its cities at the forefront of an increasingly globalized and competitive economy while addressing the cumulative legacy of urban deprivation. These two aspects are complementary' (CEC, 1997).

Thus, there is a common understanding about the seriousness of the social problems we are facing and also about the need for urgent action.

Over the last few years social exclusion has become an issue given high priority on the political agendas in most member countries. In several countries special government committees have been set up and given the task of analyzing mechanisms of social exclusion and developing strategies to promote integration. As a result of this activity we can see newly adopted and emerging programs in member countries, including improved concepts for addressing issues of exclusion and integration.

From a mapping of current social policies and programs to regenerate and promote social cohesion in neighborhoods, it is evident that issues regarding deliverance of services and governance are issues that need to be addressed. A rather common assessment in the member countries studied is that issues regarding governance, including reformulation of roles and relations between agencies, professionals and residents, and the development of new modes for delivery of services are necessary to further improve strategies to promote social integration (Allen, Cars and Madanipour, 1999).

Social and Physical Distances and Social Integration/Exclusion

The concept of social exclusion was introduced in an institutional context by Jacques Delors in the 1980s and derives from the French Government's aim to develop French social policy in that period. Today the use of the concept is widely spread throughout Europe. We argue that the introduction and use of the concept is more than merely a rephrasing of traditional concepts such as segregation, poverty and underclass. Poverty and underclass have been used as concepts to characterize the situation of disadvantaged neighborhoods. They were often used to describe a situation that could be considered a transitory accidental situation, i.e. one may be poor today but better off tomorrow, since there are mobility processes that can improve the situation. The concept of social exclusion is different. Social exclusion implies that some social groups are cut off from this possibility (Padovani, 1999). Recent years of European social development show that the concept has substantive content. In contemporary Europe it comprises a new way of analyzing and combating social injustices (Cameron and Davoudi, 1998; Atkinson, 1998; CEC, 1992). Thus, social exclusion refers to processes of social deterioration and places a focus on vicious circles of decline. Social integration refers to processes that involve individuals, households and social groups in social arenas – e.g. the labor and housing markets and participation in political processes on various levels (Lindén, 1999).

Thus, during the course of the 1990s the significance of the concept of social exclusion has deepened. This development is discernible from two perspectives. First it seems generally recognized that social exclusion is not merely a specific single problem. Being poor, or unemployed, or belonging to an ethnic minority group living in a segregated neighborhood is not a condition that, in isolation, provides evidence of social exclusion. Individuals can, despite these hardships, very well be part of a mainstream society. Having rich networks of relationships and taking part in a wide variety of social activities, individuals can have rich social and cultural lives. The absence of these networks, however, increases their risk of being isolated and excluded.

The other feature which makes the concept social exclusion distinct in comparison to previously used concepts is the strong emphasis on process rather than condition. Thus, privations of specific social or economic conditions do not necessary mean that an individual or a group of individuals is excluded. However, it means that they become more vulnerable to social exclusion. Hardship in some dimension of life means a risk of entering a process that leads from integration to isolation and exclusion (Madanipour, Allen and Cars, 1998).

The European Commission sums up the difference between poverty and social exclusion as follows. 'The concept of social exclusion is a dynamic one, referring both to processes and consequent situations.... More clearly than the concept of poverty, understood far too often as referring exclusively to income, it also states the multidimensional nature of the mechanisms whereby individuals and groups are excluded from taking part in social exchanges.... It even goes beyond participation in working life: it is felt and shown in the fields of housing, education, health and access to services...' (CEC, 1992).

Social integration/exclusion between different groups of people is to a great deal a function of social distance. The less the social distance, the greater the probability is of physical proximity between people. The relation between social interaction and social and physical distance is closely interwoven. The physical distance seems, however, to be of lesser importance today than before, especially for people with post-industrial lifestyles. However for people socially disadvantaged and with low incomes, physical distance still often functions as a barrier for social interaction with the world beyond their neighborhood.

Social and physical distances act as mutually reinforcing factors of social integration and residential segregation. Residential segregation minimizes the conflicts between social groups with different values and attitudes. It also has impacts on the social control mechanism if the area is inhabited by relatively homogeneous groups. It will not, however, minimize the conflicts between social groups in different housing areas, or within areas, that are characterized by quite different social structures. Thus, it has impacts on social integration in the small housing areas or on the local level but results in social exclusion on the regional level. This can be illustrated – in a schematic way – as in Figure 8.1.[8]

Family relations have been explicitly introduced in the integration/-exclusion process. This is especially apparent in a North-South European dimension, but this is also valid with regard to the fact that different ethnic groups have quite different family traditions and relations even within the same cities or regions, despite taking into account the North-South division. In a North-South perspective it is a well-known fact that the families in Southern Europe on average are larger, and that different generations often share the same dwelling more and have a common economy than in the northern parts of Europe (Vogel, 1997).

This has implications for the social integration process – extended families in Southern Europe serve as a substitute for the formalized public welfare systems in the Nordic welfare states and vice versa; in the Nordic countries the institutional welfare states have replaced the traditional family ties and then eroded the family as a form of social protection. However, also within the Nordic countries, large families still exist frequently among many ethnic groups.

These groups are, however, usually not integrated in the surrounding community – instead they are often socially excluded and living in segregated housing areas. Within the countries there are also significant differences with regard to kinship ties. Here, we can find an urban-rural dimension, where the kin ties are more pronounced in the rural areas than in the urban ones. The trend is, however, that small and single parent families will continue to increase even in the Catholic and Southern European countries (George, 1996).

Thus, it can be concluded that a number of factors play a role with respect to 'social distance'. As argued above there are strong arguments underlining the crucial role of working life conditions. In addition family relations, ethnicity, age, class and lifestyle are of importance for 'social distance'.

Social distance in turn impacts individual opportunities in terms of 'physical distance', i.e. if social distance is short, physical distance becomes less of a problem, and options in the housing market increases. Taken together 'social distance' and its relation to 'physical distance' and the options in the housing market constitute a basis for the analysis of social exclusion and social integration as shown in Figure 8.1.

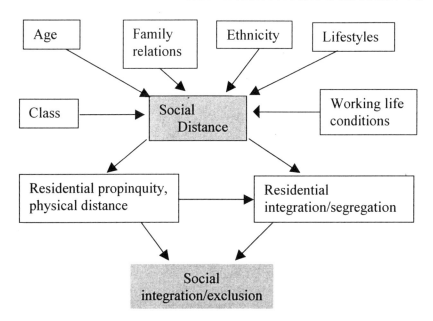

Figure 8.1   Social distance, residential integration/segregation and social interaction/exclusion – a schematic view

Source: Adapted and revised from Knox (1994).

How can Social Exclusion be Measured?

Obviously statistical indicators can provide valuable knowledge, increasing our understanding about the scope and consequences of social exclusion. However, lately there have been disagreement and discussion about the role of and function of indicators of deprivation. The British Index of Deprivation, developed for the Department of the Environment in the early 1990s, opted to avoid using indicators of the existence of vulnerable groups as a proxy for deprivation. That is, single parents or a minority population were no longer used as indicators since it was recognized that many people within such groups are not deprived, and because of the dangers of stereotyping and stigmatization. Emphasis was instead placed on the outcome of indicators of actual conditions (Stewart and Griffiths, 1998).

It is equally important to keep in mind that statistical indicators, regardless of their quality, have a limited value in understanding and explaining social developments. A qualitative component also has to be included. 'Social exclusion can never be understood by taking ... figures, however important, at face value alone. They have to be understood in their proper context and this requires, in the end, a number of case studies' (Kloosterman, 1999).

For the development of proper measures of social exclusion it is necessary to gather information about the form and structure of social integration and exclusion and then analyze the specific geographical level on which they are taking place. The indicators chosen must be represented on different levels (region-types). This is a first step in capturing the regional/spatial dimension of the problem. If it is accepted that sub-societies exist within cities and regions, the territorial scale turns out to be quite arbitrary, ranging from urban neighborhoods or small rural communities to larger regions and even nations.

In order to measure social exclusion or cohesion it might be useful to extend the differentiation of regions for certain objectives of analysis by developing a certain typology. For instance, at the EU level, there are differences according to the indicators to be taken into account in analyzing social cohesion or exclusion in, for example, the northern and the southern parts of Europe.

There are also differences within each country that ought to be analyzed in terms of social exclusion and cohesion. Here, it can be useful to work in urban/rural dimensions, with different kinds of regions in between. In this case, we have chosen the following typology – which of course can be extended or reduced – within the countries: metropolitan regions, university regions, regional service centers, old factory towns, small towns, and rural areas. This typology is based on the dominant features in the relevant regions.[9]

Dimensions (functional/geographical)	Northern Europe	Central Europe	Southern Europe
Metropolitan			
University			
Regional service centers			
Old factory towns			
Small towns			
Rural areas			

The empty spots represent different sets of indicators that differ according to the North–South divide as well as according to the urban-rural dimension. In this case, there will be 18 different combinations where the social indicators have different weights with respect to social exclusion or cohesion. Family relations, for example, seem to be much more important for social cohesion and thus for exclusion in Southern Europe than in Northern Europe.

There are also differences within these large regions. In the northern parts, family relations seem to be of much more importance in rural areas than in metropolitans ones. Even within metropolitan or rural areas, there are sub-societies where social exclusion or cohesion has different weights according to the indicators. The same is probably valid in the southern parts according to family relations in an urban-rural dimension and within these areas or regions. The same reasoning can be applied to other indicators like incomes, employment and unemployment, education, religion, political participation, social capital, or cultural heritage.

In conclusion, it could be argued that methods commonly used for measuring social exclusion are not the most relevant; furthermore the geographical units chosen are often defined in an insensitive way, not taking into account the vast differences within the unit. The 'average' figure that comes out becomes a statistical truth with little or no relevance in describing the social realities of the unit in focus. This becomes especially obvious when social issues are studied on a city level. The average picture that emerges when data are compiled can conceal the fact that there are, parallel to economic growth and prosperity, pockets or areas of decline, characterized by poverty, unemployment, dereliction and social exclusion. This physical concentration of disadvantage also often has an ethnic or cultural dimension, indicating that some groups are more vulnerable than others. It is hard to capture social diversification on the micro level (i.e. in sub-areas within cities or urban areas). An analysis of social welfare for cities or urban areas therefore requires more finely tuned statistics and analysis combined with studies of the everyday life of residents in these sub-areas.

Current Responses to Social Exclusion

As mentioned there is growing concern among European social policy makers about the social impacts of structural changes in the economy. At the same time it is realized that these changes call for new approaches to promote social cohesion. The working methods and priorities in social and economic welfare policies must be significantly revised in order to tackle the current problems in an effective manner. Two features of change are obvious in most European countries. First, government committees or similar initiatives have been set up to provide understanding and a diagnosis of the problems. Second, a radical reorganization of social and financial programs can be seen. This reformulation has been carried out with the realization that public resources are scarce and the assumption that the efficiency of measures could be improved if holistic approaches were adopted.

All member states in the Union have developed formal and informal systems for the provision and delivery of social welfare. Schematically these delivery systems can be grouped into four categories:

- The *labor market.* By participating in the labor market individuals obtain financial and other resources that can be utilized for 'purchasing' social services and other social welfare qualities, either by direct consumption or by savings and insurance to meet social needs that might occur in later stages of life.
- The *family* constitutes another system for delivering social welfare. The basic foundation of this system lies in the concepts of solidarity and redistribution. Family members help each other by satisfying social needs and in achieving other welfare ambitions. This family-based delivery system has different faces, e.g. it can involve grandparents taking care of children, members of the family with a work income financially supporting family members lacking an income, and middle-aged members taking care of older family members in need of care and support.
- *Civil society* constitutes a third system for the delivery of social welfare. Similar to the 'family system' key concepts are voluntariness and solidarity. By being part of various networks the individual, in case of hardship, can achieve social support from civil society and the voluntary sector. This system operates in different ways – sometimes it is highly informal and sometimes more formalized. Informal networks on an individual level can be constituted by friends or neighbors supporting one another in situations of hardship or to improve day-to-day life and social welfare on a more general level. Formalized networks can for example be illustrated by membership in organizations, clubs or churches, which in various ways have social obligations and tasks with respect to the social well-being of their members.

- The *welfare state* constitutes the fourth system for welfare delivery. The task here is basically is to redistribute common resources in such a way that basic social needs and levels are guaranteed to the population. The state welfare system can have a different orientation, either general or selective. The general approach includes measures applying the entire population. Selective approaches target at groups with 'special needs', normally individuals or households in a weak social position.

When the member countries are compared, two distinct patterns can be observed. First, the different systems for delivering social welfare are highly integrated. Thus, the welfare of an individual could be seen as the total outcome when delivery through the different systems is added up. This interdependence means that a change in one system impacts the welfare of the individual as well as the conditions for the other systems.

Second, when the members states are compared, it becomes obvious that the main emphasis varies. In some countries welfare delivery by the family plays a significant role; in others the welfare state has a predominant role. With respect to the focus of the welfare system, member states can be schematically organized in geographical clusters.

In this kind of approach, Esping-Anderson's typological work on national welfare regimes (1985) provides a key set of ideas informing current debates on changing national patterns of social provision. His main proposition is that there are three ideal typical models of welfare provision in Europe. The Nordic (or Social Democratic) model is based on relationships between social partners in circumstances of relative labor scarcity and seeks to ensure that the social conditions of employment support the well-being of society. The Anglo-Saxon (or liberal) model is based on a view of society as composed of atomized individuals and seeks to ensure that each person attains a minimum material standard of well-being. The Continental (corporatist or conservative) model is based on a conception of society as comprising groups with reciprocal rights and obligations.

A similar categorization has been made in a recent analysis of the market, welfare, the state and the family, commissioned by the European Union (Vogel, 1997). Vogel identifies three distinct geographical clusters with similar welfare delivery strategies:

- A Nordic cluster of advanced institutional welfare states (Sweden, Denmark, Finland).

- A Southern cluster of family and welfare states, relying on the traditional family as the prime welfare delivery strategy (Portugal, Spain, Italy and Greece).
- An intermediate Central European cluster with moderate institutional and family arrangements, in combination with corporate and social protection strategy (Vogel, 1997).

The weakness of an ideal type analysis, such as Esping-Anderson's, is that it always oversimplifies the phenomena that it is designed to reflect (Allen, 1998). However, this simplification allows the identification of issues of crucial importance when possible strategies for developing welfare regimes are analyzed.

As mentioned, it is obvious that the delivery systems are interdependent and that changes in one system impact others. Furthermore, it is clear that the main emphasis of welfare delivery changes over time. After World War II, there was a universal trend in the direction an expanding welfare state, which in turn meant a parallel decrease in responsibility for the family and civil society to deliver social welfare. The idea of welfare and freedom from poverty as a social right was established in most member states (Vogel, 1997).

In the 1990s, Europe has experienced significant structural changes and an economic recession. The globalization of the economy and financial constraints on public expenditure are two features of this change. They have in both direct and indirect ways affected the systems for welfare delivery. One direct change is the cuts in various public welfare programs, i.e. public agencies stepping back from welfare ambitions and programs developed during the post-war period. Another indirect effect is the discussion about a reconfiguration of the welfare system. This debate has emerged from various starting-points; for instance, from the claim that welfare state mechanisms for delivery are inefficient and poorly targeted, for reasons of public financial constraint, and from claims that services provided by the family and civil society contain qualities that cannot be replaced by public and professional welfare delivery systems (see e.g. Vogel 1997; Madanipour, Allen and Cars, 1998).

The outcome of the current debate and ongoing reconfiguration of the welfare system still remains to be seen. Esping-Anderson (1996) identifies threes possible routes. One is the *Scandinavian route* based for instance on the continuation of full employment and public jobs to support the infrastructure for equal opportunities and social investment. This model presupposes a high tax burden. The *neo-liberal route* stresses market distortion by welfare state intervention and advocates labor market and wage flexibility. This route is accompanied by cuts in the transfer systems. The third route is labeled the *labor reduction route* and is based on a jobless growth scenario and the growing surplus of unskilled de-industrialized labor. This route supports early retirement, and income maintenance and job security for a shrinking insider work force. The choice of route or combination of routes to large extent still remains to be made.

New Approaches to Combat Unemployment and Social Exclusion

All over Europe the realization that substantial change in social policy is inevitable has called for central government initiatives to reconsider current policies. This work has in many countries had the explicit aim of providing radically different policies and strategies. What is common for most countries is that this reformulation of policies is given a high priority.

Another feature of this work is the tendency to see these problems in a broader perspective than previously. Problems that traditionally have been handled by the social sector are now being dealt with in a more comprehensive manner. One significant feature of this change is that issues concerning work and employment have been given a central position in the new approaches currently being developed. Not infrequently, particular attention is directed towards measures to facilitate local economic development and the development of local enterprises. In many countries education and job-training programs are given a strong emphasis. This comprehensive focus is reflected in the way the formulation of new policies is organized.

The question of geographical consideration in targeting programs shows both concord and differences among European countries. What unites countries is obviously the spatial concentration of problems. Social exclusion has a geographical dimension. To a very large and increasing extent people facing social exclusion or involved in processes that might end up in exclusion, are spatially concentrated in neighborhoods with a poor reputation and relatively poor standards. Further, many of the countries witness a gradual reinforcement of the stigma of these exposed neighborhoods (Madanipour, Allen and Cars, 1998).

Common Elements in National Approaches

A comparison between countries in Europe shows great differences with respect to modes of integration. The differences lies both in the focus of the programs and in their degree of detail. What all countries seem to share is the realization that comprehensive and integrated strategies are a necessity in order to combat social exclusion efficiently. However, in some countries, this strategy has not yet been formulated. They are still stuck with a patchwork of uncoordinated measures. In other countries modes for integration have been defined, but there are not yet any clear guidelines or programs for implementation. In still other countries, great emphasis has been placed on developing and implementing new modes for integration.

In summing up, the following elements can be identified in European visions for social integration:

- *Employment* is commonly recognized as a key aspect of integration. However, the focus is split. While some countries, like Sweden and Denmark, put the emphasis on educational programs and training and local economic development, others, like the UK, also stress the need for a more flexible labor market.

- *The cash-benefit system* is an important, but politically sensitive, ingredient in integration programs in several countries. The 'unemployment trap' is a reality for many people with low incomes. This problem has a direct bearing on both tax and wage policies.

- *Physical upgrading and improvement of services* in distressed neighborhoods are commonly accepted as a cornerstone in integration policy. However, priorities are shifting between countries. While physical improvement still is seen as vital in many southern countries with substandard housing, it is considered to be relatively less important in other countries. Moreover, it is obvious that priorities have changed over time in many countries. Rather than stressing physical improvements and area based measures, emphasis today is placed on individual-based measures aimed at improving the residents' capacity and possibilities for improving the quality of everyday life.

- *Partnerships* for development are another concept, which is commonly recognized as an important ingredient in an integration strategy. There is a unanimous realization that public activities decided on different geographical levels and in various sectors of society must be co-ordinated in a better way. Further, the strategy in several countries is to actively involve private businesses, organizations and residents in promoting general welfare.

- *Democracy and decentralization* are catchwords in many of the national programs for integration. The problem of 'democratic deficit' is being addressed and new forms of decentralized neighborhood management are being put forward, i.e. capacity building, decentralization of decision-making powers and social entrepreneurship ana localized mechanisms of accountability based on resident involvement (Allen, Cars and Madanipour, 1999).

Swedish Fordist and Post-Fordist Strategies for Employment and Social Cohesion

In this final section, the Swedish way to 'full' employment and social cohesion is discussed. Since Prime Minister Per-Albin Hansson introduced the concept of 'The People's Home' (*Folkhemmet*) in the period between the wars and fostered its development during the 1950s, and then over to 'The Strong Society' during the 1960s and 1970s and finally cutbacks in the public sector during the first half of the 1990s, employment and unemployment have been central ingredients in the Swedish way to combat social exclusion and stimulate social cohesion. One of the central ingredients in 'The People's Home' was that social cohesion and 'homogenization' of the Swedish people should have the same priority as individual development (Larsson, 1994). High unemployment was a hampering factor in reaching social cohesion and consequently a hindrance to constructing 'The People's Home'. It was, however, first during the Second World War that unemployment fell drastically and 'full' employment was reached. One of the means to reach and maintain 'full' employment was the increased credence given to societal and economic planning – the 'art' of social engineering was at its zenith. This was also manifested in the establishment of 'The Strong Society' and the growth of the public sector.

Especially during the 1960s, the shortage of labor seems to have hampered industrial and economic development. One solution for eliminating this problem was increased labor force immigration and another was increased internal migration – migration from rural areas in the northern parts of Sweden to expanding industrial areas in general and to metropolitan areas in particular.

Rapid economic growth – as in the 1960s – has, as a rule, been associated with the movement of resources, which has also resulted in extensive geographical mobility. Resources had to be shifted from low-productivity to high-productivity enterprises in order not to inhibit growth. This also formed the foundation of the so-called Rehn/Meidner model, in which a 'wage-solidarity' (i.e. wage-equalization) policy was combined with an active labor market policy.[10] Upward pressure on wage levels in the least productive firms would cause them to go bankrupt while at the same time wage increases in productive firms would be restrained. For this policy to succeed it had to be possible for labor to be shifted swiftly and simply out of low-productivity and into high-productivity firms. As high production firms were not evenly distributed geographically, the consequence was great geographical mobility during the 1960s. That decade can also be said to be the last – in Sweden at any rate – to be marked by the migration patterns of the Fordist society (see e.g. Bengtsson and Johansson, 1994). If the construction of 'The People's Home' during the 1940s and 1950s had a hampering impact on social exclusion, the development during the 1960s had the opposite effect.

One of the consequences of this policy was the 'Million Program'. It was a response to the shortage of dwellings in Sweden and was reinforced by the large inflow of people to metropolitan areas. The homogenization of these housing areas was, however, not a socially cohesive factor – instead it resulted in estrangement and social exclusion. This was also a turbulent period when the Fordist society was transformed into a post-Fordist. The post-Fordist segregation problems, with social exclusion as one result, are thus, to stretch the metaphor, a child of the Fordist planning process (Johansson, 1993).

The Fordist principles for organizing the working process on the factory floor using Taylorism and assembly lines became obsolete during the end of the 1960s and beginning of the 1970s. A large number of 'wild strikes' and conflicts with respect to the labor market and working conditions showed the limits of the Fordist production processes during a time when the economy was undergoing a rapid transformation. The homogenization of the differing labor market segments has resulted in distress and misfortunes. Instead teamwork and lean production were introduced in many Swedish factories and rigid and hierarchical organizations were replaced by more flexible systems in a post-Fordist way. These 'new' organization forms resulted in the growth of productivity in many industrial plants. These neo-industrial organization forms were seen to be a mistake during the 1970s when oil shocks and structural crises dominated the economic agenda. Instead, it is first with the rise of the post-industrial society with its dependence on knowledge-based industries that these post-Fordist organization forms have yielded success, at least according to the integration of highly educated 'workers' in these firms (IVA, 1994).

There is, however, another side of the coin in the post-Fordist transformation process. The gap between different segments of the population with respect to education, competence and job opportunities has been widening. The accentuated segmentation of the labor market, where the workforce is more heterogeneous than before, has resulted in an increased mismatch in the labor market. Substantial segments of the population have lost a foothold in the labor market, and have been caught up in processes leading to social exclusion and spatial isolation. Spatial segregation has also been accentuated both between and within different local and regional areas. Long-term unemployment has come to stay and the 'full' employment of the 1950s and 1960s seems to be far away. The social pyramid has been replaced with a social hourglass, where some groups of the population are running the risk of being permanently shut off from mainstream society. During the first half of the 1990s cutbacks in the public sector accentuated this process. The constraints on public finances for social support and welfare programs have impacted traditional policies to combat social exclusion and promote integration in obvious ways; for instance, it is reported that substantial cuts have been made within housing regeneration schemes, educational programs and other public undertakings with relevance for social integration.

Reports from the European Union that indicate that people outside the labor market or with a casual role in the labor market tend to become physically segregated to a greater and greater extent (CEC, 1997) are worth taking seriously in Sweden. Being excluded from the labor market increases the risk of ending up in stigmatized neighborhoods and thereby being shut off from various activities as well as from routes for entering mainstream society. There are, unfortunately, indications that this phenomenon is on its way to becoming a reality even in Sweden unless a radical reformulation of employment policies and social polices is carried out.

It is obvious that globalization has led to subsequent changes in the Swedish economy. These changes have directly and indirectly impacted working life conditions as well as social conditions. In conclusion it should be stated that everyday life for many Swedes is very different in terms of employment and social conditions, compared to only ten years ago. The social problems we are facing today show both similarities and differences when compared to those of past generations. Poverty, deficiencies in living environments, substandard housing and deficiencies in public health and care still exist. But these 'traditional' social problems are to a large extent part of history. However, at the same time 'new' problems and inter-relationships have emerged. Perhaps the most significant change concerns employment and the social impacts of unemployment. In addition to economic hardship, unemployment is often related to other social problems. The lack of employment is an anchor dragging people into the processes leading to social exclusion. Another 'new' feature of social problems concerns race and ethnicity. It is obvious that some ethnic and migrant groups are especially vulnerable to social exclusion. A third 'new' problem is the desperation and frustration expressed by many people living in excluded neighborhoods. They see themselves as predestined for a life excluded from mainstream society, with all its attractions and arenas, such as employment, culture, education and services. In this situation both the individual and society become vulnerable to misunderstandings. The signals must be taken seriously and effective measures promptly implemented.

These changes in social welfare and living conditions have not yet been accompanied by a parallel development in policies for the economy and employment, and social welfare. The policies still in place were developed to handle a social reality that not longer exists. However, a realization of the relation between, on the one hand, structural changes and, on the other, social processes is emerging. It is understood that structural changes in the economy have fundamentally changed the social situation for substantial segments of the population, expressed in terms of increased vulnerability for some groups, and a physical concentration of disadvantage followed by exclusion from mainstream society. There is thus the realization that changes in societal conditions make it necessary to reformulate strategies to combat exclusion and to promote employment and social cohesion. Two perspectives are crucial in this work.

First, it is obvious that social exclusion is not a phenomenon caused by a single specific condition or problem. Rather it is the consequence of a number of problems and unsatisfactory conditions in an individual's daily life. However, without contradicting this statement it is obvious that *employment* plays a major role in this context. A job guarantees an income. A job also provides a social context and a social network, which we know has significant importance. It is a road to wider social activities and networks. On the other hand, the lack of employment is often a direct or indirect barrier to participation in other social arenas and activities (Madanipour, Allen and Cars, 1998). This focus on employment as being vital for neighborhood development underlines the great importance of co-ordinated action. Improvement in the employment situation can not be achieved by action solely on the local level. True success presupposes action on the national as well as the supra-national levels, parallel to local initiatives. On the national and supra-national levels the framework is established by decisions on taxes, working hours, trade and legislation. Swedish rigidity and strict adherence to the welfare model, whose labor regulations date back to after the Second World War, hampers many people's chances of obtaining gainful employment. There are reasons to suspect that the rules of the game regarding the labor market have changed in Sweden, just as in the rest of Europe. This means that the concept of 'permanent full-time jobs' just does not exist the way it used to. It also means that a company's fixed assets have decreased in importance as compared to human assets, which have become more important. Lastly, the transformation into a service and information society offers potential for new, small-scale, often locally based companies in the service, culture and information sectors (Cars and Hagetoft, 1998). Thus there is reason to review our rules and restrictions to remove obstacles to the establishment of local business and employment. This only partly applies to national laws and regulations. On the local level, education, location decisions and programs for facilitating residents' opportunities for work are of significant importance.

The second concern relates to roles and the division of responsibilities between different stakeholders. In Sweden there has been a tendency to adopt a top-down perspective on exposed neighborhoods. Experts have formed the picture of the problem and designed models, strategies and measures based on this picture. Problems have been framed in relation to ideas of 'normality' and norms have been set by outsiders. Measures have been implemented to solve these problems and return conditions in the neighborhood back to a pre-existing idea of 'order'. In combating social exclusion, a number of actors on different levels and in various sectors of society play key roles. A successful strategy to achieve integration presupposes action based on knowledge about the residents' assessments of everyday life. Furthermore, local authorities, organizations and other parties must act in a co-ordinated manner. Goals and strategies for improvement must be accepted by residents as well as other stakeholders involved (Cars and Edgren-Schori, 1998). In this perspective an argument could be raised for rethinking the relation between 'people-based' versus 'place-based' strategies.

The argument could be raised that neither of the isolated concepts has proved to be successful responses to social exclusion. People-based strategies have often been found to be inadequate. If neighborhoods have deficiencies that make them unsafe, or in other ways unattractive, improvements of an individual's situation will be hampered by the state of the surrounding environment. On the other hand, place-based strategies have also often proved to be ineffective. Improvements in housing and living environments have not had the positive effects anticipated, given that social problems among residents have counterbalanced these improvements. Thus the conclusion is that no 'place-based' nor 'people-based' strategies are sufficient to achieve effective and substantial improvements within socially excluded neighborhoods. The challenge lies in developing strategies that combine these two approaches.

Effective regeneration presupposes a carefully chosen mix of measures directed to meet the needs of individuals, as well as the needs of the neighborhood (Madanipour, Allen and Cars, 1998). Thus individual-oriented measures must be co-ordinated with neighborhood improvement measures. The need for holistic approaches is of decisive importance. The poorly blended stew of actors and policies that are directed to upgrade the daily life of inhabitants in socially excluded neighborhoods must be replaced. A formulation of holistic and co-ordinated approaches must have a starting point in recognizing the complexity of and interrelationships between the various elements that, when combined, contribute to a certain quality of life.

A starting point for such an analysis can be found in the household living space and the daily living environment. Substantial improvements in living conditions presuppose that various individual and neighborhood-related activities are taken into consideration. These considerations include an analysis of public and private service provision, education, employment, health services, and culture and leisure activities. Based on the comprehensive picture that emerges from such an analysis, specific measures for improvement can be launched.

Notes

1 The concept of 'The People's Home' (*Folkhemmet*) was introduced by the Social-Democratic leader Per-Albin Hansson in the Swedish Parliament in 1928 during the full-session debate on the Government's policy and was thereafter a very central ingredient in Social-Democratic policy and ideology up to the establishment of 'The Strong Society' in the 1960s and 1970s (see e.g. Larsson, 1994).

2 The concept of Fordism emanates from the introduction of assembly lines in Henry Ford's factories in Detroit used in the production of the Model T. Ford was inspired by the organization of the work in Chicago's slaughterhouses.

3 This description is very much in line with Tönnies', Durkeim's, Simmel's and Wirth's reasoning about 'urbanism as a way of life', where anonymous social relations and deviant aspects of daily life are pronounced (Tönnies, 1887; Durkeim, 1893, 1897; Simmel, 1905; Wirth, 1938). Their writings have to a large degree created the image of metropolitan areas as a more social deviant and unnatural society than rural ones. This reasoning has, however, been called in question in other studies, where social cohesion in rural areas and small towns has been investigated (Knox, 1994).

4 The division of the labor market into primary and secondary segments has been a central ingredient in the segmented labor market theory since this theory was introduced in labor market analysis in the beginning of the early 1970s (see e.g. Reich, Edwards and Gordon, 1973; Piore, 1975).

5 Within this framework, it can be shown that the competence of labor on the one hand and the quality of technology on the other are two processes that reinforce each other. Instead of the negative feedback processes, entailing that original inequality will result

in a process towards equality and convergence – 'spread effects' – which is a fundamental part in the neo-classical theory, the positive feedback processes will dominate, resulting in divergent development and regional polarization and consequently social exclusion – 'backwash effects'. The concepts of 'spread effects' and 'backwash effects' are taken from Myrdal (1954), and the concepts of positive and negative feedback processes are from Vietorisz and Harrison (1973).

6 For an overview with respect to mismatches in the labor markets in differing European countries during the 1970s and 1980s, see Padoa Schioppa, 1990.

7 The rise in the age-specific migration intensities is, however, partly a statistical fluke – during the 1990s it has been much more common that students are registered as inhabitants in university towns than before. This has resulted in higher migration intensities in the relevant ages but it can only 'explain' a small part of the increase.

8 For a more exhaustive discussion of these processes, see e.g. Knox, 1994.

9 For a further discussion of the measurement problems of social exclusion and cohesion, see e.g. Madanipour et al., 1998 and Cars et al., 1999).

10 The model took its name from two trade union economists, Gösta Rehn and Rudolf Meidner, who launched these ideas in the 1950s. However, it was not until the 1960s that they were translated into practice to form guidelines for labor-market policy.

References

Allen, J. (1998), 'Europe of the Neighbourhoods' in A. Madanipour, J. Allen and G. Cars (eds), *Social Exclusion in European Cities*, Jessica Kingsley, London.

Allen, J., Cars, G. and Madanipour, A. (1999), *Social Exclusion in European Neighbourhoods: Processes, Experiences and Responses*, EU, DG XII. TSER, Final Report, Brussels, forthcoming.

Andersson, Å.E. (1985), *Kreativitet. StorStadens Framtid*, Prisma, Stockholm.

Anderstig, C. and Hårsman, B. (1986), 'On occupation structure and location pattern in the Stockholm region'. *Regional Science and Urban Economics*, vol. 49.

Atkinson, R. (1998), 'Countering Urban Social Exclusion: The Role of Community Participation and Partnership', in R. Griffiths, (ed.), *Social Exclusion in Cities: the Urban Policy Challenge*, Faculty of the Built Environment, University of the West of England, Bristol.

Bengtsson, T. and Johansson, M. (1994), 'Internal Migration', in T. Bengtsson (ed.), *Population, Economy and Welfare in Sweden*, Springer-Verlag, Heidelberg.

Cameron, S. and Davoudi, S. (1998), 'Social Exclusion and the Neighbourhoods: Looking in or Looking out?' in R. Griffiths (ed.), *Social Exclusion in Cities: the Urban Policy Challenge*, Faculty of the Built Environment, University of the West of England, Bristol.

Cars, G. and Edgren-Schori, M. (1998), 'Social Integration and Exclusion: The Response of Swedish Society', in A. Madanipour, J. Allen and G. Cars (eds), *Social Exclusion in European Cities*, Jessica Kingsley, London.

Cars, G. and Hagetoft, J. (1998), *Tensta from a European Perspective - Report from an Expert Seminar and Conference,* Svenska Bostäder, Stockholm.

Cars, G., Johansson, M., Nygren, O. and Schindegger, F. (1999), *Study Programme in European, Spatial Planning: Theme 1.3: Indicators for social integration & exclusion – Final report*, Royal Institute of Technology, Stockholm, Austrian Institute of Regional Studies and Spatial Planning, Vienna.

CEC, Commission of European Communities (1992), *The Community's Battle against Poverty.*

CEC, Commission of the European Communities (1993), *Social Exclusion – Poverty and Other Social Problems in the EC*, Background Report, ISEC/B11/93 6/4/93.

CEC, Commission of European Communities (1997), *Towards an urban agenda in the European Union*, Communication from the Commission, COM(97)197 final.

Cheshire, P.C. and Hay, D.G. (1989), *Urban Problems in Western Europe*, Unwin Hyman, London.

Claval, P. (1990), 'The Spatial Evolution of France', in SOU 1990:33. *Urban Challenges. Report to the Commission on Metropolitan Problems*, Allmänna Förlaget, Stockholm.

Dunford, M. (1996), 'Disparities in employment, productivity and output in the EU: the role of governance and welfare regimes', *Regional Studies*, No. 30.

Durkeim, E. (1893), *The Social Division of Labor in Society* (1964 edition),The Free Press, New York.

Durkeim, E. (1897), *Suicide* (1951 edition), The Free Press, Glencoe, Illinois.

Ekberg, J. (1993), *Geografisk och socioekonomisk rörlighet bland invandrare*, ERU Rapport 78, Fritzes.

Esping-Anderson, G. (1985), *Politics against Market*, Princeton University Press, Princeton, New Jersey.

Esping-Anderson, G. (1996), *Welfare States in Transition: National Adaptations in Global Economies*, SAGE, London.

George, V. (1996), 'The Demand for Welfare', in V. George and P. Taylor-Gooby (eds), *European Welfare Policy. Squaring the Welfare Circle*, Macmillan Press Ltd, London.

Hall, P. (1990), 'Urban Europe after 1992', in SOU 1990:33, *Urban Challenges. Report to the Commission on Metropolitan Problems*, Allmänna Förlaget, Stockholm.

Hall, P. (1991), 'Structural Transformation in the Regions of the United Kingdom', in L. Rodwin and H. Sazanami (eds), *Industrial and Regional Transformation: The Experience of Western Europe*, United Nations, New York.

IVA (1994), *Förändringen! Utveckling av verksamhet, ledarskap och medarbetare*, Ingenjörsvetenskapsakademien, Stockholm.

Johansson, M. (1993), 'The polarization of a metropolis in a welfare state – the example of Stockholm', *Scandinavian Housing & Planning Research* 10, 1993.

Johansson, M. (1996), 'Flexibility, Rigidity and Innovation Diffusion – the Case of Northern Sweden', in M. Johansson and L. O. Persson (eds), *Extending the Reach. Essays on Differing Mobility Patterns in Sweden*, Fritzes, Stockholm.

Johansson, M. and Persson, L.O. (1999), 'Mobile Unemployment in a Postindustrial Society: The Case of Sweden', in G. Crampton (ed.), *Regional Unemployment, Job Matching and Migration*, European Research in Regional Science 9, Pion Limited, London.

Kloosterman, R. (1999), *Comments on Theme 1.3: Indicators for Social Integration & Integration*, Comment on the European Commissions Study Programme in European Spatial Planning, Theme 1.3: Indicators for Social Integration & Exclusion, OBT, University of Technology, Delft.

Knox, P. (1994), *Urbanization. An Introduction to Urban Geography*, Prentice Hall, Englewood Cliffs, New Jersey.

Larsson, J. (1994), *Hemmet vi ärvde. Om folkhemmet, identiteten och den gemensamma framtiden*, Arena, Stockholm.

Lindén, A.-L. (1989), *Vem bor i bostadsområdet? Bostadsstruktur – befolkningsstruktur – förändringsmönster*, Department of Sociology, University of Lund, Lund.

Lindén, A.-L. (1999), *Comments on Theme 1.3: Indicators for Social Integration & Integration*, Comment on the European Commissions Study Programme in European Spatial Planning, Theme 1.3: Indicators for Social Integration & Exclusion, Department of Sociology, University of Lund.

Lindén, A.-L. and Lindberg, G. (1991), 'Immigrant Housing Patterns in Sweden', in E. D. Huttman (ed.), *Urban Housing Segregation of Minorities in Western Europe and the United States*, Duke University Press, Durham, North Carolina.

Lipietz, A. (1998), 'Rethinking social housing in the hour-glass society', in A. Madanipour, J. Allen and G. Cars (eds), *Social Exclusion in European Cities*, Jessica Kingsley, London.

Madanipour, A., Allen, J. and Cars, G. (eds), (1998), *Social Exclusion in European Cities*, Jessica Kingsley, London.

Massey, D. (1995), *Spatial Division of Labour. Social Structures and the Geography of Production*, MacMillan Press Ltd, London.

Padovani, L. (1999), 'Social Exclusion in Italy', in J.Allen, G. Cars and A. Madanipour (eds), *Social Exclusion in European Neighbourhoods: Processes, Experiences and Responses*, Brussels: EU, DG XII. TSER, Final Report, forthcoming.

Piore, M. (1975), 'Notes for a Theory of Labor Market Stratification', in R. C. Edwards, M. Reich and D. M. Gordon. (eds) *Labor Market Segmentation*, Lexington, Massachusetts.

Reich, M., Edwards, R. C. and Gordon D. M. (1973), 'A theory of labor market segmentation', *American Economic Review*, May.

Rifkin, J. (1996), *The End of Work. The Decline of the Global Labor Force and the Dawn of the Post-Market Era*, G. P. Putnam & Sons, New York.

Samers, M. and Woods, R. (1998), 'Socio-Economic Change, EU Policy and Social Disadvantage', in D. Pinder (ed.), *The New Europe. Economy, Society and Environment*, John Wiley & Sons, Somerset, New Jersey.

Scott, K. (1999), *The Immigrant Experience: Changing Employment and Income Patterns in Sweden, 1970–1990*, Lund Studies in Economic History 9, Lund University Press, Lund.

Simmel, G. (1905), 'The Metropolis and Mental Life', in P. Sennet (ed.), *Classic Essays on the Culture of Cities* (1961 edition), Appelton-Century-Crofts, New York.

SOU 1989:67, *Levnadsvillkor i storstadsregioner*, Underlagsrapport från Storstads-utredningen, Stockholm.

Stewart, M. and Griffiths, R. (1998), 'Social Exclusion and Urban Policy: A Framework for Discussion', in Griffiths (ed.), *Social Exclusion in Cities: The Urban Policy Challenge*, University of the West of England, Bristol.

Tönnies, F. (1887), *Community and Society* (1957 edition), Michigan State University Press, East Lansing, Minnesota.

Vogel, J. (1997), Living conditions and inequality in the European Union 1997, Eurostat Working Papers E/1997–3.

Walker, A., Alber, J. and Guillemard, A.M. (1993), *Older People: Social and Economic Policies*, Commission of European Communities, Brussels.

Wirth, L. (1938), 'Urbanism as a Way of Life', *American Journal of Sociology*, vol. 44.

Womack, J., Jones, D. and Roos D. (1990), *The Machine that Changed the World*, Macmillan Publishing, London.

9 Quality of Life and Social Cohesion: A Methodological Discussion and their Implications in Planning

VANIA A. CECCATO

Introduction

Nowadays the term quality of life has been used in a variety of ways to characterize our daily life. In the mass media, mainly in marketing, it can be associated with the quality of a product or used as a keyword in a political platform. When considered academically, it has been given a large number of definitions based on different approaches. Evidently, the attempt to give a precise formulation to the term quality of life must capture its ambiguity and complexity rather than hide or eliminate them.

'There are as many quality of life definitions as there are people' (Liu, 1976). Regardless of what community it refers to, the quality of life question is a complex and multifaceted one. In general, the concept includes the distribution of benefits and human rights that a society, in a certain period of time, judges to be essential. It also includes a series of collective benefits of a less tangible nature but which are also very important to social welfare (Guimarães, 1984).

Because of the complexity of the term quality of life, it has often been associated with numerous other concepts, among them, *welfare, living conditions, level of living, well-being, life style, environmental amenities* (Díaz, 1985). The word *welfare,* in Swedish *välfärd*, in Danish *velfaerd*, in Norwegian *velferd*, and Finnish *hyvinvointi,* thus in all Scandinavian languages, covers basic elements of human *well being* and *level of living*, working as a general synonym for quality of life but with different connotations. Often, quality of life has been used as *level of living* (in the Swedish traditional approach) in relation to the analysis of an individual's resources, and *well being* (in the Finnish approach) has been associated with people's needs and aspirations, both called welfare studies. Quality of life studies also vary in the scale of application, sometimes being applied to a whole country (Bernow, 1982, Levnadsförhållanden, Levekårsundersögelsen, Levevilkår in the Nordic countries) or to regions (Siirilä, 1984), cities (Knox, 1982; Rogerson et al., 1989) or even residential areas (Abaleron, 1987, 1995).

The increasingly rapid changes of society have also brought about quite a radical change in the definition of quality of life. On the one hand, quality of life today does not mean simply availability of resources but also easy accessibility to and use of them. Time issues, information elements, the level of competence in using technological everyday devices, and the level of freedom in making choices between different solutions all constitute important elements to be considered in order to measure people's well being. In Sweden, real income first increased for a long period and then decreased. The country is suffering from a relatively high rate of unemployment. Those who have a job tend to travel longer distances than before to get to their place of work. People have become more mobile than in previous decades. They seem to spend time in a variety of environments. These changes have not only brought about a problem for the established service provision paradigm but also difficulties concerning the validity of methods for analyzing changes in life quality. People live in one place, work in another and may spend their leisure time in yet another part of the city.

On the other hand, large inequalities between groups of populations create places in many European cities where the effects of social *in*-cohesion are evident. These disparities are more evident between different social economic groups but are not less important than those between men and women. Gender issues associated with equal opportunities, especially in the labor market, have also become more and more important for analyzing quality of life. Even though reality nowadays requires new ways to approach social cohesion, methods applied to quality of life analysis which were developed during the last three decades seem to have potential in helping researchers face the challenge of analyzing its effects.

The purpose of this article is to argue for the inclusion of an analysis of quality of life in regional planning. The paper is divided in three parts. The first one gives a description of how the concept of *quality of life* has historically been approached in Swedish urban planning. In terms of European Community policy, social cohesion appears to be a new way to deal with quality of life issues. A discussion of regional and local policies focusing on the effects of social *in*-cohesion constitutes the second part of this paper. Finally, the third part discusses the use of quality of life methods for analyzing social cohesion issues in urban areas. Special attention is paid to case studies in Nordic countries where quality of life studies have often been an instrument for evaluating the efficiency of welfare state investments. There has also been a growing awareness of territorial bases of inequality in society, and policies designed to ameliorate these inequalities have assumed explicit spatial dimensions. Geographical Information Systems have been considered to be a useful tool for spatial assessments, with social analysis promising to be a potential research field.

For the purposes of this article, the concept of region as the unit of focus for policy will shift in size from small geographical areas to larger ones. A region will be considered to be, for instance, a *neighborhood* in a city in or a metropolitan area context and in other cases, a region will be considered as *counties* or other geographical unit which is the object of policies for regional development. At the European level, region means *NUTs* or eventually, a set of counties or a whole *country*. However, since the focus is on Swedish urban planning, region is mostly synonymous with urban spaces in this paper.

Positioning Quality of Life in Swedish Urban Planning

Studies of quality of life have a central role in the Swedish model of spatial planning. When new residential areas have been planned one of the criteria has been to provide the areas with appropriate levels of public services. The idea of this policy has been to give every district a decent starting point in the life of its residential areas. The policy has been applied throughout the country, both in the suburbs of metropolitan regions and in smaller cities and towns where the whole supply of services in the populated area is within reach. The provision of medical care, day-care centers, schools and other public services have been prominent examples of this widely practiced policy. A major concrete example of this planning philosophy was part of the so-called *million homes program* during the 1960–1970s. However, the quality of a place assessed today is not only a pure reflection of the planning philosophy behind its construction, something that is finished, completed in the past. This quality has also been part of an open process, one of continuous development and change. Locally, it is a product of the interplay between space and those who live there over time.

The living place is not an isolated entity. Its quality depends on a broader context in which the city, the region, is embedded and that also changes over time. There have been significant changes in Sweden as a whole during the last few decades that have impacted the quality of the living place. Building activity has been substantially reduced, especially regarding residential areas. The Swedish planning paradigm of equal service provision to everyone everywhere has not been generally extended to the existing building stock. Maintenance of the quality of these areas has varied from place to place, and, in some cases they have deteriorated for lack of economic resources.

As in other European countries, geographical segregation patterns[1] have become more evident during the last few years, especially in the largest Swedish urban areas. Suburban rental housing areas that have high unemployment, mainly with a less educated labor force and immigrants, are geographically separated from areas of highly educated people, mostly composed of Swedes, living in valorized areas. This socio-economic and ethnic segregation has for different groups resulted in unbalanced access to economic resources, which in the near future may produce differences in opportunities in life as a whole. Many anticipate an irreversible pattern of social exclusion.

Shifting Paradigms: Historical Overview of Quality of Life in Swedish Cities

Contemporary Stockholm County is a concrete example of how urban planning has been carried out over the decades in order to promote good quality of life for its inhabitants; see Table 9.1. The urban structure has not only been a product of economic conditions, land availability or technological developments at different periods of time. This quality has of course been part of an open process that goes beyond the initial planning. It has been a product of the interplay over time between space and those who live there, the inhabitants, which are in continuous development and change. The focus here is primarily on those responsible for urban construction. Planners, architects, builders and/or politicians have been influenced by different urban theories and models. Based on some pragmatic utopia, they decided what the city structure should be like in order to have good quality. They not only defined how many buildings the city should have but also the size of apartments, street widths, the heights and types of housing, the distances to underground stations or to main services and the configuration of open spaces.

Initially urban planning was an attempt to overcome the most urgent problems, which arose with the growth of industrialized society at the end of 19th century. Land use regulations, high density areas, increasing numbers of squatters and slums, a lack of basic infrastructure, and the risks of fire were some of the problems which needed to be solved by urban planning. The quality of life concept was a class-related concept. Quality of life was related to the difficult task of working and surviving in the city.

The housing shortage was still a problem in Stockholm during World War I. Overcrowding was often associated with high mortality rates in those places. During World War I, housing construction almost came to a complete halt. In this critical situation the State and local authorities were forced to intervene. For the first time Sweden developed a national housing policy and housing became regulated by local authorities. When government loans stopped, the National Federation of Tenants' Savings and Building Society (HSB), and the Swedish Union of Tenants were formed (Thiberg, 1990). After 1919, the Health Care Statute was adopted, which defined minimum requirements concerning indoor air standards, heating and protection against humidity. As far as overcrowded places were concerned, the committee would only intervene if there was a risk to general public health. According to Alfredsson and Viklund (1981), these ordinances had no practical effect because there were seldom replacement houses for the families who lived in this deficient housing stock.

In the economic depression of the 1930s, theories were developed about state control and regulation of the free-market economy. In this environment in Sweden, the public planning system was launched. Economic and physical planning gradually developed into a tool that would regulate larger and larger sectors related to human conditions, such as housing, living environment, services and transportation. After the World War II, considerable progress was made with the provision of housing, construction of schools and location of industries constituting important driving forces in the municipalities. The Building Ordinance aimed to increase standardization in dwellings through requirements for the housing construction industries. There was a general requirement that all dwellings should have an entrance-hall, wardrobes and suitable connections between rooms. Dark or badly lit areas should be avoided if possible and all rooms should have as much sun as possible. The ventilation of flats was required, together with a minimum room floor surface area of 10 m^2 with a minimum height of 2.5 m. Later, requirements regarding rooms, room sizes, dimensions and the furnishing of kitchens, toilets and bathrooms were also included. Overcrowding was defined as more than 2 persons per room, excluding kitchen. Housing rent for a two-room apartment was to decline so that it constituted no more than 20 percent of an industrial worker's average salary. Overcrowding would be abolished via state financing and housing allowances for families with children and retired persons.

Table 9.1   Residential quality of life conceptions and the Swedish planning

Time	Background facts	Paradigms in planning	Quality of life – QOL conception
Second half of the 19th century	Overpopulation, congestion, traffic jams, unhealthy dwellings and the return of widespread epidemics.	*Regularism*	Surviving in the city – QOL was a class-related concept.
1890 – 30	Housing shortage, overcrowded places often associated with high mortality rates. City expansion and transportation development. In the economic depression of the 1930s, theories were developed about state control and regulation of the free-market economy. First national housing policy was created.	*Garden cities*	The rural ideal, close to the city, even to workers – the 'garden suburbs'.
1930 – 50?	Building Ordinances based on functionalist ideas. Use of new technologies in housing. After the Second World War, standardization of dwellings. Non-profit housing companies were introduced in 1945. All resources were spent on new housing production.	*Functionalism-rationalism*	Everything had to be linked to the planning system, the number of houses, schools and service areas.
1940 – 60	After the 1950s, Swedish society was transformed radically from an agrarian into a highly industrial one. By the 1960s, overcrowded living conditions had been relieved and housing standards radically improved for large groups of households. Despite the improvement, problems of housing shortages in most cities persisted – the demand for housing had become considerably larger than expected.	*Functionalism-neighborhood and ABC models*	The QOL concept was subordinated to this quantitative approach to welfare, in an equality perspective, in which everybody should have a house to live in, access to the basic services in the neighborhood, access to school, transport and other services.

1965 – 75	Building companies were encouraged, in various ways, to introduce industrial methods in building, making use of prefabricated parts. Large projects were favored in the provision of state loans. Because the ideology of functionalism reflected and was part of the Social Democratic reforms of the 1930s and 1940s, it had a large influence on urban Swedish planning as a whole.	*Functionalism - one million dwellings program*	The QOL concept was subordinated to this quantitative approach of welfare. No residential area should be built without there being enough commercial and public services within reach both for the average citizen and for weaker socio-economic groups.
1970 – 80s	Construction of buildings was substantially reduced. Planning and architecture were criticized for being more focused on cost efficiency than quality of life. The maintenance of the quality of these areas has varied from place to place, and, in some cases, because of the lack of economic resources, they have deteriorated. The first renewal programs were implemented.	*Functionalism - maintenance and participatory planning*	The surplus of housing changed the market perspective, from quantity to quality.
1980 – 90s	A tendency towards economic, social and cultural segregation developed, as a serious problem in several cities. Increasing imbalance between socio-economic groups. The Swedish planning paradigm of local services provision did not seem to fit anymore; people became more mobile than ever before. Increase in environmental aware-ness. IT commuting still reaches only a marginal share of labor force.	*Ecovillages and partici-patory planning measures against segregation. Impact of IT*	QOL seems to become a function of economic resources. Local and innovative solutions contribute to maintaining/-increasing the residential QOL. Information technology defines new patterns of accessibility to information and resources.

During the 1950s, neighborhood planning, with service centers surrounded by residential districts, focused on the need for creating common interests in living places. The term *neighborhood* was often used to represent the combination of housing and other components, such as schools, day nurseries, parish halls and commercial areas as well as recreation and open spaces which were located together in a center. All these activities were given dimensions in accordance with specified standards. The neighborhood unit was to be well separated by outer boundaries in the form of, for example, main roads, railways and green belts. Traffic should be arranged so that the area contains only that traffic which directly influences the area. All transit traffic would be excluded. The number of connections between the neighborhood unit and other areas would vary based on its degree of spatial dependence (Lanesjö, 1987). This type of structure would adapt very well to the increase in cars with the help of public transportation, making it possible to overcome the distance between living and working places. For regional services, each sector of the outer-town had a main center containing department stores as well as specialized shops and social service and recreational facilities, all of which were to serve large areas, mostly representing several hundred thousand inhabitants. People were to walk to their local center but ride to the regional ones. The centers were situated at junctions of the traffic system and where the population was concentrated.

After the 1950s, Swedish society was transformed radically from an agrarian into a highly industrial one. This created a demand for housing, schools, work places, day care and medical care centers, roads, etc, which would only be satisfied in the 1970s. The policy was applied throughout the country, from the suburbs of metropolitan areas to the smallest towns. The planning perspective was quantitative, based on the number of houses, schools and town center areas. The quality of life concept was in turn also subordinated to this quantitative approach to welfare, in an equality perspective, in which everybody would have a house to live in, access to the basic services in the neighborhood and access to school, transportation and other services. The measurable data was the basis for evaluating how well off people were in their life quality dimensions.

By the 1960s, overcrowded living conditions had been relieved and housing standards radically improved for large groups of households. Despite the improvement, problems of housing shortages in most cities persisted – the demand for housing had become considerably larger than expected. Functionalist ideas were ready to be put into practice in the *one million dwellings program*, that is, the Government's 1967 program to build a million new dwelling units in ten years. Building companies were encouraged, in various ways, to introduce industrial methods in building, making use of prefabricated parts. Large projects were favored in the provision of state loans. Because the ideology of functionalism reflected and was part of the Social Democratic reforms of the 1930s and 1940s, it had a large influence on urban Swedish planning as a whole.

One important aspect in this development in Stockholm is the effect of *Lex Bollmora,* which reinforced segregation in the region. *Lex Bollmora* permitted the City of Stockholm to build outside its own borders if the neighboring municipalities invited it. Both the City of Stockholm and the neighboring municipalities were ruled by Social Democrats and most of these municipalities were located in the southern part of the region. In these areas we find many of the roots of spatial segregation problems in Stockholm region nowadays – at least regarding the effects of the planning system.

Sweden has been exposed more and more to external economic influences during the last decade. This has resulted in changes in how people behave and evaluate their conditions. Today, construction of buildings has been substantially reduced, mainly with regard to housing districts, after building production reached record levels during the 1970s. The surplus of housing changed the market perspective from quantity to quality. In the 1970s, a housing surplus developed in many cities, and the market was inundated with flats in multi-family houses. People in planning and architecture were criticized for being more focused on cost efficiency than quality of life. A tendency towards economic, social and cultural segregation arose as a serious problem in several cities in Sweden. In Stockholm, various radical movements against the city's environment were formed which tried to show the cultural value of the old buildings which were to be demolished. In the suburbs, neighborhoods with eight-story buildings or higher were not appreciated by a large part of the population. In a survey carried out in 1972 it was shown that even if the population valued the low cost and the high standard of services, it did not compensate for the poorly built environment and the long distances to workplaces from these newly built areas.

Nowadays if someone prefers to choose the service outlet which is most convenient, this person will choose this irrespective of whether it lies in the vicinity of his or her domicile. People have become more mobile. For many, the surroundings of the workplace are more convenient than the local service center in their neighborhood. For those who are not comparatively mobile, such as elderly people, there is no choice other than to depend on other neighboring centers to get access to the services that no longer exist in their own residential area. At the same time that there is an increasing demand for certain types of apartments, there is a surplus of empty apartments in many suburbs of Swedish cities. The maintenance of the quality of these areas has varied from place to place and in some cases it has deteriorated.

Segregation patterns have become more evident during the last few years, especially in the largest urban areas. Suburban rental housing areas with high unemployment, mainly with a less educated labor force and immigrants, are geographically separated from areas of highly educated people, mostly composed of Swedes, living in valorized areas. The quality of life became a function of an unequal *degree of freedom* between those who have the choice and those who do not. For those who can choose where to live, residential areas that are 'free of crime' or 'environmentally friendly' are attractive alternatives resulting, in extreme cases, in so-called 'gated communities'. Exclusion of certain groups in society is also foreseen based on recent technological development and, mostly, on the global market culture of the consumer, which is highly dependent on people's financial resources.[2]

During the 1970s and 1980s, the state and municipalities invested in renewal programs aimed at improvements in the physical environment, façades and outdoor meeting places. These initiatives have targeted segregated areas in suburban areas in the largest Swedish cities. Since 1995, the Large Cities Committee, *Storstadskommittén*, has had the main task together with those affected in large cities of suggesting and initiating measures aimed at the creation of better conditions, especially in unprivileged areas (SOU, 1998:25). Since then many studies have provided support for the committee's actions.

At the same time, people seem to have become more concerned with the environmental implications of having a car-based life style. Trends focusing on increasing urban density for a more sustainable city go against the sparser urban patterns that will persist for the next few decades. Estimations for Stockholm County project that IT commuting will maintain the sparse urban building patterns. The challenge for the Swedish planning system is to take these rapid changes which are making new demands into consideration in order to preserve the quality of life achieved during the past few decades. It requires not only maintenance of the physical environment but also measures to integrate those who are already living marginally. Geographical segregation may imply differential life opportunities for those who are living in isolation. The increasing inequality between groups plays against current efforts to recreate and maintain quality of life.

Summing up, how has the conceptualization of quality of life been handled in the Swedish planning system? One may identify different shifts in the concept of 'good quality of life' from time to time. One could also argue that the idea of quality of life in Sweden as a class-related issue has resurfaced in the political debate nowadays since segregation patterns have become apparent in large Swedish cities. The lack of accessibility to certain resources has created basically two groups, those who are able to choose whatever they wish and those who have no other choice than to be dependent on the choice of others, mainly from the apparatus of the welfare system where quality is collectively defined. Other trends have incorporated environmental awareness as part of the conceptualization of quality of life in recent years. Information technology also seems to be making some difference in people's life styles, at least for certain groups. The ever-increasing mobility should also be considered as a new aspect in quality of life studies. These current trends require new ways of thinking and assessing quality of life that are still weakly explored.

Social Cohesion: A New Way to Approach Quality of Life Issues?

In the 1990s, social cohesion has been the keyword of any strategy in research and policy initiatives for promoting a better quality of life. Governmental, inter-governmental and non-governmental bodies have increasingly concerned themselves with matters related to the theme of 'social cohesion'. One might note that this matter has been central to the United Nations, for instance, with HABITAT II conference in 1996, and to the European Community,[3] especially with the creation of a Committee for Social Cohesion in June 1998. The term social cohesion refers generally 'to some kind of identifiable condition of system stasis which societies fall from and aspire to' (Vertovec, 1997), a strategy that has been applied to different geographical scales, from neighborhoods to nations. As Table 9.2 shows, social cohesion in research has had a diffuse meaning, varying from solidarity networks of civic engagement, to national identity to the existence of citizen associations. Social cohesion is commonly defined by its opposite term, that is, social *in*-cohesion, social disintegration or simply what results in the lack of quality of life. Social *in*-cohesion can be indicated, for instance, in a neighborhood, by joblessness and homelessness, a high incidence of crime, xenophobia, an entrenchment of political apathy, manifestations of racism, growing mistrust of neighbors and of government, or the worsening quality of social services.

At the regional level, social *in*-cohesion can be indicated by disparities in infrastructure and economic conditions among regions and cities and a lack of co-operation among those acting in a certain geographical area, that is, lack of social capital. Even if there is no clear definition of this term among the EU countries (Wijkström, 1998), social capital is usually used to indicate a group of soft factors or indicators that explain the economic development of a region. In Sweden, social capital has received other denominations (Mann, 1998) and has also been the object of recent studies. In policy, social capital has been associated with as many denominations as social cohesion, from a more economically-oriented approach – with applications in labor market policies – to a more socio-cultural approach, used as synonym for social network, participation in co-operatives or local associations and in local democratic outlets.

Social Cohesion and European Community Policy

Social cohesion has been used in different contexts in the policies of the European Community. At the Community-wide level, social cohesion is often associated with reducing development disparities among European regions by investing mostly in infrastructure. '...As the recent Cohesion Report has suggested, there is still a long way from our grand goal of creating a single European area, which is competitive, regionally well balanced and firmly anchored in its social dimension...' (European Commission DG XVI, 1998). The Cohesion Fund created in 1993 '...is intended to contribute to the strengthening of the economic and social cohesion of the European Union, and to help the least prosperous Member States take part in Economic and Monetary Union...' (European Regional Development Fund & Cohesion Fund, 1998). Social cohesion according to the Cohesion Fund means *the improvement of the environment* and *the development of transport infrastructure and networks,* mainly in four countries: Spain, Greece, Ireland, and Portugal.

Sectoral policies of the European Community, such as energy policy (European Commission DG XVII, Energy and Economic and Social Cohesion, 1997), have developed special programs by integrating the objective of social cohesion into their program. In this case, '...the aim of Community action in favor of economic and social cohesion is to reduce differences between the Union's regions...'. Social cohesion is also one of the goals of the European Spatial Development Perspective – ESDP, '...a framework for spatial integration which takes account of various levels of political and spatial organization in Europe...' (European Regional Development Fund & Cohesion Fund, 1997). The general policy aims are (1) a more balanced and polycentric system of cities and a new urban-rural relationship, which involves among other things, the sustainable development of cities and diversification of rural areas; (2) parity of access to infrastructure and knowledge, for instance, by having better accessibility and more sustainable use of infrastructure and increasing diffusion of innovation and knowledge; and (3) management and development of the natural and cultural heritage.

Table 9.2   Social Cohesion: selected approaches based on Vertovec (1997)

Classic sociological concepts	*Mechanical and organic solidarity*	'Mechanical solidarity' (common values, beliefs and experiences enabling persons to co-operate successfully) or 'organic solidarity' (social integration maintained through interdependence; that is, despite individualism and a complex division of labor, a kind of collective conscience still rests in shared principles and expectations – embodied, for instance, in law and the market).
	Normative integration	The society's norms, values and morality, sanctions, roles and behaviors are highly internalized and institutionalized throughout the society (in these ways parallel to traits of *Gemeinschaft* and 'mechanical solidarity'). It has been commonly assumed in some quarters of traditional sociology that the possibilities for normative integration decrease as the size and complexity of society increase.
Key political concepts	*Civil society*	Civil society is described broadly as 'the space of uncoerced human association and also the set of relational networks – formed for the sake of family, faith, interest and ideology – that fill this space.' These networks include unions, churches, political parties, social movements, co-operatives, and 'societies for promoting or preventing this and that' (Ibid.: 90). It is through such networks and the multiplicity of people's activities which they provide that, ideally, state power is held in check.
	Social capital or social economy	Social capital is described as 'features of social organization, such as trust, norms, and networks that can improve the efficiency of society by facilitating co-ordinated actions.' 'Networks of civic engagement [such as neighborhood associations, choral societies, co-operatives, sports clubs, mass-based parties] are an essential form of social capital: the denser such networks in a community, the more likely that its citizens will be able to co-operate for mutual benefit.'

	Nation-state, national identity and nationalism	In conjunction with the construct of the nation-state, national identity – a sense of belonging to that whole – is both stimulated by and expressed through symbols (including flags, anthems, heroes) and secular rituals (such as the opening of Parliament and Memorial Day parades).
Normative political philosophies	*Marxism, welfarism*	Cohesion of a society was considered to be possible only through ensuring a baseline of political and economic equality for its members. This led to the institutionalization of mass, uniform provision of social services and financial assistance via the hands of a strong central state. Such a 'top-down' system was seen as the most assured manner of maintaining solid social cohesion.
	Liberalism	Cohesion is presumed in liberalism to flow from mutual respect of individual rights and persons pursuing their own ends in parallel. In some forms of neo-liberal thought which gained much ground in the 1980s, these ideals have been increasingly poised in terms of capitalism and the marketplace: individual citizens and their interests have come to be described largely by way of entrepreneurs and consumers, goods and quantifiable services. Social cohesion is left to the transactions of a laissez-faire market.
	Communitarianism	It rejects liberal individualism as being overly atomistic and instrumental. Communitarians believe we all have (or should have) a deep bond to a particular sort of (usually small scale) social group, a bond which in turn is supported by the group's values. Advocates of communitarian philosophy wish to see policies supporting the creation and maintenance of strong communities based on what, in this view, are thought to be the foundations of civil society: families, churches, schools and neighborhoods.
	Associationalism	It advocates the democratic value of cultivating a widespread presence of 'little associations' of voluntary participation based on a wide range of possible. The idea is that, if provided with the appropriate degree of resources and public authority, a variety of local associations could provide the common values, direction, services and activities for 'bottom-up' community building and, thereby, wider social cohesion.

There are two aspects of the ESDP involved in integration at the regional and local levels: cross-border co-operation and development of cross-border spatial strategies, and interregional co-operation on spatial issues shared by geographically separate regions. '...Action at the regional level includes, for example, co-ordinated development of transport infrastructure, action programs for the maintenance of settlements in rural areas facing population decline or abandonment of land, the sustainable development of landscapes, or the prudent management of water resources. Local action might involve joint strategies for economic diversification aimed at developing clusters of cities and urban networking, adoption of planning concepts for the sustainable city including multi-modal transport strategies, urban/rural partnerships for spatial development strategies...'

Social cohesion has also been used as a substitute or complementary term for welfare in discussions involving partnerships between the State and the private sector. In France, for instance, there are those who argue that, '...the welfare state was, in some respect, a painkiller, an anaesthetic against action. The minimum wage regulations with a *contract* would provide a source of income for those who had reached the end of their unemployment entitlements, while encouraging them to shoulder their own responsibilities. The challenge in implementing these reforms was to avoid the disintegration of families and to maintain a sense of security...'.[4]

In this context, social cohesion often seems to be used as a tool for improving the image of companies and promoting more competitive regions by creating social capital. Such a trend proclaims the engagement of the private sector in partnerships not just with trade unions but at the local level with community groups for improving their life quality and creating a *more cohesive society*. The starting point is that society, as a whole should face the challenges of unemployment and disintegration, which are the result of recent economic developments. The employment of people with reduced capacity for work, improved cohesion between family life and working life, minimizing exclusion within enterprises, strategies for educating, training, recruiting and keeping a qualified workforce, providing transitional help for workers who were displaced, and involvement in the local community are all examples of corporate social behavior. '...Experience in Ireland and in other European countries shows that the benefit is not all one way. Companies actually gain considerably from their involvement in these projects in terms *of engaged and motivated employees* and a *more favorable business image with the general public*. In short it can be a win/win situation for all concerned...'[5]

Social cohesion is suggested by the terms *social stability* and *equity* in environmental European policies. The Lisbon charter, for instance, declares the '...need of integrating environmental with social and economic development in order to improve health and quality of life for our citizens, which requires therefore cross-sectoral approaches to planning and implementation...'.[6]

European policies at the local level also consider social cohesion as a synonym for integration of immigrants and their descendants in European society. Segregation is the closest term for representing the lack of social cohesion in this case. Local governments in Europe have had a role in promoting the benefits of a multicultural society in which social cohesion seems to be a key element. This can be described in many cases as a process of looking after the community, establishing support mechanisms and networks, and living and working in an environment of trust created by individuals themselves. In this context, the contributions made by volunteers are welcomed to improve the quality of life in communities by assisting in the provision of community programs or simply the participation of inhabitants in local associations.

Analyzing Effects of Social Cohesion Using Quality of Life Methods

How can methods for measuring quality of life, either based on an analysis of hard statistics or soft data, or even a combination of both, help in diagnosing the consequences of social *in*-cohesion at the local and regional levels? The following topics constitute potential areas of research using quality of life methods, which can be further developed by taking the different denominations of social cohesion into consideration.

Social Cohesion as Equal Access to Resources

Let us take a neighborhood as an example. The analysis of resource distribution based on hard statistics can be adequate when the lower quality of life of a group becomes imminent compared with other groups. High unemployment rates, a low participation rate in elections, a lower quality of services, deficient infrastructure and a decline in housing quality and services can be used as indicators of the effects of social exclusion or social *in*-cohesion.

One of the greatest advantages of this method is that it establishes a broader background for the analysis for specific subjects, such as urban crime, public health, education and housing quality. Such a contribution can be especially important when the geographical dimension is taken into consideration. The problem of precisely identifying areas or groups which need more attention from local planning can be easily solved, or at least the method can contribute to the better timing of policy responses, so that problems are addressed before they become deeply rooted. Even if this approach is used in planning which often follows a top-down approach, its utility is in its capacity to diagnose phenomena of time and place, such as the unequal distribution of resources in a certain geographical area or between groups at a specific point in time. Such a diagnosis could provide the basis for discussion on integrating different social groups into society – especially groups of immigrants and ethnic minorities and on participation, which are the long-run implications of unequal access to resources in terms of life chances and democracy. This implies more than just identification of the problems of the effects of social exclusion, such as poverty or areas with physical deterioration. This provides a basis for the identification of other factors beyond income that impoverish people's lives, that is, the barriers that impede an individual's full participation in social and economic life.

It is worth noting that the analysis of resources began as early as the 1950s, when it was suggested that measurements of well being should be based on several components, not only on monetary measures, such as GNP per capita. During the 1960s, in the US, a new research field called 'social indicators' (the research cousin of quality of life studies) grew as a result of the dissatisfaction among academics with the quality and quantity of social information available to public policy decision-makers. This trend also spread in the Nordic countries, influencing the basic concepts of the first studies concerning quality of life. So-called objective or descriptive indicators were the main sources of data.[7] For a review of studies on quality of life in the Nordic countries, see Ceccato (1998).

The production of the so-called Index of Local Deprivation (ILD) in the United Kingdom is a recent example of such an approach applied to three spatial scales – local authority district, ward and enumeration district. Indicators are composed of data on the economic standard, health, education, the environment, crime and housing aspects and are intended to give a basis for local and regional policy. A ranking shows the UK cities listed by their performance according to the ILD (UK government, 1998).

At the European Community level, a project on urban indicators for the Committee of the Regions recently launched an exploratory study using a similar approach. The project focuses on the definition of urban indicators of quality of life to support new policies for urban areas within the Union (Craglia et al., 1998). The project involves not just classical socio-economical indicators but also indicators on technology and innovation potential, such as education and training and access to and use of information technologies, which are believed to give a picture of how these resources are distributed and accessed by the population.

It seems that environmental indicators in quality of life studies continue to be a challenge to researchers and practitioners. Not many analyses dealing with socio-economic issues have taken environmental aspects of sustainability into consideration. Those that focus on environmental aspects generally treat specific environmental indicators of quality, such as air pollution, water quality, land use demands, rather than give a general analysis of quality of life.

Social Cohesion as Social Capital

A complementary approach would be based on the identification of aspects or indicators[8] that the population itself judges as being important to their quality of life. The analysis would start out from what people themselves judge to be important instead of beginning by using aggregated statistics. Taking again the example of a neighborhood, different groups would be able to identify what resources are needed or where 'the problems' are based given their particular needs.

Bernow (1982)[9] was a pioneer in Sweden, evaluating quality of life in Swedish cities by focusing on subjective evaluations of objective conditions. His hypothesis was that '...people with different personal characteristics evaluate differentially the perceived reality...'. Personal characteristics can influence all elements of the proposed model. The author discussed how individuals evaluate the different dimensions of life: the residential area, the work place, family life, their relationships with friends and health. The results showed that the individual assessment of an aspect of reality is a function of what this reality looks like and but also the individual's background (previous experiences, aspirations, friend status, citizen status) along with the personal characteristics.

Abaleron (1987) used the population's perception as an important source of information to determine quality of life. The main objective was to evaluate the degree of association between certain objective indicators (public goods and infrastructure) and the perception of quality of life (subjective indicators) in four Argentine cities. The results demonstrate that there is no relation between infrastructure and public goods variables and the perception of quality of life in urban areas. When the distribution of these services is heterogeneous and of inferior quality, as in peripheral districts, the author verified a relationship between certain objective and subjective variables. In places with a high socio-economic level, *the vital horizon* factor also increased the capacity to make comparisons. This factor represents the different degrees of an individual's necessities at distinct social-economic levels. On the contrary, in places where the socio-economic level decreased, *the accommodation factor* developed as a response to the existing situation, stabilizing necessities and desires. The perception of public goods *per se* was not as important as the comparative perception between different places. This comparative perception approach feeds the mechanisms of necessities, desires, satisfactions and frustrations. Desires and aspirations, as opposed to necessities, depend on a specific cultural and civilian context and thus they do not have universal validity.

Subjective information can also be used to indicate regional imbalances. Studies of people's regional preferences in the Scandinavian countries from the 1980s showed the contradiction between regional preferences and the objective level of living. Results revealed a tendency for people to prefer living in medium-sized urban centers and more sparsely populated areas. In particular, people living in the main large regions would have preferred living in smaller cities if they could choose freely. This could be partially explained by the fact that the rural advantages were more heavily weighted and evaluated by most people compared with the urban advantages. There could be also dissonance between responses given to an idealized situation (hypothetical free choice, no restrictions on job and educational opportunities) and a realistic situation (restricted choice, accounting for circumstances).

Issues related to the effects of social in-cohesion make this approach particularly important in European cities, when minority needs or opinions should be valued as a fundamental key to achieving an integrated society. Equal opportunities for different social groups also include a gender-based discussion. A complete picture of the differences in opportunities between men and women in all life dimensions (and the perception of them) remains a challenge in quality of life studies. Sen (1985) developed one of the first empirical attempts to analyze differences in quality of life by gender. Gender issues are important because men and women have different experiences. A woman's perspective of quality of life should be based on women's experiences and needs since women, for instance, nowadays have double tasks; on the one hand they are still responsible for the household and children and on the other hand most women are active in the labor force.

There are many examples in the literature on quality of life showing that subjective information is able not only to indicate where the 'the problems' are but also to identify potentiality for improvement. Thus, subjective information is also capable of revealing soft aspects that compensate for the lack in quality in a certain life dimension, which hard statistics alone are normally not able to capture. This type of information is often acquired through interviews and questionnaires at the individual level. In local planning, such an approach has been labeled as a more bottom-up one, giving people themselves the opportunity to directly influence their conditions. The use of interviews instead of questionnaires sent by mail [10] can be especially important in areas where the participation process is still in its initial phase or where an entrenchment of political apathy is evident. The great challenge is to develop new techniques for acquiring information that take the heterogeneity of residents into account as well as the reasons that people have for refusing to give their opinions (Ceccato, 1998).

The use of subjective data has also been linked to the identification of social capital at the regional level. Social capital, in this case, has been regarded as the dynamic ingredient that explains why certain regions are economically more successful than others. This can be illustrated by the existence of certain indicators reflecting 'networks of civic engagement, such as neighborhood associations, choral societies, co-operatives, sports clubs, mass-based parties. For Swedish examples, see, for instance, Berggren et al. (1998) and Grut and Mattson (1998). One of the greatest challenges is to identify indicators of social capital in regions or countries where the social networks are not traditionally institutionalized but might function as an important element for economic development.

The Spatial Dimension of Urban Quality of Life

Despite the interest in spatial indicators, the main statements and reports published up to the early 1970s were almost entirely non-spatial in their content. Only since the entry of geographers into the field has the spatial dimension been added. This is important since there has been a growing awareness of territorial bases of inequality in society, and policies designed to eliminate or ameliorate these inequalities have assumed explicit spatial dimensions.[11]

What are the Advantages of Using Spatial Data Concerning the Quality of Life Studies?

One of the most important advantages in using maps in general instead of tables or diagrams is that human eyes are better able to identify patterns in a map than to read numbers in rows and columns. It is already known how long it takes and how difficult it is to describe spatial relations using only words. Maps can synthesize and aid our mind in effectively transforming data into a comprehensible form of information.

The most important advantage in using maps is to have information about different dimensions of quality in a more detailed and precise format indicating where the phenomenon occurs, its *locus*, for instance, the spatial pattern of crimes in different parts of a residential area or the identification of deprived areas in metropolitan regions. New techniques[12] are able to produce the exact geographical location, thus functioning as a diagnostic tool for an ideal distribution of resources in direct proportion to area needs.

It is believed that the adoption of the spatial dimension in policy can help to target resources to the neediest areas, and hopefully, to build future capacity for self-sustained growth. Regarding distressed urban areas, the focus on geographical areas according to Parkinson (1998) means an improvement in the prospects of excluded areas by strategically linking them to more prosperous parts of the city. This could also '...improve service delivery through the integration of policies and resources of different agencies at the local level; increasing community social capital and encouraging good practice and policy innovation...'.

Different tools are used nowadays for mapping and spatial analysis of the urban space. The most common types of tools are desktop mapping systems and Geographic Information System (GIS).[13] GIS and desktop systems have the potential to represent non-spatial data. Most of the time this is the case for socio-economic data. They can be associated with different forms, from points (x,y co-ordinates) and blocks to larger statistical entities. This representation is associated with a point or generalized as a polygon, which means a loss of information. Point data are effective in representing information about crime patterns and health analyses, where a point represents a unique case. The detail concerning the precise location is itself an important attribute for this type of geographical analysis.

There are several studies in the national and international literature confirming the potentialities of developing the spatial dimension of quality of life using GIS.[14] They can be divided in two main groups; the first is composed of academic studies focusing on methodological developments in spatial analysis while the second focuses on providing a basis for decisions in planning.

In Sweden, the most recent study using GIS for a multitemporal analysis of socio-economic conditions in Dalarna was carried out by Pettersson and Westholm (1998) and Ceccato (1998). Pettersson and Westholm (1998) show in *Gräddhyllor och fattigfickor* that segregation also exists in rural areas. They have investigated how living conditions change over time and space on a micro regional level (i.e. parts of municipalities) based on available statistics and maps from a 10-year period. The material covers a period stretching from an era of high economic growth and full employment to economic crisis. The authors claim that the period is insufficient for discussing trends in regional development but that the analysis of small geographical areas permits analysts to examine some phenomena and areas in a way which has not been possible before. Another advantage of the micro regional analysis, the authors explain, is that it gives another geographical level. That is, analysts can make their own divisions by choosing certain micro regions without taking municipal boundaries into consideration. Thus one can analyze conditions that were formerly concealed by the traditional use of municipal averages.

A focus on the spatial dimension of residential quality by Ceccato (1998) adds to the knowledge of the interrelations among objective and subjective indicators of quality of life. The empirical analysis is based on a theoretical framework which includes individual and aggregated data about housing conditions, quality of the outdoor environment, accessibility to services, social links and security. The influence of other dimensions of life on how people evaluate their residential areas as well as aspects of the perceived living environment was also explored. Spatial differences in quality as well as in people's satisfaction were mapped and analyzed statistically. Results showed that the relationship between the objective reality and the perceptive assessment is not straightforward. Objective and subjective indicators are often complementary in expressing measured and perceived residential quality of life.

The second group of studies focuses on the spatial dimension of a certain aspect of quality of life as a way of improving the quality of information handled in the planning process. Thus, GIS technology can also be classified by its use at various points in the planning process. There are those which refer to the use of GIS as a tool for helping analytical and synthesis-oriented tasks such as plan development and evaluation. A successful example was developed by Langendorf (1995) showing how computer-based information departs from traditional methods and can contribute to better utilization of information in decision making. This GIS use is very often related to a top-down approach in planning but Dunn et al, (1997) recognizes the potential of traditional mapping capabilities for enabling the participation of interest groups and improving a more bottom-up approach in local planning.

There are also other GIS applications in planning based on the availability of a model base, allowing the user to support decision-making processes in terms of various strategies. These systems are usually called DSSs, Decision Support Systems. The study by Yaakup and Healey (1994) illustrates how the usefulness of a GIS can be improved and become a DSS by adding particular features to the system in order to produce alternative solutions to squatter problems.

Internet GIS is another emerging trend since it has great potential for stimulating a more democratic planning process. One of the first attempts was described by Shiffer (1995), who illustrated the potential of the World Wide Web (WWW) as a support system for individual browsing or gathering planning-related data. A prototype was developed to aid a planning agency in discussing the potential impacts of major changes to the built environment. The basic assumption was that a greater degree of access to relevant information leads to the consideration of a greater number of alternative scenarios and consequently, it will lead to better-informed public debate. An encouraging example of such applications is an ongoing project developed in Great Britain by Kingston et al. (1999).

What are the challenges in using the spatial dimension in quality of life studies?

The challenges in using the GIS as a support in planning are not mainly linked with the tool itself but the way in which it is utilized. For example, the map may be used to create images of needs or satisfaction among the involved groups. There are, of course, limitations regarding the demand side, that is, those who are able to use these techniques in social analyses. There still seems to be an imbalance regarding GIS adoption and implementation among Swedish local authorities (Sandgren, 1993) as well as in the rest of Europe (Masser and Craglia, 1996). According to a survey made by the Development Authority for Landscape Information in 1997 of 1,090 organizations in Sweden, a lack of knowledge among those who would be potential users in these organizations and the price of data handled by the GIS system were the factors limiting the use of GIS. For the future it is expected that investments in education targeting GIS should be a priority in order to reduce the lack of competence among staff and other potential users in local governments, which is an important obstacle for its development.

Final Considerations

Social cohesion has been the keyword of any strategy in research and in policy initiatives for promoting a better quality of life. Governmental, inter-governmental and non-governmental bodies have increasingly been concerned with matters related to the theme of 'social cohesion'. Methods applied to quality of life analysis developed during the last three decades seem to have a potential for helping people face the challenge of analyzing the effects of social in-cohesion. At the same time, there has also been a growing awareness of territorial bases of inequality in society, and policies designed to ameliorate these inequalities have assumed explicit spatial dimensions. The use of quality of life methods for analyzing social in-cohesion issues in urban areas and the potential for exploring its spatial dimension have been presented in this paper as potential research areas.

Knowledge needs to be developed regarding:

- The analysis of the effects of social in-cohesion using aggregated and individual data – social cohesion as equal access to resources and as social capital.
- The development of methods that deal with the Northern–Southern contexts in Europe with respect to social cohesion, social capital and quality of life. This aspect is important since social cohesion, social capital and quality of life have different meanings and are of a different type in Southern and Northern countries as well as in urban areas and in rural areas or small towns.
- The term social capital is often used to explain differing regional economic development. New methods should assess whether these differences in social capital imply differing regional economic performance.
- The identification and incorporation of consistent indicators on quality of life which take into consideration environment quality, differentiated mobility among groups in the population and innovation potential.
- A gender perspective in quality of life studies.
- Analysis using spatial statistics linked to GIS in social analysis aimed at verifying the distribution of a phenomenon and also getting a measurement of its geographical distribution.

Notes

1 The large cities committee, *Storstadskommittén*, defined segregation in 1995 as 'socio-economic and ethnic separation of different populations groups. It can be a question of separation in different living places. When these different separations coincide segregation becomes a serious problem' (SOU 1998:25).
2 Social exclusion is a global phenomenon but in many Western countries it has been related to fundamental economic and social changes which they are undergoing at the present time. These changes are not uniform either within or between countries. Bottoms and Wiles (1997) recognize several macro changes ranging from increasing

economic polarization to a shift in gender roles, which are changing the nature of the cities and significantly affecting patterns of crime.

3 The Maastricht Treaty establishing the European Union, which entered into force in 1993, makes economic and social cohesion one of the Union's priority objectives.

4 Minister Jacques Barrot, Labour and Social Affairs, at the Annual Meeting of the World Economic Forum, 1998, *Social cohesion in a competitive world.*

5 Minister Dermot Ahern, Ireland, World's first international conference on social cohesion, 1997.

6 *Lisbon Charter*, Second European Conference on Sustainable Cities & Towns, 1996.

7 'Objective indicators are generally defined as counts of various types of phenomena, such as levels of income and residential densities. They are most often regarded as quantitative 'facts' selected from census data and other accessible official registers'. 'Objective indicators are hard measures describing the environments within which people live and work. These can deal with issues such as health care provision, crime, education, leisure facilities and housing' (Pacione, 1982).

8 Subjective indicators are, on the other hand, generally defined as being based on direct reports from individuals about their own perceptions and feelings. To obtain a direct measure of the quality of life of the people concerned, a questionnaire survey is proposed'. Subjective indicators tend to describe the ways people perceive and evaluate conditions around them' (Pacione, 1982).

9 Erik Allardt first developed the use of subjective indicators in the 1970s in Finland. His approach was focused on the level of need satisfaction rather than on resources. For a short description, see Allardt (1993).

10 This technique may not take the capacity of expression for certain groups into consideration. The questionnaire starts from the principle that everyone can read, understand and answer the questions equally. In areas where this principle does not correspond to reality, there is a high non-response rate. People can for any reason choose not to answer the questionnaire – this fact may be worth investigating for those interested in social cohesion issues, since social cohesion can also be indicated by active participation in local institutions or to some degree by attachment to the local network.

11 The adoption of area-based approaches in policy can be exemplified among European Community members by the European Spatial Development Perspective – ESDP and among OECD countries; one example is the program for Distressed Urban Areas, (OECD, 1998).

12 Such as Geographical Information Systems (GIS) and Desktop Mapping Systems. In Sweden, for instance, the total number of professionals using these types of techniques has increased from 3,822 in 1995 to 6,761 in 1997 (ULI rapport, 1997).

13 The desktop systems handle digital maps as vectors to organize data from tables. The desktop systems have more or less limited spatial analysis, data management and fewer possibilities for adaptation. GIS, geographical information in a bi-dimensional co-ordinate system, contains information about the relation among geographical elements, which is fundamental for carrying out spatial analysis. The inability to make spatial analysis, that is, a mathematical description of spatial relationships, is the main reason used by experts for not calling a desktop system GIS. As desktop systems often work as part of the GIS, many applications use both systems, which makes it difficult to separate applications using only GIS or desktop mapping. The term GIS and desktop mapping system will be used here as synonyms.

14 GIS applications reflected to some extent the development of computer technologies. GIS evolved firstly from mainframe GIS, in which GIS programs resided on the mainframe with terminal access, to independent GIS workstation units. Later came the

era of the desktop GIS in which GIS was a stand-alone program with no information exchange between computers. More recently, network GIS has been a reality, in which desktop GIS programs share data, applications, and other resources within local area networks. The recent development of Internet technology has brought another significant change to GIS, mostly shaping the ways in which traditional GIS functions.

References

Abaleron, C.A. (1987), 'Condicionantes objectivos y percepcion subjectiva de calidad de vida en areas centrales y barrios vecindarios', *Revista Geográfica*, vol. 6, pp.103–42.

Abaleron, C.A. (1995), *Calidad de vida de la poblacion marginal de San Carlos de Bariloche: problemas, efectos y complejos causales*, PIA–CONICET, Bariloche.

Alfredsson, B. and Viklund, E. (1981), *Stad och hälsa*, Stadsförnyelsekampanjens skriftserie, 5, Lund.

Allardt, E. (1993), 'Having, loving, being: an alternative to the Swedish model of welfare research', in: M.C. Nussbaum and A. Sen, (eds), *The quality of life*, Clarendon, Oxford, pp. 85–88.

Berggren, C., Brulin, G. and Gustafsson, L. (1998), *Från Italien till Gnosjö: om det sociala kapitalets betydelse för livskraftiga industriella regioner*, Nutek, rapport 2, Stockholm.

Bernow, R. (1982), *Livskvaliteten i Sverige: frågor till svenska folket*, Temaplan, Stockholm.

Bottoms, A.E. and Wiles, P. (1997), 'Environmental Criminology'. in: M. Maguire, R. Morgan, and R. Reiner (eds), *The Oxford Handbook of Criminology*, Second edition, Oxford University Press, Oxford, pp. 305–59.

Ceccato, V.A. (1998), *Assessing Residential Quality of Llife: Three Case-studies in Stockholm County*. Licentiate Thesis, Division of Regional Planning, Royal Institute of Technology, Stockholm.

Craglia, M., Leontidou, L. Nuvolati, G. and Schweikart, J. (1998), *Evaluating quality of life: theoretical conceptualisation, classical and innovative indicators*, Committee of the Regions of the European Union.

Díaz, K. (1985), Los estudios geográficos sobre la calidad de vida en Venezuela, *Revista Geográfica*, 102, pp.55–72.

Dunn, C.E., Atkins, P.J. and Townsend, J.G. (1997), 'GIS for development: a contradiction in terms?' *Area*, 29, pp. 151–59.

European Commission (1997), *European Regional Development Fund & Cohesion Fund*, Noordwijk.

European Commission DG XVII (1997), *Energy and Economic and Social Cohesion*.

European Commission (1998), *European Regional Development Fund & Cohesion Fund*.

European Commission DG XVI (1998), *Speeches of Commissioner*, Spotlight on Cohesion Policy.

Grut, K. and Mattson, E. (1998), 'Social ekonomi: om kraften hos alla människor', in K. Grut and E. Mattson, (eds), *Social ekonomi*, Utbildningsförlaget-Brevskolan, Stockholm.

Guimarães, R.P. (1984), 'Ecopolítica em áreas urbanas: a dimensão política dos indicadores de qualidade ambiental', in A. Souza, (ed.), *Qualidade de vida urbana*, Zahar, Rio de Janeiro, pp. 21–34.

Kingston, R., Carver, S., Evans, A. and Turton, I. (1999), 'Virtual Decision Making in Spatial Planning: Web-based Geographical Information Systems For Public

Participation', in *International Conference on Public Participation and Information Technology*, Lisbon, (http://www.ccg.leeds.ac.uk/vdmisp/vdmisp.htm).

Knox, P. (1982), *Urban Social Geography*, Longman, London.

Lanesjö, E. (1987), *Bygg nytt i gammal miljö*, K-Konsult, Stockholm.

Langendorf, R. (1995), 'Towards an improved information utilisation in design decision making: a case study of the Hurricane Andrew recovery efforts', *Environment and Planning B: Planning and Design*, vol. 22, pp. 315–30.

Liu, B.C. (1976), *Quality of Life Indicators in US Metropolitan Areas: a Statistical Analysis*, Praeger, New York.

Mann, C.O. (1998), 'Att ge social economi en svensk innebörd', in K. Grut, and E. Mattson, (eds), *Social ekonomi: om kraften hos alla människor*, Utbildningsförlaget, Stockholm, pp. 148–54.

Masser, I. and Craglia, M. (1996), 'A comparative evaluation of GIS diffusion in local government in nine European countries', in I. Masser, H. Campbell, M. Craglia (eds), *GIS Diffusion: the Adoption and Use of Geographical Information Systems in Local Governments in Europe*, Taylor & Francis, GISDATA 3, London.

OECD (1998), 'Distressed Urban Areas', http:/www.oecd.org/tds/old%20files/duaintro.htm

Pacione, M. (1982), 'The use of objective and subjective measures of quality of life in human geography', *Progress in Human Geography*, vol. 6, pp. 493–514.

Parkinson, M. (1998), 'The areas-based approach', in M. Conway (ed.), *Meeting the Challenge of Distressed Urban Areas*, Conference report, European Foundation for the Improvement of Living and Working Conditions, Dublin.

Pettersson, Ö. and Westholm, E. (1998), *Gräddhyllor och fattigfickor: en mikroregional analys av välfärdens geografiska fördelning i Dalarna*, Dalarnas Forskningsråd, Falun.

Rogerson, R.J., Findlay, A.M., Morris, A.S., and Coombes, M.G. (1989), 'Indicators of quality of life: some methodological issues', *Environment and Planning A*, vol. 21, pp.1655–66.

Sandgren, U. (1993), 'GIS Diffusion in Sweden', in I. Masser, M. Craglia (eds), *Abstracts of the papers presented at the specialist meeting on Diffusion of GIS in Europe* (http://www.shef.ac.uk/uni/academic/D-H/gis/absdiff.html).

Sen, A. (1985), 'Well-being, Functioning and Sex Biases: Indian Illustrations', in *Commodities and capabilities*, North Holland, Amsterdam (Lectures in economics 7).

Siirilä, S. (1984), 'Spatial structure and social well-being', *Fennia*, vol. 62, pp. 117–26.

SOU - Socialdepartementet (1998), *Tre städer: en storstadspolitik för hela landet*, SOU 1998, 25, Stockholm.

Thiberg, S. (1990), *Housing Research and Design in Sweden*, Swedish Council for Building Research, Stockholm.

UK Department of the Environment, Transport and the Regions (1998), *Index of local deprivation*, (http:/www.regeneration.detr.gov.uk/98ild/indicate.html).

ULI – Utvecklingsrådet för Landskapsinformation (1997), *GIS i Sverige 1997, redovisning och analys av ULIs enkät*, ULI – Utvecklingsrådet för Landskapsinformation, Gävle.

Vertovec, D. (1997), 'Social Cohesion and Tolerance', in *Second International Metropolis Conference*, Copenhagen, September 1997 (www.ercomer.org/metropolis/proceedings-/index.html).

Wijkström, F. (1998), Social ekonomi – om mening och identitet bortom lönearbetet, in: K. Grut, and E. Mattson (eds), *Social ekonomi: om kraften hos alla människor*, Utbildningsförlaget, Stockholm, pp. 58–70.

Yaakup, A.B. and Healey, R.G. (1994), 'A GIS approach to spatial modelling for squatter settlement planning in Kuala Lampur, Malaysia', *Environment and Planning B: Planning and Design*, vol. 21, pp. 21–34.

PART III
PROFESSIONAL CULTURES

10 An Approach to the Development of Competence for Sustainable Development in the Context of Planning

EVA ASPLUND

Introduction

This chapter focuses on municipal planning and the demands on local governments to contribute to the sustainable development of the local territory. The purpose is to elucidate and discuss the capacity at the local level to tackle these problems in planning and strategic considerations. Up to now, a great deal of attention has been given to the fact that sustainable development is an unclear and even ambiguous concept. In order to overcome the problem of unclear ends, the main interest in areas like planning research has been on operationalizing ends, which have been adapted to current ideas of planning practice. Moreover new methods and tools have been developed in order to encourage the integration of sustainability issues in planning.

Then the question arises whether we can expect planning practice to adopt these new guidelines and ideals for societal development without reflection if we regard sustainable development as a challenge both to current values and to the traditional approach to planning. The main interest in this chapter therefore is not in the institutions involved in planning but in human beings, processes and patterns at the local administrative level. The theoretical section includes a discussion of the different ways to understand the mechanisms behind the interaction between professionals with different kinds of competence in an organization. The chapter ends with some thoughts about how the conditions for the development of competence and rethinking in planning could be understood.

The arena is the Swedish municipality with its institutions, actors and activities. The municipality is the administrative unit at the lowest level of the Swedish system. Still, on average the territory is larger and the population is more numerous compared to municipalities in most other European countries. Following a reform in 1972 more than 800 Swedish municipalities were reduced to 280 for a total population of almost 9 million. This also means that each municipality as a rule consists of several densely populated areas surrounded by forests and/or agricultural land (see Chapter 2, Sten Axelsson). They also have a relatively long tradition of autonomy. It is at the local level that demands for development in terms of economic growth confront the equally necessary but more far-sighted considerations for the environment and the management of resources. This is where guiding principles which are issued centrally should be implemented. It is also the political level to which those living and acting in the local territory address their demands and expectations. Local governments have the exclusive right and responsibility to make plans for the improvement of local conditions and local development. This should help local governments to prepare themselves to meet future needs as well as avoid mistakes that could be foreseen but are often overshadowed by other, more immediate and directly experienced problems. The plan adopted is expected to be the document in which intentions for further local development are expressed.

The planning system and planning procedures are regulated by the Planning and Building Act. This legislation was thoroughly revised in 1987 and was included under the 'umbrella' of the Natural Resources Act. Compared to the earlier legislation, more stress was laid on environmental considerations in planning. This means for instance that ecological aspects should be taken more seriously and that natural resources should be used economically. In the last decade further directives have been given, emphasizing special areas of concern for the better adaptation of society to environmental conditions. Local governments are obliged to produce comprehensive plans and to continuously keep them up to date. The plans should cover the entire local territory and contain the information necessary to give guidance on more detailed planning as well as on other kinds of considerations and decisions concerning the local territory.

The demand for sustainable development is representative of a change of course in society. Valuations set in an industrial society, at least to some extent, are called in question. From an environmental point of view this means that problems that derive from the industrial period must be addressed and that new conceptions for societal organisation must be developed. Thus, rethinking in planning as well as in the stewardship of ecological conditions are necessary in many ways. Sustainable development can be understood as a general concept, originally introduced[1] in order to turn attention to the fact that society is being developed in a way that is not sustainable. The purpose was to gain broad political acceptance of the idea that some kind of change is necessary. Consequently there are a wide range of possible interpretations of this concept, depending on the interpreter's point of departure. That is to say that different sectors of society develop different views of the world and in turn different views of how sustainable development should be achieved.

However, one image of planning is that it should enable the co-ordination of different views. From this perspective it does not make sense to try and find one proper definition of the concept that could be applicable to local planning for sustainable development. Instead, one point of departure in this text is that different approaches to the concept must be seen as legitimate and that competition for the privilege of formulating the new commitment is at hand and might even be fruitful. In the following paragraphs the term 'sustainable development' will include all these possible or optional interpretations.

Nonetheless, some indices have to be chosen/identified, following the traditions of Swedish comprehensive planning and its territorial or spatial approach to problem identification and problem solving. Regarding municipalities from a territorial point of view is what allows the integration of different kinds of sectional or specialist aspects on spatial development. But it also offers a certain terminology and mental pictures of the municipality as a territory with its distinct borderlines. There are flows over these borders in both directions of necessities and remnant products, commuters and migrants, enterprises moving in and out, money and so forth.

Each municipality has its territory and at the same time depends on others. But it is what is inside the local borders that the municipality to some extent can control or at least is responsible for. It is critical in planning for sustainable development in this context to find ways to prepare for an improved balance in the exchange between urban areas and the countryside.

This paper will elucidate some of the problems that the integration of sustainability issues in planning practice gives rise to. The stress will be on the processes and conditions for development and change from the perspective of agents involved in the planning process. The following presentation is based on studies made in four Swedish municipalities of how the approach to planning and environmental issues has been affected in practice by the new demands.[2]

Conditions for the Development of Competence

As a consequence of the reduction in the number of municipalities in 1972, local administrative units were able to strengthen their professional competence. The main task for this kind of competence was to manage and develop the welfare society. Increasing resources had to be spent and distributed in order to benefit the common good. Today the economic situation has changed, resulting in a contraction of economic as well as personal resources. In addition, more emphasis has been placed on the task of promoting sustainable development.

As this concept is a very ambiguous one, there are also different views on the needs for additional competence or development of existing competence. Of course new knowledge is being developed about the conditions for a sustainable relation between society and nature, and surveys of the prevailing environmental problems and threats are currently being conducted in different scientific disciplines and institutions. Limits to growth and to man's future existence on Earth are set mainly from a natural science point of view.

Different ways to solve problems and to find new ways to achieve sustainability involve many other aspects such as social, economic, organizational and technical considerations. The problem thus, from an institutional point of view, could be described as: How do we make this information and knowledge available to those in charge of and involved in planning activities in local governments? From a planning practice point of view the problem could instead be described in terms of: What are the conditions for those involved in local planning for adopting information and knowledge concerning sustainability matters? What is it that guides different kinds of professionals in selecting and assessing different kinds of information? What makes them able to communicate knowledge and experience, to handle it in democratic processes and to transform it into action and strategies?

Tensions Between Different Approaches to Environmental Issues

Even if various aspects of sustainable development can be seen as legitimate, a natural science perspective is basic, especially at the local level. Falkenmark (1997) defines the sustainable society as one that does not undermine its resource base. When it comes to planning, the main problem seems not so much to be getting access to information and facts about environmental conditions and the sources of problems in the environment. It is rather that there are tensions between different ways of thinking and talking about these aspects. Management of natural resources, maintenance of the reproductive capacity of ecosystems and similar matters may be best discussed in terms of flows and substances. Preservation of other environmental qualities may instead be discussed in terms of biotopes and neighborhoods etc, which are more closely bound to land use. Local environmental policies emanate from specific local conditions while policies made at the central level take their starting point in accounts of general threats to the environment. In environmental politics the extent of environmental problems and the idea of a more sustainable world must be made comprehensible to the public but these matters must also be understood in a feasible way; implementation of policies also has to be considered.

Thus, work has to be done on many frontiers at the same time. One question is whether planning should be seen as one of these frontiers or whether it should be used for co-ordination of different activities.

Dilemmas Concerning the Mandate of Local Governments

In Sweden, local governments have the exclusive right – and responsibility – to make plans and strategies for future development of the territory. This could be described as a responsibility to act in favor of the desired development of the local territory and to avert threats to such development. In practice though, politics at the local level still mainly concerns conditions for social and economic welfare and is therefore by tradition very much focused on urban areas. Job opportunities for all inhabitants are as a rule seen as crucial for the sustainable development of the municipality.

At the same time the competition between municipalities and regions in order to attract enterprises both depends on and has an impact on environmental qualities. In fact all political parties have adopted ambitious environmental programs. But in their everyday work it is the immediate and directly experienced problems that attract attention. And sustainable development requires long-term perspectives.

There are also of course difficulties in getting public support for local environmental policies aimed at averting threats not yet apparent or manifest. Moreover, stewardship of the countryside to a great extent is the landowners' own business. Farming and forestry are regulated by the state and, today, also by EU rules. Part of the problem therefore is whether local authorities have the motivation and the proper mandate to maintain and develop territorial qualities and create a better balance in the exchange between urban areas and the countryside.

Shortcomings in Planning

Planning in Sweden traditionally has its focus on the development and restructuring of urban areas. Ideas related to sustainable development highlight the need for a different approach to planning. Over time different issues have been the focus of local planning. As a result of legislation, the purpose of plans is to regulate the future use of land and water. Depending on the situation, planning can also be regarded as a way to construct visions, to prepare for projects to come, to regulate and give guidance on building permits, to offer an arena for collecting information or for discussing issues concerning the future. Far-sighted issues, to which sustainable development belongs, should be handled in comprehensive plans. One dilemma is that these are not judicially conclusive and as a consequence the guiding capacity is not very strong. Still it is obvious that the earlier in the decision process the environmental or sustainability aspects are introduced, the better the opportunities are for bringing about a real integration that might affect the results, for instance in the comprehensive plan.

But there are many new issues and aspects knocking at the door of planning. Moreover, there are tensions between many different departments in the local administrative unit expected to contribute in planning activities. In addition it is a fact that comprehensive planning has not been able to attract very much interest from either politicians or the public. The main problem therefore seems to be that planning has a potential as an instrument for sustainable development but not as it is carried out today.

A Study of Four Municipalities

In order to get an insight into current ways to treat issues concerning the environment and planning, studies were carried out in four Swedish municipalities (30,000 – 60,000 inhabitants). The first step was to select two municipalities with 'moderate' ambitions[3] concerning sustainability. One of them was chosen from among municipalities with long industrial traditions and a stable social democratic majority. The other one can be characterized as having a more complex structure of economic life and a constantly changing social democratic majority. After the completion of these two studies, two more municipalities, showing the same variances with one another, were selected. The only intentional difference was that both were recognized as being at the forefront concerning ideas on sustainable development.

To begin with, interviews were carried out with officials from departments (and public companies) usually involved in planning and environmental management – planners, environmental and health officers, technicians and co-ordinators of Agenda 21.[4] Besides including simple questions about the respondents' educational background, position in the internal organization etc, the interviews covered the officials' approach to planning and the environment, ways of organizing work, the way different issues were put on the agenda, officials'/departments' relations to politicians etc. As a second step, workshops were arranged in which the chosen representatives took part in cross-sectional discussions on the same topics. Interviews were also conducted with politicians in charge of the issues in question, mainly in order to check their attitudes to the pictures given by the officials.

The method was characterized by openness, encouraging a narrative approach and focusing on interaction and processes. The purpose of the chosen course of action was to generate hypotheses in a field where theory as yet is comparatively unelaborate. We then highlighted phenomena, situations, patterns, differences and similarities from the empirical material that were worth a closer analysis. The empirical material was then used as a subject for seminars with researchers representing different disciplines, mainly in the social sciences. On these occasions the problems were viewed from different angles and the theoretical framework was expanded. Different theories have then given guidance in the search for new and fruitful ways to elucidate different phenomena and mechanisms affecting the opportunities for developing competence for sustainable development.

One central topic in interviews and workshops was the approach to comprehensive planning – both the way the process used to be designed and ideas on possible ways of adjusting it to a new situation. Comprehensive plans were developed somewhere around 1990 in all the municipalities studied. Neither politicians nor the public paid very much attention at the time. Thus, the plans were described as mainly the products of officials. Guidelines for the work were laid out in the Planning and Building Act, which had recently (in 1987) been altered.[5] This also had consequences for the way the plans were presented; each one contains a first part recounting the prevailing local conditions, mainly in the countryside, and a second, concluding part presenting strategies for the development of more densely populated or urban areas. Despite clearly stated intentions that plans for further development had to be based on ecological considerations, there was no integration between the two parts. Connections between the two parts were almost completely missing. There was one exception in the form of a plan worked out after that by the two more environmentally conscious local governments and adopted in 1996. The descriptions of the background and the planning process in that case were more thoroughly analyzed.

In the two municipalities studied first, no co-operation had been established between the Department of the Environment and Health and other departments. Environmental tasks were assigned by central government directives. The environmental and health officers gave evidence that an increasing number of tasks had been assigned to them by the state in recent years. Their opinions on plan proposals had appeared in late stages of the process and were often ignored. In one of the municipalities the Department of Planning and Environment and Health had been combined into one unit run by a leading official working in both areas. This did not lead to further co-operation. On the contrary, environmental issues lost status because of the loss of formal expert leadership. In the other municipality the division between the different sectors was strictly maintained. Every department did its own job, presenting it to their respective politicians, who were expected to make the crucial considerations and decisions. This seems to be a formally proper way of working, but in times of transition it seems to lead to an inefficient use of existing competence and constitute an obstacle for developing new ideas and approaches.

In the next pair of municipalities studied, the emphasis was placed on local environmental policies. The central guiding principles for environmental and health management were of course the same in all municipalities. But besides the compulsory tasks, environmental and health officers were involved in various projects, for instance in planning. This was managed by means of a more effective organization of the work, personal and economic resources being about the same as in the other municipalities. The leadership of the environment and health departments was shown to be crucial in allowing environmental competence to affect the work of other departments. In one of these municipalities environmental and health officers, planners and co-ordinators of Agenda 21 became allies, leaving the technicians on the side. In the other one a loose alliance of environmental and health officers, technicians and co-ordinators of Agenda 21 was established. Among the driving forces for co-operation, better opportunities for tackling complex problems was mentioned. Professional prestige and personal engagement in environmental matters were also found to be important factors. Some degree of jointly-held views on the need for more sustainable development was seen as basic in order to facilitate communication and co-operation. On the other hand, differences in the use of language, professional jargon etc were described as obstacles to communication and co-operation. These phenomena and mechanisms will be more thoroughly discussed in the following section.

In addition, political acceptance of the results of the increasing influence of the environment and health department on other departments' work was obviously necessary. One important fact seemed to be that this could be done without demands for further resources. The study also showed that the local politicians had not yet seriously considered conflicts connected with sustainability and development. We found that they left much of the conflict resolution to their professional experts. For instance, in one of the municipalities there were different opinions about which assumptions the energy program should be based upon. The planning officials made a restrictive and environmentally-friendly plan based on a long-term forecast of energy resources. The engineers responsible for fulfilling the requirements of the plan argued that it should be based on calculations of realistic possibilities of economizing with different kinds of fuels and electricity. The politicians approved the plan and left it to the engineers to make the best of it. The need for restricting car traffic is another example of an issue that politicians hand over to the expert.

The different profiles of the pairs of municipalities chosen were found to be of significance for the culture of the respective local authority. In those dominated by industry and with a stable political majority, we found an action-oriented spirit. Action capability among officials was seen to exist prior to investigation capability. Thus, planning was used mainly to describe the conditions for future action and not as a means to discuss more far-reaching strategies. In the other municipalities investigation and environmental training of the public staff were seen as existing prior to action and projects. In the more 'ambitious' of the two, environmental matters like the future energy supply, management of natural resources and nature preservation were seen as integrated parts in the planning process. Jointly-held views and cross-sectional work seemed to be essential for comprehensive planning becoming an instrument for the development of ideas on sustainability.

The Significance of Competence

Two of the municipalities were selected because of their reputation as being more concerned about the environment. One interesting question is of course what constituted their relatively greater ambitions. What made them look more 'successful'? There is as yet no clear evidence that these municipalities will turn out to be more sustainable than others. The point instead seems to be that jointly-held views and cross-sectional work are essential for comprehensive planning to become an instrument for the development of ideas on sustainability. What had happened in the two more 'ambitious' local governments was that the learning processes had already started. So what are the mechanisms that affect the development of competence?

One thing is pretty clear. In the local administrative units where environmental tasks mainly follow central guiding principles, integration is not seen as essential. In the two cases where local environmental policies were well developed, the local government as a whole felt responsible for its fulfillment. Where the support among politicians for environmentally-friendly proposals is weak, it seems that planners and technicians are the ones that restrain the initiatives taken for instance by environmental and health officers and Agenda 21. But the formulation of goals for better adaptation to environmental conditions and new ways of working, aimed at the integration of sustainability aspects in all departments, was initiated by leading officials. The elected representatives to a high degree seem to depend on professional competence to reformulate the agenda. The influence from officials became stronger when different competences were able to co-operate. In our cases the leading officials at the environment and health departments have had key roles. They are the ones that have opened people up to a change in thinking, talking and acting in matters concerning future development. Behind such kinds of action lie more or less knowledge-based professional convictions about what the right thing to do is. But efforts to strengthen their own department's power also play a role. Thus it seems that competence must be seen in relation to power.

Co-operation, meaning that different perspectives on shared tasks have been considered, has been carried out in one case without alterations in the formal organization. In the other it has caused such changes. On the other hand there is also one example that combining departments does not necessarily improve the co-operation climate or make utilization of the available competence more effective – at least not in this short-term perspective. Nevertheless, when politicians felt incapable of handling certain issues, reorganization was used to create greater freedom of action for the people involved and the competence they relied on.

Discussion Based on an Extended Theoretical Framework

This preliminary analysis gave guidance and inspiration for developing and expanding the theoretical framework. Competence of course has to do with expert knowledge and expert skill. But competence can also be seen as a product of professional cultures, explaining differences in perspectives and modes of thinking and talking. The continued analysis is aimed at developing an increased understanding of the conditions necessary for going beyond prevailing limits, by means of widening perspectives, which could affect the development of competence and in turn innovations in planning practice. Theories applicable to these matters will be accounted for in the following section (see also Chapter 11 by Dovlén & Håkansson).

Perspectives on the World

Perspective is considered to be the way we view the world, the ways we construct the world in order to make it comprehensible. This in turn affects the way we view our tasks and roles. Perspectives are of course significant for the interpretation of the concept of sustainable development. They also depend on what culture a person belongs to. There are cultural differences between occupational groups. But local governments also develop specific cultural features. Political directives concerning sustainability might be unclear or not explicit. Still there is a certain sensibility among local officials to the actual scope of ideas on sustainable development. But there are also such things as professional pride, which encourage different occupational groups to make efforts to have their respective ideas accepted. And quite obviously, different professional cultures have different perspectives on environmental issues and thus on what actions or preparations for action should be seen as reasonable.

Culture and perspective are thus of great significance in understanding the concept of competence. We therefore need more knowledge about culture and discourse, especially about professional and organizational cultures – their origin and the mechanisms affecting the development inside and between cultures.

Culture, Discourse and Power

Culture and discourse are closely related concepts. Culture is considered to be the context in which a group of individuals belongs, the shared social and ideological values which form the basis of habits and routines in the interplay between the members of the group. Everyone lives and works within a culture. Discourse or language interplay represents the conceptual organization of a meaning-relationship, the jargon and the mental figures that are valid within a certain culture. Language and the context in which it is used are central to the discourse concept. Discourses develop and find different expressions in the language and concept usage but also in perspectives on life and, for example, work assignments. According to Burr (1995), the general social discourse is based on accepted usage founded on generally accepted mental figures and a structuring of different phenomena that make the world comprehensible. Language governs our thinking and consequently our actions. Discourses also arise around concepts or mental figures such as 'sustainable development', 'the market', or for that matter 'planning'. Professional discourses and discourses related to concepts are influenced by events in the surrounding world and by interaction between and within different cultures. The gradual emergence of a new occupation, like local government ecologists, and the new and different activities that constitute the work of Agenda 21 have been made possible partly because of the development of the social discourse.

Thus, discourses offer bodies of ideas or patterns of thought that enable us to understand the world. According to Burr (1995), this makes it obvious that the prevailing discourse – in society as a whole or within a particular professional group – controls or at least influences our conceptions. Discourses that are built into the structure of society and into practical work exercise power over our thinking. They are expressions of power relations in society, which lie hidden in our way of using language. The prevailing social discourse claims to represent an outlook on the world or, for instance, on knowledge that at least for the time being is considered 'true'. It denotes what is normal or 'mainstream'. However, existing discourses are constantly challenged by alternative ways of explaining the world and always risk being dethroned. The ability to reflect on and question truths constitutes a counter-force and also an opportunity to wield power.

Each discourse thus is suited to serve some interests at the expense of others. Consequently, discourses can be considered as enclosed in power relationships. Foucault (1976) considers what is usually called knowledge to be the special construction or version of a phenomenon or relationship that has been stamped as 'truth' in a certain social situation. We can wield power by utilizing discourses which make our actions appear acceptable. Therefore, he does not view power as something some people have and others do not, but as something that emerges from discourses. To define the world in a manner that makes it possible to act in the way people themselves want to is to wield power. According to Foucault, knowledge means having power over others and defining others. But he also sees power and resistance as two sides of the same coin. The power that is hidden in one discourse does not appear until it meets the resistance in another. He thus rejects the idea of power as a purely repressive force. Instead, he emphasizes power as a constructive force capable of producing and developing knowledge.

Professional Cultures and Competence

The sectors and professional groups we investigated represent, with the exception of the Agenda 21 coordinators, long and well-established traditions, deeply rooted in the cultures of the various professions and those developed within the various administrative units. Each administrative unit's culture presents certain general features, highly characterized by the dominant professional culture, but distinctive local features can also be perceived. Moreover, the local political culture plays a role in the application of professional competence and consequently influences what professional experience will be in demand.

Within the field of sociology that studies professions, the term 'professions' is defined as organized groups of experts commanding and using specialist knowledge within a certain domain. Professions confer authorization on their expert roles by referring to generally accepted values such as rationality, efficiency, and scholarliness. Within the group, a code system for ethics or behavior often evolves (Abbott, 1988). This professional culture is something that is created and transferred to the group members. Jointly-held values evolve and are upheld or change through social processes (Alvesson, 1995). These shared conceptions enable the professional group, or the different types of administrative organizations in which the group is employed, to function and they constitute a frame of reference for the activities of the individual group members.

Differences in value systems are of great importance for the growth and development of different cultures. There is reason to believe that an individual's choice of career is to some extent influenced by his or her set of values and that these values are reinforced by one's education as well as subsequent practical work experience. Individuals are not only influenced by but can also influence the culture they join when they begin their career. Sharing a value system is part of professionalism. It is taken for granted and can hardly be called into question. Co-operation between individuals/groups belonging to different professional cultures is rendered difficult by fundamental differences of values that are not openly dealt with.

Not only earlier experiences but also values will to a large extent influence what an individual perceives as a sensible or rational approach. For instance attitudes toward nature are essential (e.g. Wandén, 1993). The human being can be seen as either subordinate to nature, a part of nature, or capable of mastering nature, which leads to differing approaches to the environmental assignment. Varying outlooks on the importance of knowledge and whether it is possible by means of knowledge to arrive at what is true or false give rise to different ways of formulating and tackling problems. Here we have one of the reasons why different administrative bodies compete for the right to interpret the sustainability assignment. This in turn also affects attitudes to change and how change should be achieved. Thus strategic competence is highly valued among planners, while environmental and health officers stress the importance of a correct understanding of the problems that have to be solved. Technical and environmental protection competences have been shown to be more focussed on solving immediate problems and executing projects that could instantly bring about some kind of change. The Agenda 21 co-ordinators, which are a heterogeneous group, lack genuine or homogeneous professional traditions and seem to move more freely between visions of the sustainable society and action-based activities. The basic idea behind Agenda 21 is that the co-ordinators should be responsible for information about what the comprehensive environmental problems consist of, whereas the local environmental issues should be identified and dealt with by 'ordinary people'.

To bring about a sustainable exchange between town and country, one thing that is needed is a link between the responsibility for production or production preparation, for which technical engineers and planners are accountable, and the reproduction or upholding of ecosystem functions, for which the environmental and health officers are responsible. Such a fruitful link can be discerned within Agenda 21 activities, which are based on the conviction that life-style changes exert pressure on producers and other actors in the community. Those who work with Agenda 21 are in a way challenging administration cultures of longer standing.

Co-operation and Competition

The professions or the professional groups can be regarded as constituents of a system of professions in which each has been apportioned control of well-defined, functionally determined tasks, often supported by rules and regulations. Thus, professional groups can also be seen as power factors. They not only defend their territories but also have an interest in inventing new needs which they subsequently make sure they will meet (Florin, 1990). Changes in work responsibilities and new assignments influence developments within and between different professions. Changes can also create scope for new professions and lead to the disappearance of established professions. In such a perspective, different professional groups sometimes contend with one another for the same mandate (Abbott, 1988). As far as the conception of sustainable development is concerned, we can see competition for the preferential right of interpretation as a manifestation of the struggle of the different professional cultures for their own survival. Developing one's own competence field, too, is a means of keeping or strengthening one's own position. Abbott also points out that these ambitions can lead to conflicts within professions. Various subcultures might arise that each maintain different interpretations and development alternatives.

Professional competence can be described in terms of professional skill or the art of carrying out one's work. In occupations with long-standing traditions, the exercising of a profession is combined with a professional code. How to undertake carrying out one's work is something that is taken for granted within that person's own group. This is often called tacit knowledge (e.g. Schön, 1991). Since this knowledge does not exist on a conscious level, it cannot be communicated to others, which causes problems when different cultures or fields of competence meet to co-operate together. What these disparities in perspective really are and why they form is something that appears to be hidden or at least is not often the subject of discussion. This is particularly problematic in regard to planning. Forester (1989) is of the opinion that it is included in the duties of planners to call attention to the information and the aspects which are relevant to the problems that are to be solved. Thus it is part of the job to make choices, but these choices are seldom unbiased. Planners' outlining of alternative solutions and the choices between them cannot be understood as a mechanical consequence of studies and consequence analyses. Ramírez (1996) describes the synthesis-making process as partly intuitive.

If we regard these choices as 'intuitive', founded on tacit evaluations and perspectives, it will be difficult for those who do not share these values to participate in the process with *their* special competence. Differences in perspective therefore must be considered as a key issue both when it comes to enabling existing competence to be utilized in the best way and to bringing about development within the various fields of competence that facilitates co-operation.

Traditionalists and Innovators

Cultures could be more or less sluggish but they are not static. They keep developing and reorienting themselves, partly due to pressure from the surrounding world and partly due to mechanisms within the culture concerned. A deeper understanding of the interplay between different individuals or groups of individuals in a culture therefore seems to be essential. From the empirical material it has been possible to distinguish two categories among the officials interviewed. They are called either traditionalists or innovators. From the interaction between these two groups, we might be able to learn something new about the conditions for the development of competence.

What characterizes the traditionalists in general in the study is that they are in favor of the continuous development of their respective competence, inside the frames of reference given by their professional culture. They are defenders of the existing culture. Innovators in the study share a tendency to be more open to and active in reformulating their work assignments. They have a readiness to view their tasks from a wider perspective and are consequently more inclined to serve other administrative bodies. This makes them open to other people's perspectives. The innovators are sometimes characterized as 'enthusiasts' by our interviewees. They are looked upon as people driven by a certain emotional devotion as well as by their professional competence.

Environmental or sustainability issues in particular also have an ethical dimension. Personal opinions on the unjust distribution of resources and feelings of responsibility for future generations play an important role. Meetings of perspectives, valuations and moral responsibility seem to be of great significance for the development of competence inside and between cultures. On the other hand there is always a risk that innovators might lose their professional identity or that they will cause a split in existing cultures.

The difference between the two categories becomes particularly evident within the field of activity of the environmental and health committee, where a clear distinction between compulsory and voluntary tasks is made. Both the scope and the aim of the latter are determined by whether or not there are innovators and how they are influenced by changes in the surrounding world. Agenda 21 as a group and as a phenomenon can be regarded as innovative. The co-ordinators of the Agenda 21 activities can be viewed as a potential innovative power, perhaps as the group that really challenges traditional environmental protection by introducing life-style aspects and linking issues concerning production and reproduction. They have a potential to loosen up the boundaries between different fields of competence.

Local government ecologists, too, can in their capacity as holders of a new profession be seen as challengers of traditional nature conservation. The ecological perspective and economizing with resources are more central to their activities. Technical engineers in general regard themselves as more restricted by technical and economic realities. They often have little motivation to question the infrastructure systems which already exist and which many of them have contributed to constructing. The traditionalists are apt to take a more defensive position. Nonetheless, there are innovators in this field, too, who consider new technology, economizing resources, new kinds of fuel, and recycling as interesting challenges. Most of the traditional planners were shown to be in favor of operative planning.

The innovators found among the planners are, according to our terminology, those who include ecological aspects and who accept a moral and emotional approach to environment problems. They work for a more open planning process and try new ways of presenting platforms for political discussions and decisions. The scope available for innovators and opportunities for co-operation between innovators with different skills is crucial for rethinking in planning as well as in environmental politics.

The Different Stages of Competence Development

Dreyfus and Dreyfus (1986) present a model of how professional skill or the ability to carry out a profession undergoes different stages of development. They identify five steps: Novice, Advanced Beginner, Competent, Proficient and Expert. Competence in the sense of the art of carrying out one's profession is thus influenced by the relationship between theoretical knowledge – practical experience – capacity for reflection. We find our innovators among those who have reached the most advanced stages. Competence development and innovation can therefore be said to be connected with whether professionals within the various administrative units are given opportunities for attaining the security in their professional roles which leads to the ability to reconsider and question work assignments. Schön (1991) also speaks of 'reflection-in-action' as a means of developing competence, particularly in creative professions.

New concepts, which are introduced into the general dialogue of the 'sustainable development' type, can be regarded as new mental imagery around which various discourses arise. Every culture tries to add new thoughts and concepts to the social discourse within the current patterns of thought. It is reasonable to imagine that each such attempt at assimilation passes through different stages. It is a question of processes in which we might speak of certain general patterns but in which it is impossible to give a verdict on what the processes will result in. In later stages of these processes, the perspectives will meet, and in these encounters, personal commitment and true enthusiasts play an important role (e.g., Sjöström, 1990).

The final phase may imply institutionalization, where new routines, based on certain patterns of thought, will be integrated.

Implications for Rethinking in Planning

Planning as an Arena for Communication and the Development of Knowledge

The idea of planning as an instrument with a capacity to guide and control societal development in accordance with clearly stated ends is no longer valid. Little by little, insights that the world is constantly subject to change far beyond this kind of control have made rethinking in planning necessary. Today it is the transition process itself that has to be handled intellectually and practically, despite continuously increasing complexity, unclear ends and inevitable uncertainty (Wirén, 1998).

In modern planning theory, planning is described as communicative action (e. g. Forester, 1989; Healey, 1997; Sager, 1996). From this point of view, it is in the interaction between different parties – experts and politicians as well as entrepreneurs and other stakeholders – that new knowledge and new ideas are developed. A deeper understanding of both preconditions and future needs in the local society by means of discussions and talk is basic in communicative planning. It is also in these conversations that different proposals of action, projects or strategies are expected to emerge. According to these theories, consensus is reached by means of discussions or negotiations.

If we want planning to work as an instrument to prepare the local society for a more sustainable future, different kinds of competence have to be involved in the planning process. There are at least two reasons for that. Firstly, it is essential because sustainable development is a complex and even ambiguous concept, which requires a comprehensive professional approach from start, when the program is discussed. It is not sufficient to collect expert opinions on proposals that have already been designed. Secondly, planning offers an arena where different perspectives can confront one another. It is easy to imagine that professionals not provoked by arguments belonging to other professional cultures tend to suggest ways of action that are familiar to them and that require skills they themselves can provide. The planning process thus has the potential to encourage learning processes and the development of competence. However, to be able to discuss possible ways of adapting the planning process to these circumstances, it is necessary to look deeper into the motives and driving forces among the parties involved, that could encourage or hinder such renewal.

Planning in general is expected to adopt a holistic perspective, by integrating different aspects and interests. But different perspectives or discourses can not easily be brought together into one holistic approach that suits all parties. As we have seen, some discourses might be superior and others subordinate. Discourses will be suppressed when they are apprehended as threats to the prevailing discourse. When different perspectives confront one another, openings might develop meaning the establishment of a mutual understanding of perspectives and respect for differences in professional skill. But this is not always the case. Communicative planning is based on the idea of dialogue leading to consensus. Emphasis is placed on the ability to listen and understand different points of view, not to persuade each other. The point is that consensus could be reached, not that all involved parties think alike. With regard to the fact that power relations play an important role in the traditional planning process – as in most kinds of activities – the ideal dialogue situation must be seen as problematic.

The general idea is that the planning process involves co-ordination of information and the balancing of different interests and demands. This might be fruitful if the situation can be arranged as an open-minded meeting of perspectives. For this to occur the roles of the participants have to be clearly formulated. The professional skills and the interests represented among the participants must be seen as equivalent. A prerequisite for this is that each expert group is able and willing to develop its specific or unique qualifications as well as general views and an understanding of different perspectives. However, when it comes to planning for sustainable development, the roles are not so easily defined. There is for instance no single occupational group or interest group entrusted to defend the needs of future generations.

As described earlier, there is also competition going on between different groups to get hold of the privilege both of defining the problem and arguing for reasonable solutions. We can also expect situations to occur where the conflicts between different perspectives are really deep. The idea that planning has to result in consensus might then lead to restraints on views and proposed actions that are seen as challenges to prevailing valuations. The consensus perspective in planning thus can be seen as an obstacle to change. It is only if the existence of differences in basic values is considered that processes of renewal can start. For this to happen, new and strict rules have to be established in order to guarantee enough scope not only for suppressed discourses but also for discourses that might have no representative in the planning process.

As stated above, the roles of different expert groups could be more clearly defined if each of them develops its unique qualities and simultaneously its ability to understand and respect other groups. This might be expected from experts that have reached the higher levels in the skill acquisition model according to Dreyfus and Dreyfus (1986) or perhaps from the innovators as described above. But how should we then understand the specific role of planners? Their unique qualification can be described as having the capacity to handle matters of concern for the future. They use methods that can be adapted to situations characterized by a great deal of uncertainty. Planners are also known to have a strategic capacity. But the role of planners also normally includes establishing the rules for the planning process. This means that they take on the role as co-ordinators of the process and at the same time function as synthesizers or producers of plan proposals. But planners are not value-neutral. They also have perspectives of their own. They have their blind spots and they are in favor of certain interests. They also normally work very close to their political principals.

These circumstances place planners in an almost unique power position, which undermines the idea of undistorted communication. In addition and as mentioned before, difficulties in communicating planning methods and valuations may make this position still stronger. These dual roles of planners – as experts with the qualifications mentioned above and as co-ordinators – can hardly be seen as compatible with the idea of planning as a potential arena for perspectives to meet on an equal basis and for learning processes to start. Therefore, the role of planners as co-ordinators of the planning process has to be questioned, especially as planning education as a rule does not include training in the management of processes.

The Roles of Politicians in the Planning Process

As long as planning is understood as a rational means-to-ends process, knowledge-based information and professional skills are central. Policy making also makes sense as it is expected to provide ideas on ends. Adopting the idea of planning as communicative action affects the way we view the role of politicians and local policy making. In any event politicians have to take on the role as those ultimately responsible for the management and development of the local territory. They thus have to give their approval to a proposed action based on consensus in the planning process. And if consensus is not achieved, conflicting ideas have to be judged by the local government executive committee. But, as we have seen, politicians tend to leave considerations about reasonable strategies for sustainable development to experts among the officials.

Nonetheless, if these matters were seen as being of great political interest, we could not expect politicians to hand over the initiative in these matters so easily. Obviously, comprehensive planning and prevention of environmental damage are judged as being less crucial than the more immediate issues that dominate the everyday life of politicians. These matters also attract more attention from the public. So, even if the planning process could be arranged in a successful way, it does not guarantee successful implementation. The many minor decisions that are made and that often concern construction permits, investments in transportation facilities and so on might in the long run lead to consequences that do not at all correspond to the intentions laid out in the comprehensive plan. Furthermore, it might be frustrating to politicians that comprehensive planning as a matter of fact has a weak guiding capacity. This might be the result of the aim to have plans rule matters that in fact are mainly ruled by forces outside the planning as well as the political arena.

Two main problems concerning the role of politicians in planning for sustainable development therefore could be distinguished – the incapability of planning first to make these matters politically urgent and second to guarantee a certain political influence over the management and development of the local territory. From a political point of view, the consequences of the fact that plans do not have the capacity to force things to happen could be to have plans work as instruments for deciding and regulating what is not allowed to happen. Apparently, planning could become a more effective instrument for local policies if its ambitions were limited to matters that the local government is able to control. At least it seems that some kind of reflection on the role of the executive committee in relation to communicative planning has to be made.

The Role of Social Science Research in the Reshaping of Municipal and Regional Planning

The point made here is that planning theory until now has to only a very small extent taken into consideration the dynamics in the planning process and the competition among professions to take or keep the initiative in planning. Too little attention has been paid to the fact that knowledge is not value-neutral. The emphasis on planning as a consensus-shaping process gives little scope for deliberation and the identification of value conflicts in planning. What we have tried to show is that tensions between different approaches to planning as well as to sustainable development under certain circumstances can give rise to openings in the form of learning processes and new ways of thinking, leading to a renewal of planning practice.

The starting point for this research project has been the idea that comprehensive land-use planning at the municipal level could assist in the transformation of society into a more sustainable balance with nature. Some of the problems connected with the reform of planning practice in this direction have been discussed in this chapter. One of the basic reasons for many of these problems and the confusion about the role of research on planning seems to be that, even if the idea of planning as communicative action is widely accepted, in practice there are still images lingering of planning as an entirely rational process. Thus, when the reshaping of planning is discussed, the conversation often tends to turn into a discussion on how society should be reconstructed or reorganized. This also affects research on planning for sustainable development. What has been requested is thus the development of knowledge about the needs for restructuring society together with methods and models for handling these issues in planning.

But planning research also has the capacity to contribute to developing and deepening different ways of viewing and understanding phenomena in planning practice. This has been the purpose of the work described in this chapter. According to Skantze (1999), there is one more step between the description of how something is, how it can be viewed, understood or explained and what has to be done. This is where the scientific results are worked through and integrated into the context of practical work. In the continued research program this will be done in dialogue with practitioners who are involved in planning practice as well as in reconstructing institutions related to planning. As a result of this process we also expect new urgent research questions to evolve. Thus, planning research could contribute to the start of a process of rethinking in planning. But, as Skantze reminds us, the power to act, the responsibility for judgments and considerations in the context of planning practice, belongs to the practitioner, whose capacity as a reflective and learning human being has to be respected.

Notes

1   The UN report 'Our Common Future', 1987 and the UN Conference on Environment and Development, Rio, 1992.

2   The study is part of a research project at the Division of Regional Planning, the Royal Institute of Technology, Stockholm, called *The Municipality and the Territory*. Preliminary results from this project have been published in Asplund et al, 1997. An English summary has been presented in Asplund, 1999. The latter also contains an outline for a developed platform for the research project.

3   Two separate ranking lists were used, which were made up by environmental journals, each using a set of criteria to assess environmental management in Swedish local governments.

4 At the UNCED in 1992 a convention was signed by the UN member states, stating that local agendas for sustainable development during the next century should be worked out and presented by the end of 1996. In Sweden local governments have been responsible for the co-ordination of programs more or less set by the public.

5 The Natural Resources Act, which came into force at the same time, introduced demands for ecological considerations in different kinds of decisions and works as an 'umbrella' for, among others, the Planning and Building Act.

References

Abbott, A. (1988), *The System of Professions, An Essay on the Division of Expert Labour*, The University of Chicago Press, Chicago.

Alvesson, M. (1995), *Kommunikation, makt och organisation*, Norstedts Ekonomi, Göteborg.

Asplund, E. (1999), *The Municipality and the Territory. Summing up, Reflecting and Looking Forward Halfway in a Research Project on Competence for Sustainable Development*, TRITA-IP FR 99–55, Department of Infrastructure and Planning, KTH, Stockholm.

Asplund, E., Dovlén, S., Håkansson. M. and Orrskog, L. (1997), *Räcker kompetensen?* TRITA-IP FR 97–27, Department of Infrastructure and Planning, KTH, Stockholm.

Burr, V. (1995), *An Introduction to Social Constructionism*, Routledge, London and New York.

Dreyfus, H. and Dreyfus, S. (1986), *Mind over Machine – The Power of Human Intuition and Expertise in the Era of the Computer*, The Free Press, New York.

Falkenmark, M. (1997), 'Från insikt till praktik. Det naturlagsstyrda samspelet', in Hilding-Rydevik, T. (ed.), *Samspelet mark–vatten–miljö, Fysisk planering för att nå samhälleliga mål*, Forskningsrådsnämnden, Stockholm.

Florin, C. (1990), *Kampen om katedern. Feminiserings- och professionaliseringsprocessen inom svenska folkskolans lärarkår 1860–1906*, Almqvist och Wicksell International, Stockholm and JÄMO.

Forester, J. (1989), *Planning in the Face of Power*, California University Press, Los Angeles, California.

Foucault, M. (1976), *The History of Sexuality: An Introduction*, Penguin, Harmondsworth.

Healey, P. (1997), *Collaborative Planning. Shaping Places in Fragmented Societies*, Macmillian Press Ltd, London.

Ramírez, J.L. (1996), 'Planeringsteori som humanvetenskaplig aktivitet', in G. Olsson (ed.), *Poste restante – En avslutningsbok*, Nordplan, Stockholm.

Sager, T. (1996), *Communicative Planning Theory*, Avebury, Aldershot.

Schön, D.A. (1991), *The Reflective Practitioner. How Professionals Think in Action*, Avebury, Aldershot.

Sjöström, U. (1990), *Tjernobyl – och sedan? Skall människan eller händelseförloppet välja framtid?* Rapport nr 49. Pedagogiska institutionen, Stockholms universitet.

Skantze, A. (1999), *Om relationen mellan samhällsvetenskaplig forskning och praktik. Några funderingar kring en problematik*, TRITA-IP FR 99–61, Department of Infrastructure and Planning, KTH, Stockholm.

Wandén, S. (1993), 'Ideologiska kontroverser i miljöfrågan', *Rapport från Natur-vårdsverket*, No. 4196, Stockholm.

Wirén, E. (1998), *Planering för säkerhets skull*, Studentlitteratur, Lund.

11 The Role of Professions in Environmental Planning

SYLVIA DOVLÉN
MARIA HÅKANSSON

Aim and Scope

This chapter analyzes the views of environmental professionals on possibilities and obstacles for the integration of environmental issues in the planning process. The aim is to provide an empirical picture of the practical experience of some Swedish environmental planners. We will focus on some of the problems that arise when new knowledge and perspectives are to be integrated in the planning process. Our aim is to describe the tension between different professional actors and describe some of the conditions for professional interaction and professional development.

We have chosen to study environmental professions because we see their knowledge and perspectives as necessary conditions for forming a basis for spatial planning, but also because environmental issues nowadays are supposed to be integrated in the planning process. Planning for sustainability (Orrskog, 1993) has become a concept in which environmental issues are one important aspect. The link between environmental issues and planning is not new. At least for the last 100 years planning has been seen by representatives of health and environmental matters as an instrument for preventing problems caused by the built environment (Törnqvist, 1961). In Sweden today, environmental issues constitute a basis for planning thought and planning activity in building and planning legislation. Thus, the aim of environmental planning is not only to limit the environmental effects of human activities, but also to support sustainable development. The actors in society will furthermore have differing perspectives on the importance of environmental issues, what they consist of and how they should be handled.

The theoretical framework takes as its starting point communicative planning theory, which emphasizes the interaction between actors in the planning process (Healey, 1997). This collaborative process mainly focuses on the interaction between the government and other actors, and takes into account public participation in the planning and policy process. The roles of professionals, their inherent diversity of interest and their impact on the planning and policy process are not well developed in the literature. We want to provide an increased understanding of factors which impact the interaction between professionals involved in the planning process and how the professional interests are balanced. Our research question is then what experience professionals with expert knowledge about environmental issues have of options and obstacles in practical planning situations.

The chapter is based on two ongoing studies[1] of environmental planning professions. The main research method applied in the studies is abductive. It entails starting with a theoretical approach to the research question. The theoretical framework is gradually developed by moving back and forth between empirical and theoretical analysis (Alvesson and Sköldberg, 1994). The method used for gathering the empirical material in both studies is semi-structured interviews of about two hours, aimed at acquiring a description of the interviewees' work situation and work experience. The number of interviews in the studies depends on when theoretical saturation is reached, i.e. when additional interviews do not provide new perspectives or themes.

A collection of questions as a basis for the interviews is used; the objective is to have the interviewees speak as openly as possible. Each interview is tape-recorded and transcribed. The method allows the interviewees to provide their own reactions and, where necessary, corrections of any misunderstandings after the interview has been analyzed (Kvale, 1997).

In this text, we have chosen to let two persons, one from each study, represent common themes raised in the nine interviews carried out. These examples are linked to a theoretical framework, which has been developed during the studies. The two interviewees are called Sven and Linnéa (Håkansson, 1999; Dovlén, 1999). Sven's profession is that of environmental and health inspector. He has a leading position today in a middle-sized municipality. He works mainly with environmental aspects in strategic planning. Linnéa works in the department of planning of a small municipality as the local government ecologist. She has an education in natural sciences, including ecology and geology. The position of local government ecologist is a rather new occupation, which has been developed during the last few decades. Sven and Linnéa represent experiences with environmental work at the local level, and perspectives and views on the integration of environmental issues in planning, with themselves actors in the process.

Planning as Interaction and Change

In the history of planning theory, there was a turn toward a more interpretative and communicative approach starting in the 1970s, in line with the intellectual ideas evolving in the humanities and social sciences – the post-modern influence. According to that theory it is recognized that planning is an interactive process, undertaken in a social context, rather than a purely technical process of design, analysis and management. These theories may be labeled communicative, argumentative or interpretative. The field has many different positions, but generally the communicative approach in planning theory focuses on social processes through which ways of thinking, ways of valuing and ways of acting are constructed by participants. This means that planning work both is embedded in its context of social relations through its day-to-day practices, and has a capacity to challenge and change these relations through the approach to these practices (Healey, 1997). Healey places the concept of culture centrally in her discussion of collaborative planning, as a key to understanding our world and the prerequisite for change, as we live in a multi-cultural world.

Communicative planning theory focuses on how thoughts and assumptions are changing through processes between people in social interaction. To get a picture of what this may imply, we use the field of theory called social constructionism, where language, discourse, knowledge, power and change are important concepts. According to Burr (1995), who gives an overview of the field, language is constantly changing and varied in its meaning. It is a site of variability, disagreement and potential conflict. Language is also a form of action which is crucial for change, both personal and social. Language is structured into discourses, which are sets of meanings, metaphorical representations, images, stories and statements. Discourses work as frames of reference, and different discourses represent one object in different ways. Each produces a particular version of events. Some discourses enjoy widespread acceptance, as common sense or a 'truth'. They will then have political implications and are connected to the way society is organized and run. Burr also states that change is possible because humans are capable of critically analyzing the discourses that frame their lives and claiming or resisting them. Change becomes possible by opening up marginalized and repressed discourses, making them available as alternatives, challenging the prevailing knowledge.

Both communicative planning theory and social constuctionism point out that common-sense knowledge is crucial for power relations in the interaction process. Opening up marginalized voices is therefore a key action for alternative discourses, for change of perspectives and action according to new thoughts. But, as Sager (1996) argues, perspectives which diverge radically from the existing policies, and which probably demand substantial change, will have difficulties taking part in the process under equal conditions, even when conflicting interests and perspectives are recognized and accepted as a natural part of social interaction. How then can the planning process work as an arena where marginalized voices are given space to formulate arguments? And what conditions are to prevail when different professions are supposed to interact in a collaborative planning process?

Healey (1997) stresses that planning has traditionally focused on the hard infrastructure of formal rules, for example laws and organization, without considering the mechanism through which the soft infrastructure of institutional capacity-building comes about, and therefore deliberately avoids considerations of how an interactive practice develops. Our aim is accordingly to focus on conditions for an interactive practice that is linked to professionals and their work. We will stress some of the conditions for interaction between different professional groups in planning practice and point at possibilities of professional development.

In the following three sections the theoretical framework and analysis are presented. The main theoretical theme is professions in interaction. This includes systems of professions, action strategies and professional roles. In the following section are the theoretical considerations linked to examples of Linnéa's and Sven's experiences related to themes from the interviews (Dovlén, 1999; Håkansson, 1999). In the third section, a case-based analysis on professional development is presented, which includes the themes of professional cultures, learning processes and reflection.

Professions in Interaction

Systems of Professions

What is a profession? Traditionally, the definition of professions is linked to attributes like academic education, legitimization, ethical codes, journals and vocational associations. But the definition may also focus on the use of knowledge, and the necessary degree of expertise. One example is the rather loose definition given by Abbott (1988): 'Professions are exclusive occupational groups applying somewhat abstract knowledge to particular cases.' As skillfulness is stressed, this definition implies that most occupational groups can be treated as professions. Later in the text the use of knowledge will be discussed further. Anyhow, the task – the work to be done – is the core for all professions and their development. Abbott stresses that the professions both create their work, and are created by themselves in an interactive process. A profession is linked to a work area, for example, by jurisdiction given by the state through legislation, but there are also work area choices made by professionals.

When changes occur in the work area, such as when new tasks arise, occupational groups have to widen or deepen their knowledge; otherwise other groups may take over all or parts of their tasks. Besides change in knowledge, other strategies such as changes in working methods may be used to maintain a professional position.

According to Flyvbjerg (1998) action strategies can, in general, be categorized into three different types. Firstly, there are considerations about what means are needed in order to reach a given goal. According to the development of planning theory (see for example Friedmann (1987)), the first category is close to the traditional strategy, technical and instrumental planning.

The second category of strategies presented by Flyvbjerg (1998) includes those cases where some part of any given interaction will involve how one party believes the other party will act, which in this chapter is called negotiation strategy. Thirdly, the confrontation strategy involves the procedures used in a confrontation to disarm the other party with the aim of getting the adversary to give up.

In an existing professional area, subgroups may develop because of changes in the work area, which consequently might form new professions over time. Sub-groups might develop for example when new tasks arise, when old tasks become re-formulated or when the profession has to deal with problems which demand new kinds of solutions and changes in established perspectives. Professions can thus be said to form systems (Abbott, 1988) which link professions with tasks in a work area.

Changes and movements in one profession will then affect other professions. Competition inside and between professions will then contribute to development of the professions. This competition can be initiated on the local as well as on the national level. Larger social forces might also affect the development. One way to develop a profession is to obtain control over emerging work areas (Abbott, 1988).

Professional Roles

Professional development at the individual level is influenced both by the individual's personality and education and occupational experience. Education constitutes a basis and framework for the professional role expected, shaping fundamental assumptions related to work and constituting a platform for that person's encounters with professional life. The role and assumptions of the individual are strengthened and further developed in occupational life by practice. The role grows stronger over time and more and more of the assumptions, values and frameworks become taken for granted. The person and the professional become more tightly integrated. Demands for changes in the role can then be seen as threats both to the profession and to the individual, thus calling for action to maintain the role and position.

In a planning situation, as in worklife in general, actors have fundamental assumptions which impact their interpretation of the situation and their subsequent action. Most of these assumptions are taken for granted, not reflected in the day-to-day work. Healey (1997) stresses the recognition that the finely woven system of the assumptions and practices taken for granted gives the relations of power a potential to work.

Changes then require transformation of the cultural frames of reference of all those involved. A change in, for example, legislation will not alone solve the problem it supposed to handle, without also changes in values. This is in line with Abbott (1988), who argued that we can not expect that general forces like bureaucratization and changes in knowledge, for example, by education, will have uniform professional effects. The effects are shaped by internal and system forces as well as by the choices of professionals.

Professions in Planning

The discussion of professional roles involved in planning theory is primarily limited to the role of planners. Forester (1989) in particular has developed this discussion. He refers to planners as 'a broad array of future-oriented actors'. Planners further work on problems, and with people within political institutions. The solving of problems depends to a large extent on the interests, perceptions, commitments, and understanding of other actors. We can conclude that Forester emphasizes that planners have their interpretations of the world as a starting-point in solving problems. Yet in Forester's definition of 'future-oriented actors' many different professions are included. Planners are accordingly not to be handled as a uniform group as Forester asserts in his deliberation.

Forester (1989) deals with power and points out in particular that planners should be aware of distorted information. He then introduces a strategic actor called the progressive planner and a method of planning called communication action. Progressive planners have to be aware that misinformation is often not accidental in planning, but rather will be a systematic problem rooted in political-economic structures. The systematic misinformation has then to be dealt with as a systematic problem. Forester suggests that planners who responded to systematic misinformation are progressive planners and that they will need technical, organizational and negotiation skills if conflicts are to be addressed without them pretending that structural power imbalances do not exist. He recognizes that the planning profession has not traditionally embraced these kinds of diplomatic skills.

The analysis also points out the problems of planners who hold more than one role in the process. They thus act as mediators, listening to and interpreting other actors' standpoints, while at the same time they have the role of negotiator for specific interests, and are simultaneously engaged as experts. Planners will then possess certain power themselves, stemming from their multitude of roles.

Forester (1989) accordingly points out that planners not only shape facts, but also shape attention, which they consider includes attention both to facts and future possibilities. Planners 'are actual pragmatic critics who must make selective arguments and therefore influence what other people learn about, not by technically calculating means to ends or error signals, but by organizing attention carefully to projects possibilities, organizing for practical political purposes and organizational ends'. The daily actions of planners are communicative in practice. They also practice 'communicative actions that build relationships, open possibilities, and shape others' interpretations of meaning and opportunity, of 'I can' or 'I can not''. Planners belong to structures of power and thus of distorted communication; they selectively channel information and attention, and systematically shape participation, services, and promises. According to Forester (1989) this means that planners have ethical and political responsibilities.

A gap to note in Forester's description of planners is that like other professions they struggle to support their position and status. This also raises questions about the conditions for co-operation when different professions are expected to contribute in the communicative planning process. In an ongoing interview study with Swedish planners who are known for their work with sustainable aspects in the planning process (Nilsson, 1999), this is one of the tentative results. The planners see that issues of sustainability have been growing during the last ten years as a part of their work; in this way they are able to strengthen their position.

Professional Experiences – Two Interview Studies

This chapter is based on two ongoing Ph D studies. In this phase of thesis work, both writers are using interviews to collect empirical material. Two of the interviews carried out so far, namely those with Linnéa and Sven, have been used here to exemplify common themes in the material. Linnéa is one of the interviewees in a study of local government ecologists and their role in the integration of environmental issues in land use planning (Dovlén, 1999).

Up to this point, six interviews have been conducted. The criteria for the interviewees chosen were that they should have more than ten years of experience in working with environmental issues in land use planning. Three of them are women and three are men. They all work in municipalities of a different character and size. In the interviews the focus is placed on how they work, and what action strategies they use. Sven is one interviewee in a sample of three included in a study of professions involved in environmental work at the local level (Håkansson, 1999). This study is focused on professions which have traditionally worked in the environmental area, environmental and health officers.

In this interview study, three leading officials have been interviewed to date. They have been chosen because of their reputation for being engaged in planning matters, and for reformulating the traditional task to some extent. They were all educated in the 1970s and thereby represent a period when environmental issues received higher priority on the political agenda. The interviews dealt with their occupational life experiences, from their choice of education to today's situation. In both studies interviews will be added over time, based on the analyses of the previous interviews.

Both studies have their starting point in a study of four Swedish municipalities and their competence for environmental planning (Asplund et al, 1997). In that study, the differences in perspectives between professional groups were highlighted as one important factor in interaction in work situations.

The study also shows that one important condition for the integration of environmental issues in planning is the environmental professional's ability to communicate environmental knowledge.

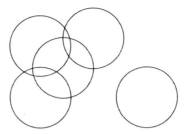

Figure 11.1 Perspectives held by different groups might be both overlapping and separated, as illustrated by the circles above

In the ongoing studies, focus is accordingly on the perspectives of environmental professions. Qualitative interviews are used as this is a valuable method for producing new knowledge and insight on existing perspectives. Snapshots from Linnéa's and Sven's stories, and analyses of them are presented below (Dovlén, 1999; Håkansson, 1999). The aim is to discuss the knowledge of environmental professionals, their perspectives and their roles in interaction with other professionals in practical planning situations.

The professional role, as mentioned earlier, might also be influenced by the professional's education, as well as work experience and the overall development in society. Linnéa describes how she has certain goals for her professional work given through her education. She believes that her individual objectives have now become goals of society as a whole as a result of policy statements about sustainable development. Linnéa is conscious about different interpretations of these goals and she prioritizes her work in order to communicate her profession's interpretations of the concept. At the same time, she stresses how her personal and professional goals have changed as a result of her work experience.

The position of local government ecologist was created in the mid-1980s. According to Linnéa, the new building and planning legislation from 1987 (PBL and NRL)[2] was the reason for the town architect's initiative to bring Linnéa's competence to the planning office. When she started, she had great difficulties. She had no clearly defined job description. She had to, as she expresses it, fight her way into the organization using her knowledge. Earlier experience in another municipality, where she had the support of her colleagues, helped her to deal with the situation. Linnéa herself has been active in formulating her tasks and role, and she has made an active choice to work with the integration of environmental issues in the planning process. PLB and NRL have provided guidelines for her work. She feels that NRL and the new demands for planning go together well with her competence.

Through her work Linnéa has gained respect among her colleagues and politicians for the knowledge which her profession represents. She stresses the importance of integrity and courage in one's professional role: 'Courage to express your opinion, courage to see your professional role in the planning process as a representative of environmental knowledge'. Linnéa has learned planning through co-operation with the town architect: 'I have learned planning as a skill by working with planning and by working with the town architect; we have supported each other'.

The interview-studies show how Sven and Linnéa use different strategies to meet different conditions that limit or support their professional work. Some of these conditions can be found in the level of competition between professions. They are also related to conflicting perspectives and differing languages. Sven brings up the problem of changes in power relations between different professions, in this case following a re-organization. In terms of the theories presented above we can interpret this as a case of competition between two professional groups in the same work area.

The main cause for this intensified competition was a change in the department's task, in this case by a political decision to give higher priority to environmental perspectives. A unification of the building and planning department and the environmental and health department then led to conflicts, which according to Sven are related to the balance of power and status as well as the differing perspectives and cultures. The political decision to give environmental issues a more central role disturbed the system of tasks.

The building and planning department has by tradition had a higher status than the environmental and health department. Sven's interpretation is that the planners at the building and planning department think of work on Agenda 21 and other recently established environmental tasks as just occasional and temporary projects They also claim that they are the ones who have the competence for an integration of environmental issues in planning.

In the light of theories on systems of professions (Abbott, 1988), the actions of the planners at the building and planning department seem to be a way of attempting to keep their position. Following the categorization action strategies of Flyvbjerg (1998), their behavior was closest to a confrontation strategy, which may entail an attempt to diminish knowledge of others, or neglect it. As of yet, we only have Sven's interpretation of the situation, and we can be sure that he also uses strategies to strengthen his position. His story thus indicates that he feels as if he is representing a marginalized voice. Sven describes the work situation as a battle of values. Different concepts of the world clash with each other, each actor wanting to keep his own perspective and get it established and generally accepted. 'It is a game. You have to be strong and believe in your mission, and be aware of the differing perspectives and the struggle to keep that position in order to succeed.'

As we learned from the theories of professions, differentiation also can take place inside a profession. One strategy might be different actions to strengthen a profession's own task. The former leading official in Sven's department seems to have had a strategy of deepening knowledge, to get more specialized, while Sven instead has the strategy of broadening the task, increasing the scope of it. Sven thinks his view on the task has been an advantage for him, and that the former leading official would have had more support in the organization taking a broader view. Sven's view is better adopted to the overall situation in the local government. A broader formulation makes the task more interesting for other groups, not just something for specialists. Legitimization of the profession in society has also stressed a broad definition in line with the rather vague concept of sustainable development, which today is used more generally. Sven's promotion to leading official might be a sign that his view, at least at that moment in time, fits in well with the overall development of the organization.

Professionals might use individual strategies to maintain or develop their position, and these can be aimed at defining the task and taking over from other actors. Linnéa does not recommend using confrontation strategies, but she does sometimes run into conflict situations when she pushes environmental issues. Linnéa does not give examples of how she uses confrontation strategies in her professional work. One colleague who calls Linnéa the 'government gynecologist' is nonetheless an example of how such a strategy is used against her. Different kinds of negotiation techniques have become Linnéa's most important strategy. She negotiates for environmental issues and ideas. She argues, for instance, that the planning committee in her local government should have environmental competence. When she meets different professionals she uses different language to support her communication and to create space for a constructive working climate.

A great deal of Linnéa's struggle is about the possibility of sitting at the negotiating table. She needs to be diplomatic; otherwise she runs the risk of being excluded. She is sure that, with aid of her knowledge, she can argue for environmental issues if she can get to the table. Sven also describes the same experience. Both describe the way they have been forced to struggle to create space for serious discussion about the environmental perspective. They also describe a number of events that have occurred during the last 10–15 years.

The environmental perspective has now been included in the traditional discourse in society: 'Nowadays it is possible to talk about environmental issues without being thought of as ridiculous'. Both stress that it is important to gain respect for ecological knowledge if environmental goals are to be reached in the field of planning. They also emphasize the importance of the work to understand different professional languages, and they are convinced of the potential for further promotion of environmental issues and that they can be a part of that change. This certainty of belief has been a driving force in their working life, despite the resistance they have met.

Case-Based Analyses of Professional Development

Professional Cultures

A fruitful way to describe the position of a profession is to use the metaphor of culture. Every group can be said to develop a culture to meet specific problems and handle situations they usually face (Frost, 1985). A culture includes shared valuations, fundamental assumptions, definitions of work and working methods, a common language, myths, and codes for behavior (Schein, 1992). Culture mainly rises from the shared needs of the members by interaction processes (Alvesson, 1995). It is affected by education and practice, as well as by personal qualities and the institutional and social context.

A professional culture can thus be characterized by the customs conceived and maintained by a profession. The main arena for the culture to develop and change is the day-to-day work. Here, the group will meet similar situations over and over again, and develop routines and ways to handle problems, until these are no longer consciously reflected and become taken for granted. The culture is also framed in the educational situation, and by other institutions linked to the profession. The culture includes the prerequisite for how to view the world and work, how to identify problems and possible solutions. The common language, the accepted way to use words and expressions and the interpretation of their meaning, are then important (Morgan, 1996; Schein, 1992). The professional role is thus maintained and developed by the culture. In times of transition when there are demands made for new working methods and new approaches arises these assumptions can be obstacles. That is mainly because of the deep-rooted acceptance, and the fact that the fundamental assumptions have become invisible to the members of the profession (Schein, 1992).

Professional Development as a Learning Process

Professionals become skilled in interpreting the situations they face. This skill usually develops as an intuitive process, through experience and natural ability, and emerges from an almost subconscious level. To be able to read situations in a successful way, the professional has to be open-minded and flexible to allow the creation of a wide range of possible solutions. A less effective problemsolver often uses the same standpoint all the time, more like a routine, which does not offer effective solutions (Morgan, 1996). Learning thus becomes important for the development of roles and professions, as well as for understanding other perspectives. The learning process is also present in the communicative planning theory, where communication is emphasized as a way for learning to take place (Healey, 1997).

An experienced professional might develop into an expert. Experts do not just have knowledge about rules and facts. It is also important for them to know how to use the knowledge, when to use it and why to act in a special way. Dreyfus and Dreyfus (1986) describe it as the difference between know-that and know-how. Know-that comprises rules and facts, simple basic information, while know-how is intuitive and taken for granted in its nature.

For know-how to develop, practice is necessary. Dreyfus and Dreyfus present a model for skill acquisition which consists of five steps: novice, advance beginner, competent performer, proficient performer and expert/excellent performer. The novices and advanced beginners depend on rules and regulations in their practice, and every step leads to an increased ability to apply rules and facts to the actual situation. With increased experience, these become taken for granted. An intuitional and experience-based fluid performance is the selection criterion for an excellent performer – an expert. The development requires practice and considerable concrete experience in real situations as well as reflection. Time is thus needed for expertise to develop. Personal engagement is also an important factor for professional development. A skilled professional is emotionally involved in the work and in the product, and feels to an increasing degree responsible for the results of actions and decisions. For a beginner just following the rules, personal responsibility and involvement are limited. For a professional, to make intuition work, the activities have to be meaningful, interesting and important.

Learning Processes through Reflection

To develop as a professional, reflection is needed. Dreyfus and Dreyfus (1986) called this the reflection phase deliberation, which is not calculative problem solving and analyzing of the situation into context-free elements, but rather critically reflecting on one's own intuition. This demands an open-minded way of being and acting, which allows the professional to look at the situation from more than one perspective. Otherwise there will be a risk of tunnel vision, leading to failure in recognizing new and more fruitful perspectives. Schön (1995) uses the term reflection-in-action and states that this is central to how practitioners cope with divergent situations in practice.

Through reflection the professional can bring to the surface and criticize the tacit understanding that has grown up around the repetitive experiences of a specialized practice, and can make new sense of the situations of uncertainty or uniqueness which he may experience. According to Schön (1995) several modes of reflection may be possible for the professional. These include an understanding of tacit norms or an appreciation behind a judgment, or of strategies and theories implicit in a pattern of behavior. They can relate to the feeling for a situation which leads to the adoption of a particular course of action or to the way in which a problem is framed, or on the professional role within a larger institutional context.

According to Forester (1989) organizations are structures of practical communication action, and they not only produce instrumental results, but also reproduce social and political relations. As organizations develop or restrict information, they shape their members' knowledge and beliefs. Just as significantly, they shape other actor's abilities to act and organize. Healey (1997) stresses that communicative planning effort seeks to debate a range of claims, but these claims come from different thought-worlds and are particular and incommensurable. Healey suggests that if we can learn more about the dialogical process of intercultural communication, we might be able to build consensus which has a multi-cultural reach, making sense and giving voice to the different culturally-constructed claims for attention which arise in a place.

Healey (1997) states that planning is a social process through which ways of thinking, ways of forming values and ways of acting are actively constructed by participants. She argues that the institutional approach would put more emphasis on how people change their ways of doing and seeing things, and thereby undertake their activities within a changed frame of reference. This will allow learning during policy development and implementation processes.

Learning Processes and Integration of Environmental Issues

Linnéa and Sven emphasize several important conditions for the integration of environmental issues in the planning process. For instance, they emphasize the importance of respect between different professional groups and the possibility of being heard and giving voice to arguments. They also note that good working relationships between different professional with different knowledge and perspectives create favorable conditions for learning processes (Dovlén, 1999; Håkansson, 1999).

Linnéa describes in different ways the need to be open-minded and reflective. She has gradually developed her own competence, depending on what she discovers about the local governmental traditions and the obstacles and the opportunities she meets. She redesigns her role and her responsibilities and uses new strategies in order to be able to do her work better. Her learning and competence development is about balancing intentions, tasks, conditions and possibilities and developing strategies. She reviews her strategies and adjusts them accordingly. Her goal is to have her perceived tasks and intentions implemented. She observes that there are different perspectives and that her own is just as limited as anyone else's. Her conclusion is that communication and conflict management in a context of co-operation are the best way to work.

As Dreyfus and Dreyfus (1986) point out, skilled professional are also emotionally involved. This engagement is the main thread in Sven's story. He has a political interest which has developed into environmental engagement during his studies. This engagement is manifested in a rather political action strategy and has become a mission for Sven: 'These issues were so important that I could not refrain from putting them forward.' For Sven his engagement is a combination of the belief in the task, the joy of living and the joy of work. It is also to be able to influence and inspire others with his perspective, both more generally and inside the department. The work is driven by enthusiasm, built on the belief in the task. Sven states that 'If you do not believe in what you do, it would not be possible to work in this way and with this task.' Working this way includes working a little on a voluntary basis, with tasks not covered by the budget, and with a broader scope. Linnéa describes how as a newly educated ecologist she wants to 'fight on the barricades and save the world with nature conservation as my main goal'. She has now put this role aside and describes her work today as being a part in a system of society where the positions are changing all the time. Linnéa believes that local government ecologists usually see themselves as having true knowledge because ecological knowledge is based on physical laws, and that kind of knowledge is more unassailable. 'It is not certain that the natural science we have learned as environmental ecologists is the right knowledge. It is some kind of comprehensive, overall view, which we as professionals can represent and interpret and which is founded on basic ecological knowledge.' At the same time, she emphasizes the need for respect for other professions: 'Other professionals do their work, and they do it correctly and appropriately from their perspective. Respect is necessary in the dialogue'.

Interaction with other people is important for the possibility to learn and to change the work situation. Linnéa gives several examples which illustrate that both meetings between people with different perspectives and conflicting interests can bring change. For Linnéa, this means that she has to take on the sometimes unpleasant role of expressing and using her knowledge: 'That is why I must have the courage to stand up for my opinions and speak up. If I lack that courage because it may put me in an uncomfortable or unpleasant position, then I have no right to criticize afterwards.' Her main strategy is to be actively involved in the work process and get something through instead of standing outside as a critical reference body. Her philosophy and strategy are to avoid confrontation and instead create conditions for communication and conversation. One might say that Linnéa forces change in her daily work by reviewing and revising her tasks and responsibilities and by trying different action strategies according to how they are received.

Linnéa thinks that if co-operation in the planning process is to be successful, it is essential that the knowledge that every profession represents is respected and considered. Being an active part in the process and being able to give voice to environmental issues is the most important task. She argues that it would be more of an insult to the knowledge she represents if she were excluded from the ongoing process than if her knowledge were ignored or rejected: 'If I have had the opportunity to bring in ecological knowledge, and if, for some reason, it is not considered or accepted, then there is no reason to fight about it. It is worse if I am not invited. Then I feel steamrolled and completely disregarded'. Sven's experience is that even if he is invited to a discussion, the opportunity to comment can be limited to some aspects, defined in advance by the people leading the process. Sven does not want to play the role as an expert, commenting on plain facts. He wants to be involved in the process by contributing his knowledge to the overall process or project, which in his opinion might lead to better quality for the outcome. Sven sometimes has a feeling of not being acknowledged for his competence.

It is in social interaction the strategies are used, but it is also here that learning takes place. Both Sven and Linnéa indicate that they have encountered power strategies, like confrontation, neglecting their issues. They both to a certain extent seem to belong to a marginalized group or discourse. This might be a reason why respect is so important in their stories. Being respected, both as a person and as a professional, is stressed by Sven. He wants to have the opportunity to voice his opinion and stand up for his task.

This also implies that he respects others, and that he is able to meet them in situations of mutual understanding in an undisturbed communication, free from prejudices and with a sense of shared knowledge: 'The most important thing is to be respected as a person and for what I stand for, and also that I respect others.' The development of the professional role for him is to a great extent described as being linked to personal development and to developing insight into his own personality. He makes a link to the work area: 'Representing these issues influences in some way your personal appearance.' This indicates that some personal qualities have influenced one's choice of profession, but also that the profession in some way will influence one's personality and life.

Concluding Remarks

With a change in theoretical perspective, in line with the communicative planning theory, there is a need to develop alternative research methods. When the aim is to affect the ongoing process in planning, methods for describing humans in interaction is necessary. In this chapter we have used interviews to capture the options and obstacles for professionals in interaction, because it is in the daily activities that change takes place. The goal of qualitative studies of this kind is to represent existing pictures of the world experienced. We recognize the development of suitable methods as being important in our thesis work. In this chapter we presented material from our studies, in which we used a method we find fruitful for gaining an increased understanding of the conditions for professional action and development in the environmental area. This method will be further developed and adopted to planning research in our future work.

Above, we discussed the processes of professions in competition, and how this will affect professions. We have also described professions as cultures, with deep-rooted assumptions, which have to be brought to the surface if substantial changes are to be possible. The theories also imply that changes in tasks, related to the awareness of maintaining the professional culture, could be a threat both to professions and individuals. Professions and professionals develop in several ways, with learning by practice and reflection playing a central role. This might be one way of fostering change, allowing marginalized voices into the process, as a way to learn from actors with other perspectives. The analysis also shows how strategies may be used to overcome existing power structures, or to maintain them. What is the impact of this knowledge for the emerging environmental planning profession?

The tentative results from our studies suggest that there is a struggle between different actors and professionals to give voice, to represent knowledge as common sense and to obtain influence and status by using varying strategies. The struggle is also to obtain respect for professional knowledge and experience. Professional competition does not have solely repressive effects. Rather it seems to be an important condition for the learning and development of professions and for defining their roles. To apply theories of professional development to the planning theories thus will contribute to the highlighting of the conflict perspective in planning. The communicative planning theory seems to overemphasize the aim of reaching consensus through collaborative efforts, neglecting the possibility of a conflict perspective, even when the theorists devote great energies to power structures and power relations.

The goal of communication and collaboration is not that professional groups should become alike, but rather that they should be able to contribute with their different experience and skills. One opening for this is to continually discuss what common sense knowledge there is and what alternative perspectives there are. The ability to listen and share each other's experiences of similar situations, and to trust the competence of other groups as well as reflecting on one's own assumptions and behavior seem important for the learning and development of professional competence.

A planning situation where some groups or professionals dominate or restrict the ability of others to formulate their arguments is an inefficient expression of power. Common sense knowledge can thus be used as power, power to define the role of others. What is important is to keep the culture and identity of the group, and develop its unique competence. The differences and the competition will then be seen as an option rather than an obstacle.

In conclusion we offer advice for professionals in the environmental area: Be aware of the gap between different professional perspectives and see it as a challenge for learning and professional development.

Notes

1 The studies are included in the research program 'The Municipality and the Territory', which is presented in this volume by Eva Asplund.
2 Planning and Building Act (PBL) and Natural Resources Management Act (NRL). This legislation is now included in The Environmental Code, which passed into law in 1999.

References

Abbott, A. (1988), *The System of Professions. An Essay on the Division of Expert Labour*, University of Chicago Press, Chicago.
Alveson, A. and Sköldberg, K. (1994), *Tolkning och reflektion, vetenskapsfilosofi och kvalitativ metod*, Studentlitteratur, Lund.
Alvesson, M. (1995), *Kommunikation, makt och organisation*, Norstedts, Göteborg.
Asplund, E., Dovlén, S., Håkansson, M. and Orrskog, L. (1997*), Räcker kompetensen? En studie av det långsiktiga miljöarbetet i fyra kommuner*, KTH, Stockholm.
Burr, V. (1995), *An Introduction to Social Constructionism*, Routledge, London.
Dovlén, S. (1999), 'The Local Government Ecologist Perspective on Environmental Issues in Land Use Planning', Paper presented at the *XIII AESOP Conference*, Bergen 7–10 July (unpublished).
Dreyfus, H. and Dreyfus, S. (1986), *Mind over Machine – The Power of Human Intuition and Expertise in the Era of the Computer*, The Free Press, New York.
Flyvbjerg, B. (1998), *Rationality and Power, Democracy in Practice*, University of Chicago Press, Chicago.
Forester, J. (1989), *Planning in the Face of Power*, University of California Press, Los Angeles, California.
Friedmann, J. (1987), *Planning in the Public Domain*, Princeton University press, New Jersey.
Frost, P.J., Moore, L.F., Louis, M., Lundberg, C. and Martin, J. (eds) (1985), *Organizational Culture*, Sage, Beverly Hills.
Healey, P. (1997), *Collaborative Planning, Shaping Places in Fragmented Societies*, Macmillan Press Ltd, Hampshire.
Håkansson, M. (1999), 'Experience of Local Environmental Work', Paper presented at the *XIII AESOP Conference*, Bergen 7–10 July (unpublished).
Kvale, S. (1997), *Den kvalitativa forskningsintervjun*, Studentlitteratur, Lund.
Morgan, G. (1996), *Images of Organization*, Sage, Thousand Oaks.
Nilsson, K. (1999), 'Strategic Spatial Planning on the Local Level – A Dilemma for Planners', Paper presented at the *XIII AESOP Conference*, Bergen 7–10 July (unpublished).

Orrskog, L. (1993), *Planering för uthållighet – från kunskap till handling*, Report R57:1993, Swedish Council for Building Research, Stockholm.
Sager, T. (1996), *Communicative Planning Theory*, Avebury, Aldershot.
Schein, E.H. (1992), *Organizational Culture and Leadership*, Jossey-Bass, San Francisco, California.
Schön, D.A. (1995), *The Reflexive Practitioner*, Ashgate, Aldershot.
Törnquist, H. (ed.) (1961), 'Hygien och samhällsutveckling', *Hygienisk Revy*, Sigtuna.

12 Planning as Discourse Analysis

LARS ORRSKOG

Problematic Planning

Introduction

Planning in Sweden – understood here as physical planning at the local level with comprehensive ambitions – is more or less out of date. We live in a post-socialist society where things are increasingly settled by the market.

The decline of planning started about twenty-five years ago through a series of partly independent circumstances. At that time nations could no longer be consolidated by the stimulation of consumption as Fordism was being replaced by flexible accumulation of capital. Production instead had to be supported for welfare to stay in the country (Nylund, 1995). Popular discontent had developed; at the same time, in what have been called the Record Years, anonymous high-rise residential areas were planned and a radical clearance of city centers undertaken. In addition, urbanization – the engine behind the planning – slowed down, mainly as a consequence of the growth of car use. Since then, the economy has gradually been globalizing and a networking society has developed at the expense of the territorially integrated society – the primary utopia of planning – which further undermines the efficiency of planning as it has been carried out.

It may be said that the original mission of planning is now finished and has been replaced by another because the world has changed, or because the mission could not actually be carried out – the dream of rational planning and a rational building process remains a dream. Nonetheless, significant parts of the legislative framework and the institutions involved in planning, as well as training programs developed during this heroic period, are still in function. This is a problem, as such things reasonably have to be reformed and replaced by other governing systems and

238

organizations; either the mission is now to develop a new type of post-socialist development planning or to build the Sustainable Society, the challenge of the day.

Planning since 1975 has been an experimental field for the development of appropriate methods for public decision-making in a world of expanding capitalism. As Judith Innes formulates it, planning has had to adapt to profound changes that have occurred in the late twentieth century: fragmented power; distrust of government and experts; multiple, seemingly incommensurable discourses; and a new tribalism, all of which are accompanied by technological change and globalization (Fishler, 1998). So criticism of comprehensive planning and disbelief in the rational calculation of futures has led to more limited time horizons and to the participation of the stake-holders who are supposed to implement the plans. Popular discontent with plans led to experiments in public participation, while recognition of an increasing dependence on external influences in local communities transformed planning into an analysis of consequences and elaboration of scenarios and alternative futures rather than proposals for land use. At the project level, the growing political and financial strength among private interests led to public negotiations with landowners and companies rather than to public planning. This was a provocation that in turn led to a growing interest among more socially concerned planners in communicative and inclusionary planning approaches.[1]

But no new method and no new strategy have yet been fully approved by planning institutions for planning for the Common Good in a post-industrial and post-socialist society, which is in contrast to the consensus that existed between 1945 and 1970 on welfare and the rational approach. Of course that has to do with the fact that consensus on planning then mirrored the consensus on development and welfare that prevailed under the Swedish compromise between capital and labor. Nothing today suggests there will be another consensus, so the field of planning also needs to be considered to be a field of heterogeneous attempts and practices.

In this text, an attempt is made to find an approach to planning originating in a post-modern conception of society and in accordance with the economic and social conditions of today. The approach examined in particular is the discourse analysis approach, which belongs to what is called the post-structural perspective on society. At the heart of that perspective lies a disbelief in essential values, that is, in a given origin, character or destiny of anything social, the ontology. Knowledge is understood to be relative and socially constructed as opposed to a belief in one reality and one truth, and there is thus a recognition of the importance of interpretation – the epistemology. Discourse analysis then is the analysis of speeches, texts and opinions, rather than 'realities', in order to better understand demands, power relations and politics. This text is a tentative attempt to transgress the fairly strong divide that exists in planning theory – not to mention in planning – between modern and post-modern perspectives on society.[2]

The argument is presented in two parts. In the first part some of the concerns at the heart of traditional planning, namely Development, the Common Good, the Rational Planning process, and the Town and Countryside idylls are examined. To a large extent this is done by giving an account of existing criticism among initiated planners and theorists. The criticism comes mainly from a modern perspective but some opinions referred to are of a post-modern character. In the first part there is also a discussion of Undisturbed Communication, on which communicationalists rely. This approach, with its strong belief in rational communication, is seen mainly as being of modern origin. In the second part of this chapter I move deliberately into a contrasting post-structural mode.

There are no specific empirical findings, that is, specific analyses of texts or talks, on which the text is grounded. It is instead general. Every now and then, however, the reasoning is exemplified with discussions about the Sustainable City, especially about the relationship between Town and Countryside, which has always belonged to the classic planning issue. [3]

Development and the Common Good

Development

The rhetoric of the industry, the market and the State is that we should develop by becoming more and more prosperous. But what is prosperity and what is development, and is society really developing by becoming more prosperous? Without answering such fatal questions, one can at least state that planners have without too much resistance taken it as their task to have cities grow and regions develop materially. But planning could be used as well to consolidate a region, to adjust a society in a better way to its local nature and culture, or to reduce segregation. This is just to mention a few examples of missions, in fact missions which are usually mentioned with regards to sustainability.

The definition of development as material growth can thus be questioned, and is in fact done so by many academics, as well as economists in favor of the modern project, such as Daly and Cobb (1989). Such modes of thought also exist in politics, although still only on the margins. Development in terms of growth, in contrast to development in other terms, thus belongs to what is discussed in politics, and if development in the future is not to be understood only as planning of growth, planning as we know it must change significantly. However, to really function constructively for planning, the discussion has to be based on a deeper understanding of the different meanings that could be given to development.

Early discussions about sustainability sometimes had such a questioning character. Given the astonishing political unanimity on sustainability, the power that the concept originally held seems to have faded. Perhaps it is the mechanical division and definition of the term into an ecological, a social and an economic threesome that have short-circuited the discussion. There was less of a debate on environmental factors in sustainability, and social sustainability was never clearly defined, which opened the way for quite a traditional economic approach to sustainability. So development in planning very much still equals growth.

In post-modern philosophy on the other hand, especially as it has been developed in France, for instance by Lyotard (1984), long-term goals rooted in long-term development narratives have been criticized in favor of more existential interpretations of society and the meaning of life. Post-modern philosophies as a matter of fact could be understood basically as a critique of the belief in development. Described in this way, post-modernism is of course a memento for all of us as planning has had as its ultimate purpose to stimulate, spread and carry out development in which people are supposed to gain a better life.

The Common Good

Planning as it has been taught at universities and used in practice, in politics and in the bureaucracy has always been legitimated for safe-guarding the Common Good. The boundary between what is private and what is public has been the firm line over which planners moved back and forth as judges and mediators. The foundation on which Plan and Building Acts are written is thus the difference and balance between public and private interests. That Common Good, as well as private interest, was born during the Enlightenment and was formalized in what is called the Social Contract (Liedman, 1997). The need to proclaim the difference between these two interests today follows from the tension that exists between politics and the markets. Thus it is often said that safeguarding the Common Good is the same as safeguarding those people that will not have a fair chance in free market situations. Poor people, people not yet born, people who are very far away as well as the environment are thus the classic concerns planners think they act on behalf of.

But the Common Good concept is becoming more and more complicated by all kinds of perspectives, and planners educated under the welfare state may feel quite uncomfortable with things as they are. There are, for instance, many versions today of public-private partnerships in large-scale building, and infrastructure – which almost by definition should belong to the public sector – is increasingly privately owned. Such things threaten the traditional basis of planning.

The Common Good must also be questioned if socialist and collectivist rhetoric are replaced by liberal and pluralistic rhetoric, the trend-setting political ideas of today. Under this line of thinking, different groups in society are in favor of different goals, which have to be tolerated as far as possible. From that perspective it should thus be a goal to reduce as much as possible what people have to come to terms with together in a society, which is also what goes on. Another way out of the dilemma would be to really try to find out what different Common Goods different sections of the population rely on, and to develop planning so that it can deliberately be arranged as a meeting between the different Common Goods.

The Common Good is furthermore a typical universalist concept, in contrast to particularist and locally adjusted concepts. The Common Good thus has normally been guaranteed through centrally formulated norms. Considering local specialties, however, the different and differing regions of Europe and local advantages in competition – these factors instead fall within the field of particularities. The Common Good and other universal virtues become indistinct.[4]

Planners can also feel very uncomfortable with how the Common Good concept is blurred by being constructed of both social and economic kinds of Good. Some Common Goods thus defend the rights of those not heard by the market while others are derived from the view that industry and capital cannot survive by themselves in a free market situation. The reason for this double-sidedness of the Common Good is that since the establishment of capitalism, the State has to not only regulate conflicts in communities but also solve problems in an economy inclined to crisis. To use the words of the German philosopher and social scientist Jürgen Habermas, there is a need for a social integrating co-ordination in the life-world and a systems integrating co-ordination of the systems of State and Capitalism, which furthermore increasingly distance themselves from each other (Nylund, 1995). In the rhetoric of planning (and politics) the same is expressed in terms of Common Good reasons for constructing a growth –

generating infrastructure as well as Common Good reasons for organizing the city so that wealth is spread among its citizens.

From a post-structural and anti-essential perspective finally, where all relations are understood to be made up of power, all decisions are interimistic and everything is negotiable; there is of course no fundamental Common Good to rely on at all. The question raised here is whether acceptance of such a perspective blurs the planning task even more or whether it would perhaps function as a relief for planners trying to adopt a post-socialist reality, torn as they are between so many different and partly conflicting loyalties to public commissioners, private landowners, entrepreneurs, users, their profession and their own convictions.

The Rationalist Approach to Planning

Rationalist Problem Solving

The art of planning can be understood as consisting of two quite different parts: the problem-solving part and the legitimating part (Fog et al., 1992). In the first part, problems are solved technically, by a planner, usually by combining aspects and solutions from different social sectors. Legitimation is handled in the decision-making or co-operative processes. This part is stressed more and more in the law, and researchers in the field are paying more and more attention to legitimation. It can be said that the problem-solving process needs to always be in touch with the legitimating process. It is through the submission of different opinions and demands during the process that solutions are developed.

In textbooks for planning, a basically linear problem solving process was presented for a long time. Although these textbooks are still around, it is commonly known that problem solving and planning do not happen that way. Problems are reinterpreted because the possible solutions did not fit the original problem. The solution to a problem often also comes intuitively and before the formal analysis is done. On the whole, problem solving processes are also full of what one may call post hoc rationalization. If such insights were considered seriously, not only would the problem solving process have to be reorganized but the relationship between problem solving and legitimating would also have to be. The parties engaged in the legitimating process would gain much more importance and planning would turn into some kind of mediating or communicative process. Although there are tendencies going on in that direction, planners are still considered very much to be oracles.

244 Reshaping Regional Planning

Also belonging to the rationalist approach is the belief in comprehensive planning, that is, long-term planning of societies in a variety of respects. That belief, however, is now shattered and for many reasons. One is that reality cannot be grasped by adding more and more facts about it. Nothing can ever be described completely, and there is an infinite number of possibilities in choosing a perspective and combinations of facts about the planning area or issue in question. With that also follows a questioning of the heavy reliance on scientific, especially positive – positivist – knowledge, that is, knowledge of a general rather than local and specific type. On the whole, the social sciences are epistemologically moving away from a firm belief in quantitative and general knowledge in favor of qualitative, interpretative and particularist knowledge. However, in the public as well as political debate, on how to construct the Good Society, traditional scientific perspectives are still very much alive.

Other reasons to have doubts about the rationalist approach is that the future is not foreseeable and that local situations to a greater or lesser extent depend on external factors. All this results in a situation where the Common Good is called into question, where the general public are reasonably given more space to maneuver in the process at the expense of expert scientists, social engineers and planners.

The Conditions of Politics

According to the rationalist tradition a planning process starts with political goals after which the task of the planner is to operationalize the goals and find suitable means by which they can be fulfilled. The goals are incontrovertible; it is only the means that can be varied. The relationship between ends and means according to that view is rational, logical and possible to calculate. Public participation in such a perspective thus has the role of achieving the goals faster, not of having the work done by planners who are critically examined and questioned by those affected by the planning.

Every experienced planner knows, however, that there is no strict relation or one-way relationship between politicians and planners. The goals are seldom formulated clearly, the means are often not consciously chosen, and everything changes during the progress of the planning process. Instead participants make the best of the situation. Along with that comes the political lack of will to know everything, count everything and decide everything.

It is indeed difficult to draw a sharp line between what planners do and what politicians do. During a planning process worth its name, planners are constantly in need of rules and goals for the game from politicians. But it is just as true that politicians need an input of proposals, as answers to questions not yet formulated, in order to stimulate the decision process. This is perhaps the case for all sectors of society, but it can be argued that it is especially difficult to draw the line requested in planning, because planning is by definition a strategic activity very near the roots of politics.

Maybe one should accept the fact that it is difficult to distinguish planning from politics and organize planning processes more deliberately, exposing different political and social wills to each other. So once again the solution seems to be to engage laypeople in the process through a dialogue both with representatives of political parties and with those who will implement or use what is planned. That is also what is happening. The difficulty of intellectually distinguishing planning from politics and from community mobilization endures, however, which among other things consistently renders public participatory endeavors ambiguous concerning the role of the participants. Are they engaged to vote for or against planning proposals, to help planners find out what the Common Good is, to react to the proposals as they are personally affected by them, or to come to terms with the ideas of others or come up with good ideas together with their neighbors or fellow citizens? One reason for the ambiguity could be that Man is most often understood among natural scientists and technicians – from whose perspective planning institutions normally are created – as a rational and autonomous entity, whereas in modern philosophy and among many social scientists he is clearly understood to be formed mainly by his relation to other people. The two different perspectives give rise namely to quite different strategies for and interpretations of participatory and politically-oriented planning procedures. Among other things consensus on the basic rules of communication and planning goals is the first step in public participation in planning according to the relative interpretation, not the last step as rationalists tend to see it (Nylund, 1995).

The Communicative Planning Approach

During the 1990s, many planning theorists have looked at planning as communication. Such theories concentrate on the role of planning as an arena for discussions between different private as well as public actors. The will of the actors is understood as depending very much on the will of other actors belonging to their own group as well as competing groups. The role of the planner as mediator between different interests is highlighted rather than his role as carrier of a political message. Among the leading theoreticians within this field are Judith Innes and John Forester from the US, Patsy Healy from England and Tore Sager from Norway.

The representatives for what is called the communicative school are all influenced by the communicative action theory of Habermas. Habermas distinguishes a life-world in which households dwell and day-to-day action in civil society goes on, which is different from the systems to which the State and its organizations and capitalism and its forms of production belong. In the life-world there is a communicative reason through which people settle their relationships and come to a consensus about common affairs. In this view, it is also said that the superiority of subject-oriented reason – which operates in market situations and on which Gallup polls and willingness-to-pay surveys rely – is negated. It is through dialogue that understanding arises and choice is made in the life-world. In the systems, on the other hand, money or power in the traditional meaning of the word reigns. The systems, however, according to Habermas depend on a functioning life-world and have to listen carefully to what happens there, as it is from there the systems derive their legitimacy (Nylund, 1995).

It is this possibility of dialogue, understood as a central feature of civil society, that the communicative school in planning theory has its focus, as it is through language more than anything else that human action is co-ordinated. There is a communicative reason to rely on, and as a result empathy is added to instrumental reason. In the Swedish context the communicative approach is in opposition both to the tradition of the Social-Democratic party of governing society with the help of strong paternalistic leaders and to the belief in the invisible hand of the market and all other expressions of belief in economic man.

According to Sager (1996) communicative action contributes as much to understanding and communication itself as to action. It contributes to a) negotiation and renewal of culturally commanded knowledge; b) social integration and the strengthening of solidarity; and c) the development of personal identity.[5, 6] Sager further declares that 'Knowledge is not seen as objective, as something given and external to man. Instead, knowledge is regarded as constructed in discourse. True knowledge is that in which a consensus is formed among informed people discussing the matter in undistorted communication' (Sager, 1996, p.8).

But there is criticism of the communicative approach, which comes from two very different camps. On the one side are the traditional interpreters of planning, who argue that it is the chosen representatives of Society who should express the Common Good, at the expense of private interests. The duty of planning theoreticians in that approach is to investigate how goals are formulated, how means are chosen and new implementation is organized, thereby guiding the efficiency of planning through experts.

On the other hand there is also criticism coming from those who disagree with what they call Habermasian idealism. Those critics are skeptical of a rational goal in planning altogether. They are more interested in society as a construction that is kept together as well as pervaded by power, and they do not think that any clear division can be made between civil society and the State. The mission of planning theoreticians in that approach is above all to describe power and raise the planners' awareness of their duties and their abilities as strategists. Flyvberg became a representative for such a theory through his investigation of planning in Aalborg. The power examined in that investigation is not power in the conventional sense of the word – that is, power coming from money or privileges – but the power that Michael Foucault taught his readers to see – that is, a culturally determined and forceful power which exists in all relations between people as well as institutions.

This illustrates the main antagonism in planning theory today, which is considered to be between a Habermasian and a Foucaultian approach.[7] This is an important antagonism because the interpretation of the whole issue of public participation and politics also depends on which side people identify with. In theory the antagonism is evident, but there are mediators also claiming that in praxis there is a need for critical and deconstructive theories as well as for positive models for building up communication between different groups in society.

Lapintie (1997) writes that it has become common to argue for a communicative approach but, as there is no accepted arena or method for argumentation, there is an obvious risk that such ambitions will be distorted and turned once again into traditional rationalist planning. Healy (1997), who relies a great deal on communicative action according to Habermas in her theory, writes in a similar way that Habermas presupposes that a fundamental purpose of democracy is to debate the validity of opposing arguments, in order to reach mutual understanding. However, she also sees the difficulties in real situations.

The Town and Countryside Idylls

Functional integration, which started with industrial society and has accelerated in our time, is growing at the expense of territorial integration. Territorial integration is defined as people and activities in an area depending on each other socially and economically. With functional integration on the other hand, businesses, institutions and households are related to each other in functional networks, rather independent of place (Friedmann and Weaver, 1979). The tendency towards functional integration has consequences among other things for the possibility of organizing a fruitful relationship between town and countryside. There is a risk that local resistance and the ability to solve problems – and the capacity to plan – also diminish with that tendency, especially as such change occurs simultaneously with the decline in local power over local resources (Mårtensson et al., 1988). In addition, urbanization has slowed down in the last thirty years, which means that people may settle down at some distance from instead of within cities, given the enormous growth in car-ownership.[8]

This description also provides some of the characteristics of what is called the networking society, that is, a society where information technology and a globalizing economy accord local relations less and less importance compared to distant relations. This space-dispersing network tendency may complicate the implementation of the Sustainable Society if it is felt that local democracy, local problem solving capacity and local circulation of materials between a city and its hinterland are important prerequisites for sustainability (Orrskog, 1998).

With that tendency the core of physical planning might be threatened as well. At the heart of such planning is the idea that the Good Society is the same as the Good City, which is a city with 'the church in the middle of it' and a city surrounded by a countryside looking like the countryside looked in the National Romanticism that flourished at the beginning of the 20th century. That might well be understood to be the utopia foremost in planning today.

The relationship between city and countryside, especially the differentiation and distinction between city and countryside, has always been important in planning. There are two essentially different reasons for this. The first and dominating one has to do with efficiency in maintenance and support of the city; the other is about respect for the countryside itself. According to the first reason, society has become concentrated and has organized towns and cities for the sake of sanitation, efficiency and social care and nowadays also very much for eco-circling, which serves the Sustainable Society (Boverket, 1994).

The other reason to keep town and countryside apart has been to keep the countryside free from development on behalf of farming, recreation, history, natural sciences and nature itself. More or less consciously, behind these considerations is the idea that the countryside is nourishing while cities are consuming.[9]

The national planning of landscapes and physical resources, which started in Sweden in the late 1960s, municipal overviews of their territories in the 1970s and strategic planning according to the Plan and Building Act from the middle of the 1980s were all consequences of conflicts between incompatible claims on the countryside. The solution was that different interests and actors were allotted different parts of the landscape. So, for instance, environmentally dangerous industries were allowed to be established along some parts of the Swedish coast whereas other parts were reserved for recreation and environmental protection.

There have, however, been integrating ambitions as well which have as long a tradition as those in favor of division. Ebenezer Howard, the superior hero of modern planning, represents this tradition. His Garden Cities of Tomorrow were to be built on virgin land and supported by farmers in the neighborhood. Although such cities were never built, the integration of green structures in housing areas has been an important theme in building suburbs with reference to Ebenezer Howard.

The program of Patric Geddes – the other English town planning theoretician with extreme significance for planning in the 20th century – consisted to an even larger extent of attempts to connect society to nature (Geddes, 1949). According to him planners should consider the natural as well as culturally determined history of a region and let towns and the countryside develop according to their own inherited tendencies and local character, but also co-operate in a way adapted to local circumstances. This was the formulation of Geddes as well as Mumford, his heir, who serve as godfathers for quite a number of the texts today on the co-ordination of town and countryside for the sake of sustainability.

Against all this, however, objections accumulate: What is the significance of dividing town from countryside when travel between town and countryside is constantly increasing and all households in the region are already urbanized in terms of life-styles? How does the dream of the Good City, with local governance, an integrated form and a high problem-solving capacity go together with the tendency to territorial disintegration? And how does the idea about local exchanges between town and countryside go together with a globalizing economy?

All this shows that the Plan – the good traditional Town and Country Plan – is becoming more and more obsolete given the political, economic and social realities of today. So, all in all, it is not only planning procedures that have to be considered once again but the use of old planning strategies as well.

How planning can avoid these dilemmas are something that is not yet known, but a crisis can be foreseen. At some point in time politicians and planners will probably try to save as much as possible both of the nostalgic dream of the agrarian society that once existed as well as the well-functioning industrial society also now dreamed of and the equal welfare society.

Another way, more in line with what is argued for in this text, would be to make a division in planning between the formulation of utopias on the one hand and organizing planning processes on the other and award different interest groups a capacity of their own to formulate those utopias. From that follows, among other things, that architects and planners would represent distinctly different professions. In a process organized this way the architects would be at the disposal of the parties involved in the process, while the task of the planner would be to organize the process, mediate and adjust.

Summary of the First Part of the Chapter

The section above includes some of the objections to the concept of development as such, and to the dominating idea that planning should contribute to expansion of the economy. In that respect there are clearly different and almost totally contradictory expectations from different actors in planning processes, not least in planning for sustainability. There was also a description of how difficult it is to come to grasp with the concept of the Common Good politically as well as philosophically, and there was found to be a conflict between the idea of a universal and a particular and more locally dependent Common Good. If the Common Good fails as a concept on which there can be consensus, much of the firm ground for traditional planning gives way as well.

It was further found that the rationalist approach to planning has been questioned and refuted in many respects. Among other things it is widely recognized among researchers trained in the social sciences that positively confirmed knowledge about the world will never be complete and that the planner's hunt for knowledge and truth could, to some degree at least, be regarded as in vain. There are always different interpretations of the truth. Nor is problem solving a straight, direct process; it is characterized by short-circuiting, feedback, intuition and post hoc rationalization to as great a degree as by consequence and mathematical logic.

A huge gray zone was then identified between politics and planning, where ends and means are intermingled and struggles for the privilege of formulating the problem persist. Such struggles persist between all parties involved in the planning process whether they be political parties, professional corps or stakeholders of different kinds. There was also a discussion of the dream of the Good Society – the Good City and the Good Countryside – as a utopia now called into question with reference to the globalizing economy and development of a networking society. Sustainability as a new grand goal in planning thus also falls into the loop. What does it look like, the Sustainable Society? Planners must most likely try to find it in a completely new manner and with new means. But there is evidently great uncertainty and competition between different perspectives and schools of thought on the issue for the moment.

To sum up, one can say that faith in planning has been slightly undermined, that there are many competing ideas not only on the Good Society but on Society, Development and Planning overall, that the road from formulation of the problem to proposals and implementation in many areas is still a mystery. It is of decisive importance who gets the privilege to formulate the problem, planners or other experts, planners or politicians, or the stake-holders in the process.

Planning As Discourse Analysis

Introduction

If the crisis in planning is as described above, critical discourse analysis may help in sorting out the situation that planning theory is in, and may also help as a method in planning. Instead of the defensive kinds of solutions mentioned earlier, there is a more offensive ambition to investigate and look deeper into the conditions necessary so that societal solidarity can be developed. Against scientifically motivated growth stands development as clarification and consolidation. Against universalistic pretensions stand particularism and anti-essentialism. Against the idea of a rational and linear problem solving process stands conditional rationality or even irrationality. Against relying on communicative reason stands the more profound insight into conditions for communication that can be found in post-structural theories of power. Against the dream of a Good Society stands the plurality of different societies with different qualities for different groups.

The rationalist approach must be abandoned and among most theorists has in fact already been replaced, as we have seen, by a belief in communicative reason. That strategy, however, has also been questioned as we saw as well. The conflict, described above, between the communicative rationality of Habermas and the power doctrines of Foucault is a very serious conflict for planning. In short Habermas argues that one can identify and master power through a critical analysis in which one distinguishes between a legitimate and an illegitimate exercise of power, in which the two types of power are handled separately. Such thinking is in conflict with the perspective of Foucault, as he argues that power is in charge over knowledge as well as over action, and that it becomes visible only through its counter-moves, counter-power (Kelly, 1994).

The debate between Habermas and Foucault can also be understood as one about belief in universal virtues such as right and wrong. Foucault rejects such notions. Habermas on the other hand seems to rely on communicative reason as a universal and essential human property and accuses Foucault of working with a self-reflecting system of criticism that has its roots everywhere and nowhere (Kelly, 1994). Discourse analysis of a more radical kind thus always runs the risk of being criticized for its disbelief in anything that is firm, some true truth to rely on and start from in the analysis of society.

In the following section Foucault's perspective will be kept in mind as a possible opening to a relatively deadlocked situation in planning theory.

Discourse Analysis

The Fundaments of Discourse Analysis

Discourse is defined as a way of talking that applies to a certain group of people, for instance in a political party or a profession, during a certain period of time and within a special area of matters. The group in question may be large or small and the area of matters can be as well. The time-span however always has to have some fixed duration since an important characteristic of discourse is its relatively long duration and stability. Within the field of environmental protection there is a discourse that has long been established, as there is in town planning.

The world we see and speak about is socially constructed. Nowadays, that is a legitimate proposal, at least in the social sciences. That means that we see the world – with its nature, environment and social structures – that we want to see; that is the one that the conventions of our society encourage us to see. We see it as we have been taught to see it. From that it follows that there is no clear-cut nature or unambiguous society existing outside of our imagination that we would all experience independent of where and when we live or who we are. At least there does not have to be such a world for us to understand each other and act in rational manners

(Rorty, 1998). It is enough if our way of living functions. With that it is also said that discourse analysts adopt an anti-essentialist attitude; no phenomenon could be said to have any one true or inner nature. This could also be described as a particularist attitude to the world in contrast to a universalist attitude. It is true that it also means that it should not be the duty of science to establish truths once and for all. The insight that the world is socially constructed is one of the fundamental insights of those working with discourse analysis.

Another fundamental insight is that language is the instrument which trains us in the convention at hand. Language is the tool with which we master the world around us, and it is through language we build up consistency in what we experience. So we see what we say. The talk about the world differs between different groups and over time. From the insight that it is language that decides what we see, it does not take discourse analysts much to be skeptical about so-called development. It is not certain that we become wiser over time, or happier.

The third fundamental idea concerns power. The reason to do discourse analysis for most researchers is to investigate and describe power in society. Through studies of how the world and society are spoken about, and more than that, they find that it is precisely through talk that the most influential form of power is exercised. But power does not remain forever with those in possession of it. New perspectives on the world may develop, whereby power moves to other groups in society. Discourse analysis thus can deliberately be used for emancipating purposes. By exposing concealed or oppressed perspectives, their legitimacy can grow. If one accepts these three characteristics as the foundations of discourse analysis, it can be defined as a scientific method to find out through analysis of language how different groups in society compete with each other, make sense of and try to master the world around them.[10]

If we go back to the dream of a territorially integrated society and that of a networking society, it could be said from a radical discourse analytical standpoint that the one as well as the other could never be anything more than an idea that can not be confirmed, and maybe not even measured. Scientists and analysts in both camps are engaged for the moment in formulating both the meaning and the consequences of their own as well as their opponents' ideas so that their own idea appears to be trustworthy and thereby true. Matters of this kind, with many different interpretations and apparently opposing tendencies and clothed in abstract definitions and explanations, seem to be especially suitable for discourse analysis. A description of a society should thus be understood not as a more or less comprehensive image, but as a description in favor of some special interests and at the expense of others.[11]

More about Discourse Analysis

The interest in how meaning is shaped, or rather, how the meaning of the world around a person is shaped, has a long history in Western epistemology. In keeping to modern times, many a philosophical starting point takes Wittgenstein and his idea about language games. He said that nothing uttered can mean anything other than for those that feel at home in the environment of the speaker. Words and sentences mean different things to different people. No proposal has a universal range. Theories of the same kind were later developed by many post-structuralist philosophers.[12]

It is typical for post-structural discourse analysis that different discourses are seen as competing. Discourses are however not easy to describe. On the contrary, according to Ernesto Laclau and Chantal Mouffe, two influential discourse analysts, a discourse is incomplete in a fundamental way, meaning that there are things within the field in question that cannot be symbolized within the discourse (Torfing, 1999). They are also without a privileged center, although they often contain nodes, that is, favored concepts and statements. Discourses thus are unstable, as are the contexts within which they occur. The play of meaning continuously expands and at least some signifiers in a discourse are floating.

Foucault devoted much of his interest to the concept of knowledge. He studied how society during different times has looked upon sexuality and crime and punishment, from which he built up a picture of society as almost totally dependant on which discourses are legitimate for the time being. Different groups of the population carry different opinions about the world and about what is right and wrong as well as good and bad, and these opinions stand against each other in competition for power, power to describe the problem and decide the agenda. Foucault thus had the opinion that power defines knowledge, not that knowledge gives power (Flyvberg, 1998). In his studies of language he was far removed from traditional linguistics.

The sociologist Bourdieu also claims that language must be understood as a tool for the exercise of power as much as a tool for communication. Language should thus be studied within its structural context, in contrast to pure linguistics, where context and power are invisible. Even the simplest exchange of sentences often holds a number of historically determined relations of power and social authority. According to Bourdieu and Wacquant (1992), it is not possible to understand what is said for someone who is outside and lacks knowledge about the structurally determined context. For instance, no conversation can be understood between a Frenchman and an Algerian without knowledge of French imperialism in northern Africa.[13]

As has been shown, the discourse analyst is usually interested not only in what is going on but also in history since almost all discourse develops and gradually changes. The town planning discourse of today for instance is better understood if it is known that it once developed as a hygienic reaction to an unbearable sanitation situation in the cities of early industrialism. Later, other meanings were layered on the original discourse, for instance when it was primarily directed at housing in the welfare society, or further on when town planning became an activity in the service of competing industries. It can thus be said that professional and other discourse is built up of sediments of earlier versions of them.

The power aspect of discourse analysis is important. Luke, writing in the 1970s, and his three types of power are often referred to: a) the classic interpretation of power as power to have people act other than they would like to; b) ignorance in handling an issue, thereby letting the 'normal' situation remain in force; and c) structural power. In post-structural literature, however, that is not an exhaustive description of power. There (Hoy, 1986; Dyrberg, 1997), power is often understood as d) what prevents people from reacting to social shortcomings by influencing their understanding and preferences in such a way that they accept the conditions, or e) what forms individuals and institutions into something we must not call either bad or good; it just defines society. In discourse analysis all those kinds of power, both 'power over' as in type a) – d) and 'power to' as in e) can be revealed. [14, 15, 16]

Ernesto Laclau and Chantal Mouffe hold a radical perspective on politics and argue that it is not rooted in any special reality or truth outside itself (Torfing, 1999). Political decisions are basically not grounded in anything outside themselves, but nevertheless involve repression and a wielding of power in reality. The ethical norms for behavior in political debates constitute an open set of undecidable claims, which are the object of endless discussions going on in a discursive framework leavened by power. In that framework, social identities change. Politics thus simultaneously constitutes and subverts social patterns.[17] Habermas and planners in general on the other hand want to assess communicative actions in the light of argumentative procedures for direct and indirect claims of truth, normality, the honesty of the subject and aesthetic harmony.

Foucault's view of the importance and power of language along with that of Laclau and Mouffe however, represents an extreme attitude in comparison with many other discourse analysts. Fairclough (1995), for instance, is more moderate and constructs his critical discourse analysis on the idea that there is reciprocity between power and language. The discursive act, according to him, is shaped by situations, institutions and social structures that at the same time are shaped by the discourse. Social and political changes not only give rise to changes in language but are also affected by language.

Whether a radical or a moderate perspective is taken in discourse analysis, analysts are engaged in how talks are constructed, that is, in linguistics. Narratives, myths, metaphors and metonyms are thus examples of what discourse analysts look for. A narrative is a story line, usually of a Great Story, in which social development is inscribed, and which organizes thinking in the field in question. The Christian and the Enlightenment narratives are forceful examples of that. The welfare society and market-oriented liberalism also have their stories without which daily talk in them can not be understood. Myths and metaphors can also be very forceful in our thinking. A myth can be understood as something invented to fill in a gap in our knowledge or in a narrative, and a metaphor is a pictorial and persuasive transcription of a central phenomenon in a discourse. As Harré et al. (1999) have found in 'greenspeak', it could also be used to compensate for the lack of relevant expressions and words in the established discourse.

A metonym finally is an expression taken over by new interpreters, often with competing perspectives, and given a new meaning different from the original. Sustainability may very well function as an example of a word that has gradually moved away from its original meaning or meanings and is regarded by many as used metonymically. In the political struggle that takes place when the welfare state is converted into a more liberal state, one can also frequently hear how words are taken over by both sides in the conflict to make their own perspective more legitimate (Torfing, 1999).

A frequent theme of discussion that arises when discourse analytical, post-structural or social constructivist theories are discussed is how change occurs (Burr, 1995). How does a new discourse arise, is there anything like learning, what is the function of pioneers, can institutions take on new missions? Foucault does not discuss such things very much. In his texts it seems as if people are prisoners of their discourse. A hegemonic discourse can, however, according to Foucault give rise to a counter-discourse, thereby influencing societal circumstances. The changes are thus of an immaterial kind (Göransson, 1998). To take another example of a researcher influenced by discourse theory Merchant (1989), who has studied changes in society's relationship to nature, argues that mental and behavioral change occur when the production system in itself has influenced and transformed nature so that our societal systems do not work.

Discussing the Merchant example in terms of agent and structure shows that people change when structure changes, but it is unclear how much freedom of action there is for the agents, for people. Agent is defined as an intentionally acting subject. Structure, on the other hand, is represented by those relatively stable circumstances that are in the surroundings of the agent, and which at least in the short run give the agent his prerequisites and set limits for his actions. Structures have a tendency to reproduce infinitely. Althusser, whose work Laclau and Mouffe take as a point of departure, only saw structures, as did many other left-wing politicians and social scientists (Torfing, 1999). According to them the State is fixed by objective structures and only reflects the interests of the dominating class in society. Class struggle makes the world go around, but classes only carry structures and the struggle between them only means that they progress along a road already staked out. According to Laclau and Mouffe, Althusser thus missed the possibilities there are in politics. Today most social scientists, however, including the influential sociologist Giddens, acknowledge the existence of both structures and agents influencing each other.

For planning the relationship between agents and structures is of decisive importance. Can a society develop according to plans that are in conflict with its tendencies to change? That is, how much room is there for acting within the context – the external circumstances for planning – which planners nowadays try to catch in series of alternative scenarios which the plans have to obey? Moreover, if there is some space for local will and action, is that not also mortgaged by the dominating description of problems and possibilities, that is, by prevailing power relations? This is not the place for a detailed answer to that fatal question. From a discourse analytical perspective however – to argue with Foucault as well as with Laclau & Mouff and Fairclough – there is some room not yet mortgaged and which can not be completely anticipated which may be taken up by discourses that are not yet established. Those can be established by being formulated and thus made visible. It is that possibility which in this text is also pointed out as a possibility in planning, through consciousness among planners about the strength that resides in discourse.

Finally it belongs to the assumptions in this article that ideas professionally inherent in an institution also define it. An institution that grew up around a certain kind of praxis, in turn rooted in some specific ideas and power relations, can not easily develop a new kind of praxis based on other ideas and other powers. No, the struggle about what ideas, what praxis and what techniques will dominate, concerning for instance energy production and distribution in society or the relationship between a city and its hinterland, is for many institutions also a struggle for survival. Institutions thus also constitute, through their relations to economic forces and training programs, obstacles for new ideas to become established.

Discourse Analysis of Planning

The main reasons to try out discourse analysis in planning research is that planning is precisely talking (Forester, 1989; Lapintie, 1997), an arena where different interests express themselves, and that planning is about the future, something we know nothing about and thus which has to be conjured up. There is, however, a struggle in planning over the formulation and handling of problems today as well. Different actors try to have their pictures of reality legitimated. A special and current reason to carry through discourse analysis of planning is that there are a number of different and competing expectations about the future arising in the vacuum after the welfare state.

For a long time the rationalist approach to planning dominated, as was shown in the first part of this chapter. This meant in part that knowledge used in planning is objective and that there is an infinite amount of knowledge to build the future on; that political boards can come to a consensus and thereby also control the implementation process; and that there is a clear-cut division between the duties of politicians and the duties of planners. The rational approach was a top-down approach.

Today the discussion gives the impression that planning is, or at least ought to be, a bottom-up procedure where the role of planners and perhaps also of politicians is to negotiate and mediate. In both cases, however, the belief in the rational decision process is unchallenged. Different experiences are expected to communicate with one another until a consensus is reached.

The focus of this text has also been on how planning bureaucracies can understand what goes on among different groups in society. The difference, however, is that whereas Habermas, whom the communicationalists and planning bureaucracies of today rely on, even 'fetishize' (Torfing, 1999) a communicative reason, we have – in the spirit of Foucault – been much more skeptical of the possibility of dialogue and consensus.

Looking at planning primarily as an arena for competition between different perspectives and demands on the world is provocative in two respects. One is that it questions the existence of incontrovertible knowledge, that is, scientific knowledge, which planning has relied upon.[18]

The discourse perspective is in opposition to established positivist beliefs among natural scientists and technicians about *one* truth. This means that the focus of our interest moves from the planning office – where those researching planning usually reside – to the assemblies and boards of politicians, as well as to arenas in civil society where planning discussions are held.

The other provocation is that consensus cannot be achieved as planning in this perspective means that different ideas about the world compete in the arena and that some special constellation of powers will dominate the plan.[19] This is against the dream of the perfect dialogue and of wise and Common Good decisions that the promoters of planning and planning acts have relied on for at least sixty years.[20]

Some of the characteristics of the discourse analysis of planning, compared to many other research perspectives – such as policy analysis, negotiation and communicative planning perspective – could be summarized as follows:

- Politics and the struggle for social hegemony are more important than the techniques of planning.
- There are no interests and actors for now and evermore; new perspectives, new interests and new coalitions may always come up.
- Disputes in planning are never settled; agreements about a plan are only temporary and during the implementation and use of the constructed environment give rise to 'renewed' discourse struggles.
- Power springs from the idea of the world that is established and from the ability to decide what planning should focus on, rather than from the ability to imprint solutions onto planning problems.
- The historical dimension is important as discourse grows and replaces earlier discourse; analysis of history can give information about the future.
- There is no utopia or any Great Story / narrative to rely on, only consistently new perspectives on the world and the future.
- No essence or inner truth is arrived at in planning; every situation and expectation have many different inherent possibilities; discourse analysis is anti-positivist.
- Structure or agents do not explain a situation or the future by themselves but together with the other.

Planning for Sustainability

Argumentation about the Sustainable Society, its outlook and realization, should be especially suitable for discourse analysis since the concept is interpreted very differently in different camps, while at the same time there is something like a tacit agreement in politics not to come into an explicit clash about the definition of the concept (Rydin, 1997). The whole issue seems to be in a rather unstable situation for the moment, and a discourse analysis of how politicians handle it would deepen knowledge about what is at stake and also give a hint of what can be expected. A special reason to look more closely at politics and power relations involving sustainability is that new reports about the greenhouse effect, the hole in the ozone layer and the destruction of rain tree forests feed both apocalyptic ideas and fundamentalism. In such a situation it is of utmost importance to focus on politics as a possible way of handling problems, which discourse analysis in reality does.

One question that immediately arises when sustainability is considered from a power perspective is whether anybody really is interested in sustainability, as it has been interpreted by green movements. Does it provide more welfare and is it profitable? The question must be asked because it is usually thought that future generations and remote nations without a voice in planning processes are those that will benefit if a sustainable relationship to life-supporting systems could be arranged. But perhaps there are those that think that they would benefit from a society not as restless and consuming as ours is considered to be among environmentalists. Asthmatics troubled by air pollution and synthetic products would welcome prohibition of a large number of products, and some people would accept a decrease in mobility if noise and other stress factors from traffic would decrease. There are also those that say that they like less but tastier meat on their plates and those that appreciate a more diverse flora. Everyone knows someone that would willingly give up some of their material welfare for the benefit of less wealthy people far away, if it could only be realized. Even more people wish that the next generation of Swedes and the generation after them would have as good access to a healthy environment as they have themselves. It is also known that there are quite a lot of people that prefer more spare time to more money.[21]

Thus there are groups – maybe large groups – that would consider there to be a better quality of life if consumption were reduced and more nature-like production processes were once again realized. In planning, those groups however are usually not seen or listened to because they are not stakeholders and not well enough established as interest groups.

Stakeholders who are allowed to influence exploitation and conservation projects are private property owners, developers, neighbors, well-established organizations and some NGOs. According to discourse analytical terminology, such interest groups represent established discourses. The groups described above, which are a kind of potential prompters of sustainability, instead represent suppressed discourses. They may themselves use that highly favored word sustainability but nevertheless are put aside as they give that word another meaning than most politicians do.[22]

This request for sustainability can be compared to the way nature and the countryside were handled in the nationwide planning of Sweden in the 1970s. That planning was initiated after severe clashes between heavy industry, cottage and recreation activities, environmental protection and farming and forestry concerning land use in attractive areas, especially along the coast. The State took it as its duty to zone the coast into areas for different use, thereby guaranteeing both the growth of industry and the different conservation purposes. Welfare could not be imagined without exploitation. That however is exactly what many advocates of sustainability doubt, which makes planning challenges today so much more difficult to handle compared to economizing on natural resources in the 1970s.

This can also be compared with what Hajer (1995) calls ecological modernization. He showed how traditional environmental politics in European countries during the 1980s was transformed into what he calls ecological modernization. From dependence on a rather passive State, industries that would not accept any external costs and a radical green movement which neither the State nor industry could come to terms with, environmental politics became successively more preventive; industry took more environmental responsibility – because of consumer demands – and the green movement came back to the table, tried as it was through a series of defeats in the 1970s and 1980s. What Hajer showed through discourse analysis was how different institutions and power centers compete with each other in environmental politics, and how one set of conceptions, with all its concepts and myths, was gradually replaced by another.[23]

In both these cases – nationwide planning of natural resources and ecological modernization – it is assumed that environmental problems can be solved through, or at least together with, economic growth. Added to the demands for sustainability, at least from environmentalists, in our part of the world, however, is the requirement that material and energy must not grow in production or consumption. We will thus not assume that there are any easy and 'fair' balances to develop, at least not in the short run. What can be done however is, through discourse analysis, find out how the struggle between different interests goes on and how they try to get their different views on the future legitimized. In this way, we can get a better view of the power relations, antagonism and hegemony involved in the sustainability issue, on the basis of which it is up to the actors to develop their own strategies. The weaker parties in particular would benefit from such an analysis.

Turning now to our own field of interest, the relationship between Town and Countryside[24] and especially the demands of cities on their hinterlands, we can, given the history of planning presented in the first part of this chapter, arrive at a set of various conceptions of the use of countryside, such as:

- the place for farming which is run like all other rationally organized industries that are under the conditions of an anonymous market;
- a place for farming mainly for local consumption;
- an area coveted by city dwellers for recreation or as a place to stay during the summertime;
- a potential area for city dwellers to settle down within commuting distance from the city;
- nature, where life reproduces itself, thereby also guaranteeing life in the city;
- a recipient for garbage and by-products from the city – a counterpart to the city in eco-circle strategies;
- a cultural relic and a beautiful background for the activities and the inhabitants of the city; and / or
- a background factor to take advantage of in competition for new tourists and companies spending money and making investments in the city.

The perspectives and expectations presented in this list are held and pronounced by more or less established institutions and organizations.[25] They could also be seen as belonging to different social contexts made up for instance by gender, age and class (Bender, 1993), and they change over time (MacNaughton and Urry, 1998). Some of the expectations are in conflict whereas others might be added together. Some combinations of perspectives could be found within one institution, while other combinations will come up rather as alliances between different actors. From the perspective of discourse analysis, however, what should be stressed is that most actors are fully occupied by their own wishes and tend to see their perspective as the true perspective. That also goes for the State and for many planning institutions. So for instance State policies in Sweden regarding people living in the countryside until recently were based on the premise that most of them were farmers engaged in production for the market (Persson and Westholm, 1994). It is highly probable that that was an effect of the very convincing and long-lasting conception of the countryside as rural, which apparently surpassed the importance of social and economic figures in statistical reports and surveys first presented long ago.[26]

Planning as Discourse Analysis

The discussion above about different interpretations of sustainability and the use of hinterlands could be developed into a study of what conceptions dominate and thus are legitimate in planning and politics. That would be to use a discourse analytical framework as a researcher. But perhaps discourse analysis can also be useful as a theoretical frame and method for planners in their profession in order to avoid some of the dilemmas planning has run into and to enrich planning situations.

In planning, for instance, of the countryside around a city, it can be said that different interest groups with their respective discourses compete for the wealth that exists in nature and the use of it as a pleasant place to live, beautiful scenery, fertile soil, a recipient or reservoir, or a refuge for bio-diversity. By analyzing that and giving special interest to power relations between the perspectives = the interested parties, one can get an idea of how much room for maneuvering there really is in planning the future of that countryside. One can also determine what power relations planning must have and how they impact whether the future that is sought will be realized as well as how institutions in society must be reformed for the desirable future to be implemented.

The questions and tasks described are all quite new or have to be carried out in a new way. Adopting a discourse analytical method, planning would thus have to be much more sensitive to different perspectives than normally. Planners would have to point out in particular the possibility of many different truths, perspectives and futures and claim that planning processes must be organized more deliberately as arenas where different perspectives meet. There is namely no fair distribution of wealth and benefits that can be calculated from outside the struggle between perspectives. And, what is crucial for this method, it must be accepted that the perspectives held by elected politicians can not be understood simply as ones that mirror all those perspectives held among people in the territory in question, and that there might be neglected perspectives worth bringing out.

Technically planners would search for different perspectives on the subject matter by engaging in discussions in the area and in texts of all sorts of kinds, and then really try to understand their origin and development. They must then try to evaluate their legitimacy, strength and implications. All this is contrast, but it can also be used as a complement to what have been normal procedures, that is, handling only those interests that are outspoken and ask for their claims in the area. The discourse is the subject, not the actors.

So what have been called interests and actors in planning should not simply be invited to state their claims in the area or other expectations formulated especially for the planning process in question. No, planners would also have to become acquainted with the more internal way of thinking and discussing of those actors, from which can be extracted their more universal claims on the landscape which come from their view on Nature and Society.

People who are involved are also understood throughout the process as being collectively constructed and participating in their roles as citizens, which of course prevents planners from reducing their goals to subject-oriented monetary claims, or to use cost-benefit or other methods where calculations of optimal solutions to planning problems are attempted. Planning as discourse analysis instead implies that the problem solving and legitimating processes intertwine in such a way that problem solving can hardly be considered to be a professional activity in its own.[27]

The perspective elaborated here may be called emancipative and stands in sharp contrast to the other two more common perspectives on planning, utopism and rationality (Lapintie, 1996). Clearly all three perspectives occur in discussions about planning for sustainability but they are very difficult to co-ordinate, although often not clearly kept apart in planning, which results in a great deal of confusion for instance about public participation.

There is the dream of the Perfect Society – the Sustainable Society – as a grand utopia; there is also the expectation of an outburst of popular engagement for the environment and for planning that would follow from work according to Agenda 21 programs; and there is the tradition of the environmental sector believing in scientific rationality (Asplund et al., 1997).

So what has been argued for in this article has really been that public planning, especially in a society where market tendencies are strong, should hold as its main duty to listen to and bring forward different popular perspectives – discourses – and hand them over to the political boards, rather than to start the process by drawing up beautiful futures or by calculating trends. In such work, planners would also have a mission to help focus the wishes and perspectives at stake on the issue, for instance land use in a municipality. That could be achieved by sensitively drawing up the contours of different futures, but such sketches should be understood as means, not ends.

Planners of course also have to calculate when to connect perspectives to the reality of the day and when to extend and implement perspectives and visions in order to clarify suggestions. But calculations are subordinated to the perspectives and can not claim to grasp any single true reality or unavoidable future.

The way of introducing discourse analysis as a perspective on and method in planning suggested here represents only a starting point. There should also be professional discussions about the implications of a discourse analytical perspective in planning, not just on planning. For instance one has to really find out what role locally elected representatives of the people – politicians in municipalities – should have in planning on discourse analytical grounds. Could they at all be seen as representatives of the discourses held in the community? Habermas maintains that the systems have become so alienated from the life-world that new arenas have to be built up in civil society where communicative reason can flourish (Nylund, 1995). The question then, however, is who has the legitimacy to build them up. Such propositions may also seem a bit idealistic from a Foucaultian perspective.

The role of the planner also comes into the loop and for many reasons. One is that planners themselves belong to a special professional discourse and can no more than any other group in society be understood as objective. Perhaps the best that can be done is to train planners to become as conscious as possible about being biased and try to handle the problem. The role so common in Sweden of being an architect as well as a planner should probably be avoided for the same reason, which would also have serious implications on how planners are trained.

How to handle oppressed discourse after it has been identified is a third very problematic issue, since even if empathy could be raised in other groups for the discourse in question the struggle probably has to be that of the oppressed group. One might also argue that it is good enough if planning is organized so that oppressed discourse could be formulated and thereby seen. Perhaps nothing more should be expected from planners working in a democracy.

To Sum Up

The kind of planning discussed in this text is the planning of land use going on at the regional and municipal level. That kind of planning has a one hundred-year history, although it took on its status as instrument for the welfare society in the second half of the century. It was consensus planning for the parallel benefits of growth and distribution of wealth. Politically the welfare society is more or less out of date and overruled by a globalizing economy and a liberal instead of community-oriented kind of democracy and State. On top of that comes the fatal request for a more sustainable Society in harmony with Nature, which is for the moment a matter of dispute.

Altogether, we should expect praxis and the institutional framework around planning to change significantly during the coming decades. Most likely there will be more conflicts, and more explicit conflicts, between different expectations on future land use. Planning and planning institutions must be renovated in order to handle that.

It is argued in this chapter that from the planning institutions' point of view, it may be constructive in such a post-consensus future to develop a post-structuralist approach. Such an approach is characterized by a disbelief in essential values and an understanding of knowledge as relative and socially constructed. In discourse analysis – the method suggested – speeches, texts and opinions are analyzed, rather than 'realities', in order to better understand demands, power relations and politics.

Planning in such a way comes closer to politics and the planner develops into a facilitator or chairman for the discussion among different interests The kind of planner with an education from a technical university now often operating would in this perspective instead find his main role as a constructor of futures in the service of one special interest group or another. With the approach chosen, planners should concentrate more on the different actors' varying perspectives on the world, not only on their specific claims, as it is through their perspectives that they try to legitimate their claims. Planners also have to try to look for oppressed discourse if there is any and bring it to the table. Planning, especially at the strategic level, should further be understood as a continuous process around never-settled disputes and not be connected too much to special plans. The Common Good also vanishes in a post-structuralist approach and utopism is referred from the hands of the planner to – if anywhere – the hands of professionals working for some special actor.

All in all, one might say that planning with the changes suggested becomes more like politics and less like calculation.

Notes

1 Inclusionary planning, by which is meant the ambition to include all the different voices that can be heard in the area planned, is a key concept in Healy's (1997) widely read book *Collaborative Planning – Shaping Places in Fragmented Societies.*
2 That divide is especially strong in planning and has only recently been discovered among planning theorists, in contrast to many other social scientists. The reason for this could be that planning is taught mainly at technical universities and that the institutions funding research in the field are closely connected to praxis. Analytically, discourse may be understood as a consequence of the strong positive values still connected to planning in Sweden. Liberals, even though they in fact oppose a strong State, may cling to the concept for opportunistic reasons. Seen in this way, planning is a metonym (see second part of this chapter).
3 This text is written within the research project 'The Municipality and the Territory', funded by The Swedish Council for Building Research.
4 The moral philosopher MacIntyre argues that it is not possible to combine Aristoteles and Nietzsche (Torfing, 1999). Either you think that there is a Common Good or you do away with all expectations of such an order. There is no Kantian, utilitarian or existentialist stop on the road between universalism and particularism.
5 The communicationalists thus go further in their criticism of the rationalist approach than the incrementalists. Sager (1996) arrived at the communicative approach while looking for an antithesis to the rationalist approach. He regarded incrementalism according to Lindblom as opposed to the belief in sensibility and rationality in the decision process but found that incrementalism also focuses on the product rather than the process. From such reasoning he arrived at the conception of dialogue as a goal in itself.
6 A 'human growth' rationale in planning was advocated by Andreas Falludi as early as the 1970s.
7 It should be said, however, that both Habermas and Foucault share the opinion that the Enlightenment meant that people could escape from superstition and mature as human beings (Fischler, 1998). Others take a more skeptical position and argue that with the Enlightenment followed instrumental logic obstructing the sensible subject.
8 Urbanization denotes different things in the text depending on the context. In talking about urbanization in general, it means that cities and villages grow at the expense of the countryside. However, one may also mean the movement from peripheral to metropolitan regions, in which sense Sweden is still a country with high-speed urbanization. In a third context it may mean that living habits connected to urban life are spread among the population. In that respect Sweden is almost totally urbanized.
9 In the landscape, nature with the help of solar energy, carbon dioxide, water and nutritive salts – builds up bio-masses and an order equivalent to life itself. What we call production in our society, on the other hand – that which goes on in the city – instead means destruction in radical natural science by breaking down and reorganizing the order of nature into different kinds of human nourishment and artefacts.
10 Discourse analysis is frequently used as a concept in two different ways. Either it is meant as an analysis of a certain discourse for linguistic reasons, or as an analysis and comparison between different discourses that are contiguous. Norman Fairclough, a linguist, calls the second type critical discourse analysis (CDA). I have chosen to call the second type, which is the type proposed here, simply discourse analysis.

11 Social constructivism and discourse theory can be used and understood in a more or less radical way. Sometimes social constructivist perspective implies only that people must acknowledge that there are different interpretations of what they see and hear and that it seems as if there will never be total consensus about anything, especially not about immaterial things such as the character of institutions or power relations. A more radical view is that there is no reality to be grasped at all, only different talks about reality. My intention here is not to choose sides in this debate but to keep the doors open to both perspectives on social constructivism. It could be that planning matures as an activity closely connected to politics if it is thought of in terms of stakes and claims handled in it without bothering about any true reality or fair deal, that is, influenced by a radical kind of social constructivism.

12 Languages are like islands. One must jump between them. There is an enormous richness in language. In a minute one may use ten different languages, jumping between them (Lyotard).

13 There is, though, a great difference between the early Foucault and Bourdieu in that Foucault did not accept any other kind of knowledge about reality than the one inherent in discourse. Bourdieu on the other hand welcomed the positivist empirical research of socio-economics as a complement and frame to what can be learned from discourse.

14 Among commentators of politics language has often been understood to be powerful. The leader of the Italian Communist Party, Gramsci, thus gave the word hegemony its modern meaning, as that which is reached by the ruling class because it rules over talking in society. In the last decade Laclau and Mouffe have developed the politically inclined discourse analysis further.

15 Foucault's power analytics can be summarized by the following propositions: '(1) power is everywhere ... comes from everywhere; (2) power cannot be acquired, seized or shared ...; (3) power comes from below, but the multiplicity of local forces form the basis for wide-ranging effects of cleavage that run through the social body as a whole; (4) power is intentional, but non-subjective ...; (5) resistance is not in a position of exteriority in relation to power, but always works within and against it ...' (Torfing, 1999, p.163).

16 It could be argued that either the first two types of power are recognizable or the third one is, since they can be seen as incommensurable (Fishler, 1998). The third manipulative one may, if understood as being unconscious, either include or repel the other two.

17 Political parties typically try to become hegemonic, that is, get power over what should be considered normal. According to Laclau and Mouffe hegemony can be described as the expansion of a discourse so that within an antagonistic context it fills up the horizon by articulating floating signifiers so that they become partially fixed (Torfing, 1999). Neo-liberals have thus managed to redefine the terms of the political debate. Through fierce attacks on a centralist and bureaucratic nanny state, and by glorifying such things as the family, entrepreneurs and the market, they have forced opposing groups to reassess their understanding of the State, the economy and civil society.

18 That is why Freedman's well-known book from 1987 is called '*From Knowledge to Action*'.

19 A land use plan and land use in itself do not however have direct implications on living standards, nature or production results. They give some preconditions for such things

but are of a more mediating and indirect importance compared to many other political instruments. That implies that there are many layers of interpretation at work in land use planning, which in turn makes land use planning especially interesting to analyze by using some kind of discourse theory.

20 Despite everything, the space that exists for planning research of a discourse analytical kind in Europe was illustrated at two conferences held in Glasgow in 1997 and 1999. At those conferences quite a number of studies were presented on how discursive practices mediate through the arena for political action and policy intervention, interacting with other kinds of social processes at work in urban areas (Hastings, 1999).

21 In these considerations it is valuable to distinguish between people as consumers and as citizens (Sagoff, 1988). It is not sure that in their role of consumers they really express the values mentioned. As citizens belonging to a community they might, however, do so. This differentiation is very important to the argumentation in this text, especially in discussing a communicative approach to planning versus planning relying on subject-oriented values.

22 In *Strömfåra och kontrapunkt i västerländsk utvecklingsdebatt* (Main Stream and Counterpoint in Western Debates of Development), Hettne (1983) has described how an earthly, bodily, sensual and decentralized relation between people and nature has been dreamed of in contrast to the dominating processes of industrialism, urbanization and etatism. He claims that these dreams, even when they are from different periods, are of one and the same origin. Presented like that, there thus seems to be an oppressed discourse about nature which I suppose it was Hettne's idea to help promote by laying it bare and thus give it legitimacy.

23 Ecological modernization is however equivalent to more effective and cleaner production. Confidence in science is still high although the task now is to guide industries and not just point out environmental problems. A good example of ecological modernization is the project going on in Sweden for the moment where huge amounts of State money are used for re-building housing areas, production processes and infrastructure for environmental reasons. Difficult questions about global justice, limits to growth and the capitalist production mode, that is, about sustainability according to environmentalists, are only touched upon in ecological modernization. A new phase in the struggles over the environment can thus be foreseen.

24 Town and Countryside should in discourse analysis be understood as a fundamental pair of opposites as much as Society and Nature. The one cannot be understood without the other according to Derrida and others claiming that our understanding is made up of opposites. Looking at town and countryside in such a way, the fundamental importance of their relationship for sustainability is stressed.

25 One of the few researchers that have studied how environmental issues are handled in planning by analyzing texts and arguments is Lapintie. In Lapintie 1996, so-called ecological architectural competitions are studied. It is shown for instance how the blend of green and development areas in a region described earlier as though developed areas stretched out into the landscape is now described rather as though green fingers reach into the metropolitan area.

26 I do not say that the statistical reports tell the truth whereas the premises for State policies were false. I just point out that those formulating State policies seem to like the

countryside to be rural while those doing the statistical surveys probably are interested in the countryside for other reasons as well.

27 Such use of planning for emancipating purposes has in fact in some cases already become legitimate. One such case is planning in marginalized regions, where people have to handle their own business. In municipal strategies in accordance with Agenda 21 it has in some cases also been legitimate to talk about the emancipating power of planning. But it is not the normal way of planning, although public participation is talked about a great deal these days.

References

Asplund, E., Dovlén, S., Håkansson, M. and Orrskog, L. (1997), *Räcker kompetensen? En studie av den långsiktiga miljöhänsynen i fyra kommuner*, Report from Department of Infrastructure and Planning, KTH, TRITA-IP FR 97–27.

Bender, B. (1993), 'Introduction: Landscape – Meaning and Action', in B. Bender (ed.), *Landscape. Politics and Perspectives*, Berg, Oxford.

Bourdieu, P. and Wacquant L. (1992), *An Invitation to Reflexive Sociology*, Polity Press, Cambridge.

Boverket (1994), *Sverige 2009 – förslag till vision*, Boverket, Karlskrona.

Burr, V. (1995), *An Introduction to Social Constructivism*, Routledge, London.

Daly, H. and Cobb, J. (1989), *For the Common Good – Redirecting the Economy toward Community, the Environment and a Sustainable Future*, Beacon Press, Boston.

Dyrberg, T.B. (1997), *The Circular Structure of Power: Politics, Identity, Power*, Verso, London.

Fairclough, N. (1995), *Critical Discourse Analysis. The Critical Study of Language*, Longman, London.

Fischler, R. (1998), 'Communicative Planning Theory and Genealogical Inquiry', Paper presented at the *Conference on Planning Theory*, Oxford, April 2–4, 1998.

Flyvbjerg, B. (1998), *Rationality and Power. Democracy in Practice*, University of Chicago Press, Chicago.

Fog, H., Bröchner, J., Törnqvist, A. and Åström, K. (1992), *Mark, politik, rätt – om plan- och bygglagen i praktiken*, Byggforskningsrådet, rapport T22:1992, Stockholm.

Forester, J. (1989), *Planning in the Face of Power*, University of California Press, Los Angeles, California.

Friedmann J. and Weaver, C. (1979), *Territory and Function. The Evolution of Regional Planning*, Edward Arnold Pbl, London.

Geddes, P. (1949), *Cities in Evolution*, Williams and Norgate Ltd, London.

Göransson, A. (1998), 'Mening, makt och materialitet. Ett försök att förena realistiska och poststrukturalistiska positioner', in *Häften för kritiska studier* nr 4.98, Stockholm.

Hajer, M.A. (1995), *The Politics of Environmental Discourse – Ecological Modernization and the Policy Process*, Clarendon Press, Oxford.

Harré, R., Brockmeier, J. and Muhlhäuser, P. (1999), *Greenspeak. A Study of Environmental Discourse*, Sage Publications, London.

Hastings, E. (1999), 'Discourse and Urban Change: Introduction to the Special Issue', in *Urban Studies*, vol. 36, No. 1, January 1999.

Healy, P. (1997), *Collaborative Planning. Shaping Places in Fragmented Societies*, Macmillan Press Ltd, London.

Hettne, B. (1983), *Strömfåra och kontrapunkt i västerländsk utvecklingsdebatt*, Naturresurs-och miljökommittén, SOU 1983:56, Bakgrundsrapport 8, Stockholm.

Hoy, D.C. (1986), 'Power, Repression, Progress: Foucault, Lukes and the Frankfurt School', in D.C. Hoy (ed.), *Foucault. A Critical Reader*, Blackwell, Oxford.

Kelly, M. (1994), 'Introduction', in M. Kelly (ed.), *Critique and Power. Recasting the Foucault / Habermas Debate*, MIT Press, Boston.

Lapintie, K. (1996), 'Paradise Lost. Rationality, Freedom and Ecology in the City', *Housing & Environment*, No. 2, University of Tampere.

Lapintie, K. (1997), 'Constructing the Environment in Planning', in K. Lapintie and M.-L. Mäsä (eds), *From Restructuring to the Ecological City*, Housing & Environment No. 5, University of Tampere.

Liedman, S.-E. (1997), *I skuggan av framtiden. Modernitetens idéhistoria*, Bonniers förlag, Stockholm.

Lyotard, J.F. (1984), *The Postmodern Conditions*, University of Minnesota Press, Minneapolis.

MacNaughton, P. and Urry, I. (1998), *Contested Natures*, Sage Publications, London.

Merchant, C. (1989), *Ecological Revolutions – Nature, Gender and Science in New England*, University of North Carolina Press, Chapel Hill, North Carolina.

Mårtensson, B., Alfredsson, B., Dahlgren, L. and Grahm, L. (1988), *Det hotade lokalsamhället*, Rapport T6:1988, Byggforskningsrådet, Stockholm.

Nylund, K. (1995), *Det förändrade planeringstänkandet*, Nordiska institutet för samhällsplanering, Avhandling 19.

Orrskog, L. (1998), 'There is no Such Thing as a Sustainable City', in L. Nyström (ed.) (1999), *City and Culture. Cultural Processes and Urban Sustainability*, The Swedish Urban Environment Council, Karlskrona.

Persson, L. O. and Westholm, E. (1994), *Europas landsbygd i förändring*, ERU rapport 83, 1994, Stockholm.

Rorty, R. (1998), 'Truth and Progress', *Philosophical Papers*, Cambridge University Press, Cambridge.

Rydin, Y. (1997), 'Can We Talk Ourselves into Sustainability?', Paper presented at a conference in Oslo 1998.

Sager, T. (1996), *Communicative Planning Theory*, Avebury, Aldershot.

Sagoff, M. (1988), *The Economy of the Earth. Philosophy. Law and the Environment*, Cambridge University Press, Cambridge.

Torfing, J. (1999), *New Theories of Discourse: Laclau, Mouffe and Zizek*, Blackwell, Oxford.

PART IV
RESHAPING THE TOOLS FOR REGIONAL PLANNING

13 Economic Guidelines for Transportation Planning

MARTIN J. BECKMANN
ÅKE E. ANDERSSON

Introduction

While land use planning may be problematical, there is general agreement among economists that the provision of transport facilities as 'public goods' is a proper task of government (Dreze, 1995). The question in each particular case is: what kind and how much? And how it is to be paid for?

In a free society in which people may use private means of transportation, the roads are the public good. The operation of van and bus systems in an urban context often falls on government, since private operators cannot supply this at a profit or even at coverage of cost. At the very least, subsidies to public transportation are now considered indispensable. The planning of government activities in transportation for a metropolitan area is a complex task. Its difficulties are multiplied when transportation planning is embedded in a larger scheme of land use and urban development programming.

While it must be considered within the larger framework of urban land use this can be done, however, independently of the details of land use plans through the observation of suitable parametric conditions in the form of designated land values to be assigned to amenities and historical monuments of mandatory constraints. Within this formulation, traffic planning can then be considered autonomously and to some extent, free from controversies over particular land use plans.

Objectives

Although transport planning for major urban areas raises challenging engineering problems, it is ultimately an economic decision problem.

What should be its objectives? While various objective functions including entropy and other measures of diversity or robustness (Mattsson, 1984) have been suggested, economic theory tells us that it should be benefits minus costs, broadly considered, properly measured and discounted to the present, i.e. the time of decision making. The time horizon should extend at least as far as the expected life of the facilities being considered. Reasonable discounting benefits and costs in the distant future become negligible, so a precise time frame is not required. Decisions based on predictions beyond, say, 30 years are hazardous in any case.

It is well known that the public's perception of transportation is ambiguous. On the one hand mobility, the opportunity to travel and move about freely and easily, is a highly valued aspect of modern life. On the other hand there is the horror of its cost, in terms of the impact of the transportation facilities on accident rates and on the environment, man-made and natural, and of the expenses of money and time spent. A rational plan that achieves an optimum of benefits over costs is all the more desirable.

Whose benefits? In a democratic society all government planning, particularly in areas that immediately touch people's lives, is now a matter of *public choice*. Political support is needed, no matter how the economic optimum is calculated. Therefore it is not just a question of total benefits and costs in the aggregate, but also of their incidence in any specific groups homogenous enough to express their particular will and exercise it through political processes. To allow for this, a careful weighing of both benefits and costs is needed with regard to identifiable groups, paying attention to who benefits, who pays, and how much they are paying.

When travel demands are given and fixed, the measurement of benefits is straightforward and, when considered as an economic problem, easy. It is also of long standing in traffic engineering practice: the savings in travel time from the given origins to the desired destinations of the known travelers. But the assumption of fixed demands is theoretically untenable and empirically invalid. Better transport facilities generate additional trip demands, as is well known.

The economic criterion that is meaningful and operational is the so-called consumers' surplus (CS), which has been used since Dupuit (1844), see also Ekelund (1987). While not perfect from the point of view of the advanced theory of demand (Hicks, 1950) it is justified as long as questions of income distribution are set aside – and transportation is a poor instrument for achieving changes in income distribution in pursuit of whatever social objectives. The CS is measured as the area below the demand curve and the horizontal that describes the price charged. In the present application price must be replaced by time.

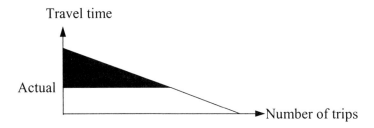

Figure 13.1 Consumers' surplus

Behind this demand curve are the perceived individual benefits realized by the purposes of each trip. The question arises whether in addition to time savings and the benefits of additionally generated trips, other matters should be considered that contribute to human welfare such as better living conditions in less densely populated places made accessible by improved transportation. Does a long run demand curve for trips contain this already, so that a separate listing would be economic double counting?

The demand curve states what the expense of time is worth to achieve the trip's purpose. Therefore if the purpose is to enable a person to live at a certain distance from work (for instance) then the value of the benefits of living there exceeds or at the margin equals the value of the expense of time. That is the meaning of demand curves and consumer surplus in the long run when locational choices are possible. There is no need for an additional counting of these benefits, since the long run demand curve reflects this all.

Complications with this procedure can only appear in regions of sufficiently low economic density to allow for a high degree of monopolization of economic activity. In such regions a radical improvement of the transportation infrastructure might change the market structure from monopoly to monopolistic competition, improving the general efficiency of the regional production system as a whole (Blum, 1998). However, in metropolitan areas with large numbers of economic agents this factor is of minor importance.

This means, of course, a great conceptual simplification of the planning problem, but it shifts the burden to the practical problem of determining the long run demand curve. As a practical matter it may be easier to assess the underlying factors directly – like amenities of suburban living – that enter into the demand curve rather than the demand curve itself. This is a question of practical procedure rather than of principle, as long as one is aware of the relationship of underlying factors to the demand curves and avoids double counting.

The Valuation of Time

To make benefits and costs comparable the time savings or the time integral as consumers' surplus must be converted into money units (or alternatively the money cost into time units). This is even more apparent when travelers' choices are affected by road tolls or other money charges.

The economic solution is straightforward only when the individuals concerned are free to choose their working hours, as in the case of the self-employed or senior partners in business and other professions. For then the marginal utility of their leisure time equals the marginal utility of their hourly wage. It may be postulated that society's choice of working hours reflects these same preferences, at least in the long run. Thus for a first approximation, the money value of one hour to an average or representative individual should equal the average hourly wage rate. (In conservative practice sometimes only half that value is used, with or without proper theoretically motivated arguments for this procedure.)

The valuation of time is seemingly avoided when a fixed budget is to be allocated so as to maximize total benefits measured in time units. However, this leaves open the question of the appropriate size of this budget. In order to determine this, the question of the value of time savings is opened up once more.

Alternative Objectives

The goal of maximizing net benefits (gross benefits minus costs) is older than the welfare state but congenial to it. Other objectives for transportation planning can be put forward and have been used in various government activities. The fiscal goal of maximizing state revenue or minimizing state losses, which goes back to mercantile economic doctrine, has been applied to state monopolies as sources of government income. The objection to this, raised by economic theory, is that user charges in the transportation system would then deviate from marginal social cost, causing user decisions to be distorted and thus to generate welfare losses which are particularly grave in view of the crucial role that transportation plays in the smooth working of a modern economy and in economic growth as demonstrated in Andersson (1990).

In fact, when determining systems costs, it is not sufficient to just add up the various money costs incurred by privates and by government, but for each tax Euro spent, the cost of raising that Euro must be included. While we will not go into matters of finance in detail, and will leave out the important issue of how the burden is to be distributed among generations through, say, debt financing rather than taxation, it needs to be pointed out that each unit of tax spent requires a cost to society larger than that unit, since economic costs are incurred through the undesired consequences of the incidence of taxation for economic behavior.

That the operation of the transportation system is an unsuitable means of redistributing income has already been noted.

In connection with financing, a brief word is needed on the desirability of the transportation system paying for itself. This would make sense if the transportation system and its users were an identifiable autonomous sub-system within the economy at large. But this is not the case. Every member of contemporary society depends on and participates in transportation. When it comes to particular, say regional, sub-sets a case could be made for a club-type arrangement. Each member of the club pays a fee to cover the overhead or fixed cost so that the system can then be operated by charging its users only the (economy-wide) marginal cost, just as a social club having assessed its fixed costs through annual fees can offer food and drink at (low) marginal cost to the benefit of all its members.

An attempt in this direction has been made by the German State railways (Deutsche Bundesbahn). For the price of a Bahnkarte of about DM200 in annual fee, the traveler is charged half the official ticket price (which presumably is still somewhat above the true marginal cost).

Travel Demand

We now return to the enumeration and valuation of benefits from transportation. It was proposed that we avoid using the long run demand curve for travel as it is too difficult to discover and instead focus on its underlying factors. To get a handle on this a first step is to classify trips and transportation activities by their purpose.

First one must distinguish between goods and person transportation. For goods the demand curve results in, or is a reflection of, potential profits, and in this case the demand curve is more accessible than any information about potential or actual profits which firms will be reluctant to disclose. A distinction that runs across goods and persons is that between transit traffic and traffic either originating or terminating in the metropolitan area under consideration. This distinction is useful in regard to the routing choices available and their responsiveness to road user charges (section Road Pricing).

In personal transportation we must then distinguish types of transportation by trip purposes. Numerically the most important is home to work place and work place to home transportation, known as commuting. It is this traffic that generates peak loads, typically 7 to 10am in the morning and 4 to 7pm in late afternoon. Efforts have been made to reduce these peaks somewhat through flextime, i. e. flexible working hours.

Typically they require office workers to all be present during certain core periods (say 11–12am and 2–3pm) and to allow flexible arrival and departure times but with advance commitment made by filing a plan, say at the end of the previous week, within an allowed range of say 6 – 20 hours for most working days, with the requirement that the total work time goal of 40 hours per week, for instance, is met.

In some US cities (e.g. Detroit) this has led to a significant flattening of the peak traffic profile in particular in certain locations and critical sections of the transportation network. In some US communities, local governments have encouraged the use of flextime with the promise of some tax abatements on local (real estate) taxes. Also exhibiting a distinct peak load profile is the school bus traffic as well as private cars. But here the issue of flextime has not been raised. Event traffic, occurring mainly on weekends, tends to raise only local problems and these are related more to parking rather than traffic flow.

The following leisure-related types of traffic show some discretion both in regards to destinations and times: shopping, (sports) recreation and visits to friends and relatives. This classification by trip purposes is relevant mainly in consideration of the elasticity of user demands in regards to timing and destination.

In every case there is a choice of transportation modes – provided available public transportation systems offer such alternatives – and routes. In public transportation route choices are made primarily by the carrier, but travelers sometimes have options and may even be able to choose among cheaper and more expensive routing, the latter usually associated with faster travel.

In private transportation optimal route choices are a critical issue to be handled by road pricing (see below) or otherwise by prohibitions (no through traffic, no trucks, no left turns at certain hours).

Supply

On the supply side we must list not only the basic types of transportation available – rail, bus, private passenger car – but also their combinations on trips.

When private car traffic feeds its passengers into a public transportation system two basic types are known as *park and ride* and *kiss and ride*. In the latter case the car is driven home again by the spouse or partner.

Ride sharing has, in spite of great efforts at promotion, not really caught on in the US because of the incentives: lower toll charges and parking fees have so far not outweighed the inconvenience of less flexibility particularly with respect to the timing of the home journey. Park and ride has been encouraged by low or no parking fees plus sometimes free bus rides and has been moderately successful. A number of new modes of transportation have been proposed ranging from the conventional to the esoteric:

- shared or communal taxis
- 'dial a van' for transportation between home and airports
- 'people movers', an automatic vehicle traveling on a rail network. Even when tried out for baggage at airports this has so far suffered from technical flaws
- loading passengers and automobiles on trains over strategic corridors
- automated highways in which cars are steered, accelerated and braked through an automatic guidance and control system, electronically operated.

While the first two are existing institutions requiring no significant technical innovations or investments, the other proposed schemes and modes have suffered from high fixed and variable cost and user resistance in the light of cost and uncertainty. Of considerable promise, however, are intelligent highway systems that offer drivers of private cars information on their location and upcoming route choices, taking full account of prevailing traffic conditions. It is tempting to utilize such information systems so as to steer travelers' choices to the system's optimal choices, but this should be approached with great caution, since travelers on the same network will soon get wise to such efforts to steer them away from choices that they would consider best for their own trips. Consequently such route recommendations by the information system will be overruled by the traveler or cause an even less predictable and possibly more harmful traffic equilibrium and even disequilibrium as a result.

Prediction and Planning: Equilibrium Analysis

Travel demand, the decisions to make trips, the choices of their time, mode and route are all influenced by the travel times, or more generally, the generalized trip costs, expected by the traveler as decision-maker. In turn the travel times that actually occur depend on the traffic flows on the various links of the transportation networks. These can be calculated based on the trip, mode and route choices.

This feedback process ends either in a chaotic situation that signifies a general breakdown of transportation activities, or, under normal conditions, in the emergence of a traffic equilibrium, see Fisk and Boyce (1983).

Figure 13.2 provides a classification of different aspects of transport modeling and planning.

		Process time scale	
		FAST	**SLOW**
Efficient decisions	**PRIVATE**	Trade, transport and communication flow equilibrium, rational expectations of congestion and accidents	Mobility of people
	PUBLIC	Non-equilibrium flows with unpredictable unexpected disruptions, congestion and accidents	Physical networks

Figure 13.2 Efficiency of private versus public decisions on transportation

The chaotic situation as depicted in the lower left corner of the figure occurs when the growth of mobility outstrips the investments into physical network capacity, as can be observed in Taipei, Cairo or Bangkok. Here as always in economic analysis, equilibrium denotes a state of the system in which decision makers stick to their plans as best choices under the prevailing conditions and these conditions, in turn, remain constant. In short, equilibrium is a state of no absolute or relative changes. Flow equilibrium in traffic networks is thus a particular instance of an economic sub-system in equilibrium. Moreover, this equilibrium tends to be stable, and small and random deviations will be corrected through a return to equilibrium. There is however one important difference between traffic equilibrium and market equilibrium of the more familiar type in economic analysis. It cannot be taken for granted that such an equilibrium represents a Pareto optimum, i.e. a situation in which no one can be made better off except by making someone else worse off.

Equilibrium versus Optimal Utilization

Having discussed the demand and the supply side of a metropolitan transportation system we turn to the crucial issue: equilibrium versus optimum; see Beckmann et al (1954) or Leblanc and Boyce (1986).

Consider first the short run. Here the supply side is fixed, transport users reside in their chosen locations and work at their chosen work places. The equilibrium problem concerns the prediction of travel destinations, modes of travel and route choices and from these the traffic flows on the various links of the transportation network (traffic assignment). For this there is an established methodology involving the calibration of gravity models, modal split by random utility modeling, and route assignment by shortest path algorithms or entropy maximization; see for instance Brotchie et al (1980) and Kim (1989). Their details do not concern us here. The important point is that the traffic equilibrium is not economically optimal.

The underlying reason is that in the presence of congestion, private costs fall short of social costs because the delay suffered by an additional vehicle, or rather its driver, is less than the delay caused to others. As a result, more use is encouraged of congested facilities than is socially optimal and longer but less congested paths are under-utilized. Similarly travelers at times of maximum flow are not sufficiently encouraged to shift to less congested hours.

Road Pricing

Having stated the problem, the question is what to do about it. In a market economy commands and prohibitions should be used sparingly, and measures which are consistent with individual decision making should be sought out.

The first best solution is that of collecting road user charges on congested facilities where amounts depend on the state of congestion. The technical means for doing this have been described in the famous Smeed report.

Objections to this type of road pricing have arisen from political opportunism rather than on technical or economic grounds. Only under the benevolent dictatorship of Singapore has road pricing been practiced so as to bring about a socially optimal utilization of its transportation network. The road user charges are set to equal as closely as possible the difference between social and private marginal cost of congestion.

Considering Stockholm as a relevant example for the planning of advanced metropolitan regions, it would seem desirable to route transit traffic around rather than through the metropolitan area. Tolls should be charged at the entry ports to the city and their level should be sufficient to make detouring around the city the less costly alternative to transit traffic. For traffic that originates or terminates in the city the function of tolls that depend on congestion levels is 1) to encourage route choices that channel traffic into the principal through route (tunnel), and 2) to invite a more even distribution of traffic loads over the day and week.

The *longer* the proposed detour route for north-south traffic around the Stockholm metropolitan area, the *higher* must be the toll needed to discourage traffic straight through the Stockholm metropolitan area. It is therefore of prime importance to study feasible investment alternative routes between, say, Uppsala or Märsta in the north and Södertälje or Gnesta in the south of the region and the transportation investments required for these.

Other Pricing Issues

In connection with road pricing one must also consider the pricing of public transportation systems. For clearly both will determine modal choice.

There is a general disposition by government and the public to encourage greater use of public transportation (for everybody but oneself) in view of its perceived lower *social cost*. We should distinguish between promotion of demand for public transportation in general and specific measures for encouraging the use of public transportation on specific critical routes, notably the critical links through an urban center. Under the general methods of promotion it has been proposed to lower fares on public transportation through subsidies to the point of even making it free. This has been tried for a bus route in downtown Denver (with mixed results) and has been proposed for the New York subway system during non-peak hours by the eminent transportation economist Vickrey (1967, 1971).

Park and ride systems with free parking and free bus transportation from parking lots located near the CBD on arterial freeways are another conspicuous example. Should the toll revenues from road pricing be used to subsidize public transportation? This sensitive issue would certainly raise political hackles. Actually, no particular designation for the use of toll revenues is needed as long as they go into the general budget for transportation investments and systems maintenance.

On general economic principles, once tolls have bridged the gap between private and social cost in automobile transportation, the case for subsidizing public transportation on these grounds evaporates. The guiding principle in pricing public transportation should be charges at marginal cost, and any remaining deficits in covering general overhead or fixed cost are to be raised by means of club fees from all users of the transportation system (private or public), that is essentially from all tax payers.

Investment

Investments in transportation systems are needed when existing facilities wear out or become obsolescent, and when transportation demand increases beyond existing capacities. As an economy's GNP grows, the demand for transportation grows at an even faster rate. Hence, at periodic intervals transport capacities must be expanded – or at the very least the system's utilization must be improved. But there are definite limits to this latter option. The types and locations of new facilities depend of course on local geography and the system in place. What all metropolitan areas have in common is a need for a circumferential or through route to handle transit needs and a system of spokes (possibly just one) to enable greater access to the center without congesting the main areas between center and circumference.

When a city is located in a plain of uniform constituency, presenting no natural obstacles, the preferred solution turns out to be a circular ring of freeways and/or rails intersected by radial routes (freeways or rail routes) that run to the center; see also Fujita (1989). A complete ring may not be feasible for cities located on rivers, lake shores or between lakes. In that case a semi circle or straight route may have to do duty for a complete ring. At the extreme opposite to the city in a plain one finds a corridor situation where traffic must be channeled into a single linear route defined by the natural obstacles that surround the metropolis. The ultimate case is, of course, where the city forms a cul-de-sac with only one opening. This is the situation of Bombay, India, where highways must all pass through a single bottleneck.

A Preferred Choice for the Case of Stockholm

Stockholm, located between the Baltic and the Mälar lake system, falls into the category of corridor cities. Even though its land use pattern does not show an extreme elongation, its metropolitan area including suburbs does exhibit a north–south axis. A ring road solution is thus an obviously natural or economical case. Transit traffic is essentially north–south oriented since destinations east of Stockholm, that is, between Stockholm and the Baltic, are few in number and significance. Even without a detailed analysis a principal north–south transport route through or alongside the center seems to be indicated. The principal decision then hinges on the question of locating this traffic facility in the third dimension: on level ground, above ground or below ground.

Consider first the solution that seems to require the least amount of construction and investment activity, a freeway or rail facility above ground level. While its construction cost may be cheapest, the cost of land acquisition is highest and so is the interference with existing land use. Adjacent areas are separated and access across the transport facility is severely restricted or even disrupted entirely. Pollution and noise downgrade the adjacent land areas, causing severe losses in land value. In the case of historic areas and those in possession of natural, architectural or landscaped beauty, the damage is irreversible and incalculable.

Granting that progress has been made in the construction of elevated facilities and bridges that allow transportation to be carried out above ground level, and that access restrictions, pollution and noise are less obtrusive in this case, land cost also being considerably less, land values will still decrease and the impact on amenities, cultural and natural, while not as extreme as for ground level facilities, are still substantial and critical. Here the choice is essentially between single or double lanes in either direction. If buses and trucks are to be allowed and this is unavoidable, then in view of the length of the underground facility, double lanes become a technical necessity. Intermediate stretches of double lanes for paving, while useful to some extent, are not a foreward-looking solution. Underground transportation systems were first tried out in Boston, then Budapest and such world class cities as Paris and London. A ring road through tunnels now exists in Brussels, the city that is preparing for its role as the European Union's capital. The underground solution requires considerable investments but avoids the cost of land acquisition, which is highest in the most densely occupied parts of the city.

The cost of tunnels under water is comparable in order of magnitude to the cost of the bridges that would be required in the ground-level and above-ground solutions. An important decision remains: How far from the center should a tunnel be extended or, coming from the outside, at which point should a ground-level facility be placed in an underground tunnel? Unless amenities that should not be touched dictate otherwise, this is a question of the density of land use as reflected in the level of land values. At the point of transition, the optimal solution requires that *investment cost of one kilometer of ground facility + land cost = investment cost of one kilometer of underground facility.* This equation is of course nothing but the well-known principle of marginal cost that follows from the minimization of total cost. Since land values tend to fall with the distance from the center, the application of this cost minimization principle indicates that transportation should be in tunnels under the most central areas of the city, with the entry and exit points placed at critical distances determined by the marginal cost condition.

Where do benefit considerations enter? They are needed essentially when considering the size or capacity of the facilities that should be constructed. Otherwise we are dealing with a straight case of minimizing total social cost. In the case of roads, the choice is essentially between one or two lane facilities (in each direction). In the case of mixed traffic, tolerable speeds for passenger traffic require opportunities for passing that are available only with two lanes. When traffic is squeezed into one lane on critical sectors, this is apt to generate queues at the point of compression. As a general rule, total travel time decreases with the frequency and length of two-lane stretches. This benefit should be weighed carefully against the additional cost of two-lane facilities. A forward-looking solution would undoubtedly be to have two lanes in each direction throughout.

Dynamics and the Evaluation of the Large Scale Transport Projects of Stockholm

Transport system improvements in central districts of a large metropolitan region generally tend to have limited impacts on patterns of location of economic activities. The introduction of a new and more efficient thoroughfare, e.g. a city tunnel or bridge, will normally be filled to capacity within a short period of time. The greatest advantages of a new thoroughfare will be recorded as time savings for commuters to and from work places and for people involved in work-related trips to customers, business meetings and similar productive activities in different locations within the metropolitan region. It has been calculated that approximately 130,000 cars will use a new city tunnel through the central parts of Stockholm on a typical weekday. If we assume that half of these trips are either for commuting or social purposes and the other half is for work-related trips, then the value of time savings is the average of the marginal productivity of work and the marginal private value of time. The marginal productivity of working time equals marginal cost of labor to the firm, e.g. the hourly wage rate plus social and other costs, mostly proportional to the wage costs.

At the time of completion of a new tunnel in a central location (for example slightly to the east of Gamla Stan) the marginal cost of labor would surely be no less than SEK 300 per hour and the private value of time would then be something between SEK 50 and 100 (at constant prices). The average hourly value of time, saved by the new possibility of transport would thus be some value between SEK 175 and 200. The number of passengers would be approximately 140,000 per day (based on normal occupancy per car). On average there will be time savings of at least seven and at most ten minutes attributable to the completion of the tunnel. These time savings will occur only for two thirds of the year, when the transportation system is close to full capacity use. The annual time savings would thus be in a range between SEK 900 million and SEK 1,300 million. Assuming a rate of growth of annual benefits at two percent per year and a real rate of interest of seven percent, the discounted value of the stream of benefits would thus be between SEK 18 billion and 26 billion SEK, as a consequence of time savings associated with the increased transportation capacity close to the city center.

In the construction of new tunnels there are normally substantial *economies of scope* to be reaped by combining the construction of new roads for car traffic through the tunnel with new subway tracks. The basic gain from such joint investment strategies is of course the possibility to spread the slightly larger investment costs on a much larger number of future users of the new tunnel.

The Calculation of Long Term Environmental Benefits

In the evaluation of the benefits of diverting surface traffic into a new tunnel, there would be substantial environmental benefits associated with noise reduction and improvement of aesthetic qualities, qualities that are highly valued by tourists and the inhabitants of the Stockholm region. These advantages would primarily be notable in Gamla Stan (the medieval Old Town) and its immediate vicinity. This is also the area where gains in time savings would be rather limited, compared to traffic from further distances in the Stockholm region. However, the evaluation of such environmental benefits is neither impossible in theory nor in practice. The key to understanding the environmental benefits (and costs) is their *impact upon the value of landed property*.

Any hotel manager would know the increased willingness of customers to pay for hotel rooms, if the environment were cleaner, quieter and more aesthetically pleasing to the guests. And any shop or restaurant owner would appreciate the same qualities, because the customers would be greater in number and more willing to stay in the area for shopping, eating and other entertainment. In short, any user of this currently disturbed city space would be willing to express a higher willingness to pay for the use of property in this area, if it were less environmentally disturbed by surface traffic.

The increasing willingness to pay rents can be estimated by examining the difference in rents at similar points of accessibility, experiencing different disturbances from the traffic in Stockholm. Rough comparisons of office rents and hotel rents indicate differences in the range of ten to twenty percent, due to environmental disturbances in the central parts of Stockholm. The value of improving the environment of Gamla Stan and its vicinity would thus currently be in a range between SEK 100 and 300 per square meter of currently disturbed property. In discounted value this would amount to a sum ranging between SEK 2,000 and 6,000 per square meter (corresponding to the increase in the sales value of the property).

The total value of an improvement to the environment due to the diversion of the traffic into tunnels and the demolition of the current disturbing and ugly transportation infrastructure can be assessed by a careful study of the impact on property values, using the methods sketched above. We must at this point stress the importance of separately estimating the environmental impacts, so as to avoid double counting through the increase of property values due to improved accessibility.

Long Term Consequences of Alternatives to New Central Highways in Tunnels

Over the decades there have been a number of alternative plans for relieving the bottleneck problems of central Stockholm. These different variants of *Österleden* would have a slight advantage in construction cost compared to the extensive construction costs of the centrally located city tunnel alternatives. The advantage of tangential metropolitan highway solutions is obvious in metropolitan areas like Vienna or Paris. In these cases there are considerable dynamic benefits gained by owners and users of land formerly lacking good accessibility to the metropolitan region. In a certain sense such new infrastructure becomes a factor of production for new metropolitan land.

But this is hardly the case in the Stockholm region. The region does not have the potential advantages of topography typical of inland regions. The expansion possibilities are limited in the east. However, this does not preclude potential increases in land values, for instance in the city of Nacka. It is disputable whether these increases in land values can only be achieved by Österleden. It seems to be a rather straightforward engineering task to construct the necessary access roads, connecting large parts of Nacka with the new city tunnels, thus reaping most of the benefits of Österleden, while simultaneously avoiding the aesthetic value losses of the system of bridges and tunnels needed for Österleden, as it has been sketched by architects, engineers and planners.

Although some qualitative conclusions of this nature can be drawn in this context, quantitative calculations are recommended in order to base decisions on correct estimations of benefits and costs. In such a quantitative evaluation the key factor in determining long-term benefits (including most of the external economies) will be reflected in increases of land values in areas experiencing increased accessibility as a consequence of the construction of Österleden.

References

Andersson, Å.E. (1990), 'Knowledge and communications infrastructure and regional economic change', *Regional Science and Urban Economics*, vol. 20, pp. 359–76.

Beckmann, M., McGuire, C. and Winsten, C. (1954), *Studies in the Economics of Transportation*, Yale University Press, New Haven.

Blum, U. (1998), 'What benefits of transport must be considered, and when?', Paper presented at a *Workshop on Measuring the Full Social Costs and Benefits of Transportation*, The Beckman Center, Irvine, California.

Brotchie, J., Dickey, J. and Sharpe, R. (1980), 'TOPAZ – General planning technique and its applications at the regional, urban and facility planning levels', Lecture Notes in *Economics and Mathematical Systems*, vol. 180, Springer-Verlag, Berlin.

Dreze, J. (1995), 'Forty years of public economics: a personal perspective', *Journal of Economic Perspectives*, vol. 9, 2, pp. 111–30.

Dupuit, J. (1844), 'De la mesure de l'utilité des travaux publics', *Annales des Ponts et Chaussées*, 2e sem., pp. 322–75.

Ekelund, R.B. (1987), 'Dupuit, Arsène, Jules, Emile, Juvénal', in *The New Palgrave Dictionary of Economics*, vol.1, MacMillan, London.

Fisk, C.S. and Boyce, D.E. (1983), *Optimal transportation systems planning with integrated supply and demand models*, Publication No 16, Transportation Planning Group, Department of Civil Engineering, University of Illinois, Urbana-Champaign, Illinois.

Fujita, M. (1989), *Urban Economic Theory – Land Use and City Size*, Cambridge University Press.

Hicks, J. (1950), *A Revision of Demand Theory*, Cambridge University Press, Cambridge.

Kim, T.J. (1989) *Integrated Urban Systems Modelling: Theory and Applications*, Kluwer, Dordrecht.

Leblanc, L.J. and Boyce, D.E. (1986), 'A bilevel programming algorithm for exact solution of the network design problem with user-optimal flows', *Transportation Research*, vol 20B, pp. 259–65.

Mattsson, L.-G. (1984), 'Equivalence between welfare and entropy approaches to residential location', *Regional Science and Urban Economics*, vol 14, pp. 147–73.

Vickrey, W. (1967), 'Optimization of traffic and facilities', *Journal of Transport Economic Policy*, vol. 1, pp. 123–35.

Vickrey, W. (1971), 'Congestion theory and transport investment', *American Economic Review*, vol. 59, pp. 251–60.

14 Spatial Interaction in Multi-Regional Modeling – A Review

PATRIK AROUSELL

Introduction

The current paper provides an analysis of the theoretical basis of some commonly used spatial interaction models in regional economics. The reviewed models are the gravity, the entropy, and the minimum information model. The aim of the text is to give examples of different contexts in which the models have been applied and to suggest further extensions.

One area in which the spatial interaction models have been used is to analyze the implications of globalization. Globalization in this text refers to the ongoing trend in the reduction of trade barriers between nations. A reduction of trade barriers may imply a growing need for quantitative economic analysis on the regional level. Interaction between regions within and between nations becomes more and more important. A paper which presents a model for the analysis of a reduction in the trade barriers is Bröcker (1988). The basis of the paper is the explicit use of a gravity formulation for spatial price equilibrium. The analysis in the paper is then made for the consequences related to production changes within regions by lower tolls.

An equally important area in regional economics is the functioning of the labor market. The second model reviewed is one in which the entropy formulation is used to forecast the commuting patterns between municipalities. The basis of the model is a national input-output model. The model is then combined with a shift-share analysis to forecast the demand for labor by municipality while the supply of labor is forecast by an econometric model. The information on the demand and supply of labor then constitutes the information on the macro-level used in the entropy model.

A large portion of the models for economic forecasting is made up of national input-output models. The benefit of the national input-output model is the model's ability to provide detailed forecasts of production on the sector level with a given demand. One extension has been to apply the national input-output concept on the regional level in a multi-regional input-output context where the interaction between the regions is assumed to take the form of trade flows. The main objection to the direct application of the multi-regional input-output model has been the cost of data needed in the estimation of the model. By transforming a national input-output model into a partial regional input-output model, this deficit may be circumvented.

The third model reviewed constitutes an example of how a national input-output model may be partially regionalised with the application of the minimum information principle. In addition, a review is made of how the trade coefficients may be estimated within a multi-regional modeling framework when only partial information is available of the trade flows.

The Multi-Regional Framework

The general setting for the structure of the system within which the gravity, the entropy, and the minimum information model may be applied is characterized by three features. The first feature is the flows existing within the system. The flows begin from a discrete number of places and terminate in a discrete number of places. The flows may either begin or terminate in the same node so no a priori restriction is given on the flow directions. The second feature of the system is the assumed linkages between the nodes. The system of nodes and linkages then constitutes the network of the system. The third feature is related to the cost of travel on the linkages between any pair of nodes where the cost is the main determinant for the flow. By translating the general system above into a regional economic one, regions are represented by nodes, transport infrastructure makes up the linkages, and movement between the regions by using the transportation infrastructure incurs the cost.

The definition of regions is mainly based on the assumption of a closed geographical unit as given in Rietveld (1985). The assumption of closed regions will be equivalent to the premise of a discrete number of regions in the sequel of this paper.

The question of what a closed region is within the modeling framework may be related to supply within a region. The relevant definition of a region referring to the supply side should be related to the establishment's use of input factors. A closed region on the supply side may then refer to a labor market region that corresponds to the scope of commuting patterns. In practice, commuting also occurs between labor market regions but as an approximation of a closed region, the labor market regions are close.

If it is not feasible to define a set of closed regions, the preferred modeling approach is to work with continuous variables. In reality, the assumption of closed regions is more often violated than confirmed. Commuting occurs across labor market regions. This may invalidate the use of spatial interaction models.

The central feature in multi-regional economic models which separates them from national economic models is the explicit modeling of the linkages between the regions and across the national-regional level. In the literature (Nijkamp, 1986), four main reasons have been given for the existence of the linkages. First, the market area is larger than the regions. Second, there exist multi-regional actors such as the central government. Third, information flows occur in space, giving rise to region-specific adoptions of innovations, and fourth, physical pollution occurs. The following arguments will explicitly deal with the first fact, that the market area is larger than the regions, which implies flows based on demand and supply interaction.

The discussion on the type of linkages also gives a model benchmark for the classification of the model structure in three different categories, the top-down, the bottom-up, and the mixed. In the top-down approach, the only existing link is the national-regional one, where the outcome in the regions is seen as a part of the national whole. In the bottom-up approach, the national variables are seen as an aggregation of regional variables. In the mixed approach, linkages are assumed to exist in both directions. It has been argued that the preferred modeling approach is the bottom-up approach based on the notion that all activities are based on the regional level. In practice, this modeling strategy has seldom been implemented given the lack of adequate data on the regional level compared to the national. In practice, the most extensively used modeling approach has been the mixed approach, where the main variables which affect the two different levels, are explicitly modeled within a multi-regional framework (Nijkamp, 1986).

The flows, once determined, are directed among the different linkages by the cost related to the flow. The cost of moving has mainly been related to the monetary and/or time cost, or the distance between the regions. The cost could also be translated into a friction cost if the flow is related to abstract networks.

The problem in the specification of the flow cost is to identify a functional form of the interaction cost and to find the variables which best explain the interaction given the functional form. In practice, a convenient form for accessibility to a particular variable is given by Keeble (1982):

$$x_i = \frac{\sum_{j=1}^{s} A_j}{e^{\beta d_{ij}}} \tag{1}$$

where x_i is accessibility to the variable A in region i, A_j is the total number of units of variable A in region j, β is a parameter which measures the impact of the distance between the regions, and d_{ij} is the distance between region i and region j.

The distance decay function, and thus the functional form for the impact of the distance, is given as:

$$f(d_{ij}) = e^{-\beta d_{ij}} \tag{2}$$

which is a widely applied formula for the interaction cost between regions.

The most relevant variables are those related to either the Euclidean distance, the time distance, or the monetary cost. Which one of the variables is to be preferred is then a question for empirical research.

The Gravity Model

The following section summarizes the theoretical basis for the three spatial interaction models. Different multi-regional models are presented in which each one of the formulations has been applied. There is a bias in favor of the Nordic modeling perspective, where two of the three models are taken from Norway and Sweden respectively, while the third model investigates the implications for Denmark, Germany, and Sweden of the creation of a custom-union. The model taken from Sweden is not a full multi-regional one but gives an example of how a national model may be modified to incorporate the flow aspects with a minimum information formulation.

The derivation of the well-known gravity model is done using a basis from Newtonian gravity, defined as:

$$F_{ij} = k \frac{M_1 M_2}{d_{ij}^2} \qquad (3)$$

where F_{ij} is the force of interaction, M_1 and M_2 are body masses, and d_{ij} is the distance between the bodies.

The gravity model used in spatial interaction studies has then been defined as:

$$T_{ij} = kO_i D_j f(d_{ij}) \qquad (4)$$

where k is a constant, O_i and D_j are mass variables, and $f(d_{ij})$ is a distance decay function.

Or, flows are generated as more general functions of origin and destination functions:

$$T_{ij} = kO_i^\alpha D_j^\gamma f(d_{ij}) \qquad (5)$$

where α and γ are parameter values.

The difference between (4) and (5) is that (4) is an unweighted arithmetic mean and (5) is an weighted geometric average of O_i and D_j, (Nijkamp et al., 1985). By taking the logarithm of (5), the OLS estimation procedure could be used to estimate the parameter values and if the parameter values of α and γ equals one, the original gravity model is obtained.

An example where the gravity model has been used to circumvent some theoretical problems related to the flow of goods between regions is given in a paper written by Bröcker (1988). The paper considers a static model for a partial equilibrium analysis of the creation of a custom union with the inclusion of a gravity formulation for the distribution of goods between regions. The basis of the model is the spatial price equilibrium model originating from Samuelson (1952) and Enke (1951).

The drawback related to the Samuelson-Enke model is the unrealistic trade patterns observed by direct implementation of the model. To overcome this, a formulation based on the attractiveness of the supply region, the fob price, the cif price, and the tariffs for importing a commodity from country i to country j are used to explicitly model the heterogeneity of the goods on the market.

The Samuelson-Enke model in its original form is given by:

$$\sum_j x_{ij} = S_i\left(p_i\right) \tag{6}$$

$$\sum_i x_{ij} = D_j\left(v_j\right) \tag{7}$$

$$q_{ij} = p_i + d_{ij} + t_{ij} \tag{8}$$

$$v_j \le q_{ij}, \quad x_{ij}\left(v_j - q_{ij}\right) = 0, \quad x_{ij} \ge 0$$

where x_{ij} are trade flows from region i to region j, $S_i(...)$ is the supply from region i, $D_j(...)$ is the demand in region j, q_{ij} is the cif price of a commodity from region i to region j, p_i is the fob-price in region i, v_j is the cif price in region j, d_{ij} is the transfer cost per unit of the commodity from region i to region j, and t_{ij} is the tariffs paid for importing one unit of the commodity from region i to region j.

Since trade is directed to the sellers with the lowest cif price, the direct application of the Samuelson-Enke model could only be assumed for homogenous goods where the price has a decisive influence of the purchasing patterns. For more aggregated goods or under conditions of imperfect information, the resulting trade flows from the direct application of the model will be unrealistic.

The paper by Bröcker (1988) gives an example of how structural change in the institutional area in the form of creating a custom union between different countries may be analyzed on the regional level. The basis of the study is the implications of a reduction in the tolls between EEC and the former EFTA for regions within Denmark, Germany, Norway, and Sweden.

In total, the model consists of 80 regions, where the regions are approximately on the county level. To measure the effects of the creation of the toll union, we use a welfare measure based on the surplus from monetary measures for consumers and producers in each region before and after the custom union. This is based on works by Mead (1955) and Johnson (1958), where the benefit of the country as a whole is the sum of the consumer and producer surplus modified by the loss of toll revenues at the national level. The explicit details for the calculation of the welfare measure are left out in the sequel.

The first modification made by Bröcker (1988) of the Samuelson-Enke model is to reformulate the flows between region i and j for a good by applying a log-linearly decreasing function of the cif price:

$$x_{ij} = \frac{A_i e^{-\beta q_{ij}}}{\sum_i A_i e^{-\beta q_{ij}}} D_j \tag{9}$$

where A_i is the relative attractiveness of region i as a supply source and β is a parameter quantifying the sensitivity of choice with respect to cif-price differences.

The second modification of the Samuelson-Enke model is the assumption of a constant total demand. Therefore, the demand does not react to price variation. The formulation of the price of a commodity in region j is then given by a composite price, which may be defined as the average price of a commodity in region j, derived from (9):

$$v_j = -\frac{1}{\beta} \ln\left(\sum_{i=1}^{n} A_i e^{-\beta a_{ij}} \right) \tag{10}$$

The resulting reformulation of the Samuelson-Enke model is then given by:

$$x_{ij} = A_i e^{\beta(v_j - p_i - d_{ij} - t_{ij})} D_j \tag{11}$$

$$\sum_j x_{ij} = S_i(p_r) \tag{12}$$

$$\sum_i x_{ij} = D_j \tag{13}$$

where the interpretation of the model is related to the doubly constrained gravity model derived by Wilson (1970) with inelastic constraints on the demand side and elastic constraints on the supply side. The model is transformed into the Enke-Samuelson model if the parameter β tends toward infinity.

The Entropy Model

The interpretation of the entropy model has been developed in a number of directions. It has been related to probability and uncertainty and to information theory. In the entropy model, a distinction is made between the micro- and macro-states of a system. A micro-state in the system is related to each one of the possible permutations of the allocation of n units in k boxes and the macro-state is related to the number of possible micro-states. Each macro-state can be derived with one or more micro-states and the most probable macro-state is the one that is associated with the largest number of micro-states. See, for example, de la Barra (1989).

The calibration of parameter values in the entropy model is made via assumptions about the state of the system of the macro-level. No assumption of the system is made on the micro-level except that the allocation of each individual object in each one of the k boxes is equally probable.

Examples of the information about the system at the macro-level may be related to knowledge of the number of objects originating from a given zone and arriving in a given destination zone. Another commonly assumed piece of information on the macro-level is related to the flow cost. The assumption is that the total flow cost is known for the system and that the cost of moving between each one of the k boxes is known. By placing different constraints on the model, the number of macro states will change and thereby the number of possible outcomes.

The estimation of the flows between the regions within the system is done by maximizing:

$$W = \frac{X!}{\prod_{i=1}^{m} \prod_{j=1}^{n} x_{ij}} \qquad (14)$$

where X is the total number of flows, x_{ij} is the total number of flows between box i and box j, and m and n are the number of origin boxes and destination boxes respectively.

As an example of the calibration of the parameter values, assume that information about the system is given on the macro-level by the flow origins and destinations as well as the total transportation cost within the system and the cost for the flows between the boxes. The objective is then to maximize (14) with respect to the different constraints imposed.

In the case of known origin and destination margins, and with the knowledge of the flow cost between the boxes and within the system, the macro information is given by:

$$\sum_{j=1}^{n} x_{ij} = O_i \tag{15}$$

$$\sum_{i=1}^{m} x_{ij} = D_j \tag{16}$$

$$\sum_{i=1}^{m}\sum_{j=1}^{n} c_{ij} x_{ij} = C \tag{17}$$

where c_{ij} is the flow cost between box i and j, and C is the total flow cost within the system.

By taking the logarithm of (14) and using what is called Sterling's approximation the maximization problem is given by:

$$\max W = -\sum_{i=1}^{m}\sum_{j=1}^{n} x_{ij}\left(\ln x_{ij} - 1\right) \tag{18}$$

subject to

$$\sum_{j=1}^{m} x_{ij} = O_i \tag{19}$$

$$\sum_{i=1}^{n} x_{ij} = D_j \tag{20}$$

$$\sum_{i=1}^{m}\sum_{j=1}^{n} c_{ij} x_{ij} \tag{21}$$

The solution of the problem is given by:

$$x_{ij} = e^{-\left(\lambda_i + \beta_j + \gamma c_{ij}\right)} \tag{22}$$

where λ_i, β_j, γ are the Lagrangean parameters associated with (19), (20), and (21).

An Input-Output Model Combined with an Entropy Model

In the development of input-output modeling, two different approaches have been taken to extend the framework given by Leontief to a multi-regional setting. The approach has been either to apply the national input-output modeling framework to a pure regional framework where, in the ideal case, the regions are modeled as separate entities and where the linkages between the regions are given by trade coefficients similar to the technical coefficients. The other approach is based on a national input-output model where the model may be partially regionalized by applying different theoretical methods such as one of the spatial interaction models. The following section gives an example of the latter approach where a national input-output model is combined with an entropy model for the forecast of commuting patterns between the municipalities.

The PANDA was developed at SNITEF in Norway with the objective to forecast commuting and migration patterns (Stokka and Støland, 1989). The model is an example of a combined approach where a national input-output model, the REGNA module, is used to forecast industrial production which by using a shift-share distribution gives the labor demand at the regional level. An econometric model, the REGBEF module, forecasts the development of the population within a municipality. The equilibrium flow between the demand and supply of labor is then solved by an entropy model.

The REGNA module is a national input-output model where the exports, national and local public consumption, imports and part of the investment are given exogenously. The private consumption within the model is endogenously determined by the income given to the households via the gross product from industry and via transfers. The gross product within industry also determines labor demand by industry which, in turn, is distributed among the municipalities by a shift-share analysis determining local labor demand.

The REGBEF module in PANDA is based on a demographic model consisting of the module aging, birth, and death, the labor market module, the gross migration module, and the housing market module. Of these modules, the labor market and the housing module are based on an entropy formulation for the interaction among the regions with regard to commuting and migration. The aging, birth, and death module is given by transition frequencies, and external migration is calculated from migration rates and from the labor market module. Only the entropy model for the commuting patterns between the municipalities is reviewed in the following sequel.

The basis of the labor market part of the PANDA model is given by the demand and supply of labor for time t and municipality k. The labor supply within the model is determined by participation rates for the population at time t in municipality k by sex and age. The demand for labor is exogenously determined by the shift-share analysis.

From these formulations, the supply and demand for labor are given by:

$$S_{kt} = \sum_{s} \sum_{a} l_{sa} P_{sakt} \qquad (23)$$

$$D_{kt} = \sum_{i} N_{ikt} \qquad (24)$$

where S_{kt} is the labor supply in municipality k at time t, l_{sa} is the labor activity frequencies for sex s and age a, P_{sakt} is the population by sex s, age a, municipality k, and time t, and D_{kt} is the labor demand in municipality k, at time t. Also, N_{ikt} is the exogenous labor demand for industry i, municipality k, and time t.

S_{kt} and D_{kt} form the margins in the entropy model and are interpreted as the information given on the macro-level of the system. Before the margins are determined, the model is modified for the groups within the population which do not participate in the labor market.

In addition, a turnover percent is given where the model user determines the proportion of the labor force which is participating in the labor market interaction every year. This is defined as TOV_t. The number of people who still need to be added to the interaction matrix in year t after the model distribution is given by:

$$RT_{ijt} = (1 - TOV_t) T_{ijt-1} \qquad (25)$$

where T_{ijt-1} represents the elements of the interaction matrix between the previous year for industry i to industry j.

The margins to be distributed by the entropy model are then given by:

$$MS_{it} = \sum_{j} TOV_t T_{ijt-1} + (S_{it} - S_{it-1}) \qquad (26)$$

$$MD_{it} = \sum_{j} TOV_t T_{ijt-1} + (D_{it} - D_{it-1}) \qquad (27)$$

In (26) and (27) S_{it} is the supply of labor by industry i at time t, S_{it-1} is the supply of labor by industry i at time $t-1$, D_{it} is the demand of labor by industry i at time t, and D_{it-1} is the demand of labor by industry i at time $t-1$.

The solution of the system of equations is given by:

$$MT_{ijt} = a_i b_j MS_{it} MD_{jt} f(d_{ij})$$

(28)

$$a_i = \left(\sum_j b_j MD_{jt} f(d_{ij}) \right)^{-1}$$

(29)

$$b_j = \left(\sum_i a_i MS_{jt} f(d_{ij}) \right)^{-1}$$

(30)

The formulation of the travel distance function in the entropy model, $f(d_{ij})$, is either given as a power or an exponential function, defined as:

$$f(d_{ij}) = d_{ij}^{-\beta} \text{ or } f(d_{ij}) = e^{-\beta d_{ij}}$$

(31)

where d_{ij} is the distance between municipality i and j depending on the systems estimate of the best fit of one of these functions.

The distribution among migrants by municipality is given by the following function:

$$lm_{ij} = \alpha e^{-\beta(\delta - d_{ij})} \qquad \text{for } d_{ij} \leq \delta$$

and

(32)

$$lm_{ij} = \alpha\left(2 - e^{-\beta(\delta - d_{ij})}\right) \qquad \text{for } d_{ij} > \delta$$

where α and β are parameters, and δ is the distance.

The number of those who choose to commute is given by:

$$lc_{ijt} = 1 - lm_{ijt}$$

(33)

The Minimum Information Model

The interpretation of the entropy function has been extended to be a measurement of the amount of uncertainty or lack of information associated with a probability distribution. By defining:

$$p_{ij} = \frac{x_{ij}}{X} \tag{34}$$

the most probable flow distribution is determined by maximizing the function:

$$S = -\sum_{i=1}^{m} \sum_{j=1}^{n} p_{ij} \left(\ln p_{ij} - 1 \right) \tag{35}$$

subject to the set of constraints containing the available information.

The weakness in the interpretation as an information-theoretical concept is that the a priori assumption of probabilistically equal flows between regions is often unrealistic. Second, entropy-maximizing is generally seen as a statistical approach which apparently ignores the underlying principles of individual human behavior.

The solution to the first problem is to incorporate a priori information within the framework of entropy maximization. The information gain is then given by:

$$I(P,Q) = \sum_{i=1}^{m} \sum_{j=1}^{n} p_{ij} \ln \left(\frac{p_{ij}}{q_{ij}} - 1 \right) \tag{36}$$

where q_{ij} is the previous observed distribution of the values of p_{ij}.

The derivation of the expression may for example be found in Snickars and Weibull (1977).

The PANDA model provided an example of how information given by a national input-output model combined with a shift-share analysis may provide information on the macro-level of the labor flows distributed by an entropy formulation. The information given by the input-output model may also be used to determine the flow of goods between regions. The basis of the analysis is, as in the PANDA model, a national input-output model, ISMOD, used in Sweden for forecasts of industrial production.

The ISMOD model is an example of a national input-output model which may be extended to a partial regional model with respect to trade flows between regions. The ISMOD model has been developed by Johansson and Persson (1987) and relates to the tradition of computable general equilibrium models based on an input-output structure which allows detailed analyses on the sector level. The dynamic of the model is given by a vintage structure and there, the model is suitable for analyses in the medium term of structural change within industry. The explicit use of econometric methods in the ISMOD model is related to the modeling of the development in the industrial sector. What is given in the modeling framework is that different vintages are attached to each one of the industrial sectors. The partitioning of industrial sectors into vintages is done with regard to labor and intermediate inputs in the production process. Then, by defining an econometrically estimated loss and updating function, the demand for production factors is updated as an average of the best available technologies. The loss of capacity is determined by relating changes to the value added within the vintages. A more detailed discussion of the vintage approach is given, for example, in Johansson (1989) and Westin (1990).

The ISMOD model is defined on the national level but may be extended to incorporate regional aspects with regard to the flow of goods within the system. From a set of defined regions, the application of the entropy, or the minimum information formulation could be used as tools for forecasting the regional production flows. The basis of a partially regionalized model is to derive demand and supply functions in each of the regions. The determination of the demand for products may be given by the national accounting framework:

$$Y^r = I^r + C^r + G^r + Ex^r - Im^r \qquad (37)$$

where Y^r is regional gross product, I^r is regional investments, C^r is regional private consumption, G^r is regional public consumption, Ex^r is regional export, and Im^r is regional import.

Knowing total demand within the region, the demand per industrial sector could easily be derived by applying the Leontief inverse:

$$\mathbf{x}^r = \left(\mathbf{I} - \mathbf{A}^r\right)^{-1}\mathbf{Y}^r \qquad (38)$$

where $\mathbf{x}^r$ is the production by industry in region r, $\mathbf{I}$ is the unit matrix, $\mathbf{A}^r$ is the matrix of technical coefficients for region r, and $\mathbf{Y}^r$ is the regional demand.

Knowing total demand within the region and by assuming a fixed supply capacity, the margins for an entropy or a minimum information formulation are derived. They constitute the information given on the macro-level.

An example of a modified system related to the one above has been used in Bjurklo (1995), where the inter-regional input-output balance is given by

$$X_r^v + M_r^v = \sum_j x_{ij}^v + \sum_j F_{ij}^v + E_i^v \qquad (39)$$

where X_r^v is the production value of commodity group v in region r, M_r^v is the import value of commodity group v in region r, x_{ij}^v is deliveries of commodity group c from region i to region j, F_{ij}^v are deliveries of final consumptio n of commodity group v from region i to region j, and E_i^v is exports abroad by commodity group v and region i.

The origin and destination margins within the model may now be derived where the left hand side of (39) is defined as the absorbed supply and the right hand side is defined as the absorbed demand within the region. The question then is whether the entropy or the minimum information model should be used to find the equilibrium flows on the market. Once again referring to Bjurklo (1995), the observation is that trade flows of manufacturing goods are to a large extent determined by personal networks. The implication of these connections is that the existing trade patterns for manufacturing goods may to a large extent explain the future flows. Under these considerations, applying the gravity model governed by strong transportation cost constraints should give a plausible ex ante result.

The preferred model should then be the minimum information model, given as:

$$I(P,Q) = \sum_{i=1}^{m} \sum_{j=1}^{n} P_{ij} \ln\left(\frac{p_{ij}}{q_{ij}} - 1\right) \qquad (40)$$

subject to:

$$\sum_j p_{ij} = \frac{O_i}{X} \qquad (41)$$

$$\sum_i q_{ij} = \frac{D_j}{X} \qquad (42)$$

$$\sum_i O_i = \sum_j D_j = X \qquad (43)$$

$$p_{ij}, q_{ij} \geq 0$$

In these functions x_{ij} is the trade flow between i and j, X is the total trade flow, y_{ij} is the a priori trade flow between i and j, and Y is total a priori trade flow.

By this formulation, the regional transportation pattern could be derived from a national model.

We have reviewed how the minimum information model can be used in the reformulation of a national input-output model into a partial regional model. The minimum information model could also be used in a multi-regional input-output model in reducing the data needed in the estimation of the trade coefficients between the regions.

The basis of the multi-regional input-output model is the initial work of Leontief, where the accounting framework in the national input-output model is used and extended to a multi-regional framework. Within the multi-regional input-output modeling framework, the linkages between the regions are given by the import and export relations, where the theoretical framework for the inter-regional input-output model was first formulated by Isard (1951). The theory developed by Isard is a straightforward extension of the Leontief national model. The accounting balance in Isard's model is given by:

$$x_i^r = \sum_s \sum_j b_{ij}^{rs} x_j^s + \sum_s y_i^{rs} \qquad (44)$$

where x_i^r is total production of industry i in region r, b_{ij}^{rs} is shipment from industry i to industry j from region r to region s, x_j^s is total demand of industry j in region s, and y_i^{rs} is total final demand from region r to region s by industry i.

The problem with the model above is that it is virtually inoperable given the large amount of data demanded for estimating $b_{ij}{}^{rs}$. To overcome the problem, a further disaggregation may be done as:

$$x_i^r = \sum_s \sum_j a_{ij}^s t_i^{rs} x_j^s + \sum_s y_i^{rs} \tag{45}$$

where t_{rs}^i are the technical coefficients which measure the trade flows between region r and s by industry i, and a_{ij}^s is the technical coefficients for region s by industry i and j.

As been argued by Snickars (1979) and by Batten and Martellato (1985), if only limited information is known about the trade patterns, the minimum information principle could be applied. The benefit of using the principle is that a combination of survey and non-survey data could be used in the estimation of the shipments from industry i in region r to industry j in region s in Isard's model and thus the full model could be applied. Snickars (1979) wrote a paper which examines this possibility, where the requirement for estimating the trade coefficients is that available information should be given by the national input-output coefficients, the final demand, the production of sector i, the value added in sector i, the total export from sector i for region s, the value added in region r, the export from region r, and the import to region r. By using these data, the shipments from industry i in region r to industry j in region s could then be estimated by the application of the minimum information principle where non-survey data are included as an explanatory factor. The procedure amounts to an econometric estimation of the classical model by Moses (1955).

Conclusions

This paper has presented some spatial interaction models used in modeling and forecasting linkages between regions. As has been shown from the examples, the approaches used in these models may be seen as either substitutes or complements. In the gravity model and the minimum information models in the paper by Bröcker (1988) and Snickars (1979), the models have been used as complements to an existing modeling framework. In Bröcker (1988), the model was used to reformulate an existing model into a model which considered the heterogeneity of the goods but preserved the modeling framework. In the paper written by

Snickars (1979), the minimum information formula was adopted to reduce the amount of data needed to estimate the coefficients within a multi-regional modeling framework. The two models could also be used as substitutes as shown in the example of the ISMOD model, where a partially regionalized national input-output model could be derived instead. The strength of using the models in this context is that a partially regionalized model may be created within an existing input-output framework without the costly and cumbersome estimation of the full Isard model or the trade coefficients. Therefore, by adopting the spatial interaction models, partially regionalized models may be created at a relatively low cost.

In a national input-output model, the technical coefficients are given as averages of the regional technical coefficients. The assumption then has to be made that the national technical coefficients are equal to the average regional coefficients. Otherwise, the regional technical coefficients have to be estimated and used within the framework. If the average national and the regional technical coefficients are not equal, the question is whether a partial regional model is stronger than a traditional multi-regional input-output model.

Another question of importance in combining two modeling frameworks is related to the forecast error of the investigation. In any forecasting, there is some error in the forecast values. In the derivation of the margins of the spatial interaction models, there is an error in the forecast related to the estimated parameter values within the model. The error is then transferred to the spatial interaction model which itself is subject to forecast error. Therefore, the accuracy of the forecast is less than the initial forecast. The critical question then is whether the errors are of such a magnitude that the forecast becomes less valuable. In that case, the use of the spatial interaction models does not provide any additional information to the system and a regionalized model is not feasible. To evaluate the performance of a partially regionalized model, comparisons should be made between a multi-regional model and a partial regional input-output model.

In relation to the formulation of the minimum information model, the question is also how disaggregated the formulation of the model should be. In Bjurklo (1995), the model is a top-down one where there is only one manufacturing sector in which transportation occurs. The implications of a one-sector top-down model is that no detailed analysis may be made at the sector level and that no information is transferred from the regional to the national level. Should the aggregation be on the one-sector level, on the level of the transportation modes or on the level of each individual sector?

The question is also which of the models will be used in a particular case. The relevance of using the models in applied work can only be evaluated after their accuracy in the prediction of flows under investigation has been tested. For example, it has been shown in an investigation by Anderstig (1982) that the minimum information formula has given better results in the estimation of trade flows between countries related to the gravity model.

This may be related to the results from Bjurklo (1995). Both these investigations were made for aggregation of the sectors. If a disaggregation is made of the manufacturing sector, the question is whether the minimum information formulation is superior the other formulations. Since no answer may be given a priori on which formulation gives the best explanatory power, different models have to be formulated and tested against each other.

Relating to the theoretical formulations of the models, the question is whether there are statistical methods for deriving the most probable flows within a system or whether the models could be assumed to give equilibrium flows. In the entropy and the minimum information formulations, the information about the system is assumed to be given on the macro level and was mainly related to the distribution's marginal. Then, with the given information on the macro level, the models find the most probable flows with respect to the underlying assumption.

The question of how feasible this assumption is relates directly to the second question given in the section of the minimum information model, namely, whether this assumption reflects underlying human or economic behavior. The problem could be minimized if more information about the system was incorporated on the macro level. The implication of more restrictions at that level means that the estimation becomes less dependent on the underlying assumption and more deterministic in nature. The inclusion of prior information in the minimum information formulation is clearly a step in this direction.

The underlying probabilistic assumption is reduced here to the assumption that flows from the previous period have a conserving influence of the system. The model could be assumed to reflect the actual flow patterns more realistically.

References

Anderstig, C. (1982), *Actual and Predicted Trade Flows of Forest Products*, Department of Economics, Umeå University, Umeå.

Batten, D. and Martellato, D. (1985), 'Classical versus modern approaches to interregional input-output analysis', *Annals of Regional Science*, vol. 19, pp. 1–15.

Bjurklo, L.G. (1995*), Assessing Methods to Estimate Delivery Flows and the ERG Model*, Royal Institute of Technology, Division of Regional Planning, TRITA-IP FR 95–9.

Bröcker, J. (1988), 'Interregional trade and economic integration', *Regional Science and Urban Economics*, vol. 18, pp. 261–81.

de la Barra, T. (1989), *Integrated Land Use and Transport Modelling*, Cambridge University Press, Cambridge.

Enke, S. (1951), 'Equilibrium among spatially separated markets', *Econometrica*, vol. 19, pp. 40–8.

Isard, W. (1951), 'Interregional and regional input-output analysis: a model of a space economy', *The Review of Economics and Statistics*, vol. 33, pp. 318–28.

Johansson, B. (1989), *Vintage Analysis of Regional Economic Change: A Nordic Tradition*, CERUM Working Paper, CWP-1989:18.

Johansson, B. and Persson, H. (1987), *ISMOD – systemets flersektormodeller av den svenska ekonomin*, SIND PM 1987:3.

Johnson, H.G. (1958), 'Marshallian Analysis of Discriminatory Tariff Reduction: An Expansion', *Indian Journal of Economics*, vol. 39, pp. 177–82.

Keeble, D., Owen, P.L. and Thompson, C. (1982), 'Regional accessibility and economic potential in the european community', *Regional Studies*, vol. 16, pp. 419–32.

Leontief, W. (1953), 'Interregional Theory', in W. Leontief (ed.), *Studies in the Structure of the American Economy*, Oxford University Press, New York.

Leontief, W. and Strout, A. (1963), 'Multi-Regional Input-Output Analysis', in T. Barna (ed.), *Structural Interdependence and Economic Development*, MacMillan Ltd, London.

Mead, J.E. (1955), *The Theory of Custom Unions, a General Survey*, North-Holland, Amsterdam.

Moses, L.N. (1955), 'On the stability of interregional trading patterns and input-output analysis', *American Economic Review*, vol. 45, pp. 803–32.

Nijkamp, P. (ed.) (1986), *Handbook in Regional and Urban Economics. Volume I Regional Economics*, North-Holland, Amsterdam.

Nijkamp P., Rietveld P. and Snickars F. (1985), *Regional and Multi-Regional Economic Models: A Survey*, Umeå University, Working Paper from CERUM, 1985:10.

Samuelson, P.A. (1952), 'Spatial Price Equilibrium and Linear Programming', *American Economic Review*, vol. 42, pp. 283–303.

Snickars, F. (1979), 'Construction of Interregional Input-Output Tables by Efficient Information Adding', in C.P.A. Bartels and R.H. Ketellapper (eds), *Exploratory and Explanatory Statistical Analysis of Spatial Data*, Martinus Nijhoff, The Haug.

Snickars, F. and Weibull, J. (1977), 'A minimum information principle: theory and practice', *Regional Science and Urban Economics*, vol. 7, pp. 137–68.

Stokka, A. and Stølan, A. (1989), 'Development and Organisation of a Tool for Regional Planning: the PANDA System', Paper presented at the *IVth World Congress of the RSAI*, Palma de Mallorca Spain, May 26-30, 1992.

Westin, L. (1990), *Vintage Models of Spatial Structural Change*, Umeå Economic Studies No. 227, University of Umeå.

Wilson, A.G. (1970), *Entropy in Urban and Regional Modelling*, Pion, London.

15 Emerging Trade Patterns in the Baltic Sea Region

PONTUS ÅBERG

Introduction

During the last ten years the Baltic Sea region[1] (BSR) has undergone a rapid transformation, with the situation changing from one where there is a clear division between market economies and planned economies to one with interacting market-oriented economies. Economic and political development in several transitional economies has stabilized in a positive way in the last few years. The growth rates in countries bordering the Eastern shore of the Baltic Sea first dropped dramatically but have recently recovered in nearly every state. Knowledge about critical development conditions in transitional economies has also improved substantially in recent years. There is currently a considerable amount of comprehensive research on the economic development of transitional countries.

This new body of literature and the introduction of market-oriented forces in transitional countries have created a significantly better basis for more systematic analyses and projections of trade and transportation demand in the Baltic Sea region. The current long-term outlook for economic development in transitional economies is one of clear optimism. The impact on trade between transitional countries and market economies has been vast and is continuously changing. The change stems from at least two sources.

The former Soviet republics were, roughly speaking, incorporated in an extensive trade plan or a socialist division of labor based on non-market principles. Republic A could be more and less forced to produce commodity X and export it to republic B, which produced commodity Y according to a plan, and sold it to other republics. Free trade creates trade in relation to planned trade from a world trade perspective. Second, the market economy allows countries to grow in a 'natural' way and if this happens to be successful, it will stimulate trade.

The intention of this chapter is to build a trade model and apply it to trade in terms of value and trade in terms of tons. The chapter also forecasts future trade flows and future transportation demand. We apply work on the Baltic Sea region and study its development towards the year 2015.

Outline of the Study

This chapter is divided in five sections. The second section discusses global trends in economic growth and international trade in various regions. The third section presents different spatial interaction models and gives an overview of earlier contributions in forecasting trade flows. This chapter presents a gravity-type trade model for estimating trade in tons and values and between European countries. The estimated parameters will then be applied to countries on the Baltic Sea.

The fourth section presents the estimation results, with regards to trade both in tons of value and in tons and trade predicted by the gravity-type trade model. This section also analyzes gaps between predicted and observed flows as indicators of affinity differences. The final section summarizes the chapter and suggests some conclusions.

GDP and International Trade

GDP

Two general observations on world economic output can be made on the basis of historical experience. Firstly, the process of economic growth is uneven across regions and over time. Secondly, there is a certain convergence of economies over time; developing and transitional economies are in the process of 'catching-up' with industrialized economies. Successful cases of economies industrializing and 'catching-up' all appear to follow a similar dynamic pattern. Once a particular threshold of economic and infrastructural conditions is passed, economic growth accelerates, reaches a maximum level, and then declines. The observation on convergence is also supported by β-convergence studies that find positive levels of β, indicating that income over time in different economies is converging (Barro, 1995; Persson, 1998). The convergence observation holds true if we exclude Africa, particularly Sub-Saharan Africa. Thirty-two countries in that region are poorer now then in 1980. Sub-Saharan Africa is the lowest income region in the world.

Advanced economies such as Western Europe and North America have realized slower growth during the last 40–50 years compared to most of the regions around the world (Maddison, 1989). The growth does not tell us the story behind the growth rates. GDP and GDP rates are influenced by a number of variables.

It is beyond the scope of this chapter to examine the factors driving changes in GDP. However, we could note that in most cases, trade between regions or nations affects GDP positively. Trade allows countries to import technology and knowledge; foreign competition spurs domestic companies to become more productive and domestic resources are used more efficiently.

Table 15.1 below summarizes the IMF's baseline scenario concerning economic growth rates. It also gives an indication of medium-term growth prospects, which will be important later on in this chapter. World economic growth is expected to increase to an average annual rate of 4.1 percent in the period 2000–2003. This may be compared with the long-term trend growth rate of just over 3 percent that is documented for the past quarter century. Transitional countries are expected to grow at an annual rate of 4.1 percent as well, up from an average of 0.1 percent in the period 1996–99.

Table 15.1   Historical economic growth rates and summary of IMFs baseline scenario

| | Eight-Year Averages | | Four-Year Averages | |
	1980–87	1988–95	1996–99	2000–2003
World real GDP	3.1	3.2	3.2	4.1
Industrial countries	2.6	2.6	2.5	2.8
Countries in transition	2.7	-4.5	0.1	4.1
Developing countries	4.2	5.5	4.5	5.6

Source: IMF (1998).

International Trade

Globally, international trade has grown considerably in recent decades. For example during the period between 1963 and 1979 the rate of world expansion of real merchandise exports (that is, the value of exports deflated by changes in export prices) averaged 11.8 percent per year. This is a remarkably high growth rate by historical standards. Indeed, this figure likely underestimates true growth in the real volume of exports because available price data do not adequately account for improved product quality. At the same time, global growth in real output, measured as the gross domestic product (GDP) in each country, averaged 6.1 percent per year, which is also high by historical standards. This implies that the elasticity of world merchandise trade with respect to global output was 1.9, when trade elasticity is calculated as the annual percent change in world trade divided by the annual percent change in world GDP. Thus, during the period between 1963 and 1979, the world experienced a rapid rise in integration among countries as they became more interdependent through the international trade of goods. This trend continued after 1979, although economic activity grew at markedly slower rates. In the period between 1979 and 1991, real export growth averaged 4.4 percent per year. During the 1990s world trade has grown substantially faster than world output, with an elasticity above 2. It is faster than in previous years. The average elasticity between 1970 and 1979 was 1.4. The corresponding relation during the 1980s was 1.1 (IMF, 1996). The IMF's medium-term scenario for 2000–2003 projects an annual growth of 6.2 percent. Developing countries and transitional economies are projected to maintain a growth rate above the world average, while growth in industrial countries will be below average. Actual current projections are summarized in Table 15.2.

Table 15.2   Historical world exports and imports and summary of IMFs baseline scenario (percent per year)

| | Eight Year Averages | | Four Year Averages | |
	1980–87	1988–95	1996–99	2000–2003
World trade	3.3	6.6	6.2	6.2
Exports				
Industrial countries	4.6	6.9	6.0	6.1
Countries in transition	3.0	-1.0	6.2	7.3
Developing countries	0.6	9.1	7.2	7.2
Imports				
Industrial countries	4.3	6.5	6.1	5.6
Countries in transition	1.9	-0.8	6.3	7.6
Developing countries	1.1	8.0	6.1	7.6

Source: IMF (1998).

The current forecast for growth in world trade suggests a potential trade growth rate for countries bordering the Baltic Sea of six to seven percent per year for the next five years. Trade growth in Baltic transitional economies could be closer to seven percent annually, and that of industrialized economies about six percent per year.

A Gravity Model on Trade

There are various approaches available to estimate future trade flows in the Baltic region. In this chapter, an unconstrained open gravity trade model is applied. A spatial interaction model in the form of an open gravity model of international trade has various features including the volume or value and direction of trade. The model formulation presented below is a standard gravity-type trade model, including 'mass factors' and link attributes. The model describes the trade flow X_{ij}, from a particular origin country or region *i* to a particular destination country *j*. Three types of factors are included which contribute to a quantitative explanation of the extent of the trade flow between any two countries:

- *Supply factors* indicating the total potential supply of the exporting country *i*.
- *Demand factors* indicating the total potential demand of the importing country *j*.
- *Link attributes* representing economic conditions that either facilitate or restrain the flow's movement between any two countries. These factors reflect trade friction or transaction costs. Moreover, the economic affinity between two countries will reduce the friction.

The major factor determining the potential supply of country *i* is its production capacity (Y_i), and the ratio of its production for exports to total production (the 'openness ratio'). The former figure is usually represented by GDP, while the latter is represented by the size of the population. GDP varies positively with trade while the openness ratio tends to vary negatively with population.

The population variable serves as a proxy for the scope of the economy – the extent to which the country could satisfy its own demand under autarchy or basically home market demand. The same economic forces that determine potential supply govern a country's potential demand. Higher income therefore suggests greater demand. A larger population in the importing country implies greater self-sufficiency.

GDP and population could also be included using GDP per capita as a variable. The importing country's GDP per capita should be taken as another measure of income, which is positively correlated with the quantity and quality of trade. The exporting country's GDP per capita implies a larger variety and a better quality of goods. Transaction costs reflect trade resistance, and comprise a great variety of variables. Forces resisting – or facilitating – trade determine transaction costs, which can be divided into three main categories:

- natural impediments (for example oceans),
- artificial obstacles (administrative borders) and
- affinities (countries with the same speech and/or cultural area, historical ties or the like).

Transaction costs are often expressed in terms of the geographical distance between two economic zones within a country. Increasing distance results in higher transaction costs and smaller trade. However, distance must be defined in broad terms, because direct transportation costs may for many commodities be a minor part of total interaction costs.

Market information and customer contacts are important elements of trade transaction costs. We are still better informed about markets in our region than conditions prevailing in faraway countries, despite improvements in world information and communication systems. The general model has the following form:

$$X_{ij} = A(Y_i)^{\alpha_1}(Y_j)^{\alpha_2} F_{ij} \tag{1}$$

where X_{ij} is the trade flow from country i to j. A is a constant, Y_i is attributes related to origin node i or a measure of supply capacity in i. Y_j is attributes related to destination node j or a measure of demand capacity in country j. F_{ij} represents link attributes between i and j, reflecting various transaction costs of doing business. The elasticity of supply is denoted by α_1 and α_2 is the demand elasticity. The link-related function F_{ij} is specified as follows:

$$F_{ij} = \exp\{\alpha_3 D_{ij} + \alpha_4 EU + \alpha_5 Nordic\} \tag{2}$$

D_{ij} represents distance-related costs, such as transportation costs from i to j. This average distance is often approximated as the distance between the main airports. EU is a 0/1 variable denoting EU membership, and in the same way Nordic means that i and j are both Nordic countries. Table 15.3

presents variables describing node-related attributes and variables, which characterize link attributes.

Table 15.3 The gravity model and its components

Variable	Proxy variable	Hypotheses: The volume of trade from i to j correlates ....
Potential supply of the exporting country i	GDP of i (Y_i)	Positively with GDP in i
Potential demand of the importing country j	GDP of j (Y_j)	Positively with GDP in j
Transportation costs from i to j	Air distance from i to j (D_{ij})	Negatively with increasing distance from i to j
Trading preference	EU dummy, Nordic dummy	Positively with trade preferences

There are nine countries in the BSR. One way to predict future trade flows would be to estimate current trade between these countries, use the estimated coefficients and introduce forecast values for the independent variables. However, the estimated parameters may not be invariant over time, since some countries are still in the transformation process, changing from planned to market-oriented economies.

This study is mainly interested in the market potential of trade flows and transportation demand and should therefore use coefficients referring to market economies only. To do this, one could use EU countries together with other market economies in Europe. An estimation of these countries would yield 'market' coefficients, which we then could apply to current and future statistics concerning the Baltic Sea region.

This is the same method that Hamilton and Winters (1992) use. We have three years, 1995, 1996 and 1997, and fourteen EU members plus Norway and Switzerland. To overcome time-related auto-correlation and business cycle fluctuations, we use the average of the three years. The total number of observations amounts to 240. If we add a log-normally distributed error term to equation (3), then the ordinary least square (OLS) method can be used to estimate the elasticities after a logarithmic transformation. The following regression equation has been estimated[2]:

$$\ln X_{ij} = \alpha_0 + \alpha_1 \ln GDP_i + \alpha_2 \ln GDP_j - \alpha_3 D_{ij}$$
$$+ \alpha_4 EU_{ij} + \alpha_5 Nordic_{ij} + \varepsilon_{ij} \tag{3}$$

where X_{ij} is country i's exports to j, measured in production USD million. GDP in country i (j), is in USD million, D_{ij} is the air flight distance in km between the capitals of the countries, EU is a dummy variable, where 1 indicates membership in the EU and 0 indicates non-membership, Nordic is another dummy variable which technically operates similarly to the EU dummy. α_0 to α_5 are parameters to be estimated.

The corresponding formula for trade in metric tons has the following expression.

$$\ln XT_{ij} = \alpha_0 + \alpha_1 \ln POP_i + \alpha_2 \ln POP_j - \alpha_3 D_{ij}$$
$$+ \alpha_4 EU_{ij} + \alpha_5 Nordic_{ij} + \varepsilon_{ij} \tag{4}$$

where XT indicates trade in tons. The supply factors have been changed from GDP to population for two reasons. First, using population instead gives a slightly better fit.[3] Second, trade in values is a monetary measure driven by aggregated income (GDP), while trade in tons is a quantity measure driven by the number of agents (population). As income rises, trade in values would probably increase but trade in tons could decrease since heavier and low-value goods could be out-competed by lighter and high-value goods.

Equation (3) and (4) constitute the basic approach with one average observation on each link. These models will be compared with a panel model with three observations (three years) on each link and a random effect measured by the number of links, export node or import node, like equation (5) and (6).

$$\ln X_{ij,t} = \alpha_0 + \alpha_1 \ln GDP_{i,t} + \alpha_2 \ln GDP_{j,t}$$
$$- \alpha_3 D_{ij} + \alpha_4 EU_{ij} + \alpha_5 Nordic_{ij} + \varepsilon_{ij}, t + u_{ij} \tag{5}$$

$$\ln XT_{ij,t} = \alpha_0 + \alpha_1 \ln POP_{i,t} + \alpha_2 \ln POP_{j,t}$$
$$- \alpha_3 D_{ij} + \alpha_4 EU_{ij} + \alpha_5 Nordic_{ij} + \varepsilon_{ij}, t + u_{ij} \tag{6}$$

where t indicates 1995, 1996 and 1997 and u_{ij} is the random effect. For each model, best output is presented and chosen before we enter the next stage and project future trade flows. In a panel model setting like this, one might consider the fixed effect model instead of the random effect model.

However, the objective here is to translate the estimated coefficients and market-oriented functions to the BSR and with this approach, the fixed effect model drops out because the individual effects can not be transferred to other countries. It might be more appropriate to view individual specific constant terms as randomly distributed across cross section units (links), origins (export-nodes) or destinations (import-nodes).

This would be appropriate if we believed that sampled cross-sectional units were drawn from a large population (Greene, 1993). In this perspective when parameters from one area are transferred to another area, this path would be a fruitful alternative. The random effect could be seen as market effects influenced by Western economies, which should be used in a BSR setting.

This type of gravity model has been widely used for the past 30 years. The following section describes a sample of these earlier studies and its different objectives. All except one in this sample have been estimated based on value.

The exception is Johansson and Westin (1994) who estimated trade measured in metric tons. We will therefore pay special attention to that paper. We will also focus our interest on earlier studies of the Baltic states and East Europe like Hamilton and Winters (1992), and Baldwin (1995).

However, first an overview is presented showing typical parameter values obtained in estimated trade models of the gravity-type. Table 15.4 presents the main parameters. The studies include far more variables than those presented here but our concern so far is these variables. In one sense they are not comparable, since these estimated coefficients are affected by other variables that are included. However, it gives a rough overview of how the main coefficients normally appear. A review of some selected studies is also presented.

Tinbergen (1962) is interested in determining the 'normal' pattern of international trade that would prevail in the absence of discriminating trade impediments and he looks for deviations from the normalized trade pattern. He uses a log-normal function on trade, which is explained by GNP in each country, distance and dummy variables with one for neighboring countries, one for a Commonwealth preference and one for Benelux preference. Pöyhönen (1963) builds a model for the volume of trade between countries, based on the same ideas as Tinbergen explained above. Linnemann (1966) tries to answer the questions of why the size of international trade flows differs so widely between pairs of countries and what factors determine the size of the trade flow. He follows the same scheme as Tinbergen, as he was in the research team that carried out the analysis reported in the work of

Tinbergen (1962). Additionally, Linnemann introduces population as a size variable together with GNP.

Table 15.4 A sample of earlier gravity trade studies

Study	Income-related supply	Income-related demand	Distance[4]
1. Tinbergen 1962[(1)]	0.74	0.62	-0.56
2. Pöyhönen 1963	0.52	0.50	0.0016
3. Linneman 1966[(2)]	0.99	0.85	-0.81
4. Aitken 1973	0.91	1.05	-0.35
5. Sattinger 1978	0.91	0.79	-0.97
6. Abrams 1980	0.76	0.65	-0.25
7. Sapir 1981	1.40	1.99	-1.15
8. Bergstrand 1985	0.84	0.56	-0.72
9. Thursby, Thursby 1987[(3)]	0.50	0.41	-0.99
10. Bergstrand 1989[(4)]	1.35	0.69	-0.44
11. Hamilton, Winters 1992	1.17	1.02	-0.75
12. Hellvin 1994	0.91	0.53	-0.72
13. Baldwin 1995[(5)]	1.16	1.22	-0.88
14. Johansson, Westin 1994[(6)]	-0.99	0.96	-0.0002
15. Johansson, Fischer 1996	0.96	1.01	-0.36
16. Strömquist, Åberg 1998	0.67	0.61	-0.0012
17. Torstensson 1998	0.66	0.72	-0.61

(1) Estimation A-3. (2) Calculation AC 1. (3) Coefficients related to Sweden. (4) SITC 6 1976. (5) AR1. (6) Sweden is the only origin country.

Abrams (1980) examines the macroeconomic determinants of international flows between developed countries, paying special attention to the effects of exchange rate variability. The purpose of Sapir (1981) is to test for the existence of statistically significant effects of the EEC Generalized System of Preference (GSP) on actual trade flows between developing countries in the EEC. Bergstrand (1985) presents a critical examination of the gravity formula. Based on certain assumptions, he derives a gravity equation from a general equilibrium model of world trade. Thursby and Thursby (1987) use the gravity formula to examine the Linder hypothesis and the effects of exchange rate variability on trade in values.

Hamilton and Winters (1992) use their model to project future flows in goods traded between Western and Eastern European countries. The method they use is to apply a gravity trade model with coefficients referring to OECD countries. The estimated regression equation they use is

$$\ln X_{ij} = -12.5 - 0.38 \ln pop_i + 1.17 \ln GDP_i - 0.22 \ln pop_j + 1.02 \ln GDP_j$$
$$-0.75 \ln DIS_{ij} + 0.78 adj + 0.7 EC - 0.02 EFTA - 0.31 ECOWAS + 1.25 SADCC$$
$$+2.1 CACM + 0.38 AG + 0.96 LAIA + 2.25 ASEAN + 1.91 UKexcol + 0.73 Frexcol$$
$$0.35 GSP + 0.89 ACP + 1.05 ACP*$$

The second line in the estimated equation starts with dummy variables like adjacency and a number of trade and organizational arrangements. These are the EC (European Communities), EFTA (European Free Trade Association), ECOWAS (the Economic Community of West African States), SADCC (the South African Developing Co-ordination), CACM (Central American Common Market), AG (the Andean Group), LAIA (Latin American Integration Association), and ASEAN (Association of South East Asian Nations). Ukexcol and Frexcol refer to ex-colonial relationships of UK and France. GSP is the Generalized System of Preferences. ACP is the EC's preferences under the Lomé Convention (ACP for ACP exports to the EC and ACP* for the reverse flow). All variables except EFTA, ECOWAS, SADCC, CACM, AG, and French Ex-colonial are statistically significant.

Johansson and Westin (1994) estimate Swedish exports to Europe, measured in metric tons. They use seven years between 1970 and 1987 in a combined time series and cross-section analysis. They divide the data into four different categories: product-competitive commodities with increasing employment, product-competitive commodities with decreasing employment, price-competitive commodities with increasing employment, and price-competitive commodities with decreasing employment. The last group is the largest by far, both measured in value and in metric tons. The following results were obtained for that group:

$$\ln X_{SE} = 6.15 - 0.99 \ln GDP_S + 0.96 \ln GDP_E + 0.03 t + 0.69 D_L$$
$$- 0.0002 d_{SE} + 1.18 D_B + 0.67 D_A - 0.78 \ln P_{SE}$$

where D_L = dummy for language and cultural similarities, d_{SE} = distance, D_B = dummy for common border, D_A = dummy for Atlantic export region, P_{SE} = price of a commodity produced in Sweden and exported. All the coefficients are statistically significant and the R^2 = 0.98. The negative coefficient for the Swedish GDP variable reflects how the exported quantity goes down and value goes up as GDP increases. This means that heavier products are substituted for lighter products when Swedish GDP increases.

Baldwin (1995) uses the same technique as Hamilton and Winters and estimates future trade flows between Eastern and Western Europe. To obtain the gravity elasticities, the model was estimated on trade flows among the EC and EFTA nations and between these nations and the US, Japan, Canada and Turkey, over 10 years (1979–1988). Baldwin obtains the following formula:

$$\ln X_{ij} = -17.5 + 0.77\ln pop_i + 1.16\ln GDP/cap_i + 0.79\ln pop_j$$
$$+ 1.22\ln GDP/cap_j + 0.28adj + 0.53EEA - 0.88DIS$$

All the coefficients are statistically significant and $R^2 = 0.99$, and DW = 2.39. Baldwin studies the potential trade for 1989, but also forecasts trade to 2020. The methods used by Hamilton/Winters and Baldwin are very similar to each other but also to the method presented subsequently in this chapter. Finally, Callsen (1998) makes a forecast to the year 2010 of the trade pattern of Northern Europe or the BSR. He also draws some qualitative conclusions about future transportation demand. He uses a gravity model to estimate trade. The study works with two scenarios, like this chapter, one optimistic where the best performing country (Estonia) is assumed to reach the income level of Greece. In the pessimistic scenario, the per capita income is only between 50 and 60 percent of those in the optimistic case. The optimistic scenario also includes EU membership for Poland and the Baltic States, and lower transportation costs. Callsen finds that total trade in the area will expand by 8 percent annually between 1994 and 2010 in the optimistic case, while the pessimistic case shows an increase of 7 percent annually. Callsen roughly estimates that freight transportation in the BSR is likely to increase by 2 to 4 percent annually.

Estimation of a Trade Prediction Model for the Baltic Sea Region

Background

The BSR comprises nine countries. Four of these – Denmark, Finland, Germany, and Sweden – are modern industrialized countries. Five of the countries bordering the Baltic Sea – Estonia, Latvia, Lithuania, Poland and

Russia – are so-called transitional economies, economies making the transition from a centrally-controlled economic system to a market-based system. There is great variation in the living standards between industrial and transitional economies.

The industrialized countries around the Baltic Sea have a total population of 101.3 million. The transitional economies have a total population of 193.6 million, including all of Russia. Measured in terms of GDP, production capacity in the industrialized countries is four times that of the transitional economies; GDP per capita is almost eight times higher. The variation among these economies is, however, somewhat smaller if one compares GNP per capita in terms of purchasing power parities. Compared on this basis, industrialized countries bordering the Baltic Sea have a GNP per capita about four times higher than that of Baltic transitional economies, see Table 15.5.

Table 15.5   Key statistics and trade performance in the Baltic Sea region for 1997

Statistics	Industrial countries	Transition countries
Population (million)	101.3	193.6
GDP in USD (billion)	2,605.2	648.2
GDP per capita in USD:	25,718	3,348
Export USD (billion)	682,517	122,965
Import USD (billion)	584,974	129,474
Export share of GDP	26 %	19 %
Import share of GDP	22 %	20 %
Export per capita, USD	6,738	635
Import per capita, USD	5,775	669

Source: IMF; EIU.

There is also significant variation in the capacity for international trade among industrial and transitional countries in the Baltic region. Exports and imports per capita in the industrialized countries are about ten times higher than in transitional economies. This indicates a strong potential for increased trade between industrialized and transitional countries. Since the GDP elasticity of international trade has a value greater than 1, the trade per capita will in all likelihood increase more swiftly than GDP per capita in transitional countries. Raw materials and fuels dominate exports from transitional economies in the BSR. This is especially true of Russia, where raw materials and fuels represent over 60 percent of all exports. The economic structure of transitional economies is also strongly reflected in Sweden's imports from these countries.

The figures also show that the structure of imports has changed drastically during the 1990s (figures from the Swedish National Board of Trade). Only exports from Russia and Denmark to Sweden of raw materials and fuels have increased. Swedish imports from all other transitional economies include an increasing share of finished and semi-finished goods. This also indicates an increased demand for transportation shipment services suitable for more sophisticated goods. In recent years, several evaluations have been produced analyzing the potential of transitional economies for producing conditions more conducive to exports.

The general conclusion of these studies (see for example Kaminski, Wang and Winters, 1996) is that among the twenty-some transitional economies, the countries bordering the Baltic Sea have developed conditions most favorable to export growth. This is especially true of Poland and Estonia, whereas Russia lags behind. Speed of adaptation to modern market conditions varies considerably among transitional economies. Among the countries bordering the Baltic Sea, this adaptation has been most successful in Poland and Estonia, while Latvia and Lithuania are developing at a slower pace. Russia has experienced the slowest pace of change. These variations are clearly reflected in GDP growth during the 1990s, as noted in Table 15.6.

Table 15.6   Real GDP growth rates in percent. Transitional countries in the Baltic Sea region. Observations and projections.

Country	1991	1992	1993	1994	1995	1996	1997	1998	1999
Poland	-7.0	2.6	3.8	5.3	7.0	6.1	6.9	5.3	5.4
Lithuania	-13.4	-35.0	-30.4	1.0	2.7	3.6	3.8	4.0	6.0
Estonia	-11.0	-23.3	-8.5	-1.8	4.2	4.0	8.0	4.1	4.0
Latvia	-8.3	-32.9	-14.9	0.6	-1.6	2.8	4.0	5.0	6.0
Russia	n.a.	-14.5	-8.7	-12.6	-4.0	-5.0	0.4	1.0	3.0

Source: World Bank; EIU; Federation of Swedish Industries. Note that rates for 1999 are projections.

From a global perspective, the BSR is a small trading area. Trade among countries bordering the Baltic Sea comprised only 2.5 percent of global trade in 1997. Total global trade amounted to USD 5,469 billion in 1997. The Baltic Sea region is also a relatively small trading area compared to individual countries.

Total trade among Baltic countries totaled USD 137.8 billion in 1997, or only about 31 percent of Germany's total exports.[5]

Table 15.7 describes the trade structure of the Baltic countries, with countries classified as industrial Baltic countries, transitional Baltic countries, and the rest of the world.

Table 15.7   Baltic trade structure for 1997. Percent of total world trade

Exports from	To			Total Exports
	Industrial countries	Transitional countries	Rest of the world	
Industrial countries	1.3	0.6	10.6	12.5
Transitional countries	0.4	0.2	1.6	2.2
Rest of the world	9.0	1.4	74.9	85.3
Total imports	10.7	2.2	87.1	100%

Source: IMF Direction of Trade Statistics Yearbook 1998.

Of the total exports from industrial countries in the Baltic region, only 15 percent was exported to countries within the region. The industrial Baltic Sea countries are an important market for goods from transitional countries; of the total exports from transitional economies, 19 percent go to countries in the Baltic region.

For several countries, the Baltic market is much greater than this average. More than 60 percent of Estonia's exports go to countries in the Baltic region. Corresponding shares for Latvia and Poland are about 50 percent. Of Lithuania and Finland's total exports, 42 and 36 percent respectively are sold to the Baltic market.

The Baltic market is even smaller for exports from Sweden and Denmark, for which 29 and 23 percent respectively go to the region. The BSR is of least importance for Russia and Germany. For these two countries, only 17 and 9 percent respectively of total exports reach the

Baltic region. Table 15.8 describes the trade pattern among the nine Baltic countries.

Table 15.8 Trade pattern in the Baltic Sea region for 1997

Exports From	(Billion USD) Germany	Finland	Denmark	Sweden	To Estonia	Latvia	Lithuania	Poland	Russia	Total
Germany	XX	4.7	9.0	11.9	0.4	0.5	1.0	11.9	9.4	48.8
Finland	4.3	XX	1.2	3.9	1.2	0.3	0.2	0.7	2.8	14.6
Denmark	10.4	1.3	XX	5.7	0.1	0.1	0.2	0.9	0.9	19.6
Sweden	9.1	4.4	5.1	XX	0.4	0.2	0.2	1.3	0.9	21.7
Estonia	0.2	0.4	0.1	0.4	XX	0.1	0.2	0.02	0.2	1.7
Latvia	0.2	0.03	0.1	0.1	0.1	XX	0.1	0.02	0.4	1.0
Lithuania	0.5	0.03	0.1	0.1	0.1	0.2	XX	0.1	0.4	1.5
Poland	8.5	0.3	0.8	0.6	0.1	0.1	0.3	XX	2.2	12.8
Russia	6.5	2.8	0.2	1.0	0.6	1.2	1.3	2.5	XX	16.1
Total	39.9	13.9	16.4	23.7	2.9	2.7	3.4	17.4	17.2	137.8

Source: IMF Direction of Trade Statistics Yearbook 1998.

Measured in absolute value, the largest trade flow is from Germany to Poland: USD 11.9 billion. This is followed by German exports to Sweden and exports from Denmark to Germany. Because of its economic size, Germany is the most important trading partner in the BSR, both as an export node and as an import node.

Germany is either an exporter or an importer in eight of the largest trade flows in the region, and is the largest destination market for all countries except the Baltic States (Estonia, Latvia and Lithuania). After Germany, Sweden and Russia are the most important markets for countries in the region. Finland exports 27 percent of its total to Sweden, and Denmark, 29 percent. Exports from Estonia to Sweden are 26 percent of Estonia's total Baltic Sea exports.

Russia is a major market for exports from Germany (19 percent), Latvia (34 percent), Lithuania (28 percent), and Poland (17 percent). Exports from Poland are heavily dependent upon the German market; almost 66 percent of Polish exports are sent to Germany. It is also interesting to see that Poland has become a large market for German products. In 1997, almost USD 12 billion was exported to Poland, which is 24 percent of total

German exports in the region. In analyzing the trade flows described above, it is equally important to note small and large trade flows. Small trade flows represent areas of significant potential growth. This is the case with all trade flows in the region of less than USD 100 million, or about 14 percent of the region's trade flows.

Noting trade per capita in exporting countries can also elucidate the trade pattern for all the Baltic Sea countries, Table 15.9. Among industrial countries in the region, trade totals USD 701 per capita. Trade among transitional economies is about 7–8 percent of this amount or USD 53. From industrial countries in the region to transition economies, exports total USD 332 per capita and flows in the opposite direction total USD 118 per capita.

Table 15.9   Trade structure per capita in the Baltic Sea region for 1997 in USD

Exports from	To	
	Industrial countries	Transitional countries
Industrial countries	701	332
Transitional countries	118	53

Source: IMF Direction of Trade Statistics Yearbook 1998 and World Bank.

Parameter Estimation on Trade in Values

The following section describes a specific trade model for the Baltic Sea region. Based on assumptions of long-run GDP estimates and other driving forces, the model is used to specify and evaluate two scenarios of future trade growth in the BSR. The data is obtained from the following sources.

Trade values are export figures from the IMF, Direction of Trade Statistics Yearbook 1998, measured in USD millions. Export data for individual countries are reported f.o.b. (free on board). Distance is measured in km (flying distance according to the grand circle) and comes from IATA. GDP, measured in USD millions in current prices are from the World Bank Atlas and International Financial Statistics (IMF). The following results are obtained from equation (3) and (5).

The base mode refers to equation (3) while the random effect models refer to different applications of equation (5). The correlation coefficients are high and most of the individual t-statistics imply significant relations between the independent variables and trade.

The results in Table 15.10 show rather large differences between the models. It seems from the size of the coefficients that the base model and the random effect model with import-nodes as indicator produce similar results.

The real total flows in the whole area amount to USD 1.44 billion on an annual average, while the predicted total flows for both the models amount to USD 1.3 billion or an underestimation by 10 percent.

Table 15.10 Regression results on trade in values

Variable	Base model	Random effect models		
		Link	Export node	Import node
Constant	-12.29 (-14.28)	-3.38 (-5.64)	-10.69 (-7.26)	-11.48 (-12.52)
GDP, export	0.81 (19.98)	0.42 (13.45)	0.64 (5.56)	0.79 (33.94)
GDP, import	0.82 (20.11)	0.54 (-18.43)	0.86 (65.57)	0.79 (12.22)
Distance	-0.00082 (-10.53)	-0.0011 (-18.43)	-0.00067 (-29.18)	-0.00092 (-22.52)
EU	0.34 (3.59)	0.53 (5.66)	0.34 (9.11)	0.30 (4.70)
Nordic	0.84 (5.94)	0.16 (0.84)	0.94 (14.34)	0.82 (7.02)
Observations	*240*	*720*	*720*	*720*
R^2	0.86	0.79	0.83	0.85
Adj. R^2	0.85	-	-	-

Note: t-values in brackets. Estimation uses White's heteroscedasticity-consistent covariance matrix estimator.

Which model should one choose? The more sophisticated model (the random effect model) is more disaggregated than the base model and would therefore be more volatile and harder to predict. Despite this, the import node model reaches approximately the same results as the base model, regarding both coefficients and R^2.

In addition, the import node model fulfils all our requirements for expected results and significance levels. Based on this, the following analysis will be based on the import node model above for trade in value.

Parameter Estimation on Export in Tons

Table 15.11 presents the results from equation (4) and equation (6) where XT_{ij} is expressed in flows in metric tons. Table 15.11 reports the results from two models, one with all variables included and one with only statistically significant variables. The total fit (0.68) is lower compared to trade in value (see Table 15.10). Total trade in tons amounts to 1,205 million tons on average each year. The predicted trade in tons in a EU setting amounts to approximately 806 million tons for both models or an underestimation by 33 percent. The friction is higher for trade in tons than trade in value. The results also show that trade by this measure is demand driven. The demand elasticity is higher than the supply elasticity. Overall, equation (4) produces good results despite an EU coefficient that is statistically insignificant. Estimation without the EU variable does not change the outcome based on the other variables. However, in the comparison with the random effect models reported below, we use model 2 and consequently, the EU dummy is excluded.

Table 15.11 Regression results on trade in tons. Base model

Variable	Base model 1	Base model 2
Constant	-1.97 (-1.78)	-1.89 (-1.67)
Pop, export	0.81 (12.36)	0.81 (11.15)
Pop, import	0.99 (12.98)	0.98 (14.04)
Distance	-0.0010 (-9.74)	-0.0010 (-9.81)
EU	-0.055 (-0.23)	
Nordic	2.09 (8.04)	2.09 (7.95)
Observations[6]	238	238
R^2	0.68	0.68
Adj. R^2	0.68	0.68

Note: t-values in brackets. Estimation uses White's heteroscedasticity-consistent covariance matrix estimator.

All variables in each estimation are statistically significant except the constant term in model (2), with export node as indicator. The constant term varies from –0.85 to –3.28. This is partly corrected by the variation in the Nordic coefficient, which fluctuates from 1.20 to 2.26, and partly corrected by the mass factor coefficients.

In a BSR setting, a low constant together with a high Nordic parameter would probably dampen trade overall but boost trade between Nordic countries. The distance coefficients are nearly identical. The mass factor coefficients varies from 0.76 to 0.88 (supply variable) and from 0.94 to 1.06 (demand variable). Predicted trade in an EU setting is estimated at 887 million tons (link), 776 million tons (export node) and 791 million tons (import node) each year. Based on the size of the coefficients, R^2 and total predicted trade, it seems that base model 2 and the import model are nearly identical (Table 15.12). Further analysis will therefore use the import model for trade in tons.

Table 15.12 Regression results on trade in tons. Random effect models

Variable	Link (1)	Export (2)	Import (3)
Constant	-3.28 (-2.97)	-0.85 (-0.51)	-2.10 (-2.02)
Pop, export	0.88 (12.17)	0.76 (4.50)	0.82 (10.46)
Pop, import	1.06 (14.71)	0.94 (28.44)	0.99 (10.46)
Distance	-0.0010 (-9.49)	-0.0011 (-19.47)	-0.0010 (-14.65)
Nordic	2.26 (6.33)	1.20 (6.78)	2.09 (9.87)
Observations	*714*	*714*	*714*
R2	0.68	0.67	0.68

Prediction of Trade Values

Before we enter the stage with projections of future trade flows, a residual analysis for 1997 will be presented. This procedure will be performed only on trade in value. Discrepancies between real flows and predicted flows reveal some affinity characteristics. Predicted flows should be regarded as 'normalized' flows or market-oriented flows. Higher real flows than predicted flows therefore indicate some affinity properties, which is not captured by the model.

Such properties are for example adjacency, cultural affinity, language and religious similarities, historical ties, foreign investments, personal relations, different types of international organizations, income structure and life style. Table 15.13 presents the relations between real and predicted flows.

Three countries, Denmark, Russia and Sweden, show less exports than expected, indicating less affinity. The interpretation could be that these countries have their main export markets in other areas because of some affinity properties. On the demand side, only Denmark and Germany import less from this region than expected. Estonia has the highest trade affinity on both imports and exports, given its strong links with Finland, Latvia and Lithuania. Intra-Baltic State trade reveals strong trade affinity. Observed flows are for some links up to 20–25 times greater than predicted trade. This implies that there is some important information missing in this model, which would describe the specific trade between these countries.

Table 15.13 Ratios between observed and predicted trade flows in values for 1997 (O/P)

EXPORTS FROM	IMPORTS TO									
	Den-mark	Estonia	Finland	Ger-many	Latvia	Lithu-ania	Poland	Russia	Sweden	Total
Denmark	XX	2.04	0.67	0.78	1.49	2.62	1.03	0.64	1.28	0.89
Estonia	1.37	XX	4.95	0.77	25.74	21.51	0.53	1.28	4.60	2.18
Finland	0.62	15.93	XX	0.87	4.70	1.89	1.33	1.18	1.01	1.05
Germany	0.68	1.21	0.94	XX	1.20	1.39	1.65	1.07	1.11	1.05
Latvia	1.00	12.17	0.46	0.54	XX	12.45	0.32	2.00	1.31	1.14
Lithuania	1.17	18.80	0.33	0.69	15.61	XX	0.90	1.79	0.65	1.11
Poland	0.88	1.27	0.65	1.17	1.84	2.97	XX	1.62	0.67	1.16
Russia	0.12	3.08	1.16	0.74	7.01	5.72	1.89	XX	0.36	0.93
Sweden	1.14	4.20	1.14	0.86	2.26	1.35	1.45	0.34	XX	0.94
Total	0.74	3.79	1.00	0.86	3.04	2.56	1.58	1.00	1.03	1.01

One way to correct the differences would be to add a fixed effect or a dummy variable on only intra-Baltic States flows. That would give these flows an extra injection. Other interesting differences are exports from Denmark to Finland and Germany, and Finland's exports to Denmark and Germany. All these flows are lower than expected. Similar relations exist for German exports to Denmark and Finland. Trade among these three countries reveals a low affinity but also a potential for increasing trade.

In contrast to these flows, observed Swedish imports from Denmark, Finland and Germany are higher than expected. Swedish exports to Finland and Denmark are also higher than predicted while exports to Germany are lower than expected. It is particularly interesting to note that some links among the Nordic countries are still higher than predicted. Observe that for

Denmark and Sweden the affinity dummy Nordic variable is already included in the model. Despite this, real flows are higher than expected.

The trade with Poland also shows interesting differences. The export from Poland to Sweden, Finland and Denmark are lower compared to what the model indicates. It shows trade affinity with all other destinations. It seems that Poland uses rich countries in an import strategy. All flows from the industrialized countries in the region to Poland are higher than expected. Trade with Russia seems to be more historical and distance-dependent than the model expects. Considering both exports and imports, Russia trades more than expected with Poland, Finland and the Baltic States and less with the other nations.

The next part in this section takes a broader and longer perspective on the following crucial questions: What can we realistically expect in terms of long-run economic growth for the transitional countries bordering the Baltic Sea?

Estimating the long-run growth potential for the transitional countries is obviously a difficult exercise because the very aim of the structural reform process is to transform the fundamental of these economies. Since this implies that historical relationships for the transitional countries are of little use, the following analysis draws extensively on the experience of other countries.

The discussion below concludes by summarizing our main assumptions about growth rates, which are adopted as driving forces in our estimated trade model for the BSR. For a number of years the growth performance of transitional countries will reflect the gradual absorption of the economic slack that developed during the initial transition phase. However, the current slack is difficult to estimate, since so much of the capital stock is economically obsolete as a result of the shift to market-determined conditions.

Nevertheless, the currently high rates of open or hidden unemployment imply that growth in the transitional countries is likely to exceed the underlying long-term potential for a substantial period growth rate. While the transformation of centrally-planned economies represents a great challenge, the underlying economic problem it poses is not substantially different from the current economic problems of many developing countries or those experienced by industrial countries at an earlier stage of their development.

Therefore it is useful to draw on empirical analyses of the relationship between economic growth and key determining variables for other countries in various stages of economic development.

Table 15.14 summarizes some key economic growth performance figures.

Table 15.14 Long-run growth of GDP per capita. Percent per year

Group of countries and period	Percent per year
Industrial countries	
1900–1990	1.2
1950–1970	3.7
Rapidly growing economies	
1970–1995	5.6
1985–1995	6.9
Developing countries 1985–1995	3.4

Source: IMF (1998); Barro and Sala-i-Martin (1995).

The per capita growth rates that have been achieved by industrial and developing countries over the past century as a whole appear to be relatively modest, but there have been extended periods with substantially higher rates. These periods include the so-called 'golden age' of industrial countries from 1950 to 1970, when per capita growth averaged 3.7 percent per year. A more recent example is the growth performance in the developing world since the early 1980s.

The remarkable economic growth rates of the most successful emerging market countries during the past decade, before the crises, are of particular interest for the transitional countries. Chile, Hong Kong, Korea, Malaysia, Singapore, Taiwan and Thailand, as a group, experienced an average per capita output expansion of about 7 percent.

One question is whether the conditions that led to rapid growth in certain periods in these countries are also present in the transition countries of the Baltic region. The answer depends on the elements that determine long-run economic growth.

A major issue is the capacity of the transitional countries to increase national savings rates, which are quite low, compared to the most successful emerging market countries.

Table 15.15 Countries in transition and rapidly growing economies. Comparison of factors influencing growth

	Rapidly growing economies 1985–1995	Advanced transitional countries 1985–1995
Real GDP growth	8.3%	4.9%
Inflation	6%	22%
Gross fixed investm share of GDP	30%	21%
Gross national saving of GDP	32%	20%
Openness to trade[*]	57%	39%
Government consumption of GDP	12%	18%

*Total exports plus total imports divided by GDP times two. Source: IMF (1996).

However, the average national savings ratio in the transitional countries has increased somewhat during recent years and is expected to further increase, as economic expansion becomes more stable. But partly unfavorable demographic trends in most of the transitional economies make it unlikely that they will attain saving rates at the high levels recorded by the most successful emerging market countries. Another major factor of growth is openness to foreign trade. There have already been important increases among the transitional economies bordering the Baltic Sea in this respect and we expect further rapid development boosted by economic expansion. With this background IMF has reported two scenarios of long-run growth potential for a select group of transitional economies. For Poland and other advanced transitional countries, application of these models implies long-term growth rates of GDP in the range of 4 to 5 percent per year. The factors influencing growth potential in these scenarios are primarily domestic factors of growth such as human capital and investment ratios.

These scenarios are based on the adoption of high-growth policies, or 'enhanced transition' policies. In these scenarios, investment ratios are raised to 30 percent of GDP. There are also external factors influencing growth. Recent empirical evidence from a broad range of countries shows that growth in the volume of trade itself leads to long-run output growth. This suggests that further liberalization of remaining barriers to trade and more efficient transportation systems, both in the transitional countries in the region and in their EU trading partners, can provide continuing incentives for GDP growth, see Table 15.16.

Table 15.16 Scenarios of long-run economic growth in transition economies in the Baltic Sea region 1997–2015

EU growth	Transition policies	
Prospects	Enhanced	Retarded
Reasonable (2.5%)	A. 6	B. 4
Low (1.5–2.0)	C. 4	D. 2

Based on these considerations, we have formulated four scenarios of the rate of potential GDP growth in the transitional countries in the Baltic region. We assume that 'enhanced transition' policies together with a reasonable growth performance in EU countries will generate a growth rate of 6 percent per year in the transitional countries. Since slippage in transition policies cannot be ruled out, we also consider a scenario of lower growth – 'retarded transition'.

Assuming low growth prospects in EU countries – that is, $1.5 - 2$ percent per year – we assume that enhanced transition in the transitional countries can induce a long-run growth rate of 4 percent. As a fourth possibility, we considered a retarded transition and unfavorable EU growth prospects. In this case, the potential for growth in the transition countries is assumed to drop to 2 percent per year. The following analysis is based on two cases:

Case A: Enhanced transition policies in transition countries and reasonable growth in EU countries.

Case B: Retarded transition and reasonable growth in EU countries.

In the first case, Poland and the Baltic States are assumed to reach the growth rates mentioned above during the period 1998–2010, which will fall 1 percentage point during the period 2010–2015. In the second case, Poland and the Baltic States are assumed to achieve growth rates of 4 percent during the period 1998–2015. Development in Russia is assumed to lag five years. Russia is assumed to have somewhat lower growth rates between 1998 and 2000. We will use real growth forecasts whenever possible from institutions like the IMF, World Bank and EIU and apply the figures given above to the remaining years. It is also assumed that all countries except Russia will become EU members by 2005. In both cases, the EU will experience a long-term economic growth rate of 2.5 percent per year.

The previous section reviewed the conditions for two scenarios of future trade in the Baltic Sea region. This includes expectations of:

- Reform policies in the transitional economies.
- Long-term economic growth within the EU and the transitional economies.
- Interdependencies between economic growth within the EU and growth in transitional countries.
- Enlargement of EU membership.
- Trade relationships in the Baltic Sea region.
- Development in the factors determining trade.

Growth in trade during the first eight years is almost the same compared to growth in the next ten years, until the year 2015. One could have expected higher growth rates during the first period for at least three reasons. Firstly, trade among transitional economies and industrial economies in the Baltic Sea region is starting from a level slightly lower than that of a naturally operating market: USD 137.8 billion in real trade compared to USD 136.8 billion in predicted trade for 1997. Secondly, growth in the transitional economies is expected to be faster in the first period than the second because of significant opportunities to mobilize slack in the transitional economies. Thirdly, membership in the EU will have a growth effect on trade during the first period – that is, until the year 2005. During the period 1997–2005, trade within the Baltic Sea region is expected to increase by 5.4 percent per year from USD 137.8 billion to USD 208.4 billion in 2005. During the period 2005 to 2015, trade is expected to grow to USD 353.9 billion in 2015 (Table 15.17).

Table 15.17 Growth of trade in the Baltic region. Both scenarios. USD Billion

	1997	2005	2015
Optimistic scenario	137.8	208.4	353.9
Percent per year		5.4	5.4
Pessimistic scenario	137.8	203.1	318.9
Percent per year		5.1	4.6

The second scenario is less optimistic. It is based on the notion that reform policies and resulting economic growth will slacken. This scenario estimates economic growth in the transitional economies at a rate of 4 percent per year.

In this scenario, however, the same rate of economic growth will characterize the entire period 1998–2015. Economic growth in Russia is presumed to increase at the same rate, albeit with a five-year lag behind the transitional economies.

The invitation of EU membership is assumed to be extended to the Baltic States and Poland in 2005, and the EU is expected to experience a long-term economic growth rate of 2.5 percent per year. In this scenario, trade in the Baltic Sea region will increase by about 5.1 percent per year between 1998 and 2005, and 4.6 percent annually between 2005 and 2015, and total trade is expected to increase to USD 318.9 billion.

During the entire period (1997–2015), trade growth is likely to be most dramatic between transitional economies and mature economies – 7.8 percent per year in the optimistic scenario.[7] Growth in trade among industrial countries in the region will be 4.5 percent per year. Exports from industrial countries to transitional countries are expected to increase by 5.6 percent annually while exports between transitional countries will expand by 3.5 percent per year, according to the optimistic case, compared to real flows for 1997.

This is in stark contrast to predicted values for both 1997 and 2015. These figures project annual growth between transition countries of 8.5 percent. In the less optimistic case, trade between industrial countries will be unaffected compared to the optimistic scenario since the economic growth rates are the same.

Trade between transitional economies will grow by 1.4 percent annually. Exports from transitional to mature countries is expected to grow 6.8 percent annually while exports from mature to transitional nations are expected to expand by 4.5 percent annually.

Prediction of Trade in Tons

The prediction of trade in tons is determined by population figures and population growth estimates. The Department of Economic and Social Affairs at the UN calculates these projections (UN, 1999). The estimates are the medium-variant projections.

Table 15.18 presents a likely scenario for the development of trade in tons.

Table 15.18 Total predicted trade in millions of tons in the Baltic Sea region

Model		Estimated trade in 1,000 tons	
	1997	2005	2015
Base model 2	374,716	372,460	366,944

The level of tons traded in 2015 is approximately 98 percent of the level in 1997 for the model. The diagram below supports the slow and negative change of total tonnage traded in the area.

Figure 15.1 shows that Swedish exports in tons are approximately the same for 1994 as for 1974. The distribution of trade in tons between industrialized and transitional countries is unequal compared to trade in value. The shares between the two groups of countries are expected to be stable over the years 1997 to 2015 since changes in the population will be slow in all countries.

Approximately one-third of total trade in the region goes from industrial to transitional nations. 25 percent is traded between transitional nations while almost 30 percent is exported from transitional countries to industrialized countries. The remaining share, about 15 percent, is traded within industrial countries. In total, exports from transitional countries constitute 54–55 percent of trade while exports from industrial nations accounts for 46–47 percent.

The results from the estimates on value and tons could be combined to calculate trade values per weight. Trade in value is a monetary measure, trade in tons is a quantity measure and a combination of these two might be a measure of quality. The quality of trade can be expressed in terms of export value per ton and import value per ton.

Long-term development can be exemplified based on the experience of Sweden's exports. The development of Swedish exports has been characterised above all by growth in quality. Higher value per ton implies higher quality.

Figure 15.1 describes the long-term development from 1974 to 1997 in three dimensions: total export value, total export tonnage and value per ton. While the level of tonnage exported for 1997 is 13 percent above the level of 1974, exports measured in value increased by 164 percent. The export value per ton consequently increased by 132 percent. As seen from the diagram, exports in tons 1994 are about on the same level as for 1974, 62.5 million tons and 64 million tons respectively. In the same time period, the value of Swedish exports increased from SEK 242 billion in 1974 to SEK 639 billion in 1997, in 1995 prices. With this as a background, it is not surprising that export value per ton has increased from SEK 3,875 to 9,003 per ton during the same period in 1995 prices.

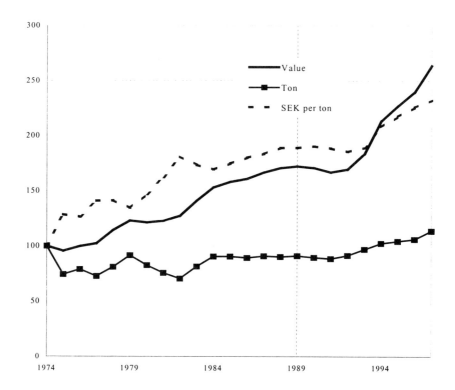

Figure 15.1 Swedish exports 1974–1997. Index 1974=100. 1995 export prices

Source: Statistic Sweden.

Export value per ton should reflect the value of inputs and can hence represent quality. This form of price indicator is closely related to the economic structure and development level of different economies. In countries with a large output of and trade in knowledge-intensive goods, export value per ton is high. For economies dominated by trade in raw materials and staple commodities exports tend to have relatively low export value per ton.[8] The highest export value per ton in Europe, as most likely in the world as well, is enjoyed by Switzerland, with an export value in the mid 1990s of about USD 8,000 per ton.

The average export value per ton in Western Europe is about USD 1,300 per ton. Germany's exports have a value of USD 2,500 per ton, and Great Britain USD 1,250 per ton. In transitional economies around the Baltic Sea, the export value is between USD 200 and 330 per ton – or about 20 percent of that of Western European countries. This is a direct reflection of the fact that trade from these countries is dominated by raw materials and other low-value goods. With modernization and rapid economic growth in the transitional economies bordering the Baltic Sea, it is likely that export value per ton will increase as exports 'dematerialize'. The trade value per ton is crucial in an analysis of transportation demand. It has been found that goods with higher trade values use more expensive transportation modes. The most valuable goods have always used the most superior mode of transportation (Andersson and Strömquist, 1988). An increasing value implies a gradual transition from ship to rail, roads and finally air. An increasing value for trade goods between countries in the Baltic region will therefore have an essential impact on the transportation system and transportation infrastructure.

What can we expect in terms of future trade values per ton in the Baltic Sea region? This analysis is based on the optimistic scenario on value and the only scenario on tonnage traded. Together, these two models yield an export value per ton in the Baltic Sea region in 1997 of USD 368 per ton. It increases to USD 570 per ton in 2005 and to USD 994 per ton in 2015. The value will be highest between industrialized countries. In 1997 it is predicted to be USD 1,453 per ton compared to USD 42 per ton, which is the value between the transitional countries.

Conclusions

This chapter suggests a method to predict long-term trade in value and tons between countries surrounding the Baltic Sea. It relies on a robust and reliable model for trade in value, but a slightly weaker model for trade in tons. Both models stem from the gravity trade model tradition. The gravity model results give us some scenarios of future trade patterns to the year 2015 in the Baltic Sea region. These scenarios may be regarded as 'normalized' or market-oriented trade patterns in the region.

There are strong reasons to expect high rates of economic growth in the transitional economies bordering the Baltic Sea. Comprehensive research by the IMF, OECD, EIU and others supports our assumptions about a long-run rate of growth in the range of 4 to 6 percent per year. We conclude that economic growth in the Baltic region will boost trade. Two applied scenarios predict that total trade in the Baltic Sea region will increase from USD 137.8 billion in 1997 to USD 318.9 and 353.8 billion, respectively in 2015. Formulated scenarios imply an average growth rate of trade in value in the Baltic Sea region in the range of 5 and 6 percent per year between 1997 and 2015. There are no corresponding changes in trade in tons since the level of tons traded in 2015 is likely to be the same as in 1997, or around 370 million tons.

These scenarios raise questions about the transportation system and infrastructure connected to the transportation system. It seems that the region will experience higher trade values per ton in the future, which will certainly influence the structure of the transportation system. What are the implications of these findings? Is it realistic to expect that current facilities are capable of handling such growth in trade or will these predicted scenarios create bottlenecks in the system? The long-term development of trade is heavily dependent on the potentials of the transportation systems. It will also be important to build an environment around the ports that connects the ports to other transportation infrastructure, like the road and rail network. It is crucial that production, and land-use and sea transportation work together and are convenient and efficient in order to manage the increase in trade. A system that combines different types of modes, like ro/ro (roll-on/roll-off) in favor of lo/lo (lift-on/lift-off), is likely to increase. This will certainly also affect the environment and the economies involved but it is beyond the scope of this chapter to incorporate such questions and answers.

The deliberations above suggest further research that can distinguish between regions and different transportation modes and what kind of products will be transported, as well as from and to whom. What kind of 'division of production' between countries in the region is expected if these scenarios were to apply? And how will ferries, air, road or rail transport these products? Changes in the unit price tell us some of the story. There is likely to be a transformation from low-skilled, raw material-based production to more skilled and capital-intensive production in the transitional countries. As a consequence, time, accessibility, reliability and flexibility will be more important than costs in the demand for transportations.

It is crucial for the long-term development of trade sketched out here that the ongoing reform and liberalization policies continue in the transitional countries. A successful policy will probably bring some of the transitional nations into the EU family. It is also important that average economic growth in the EU over the whole period reach a reasonable level.

Notes

1   The Baltic Sea region as it is defined here is comprised of nine countries – Denmark, Estonia, Finland, Germany, Latvia, Lithuania, Poland, Russia and Sweden.

2   We use an unconstrained model in this chapter. In general, constrained formulations are worthwhile alternatives. However, since we are interested in future trade flows and their possible expansion and contraction, it is useful to apply an open gravity model which we allow to grow, in both the origin (exports) and destination (imports) nodes. Using the open model allow us to immediately estimate different trade flows. If we use a singly or a doubly constrained gravity model where the focus is projecting future trade flows, we need additional equations that estimate future row and/or column sums. These are then used in a constrained framework in order to distribute exports and imports into specific link flows.

3   The adjusted R^2 increases from 0.66 to 0.68 and the F-value increases from 118.4 to 126.29 when population is used instead of GDP.

4   Note that only three earlier studies (no. 2, 14 and 16) use $e^{-\lambda D_{ij}}$ and not $\lambda \ln D_{ij}$.

5   USD 438,963 million in 1997.

6   The number of observations here is 238 and 714 since trade in tons between Norway and Switzerland is missing.

7   Real trade flows for 1997 compared to estimated trade flows for 2015.

8   Strömquist and Åberg (1998) estimate the correlation between aggregated export value per ton and GNP per capita based on a sample of countries and find a positive and statistically significant elasticity of 0.7.

References

Abrams, R.K. (1980), 'International trade flows under flexible exchange rates', *Economic Review, Federal Reserve Bank of Kansas City*, vol. 65.

Aitken, N.D. (1973), 'The effect of the EEC and EFTA on European trade: a temporal cross-section analysis', *American Economic Review*, vol. 5.

Andersson, Å.E. and Strömquist, U. (1988), *K-Samhällets Framtid*, Prisma, Stockholm.

Baldwin, R.E. (1995), *Towards an Integrated Europe*, CEPR, London.

Barro, R. and Sala-i-Martin, X. (1995), *Economic Growth*, McGraw Hill, New York.

Bergstrand, J.H. (1985), 'The gravity equation in international trade: some microeconomic foundations and empirical evidence', *The Review of Economics and Statistics*, vol. 67, No. 3.

Bergstrand, J.H. (1989), 'The generalised gravity equation, monopolistic competition and the factor proportion theory in international trade', *The Review of Economics and Statistics*, vol.71, No. 1.

Callsen, S. (1998), 'Trade Potentials in Northern Europe and Consequences for Traffic Flows' in *NEBI Yearbook 1998*, L. Hedegaard and B. Lindstrom (eds), Springer-Verlag, Berlin.

EIU 'Country Forecasts', various issues, *The Economist Intelligence Unit*, London.

Federation of Swedish Industries (1997), 'Nordic Economic Outlook', No. 1, *Industriförbundet*, Stockholm.

Fischer, M.M. and Johansson, B. (1996), 'Opening up international trade in Eastern European countries', *Papers in Regional Science*, vol. 75, No. 1.

Greene, W.H. (1993), *Econometric Analysis*, 2nd ed., Prentice-Hall, New Jersey, pp. 469.

Hamilton, C.B. and Winters, A. (1992), 'Opening up international trade in Eastern Europe', Seminar paper No. 511, *Institute for International Economic Studies*, Stockholm.

Hellvin, L. (1994), 'Trade and Specialisation in Asia', *Lund Economic Studies*, No. 56, Lund.

IATA (1995), *Air Distance Manual*, International Air Transport Association, 22nd ed, Montreal.

IMF (1996), *World Economic Outlook*, Washington, D.C.

IMF (1998), *Direction of Trade Statistics Yearbook*, Washington, D.C.

IMF (1998), *International Financial Statistics*, Washington, D.C.

IMF (1998), *World Economic Outlook*, Washington, D.C.

Johansson, B. and Westin, L. (1994), 'Revealing Network Properties of Sweden's Trade with Europe', in *Pattern of a Network Economy*, B. Johansson, C. Karlsson, and L. Westin (eds), Springer-Verlag, Berlin.

Kaminski, B., Wang, Z.K. and Winters, A. (1996), 'Export performance in transition economies', *Economic Policy*, October.

Linnemann, H. (1966), *An Economic Study of International Trade Flows*, North-Holland Publishing Company, Amsterdam.

Maddison, A. (1989), *The World Economy in the 20th Century*, OECD, Paris.

Persson, J. (1998), *Essays on economic growth*, IIES, Stockholm University, Monograph Series No. 36.

Pöyhönen, P. (1963), 'A tentative model for the volume of trade between countries', *Weltwirtschaftliches Archive*, vol. 90.

Sapir, A. (1981), 'Trade benefits under the EEC generalized system of preferences', *European Economic Review*, No. 15.

Sattinger, M. (1978), 'Trade flows and differences between countries', *Atlantic Economic Journal*, vol. 6.

Statistical Yearbook of Sweden, various years, *SCB*, Stockholm.

Strömquist, U. and Åberg, P. (1998), *Trade and Modal Change in the Baltic Region*, Department of Infrastructure and Planning, KTH, TRITA-IP AR 98–61.

The Economist Intelligence Unit (EIU), *Country Report*, various issues.

Thursby, J.G. and Thursby, M.C. (1987), 'Bilateral trade flows, the Linder hypothesis, and exchange risk', *The Review of Economics and Statistics*, vol. 69.

Tinbergen, J. (1962), *Shaping the World Economy*, Twentieth Century Fund, New York.

Torstensson, R.M. (1998), 'Empirical studies in trade, integration and growth', *Lund Economic Studies*, No. 81.

United Nations (1999), *World Population Prospects – The 1998 Revision*, Department of Economic and Social Affairs, UN, New York.

World Bank Atlas, various issues.

16 Telecommunicators in the Multinuclear City[1]

MATTIAS HÖJER

Introduction

The ecological threats to sustainable development are a starting point for this text. The effects from global warming on the ecosystems that many researchers claim may occur are so serious that they must not be neglected. Therefore, a number of different approaches to investigating how the emission of greenhouse gases can be reduced should be applied.

One of the major contributors to greenhouse gas emissions is the transportation sector. This is because of the sector's extensive use of energy, and its heavy dependence on fossil fuels. A shift from fossil fuels towards renewable energy may be possible, but the renewable energy available is not unlimited.

Moreover, sustainable development requires that resources be distributed fairly among individuals. Therefore, it seems that like energy use from transportation in industrialized countries will have to be reduced if the global warming issue is to be taken seriously. And if energy use from transportation is to be radically reduced, technological improvements may not be enough. Travel will have to be limited as well (Steen et al., 1999). But there are no indications of reduced travel in the future. On the contrary, trends and forecasts indicate continued traffic growth.

The main task of transportation is to reduce geographical barriers, in order to facilitate physical mobility. Increases in mobility have traditionally been interpreted as indications of increases in welfare. But is mobility really a suitable welfare indicator? Obviously, increases in physical mobility lead to higher accessibility, if nothing else changes. But if a similar level of accessibility can be achieved without any physical transportation, accessibility can be seen as a more relevant welfare indicator (Gudmundsson and Höjer, 1996).

So, if the emissions of greenhouse gases from transportation are to be reduced more than marginally, it seems that transportation will have to be reduced. But reduced mobility can be seen as a threat to welfare. In looking for solutions to this dilemma it seems reasonable to take rapidly changing information technology as one starting point, since the completely new opportunities for handling and transmitting quantities of information change the conditions for everyday life.

If traffic had to be reduced drastically and immediately, people would be forced to reduce leisure trips, since trips related to work and service are embodied in the prevailing physical and organizational infrastructures of a society. But if it was possible to choose what kind of trips to reduce, it is likely that many would prefer to cut commuting instead (Steen et al., 1999). Thus, it seems reasonable to put some effort into investigating the opportunities for reducing commuting with the help of information technology.

In this chapter, a scenario of a city is described where commuting distances are short at the same time as accessibility to workplaces is high. The basis for the scenario is land-use changes combined with changes in the organization of enterprises, partly based on information technology.

The approach used in this study is inspired by backcasting (Dreborg, 1996; Höjer and Mattsson, forthcoming; Robinson, 1990). In backcasting, goals for the future are determined. If these goals do not seem to be fulfilled, scenarios fulfilling the goals are generated and then analyzed. The idea is that by producing scenarios that illustrate alternatives to the forecasts, it will be easier to find alternatives to current trends.

As opposed to a great deal of related research, this chapter does not aim to forecast the future. Instead, the aim here is to present some of the new opportunities that can be realized by combining research on energy-efficient urban forms with research on emerging organizational forms. By presenting these options, alternatives to action following current trends are visualized and thereby created. Solutions to transportation-related problems might be found in a wider area than the traditional traffic and transportation field. New transportation patterns may appear. Forecasts may be wrong. Development does not follow a predestined path.

Here the focus is on accessibility instead of mobility, and on IT's effects on work rather than on traffic, i.e. beyond the traditional traffic planning field. For example new patterns of contact may appear and the location of activities can become dependent on new factors. IT may induce changes in organizational structures and thereby change the conditions for how work-places can be located.

The second section presents some ideas from the literature regarding the relation between urban form and transportation demand. The third section includes a presentation of some researchers' thoughts on how information technology changes the conditions for organizational forms. In the fourth section the presentations in the second and third sections are synthesized into a scenario. The scenario illustrates how the development of information technology, described in the third section, changes the conditions for the analysis of the relation between urban form and transportation demand, which is described in the second section.

Transportation Demand and Urban Form

Many researchers in planning agree that there are several advantages from reduced travel. Reduced travel could give social, environmental, safety- and health-related benefits. However, researchers have different opinions on how this could and should be achieved. The problem is that when travel is reduced, accessibility to workplaces, for instance, is often lost. Therefore, much of the analysis in this field is concentrated on the balance between accessibility and travel in different urban structures.

There seems to be a consensus that high density and multinuclear cities have better opportunities than low-density cities, to keep the energy use for transportation low. In some parts of the literature (Hayashi, 1996; Newman and Kenworthy, 1989; Næss, 1996), the density's importance for energy efficiency is emphasized. This literature is mainly based on empirical findings. Another part of the literature (Banister, 1997; Brotchie et al., 1999; Cervero, 1989; Owens, 1992; Wegener, 1996), emphasizes the importance of decentralized concentration, with mixed-use areas in smaller sub-centers around the city nucleus.

The different opinions can be related to Brotchie's urban triangle (Figure 16.1). Proponents of higher densities recommend that cities should aim to get as close to A in the figure as possible. Implicitly, they claim that if workplaces are spread out (the city moves right on the x-axis), commuting lengths will increase, i.e. the path will follow the A-B line. The point of decentralized concentration is that such a structure may lead to a development along the A-C line instead.

However, a number of researchers emphasize that for the commuting distances to decrease with this structure, changes in attitudes in choosing where to live, and the enforcement of different restrictions and/or economic measures, may prove to be necessary. In the worse case an increased share of workplaces outside the city nucleus may result in a higher degree of travel between suburbs (the path in Figure 16.1 leads towards B). This is stimulated by low costs for driving and good capacity for the road network.

At the same time, it is difficult to arrange high-quality public transportation, since travel would be more spread out.

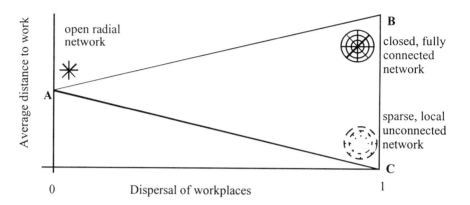

Figure 16.1 Brotchie's urban triangle (Brotchie, 1984)

The possibility of living near the workplace depends on the urban structure and on the location of functions. But there is also a problem of matching in a couple of different senses.

First, housing prices must be such that workers in an area can afford to live there. Second, it may be difficult for households where more than one person is working to find a home that is close to the two workplaces. Third, people tend to change jobs more often than they move. Thus it may be difficult to maintain a short commuting distance over a longer time period (Cervero, 1989).

In sum, it seems like a decentralized concentration could be efficient in terms of commuting distances. However, there are a number of obstacles to this. The problem is to find out how commuting can be reduced, while accessibility is kept high. It is then evident that the matching problems must be handled, if the condition of high accessibility is to be fulfilled, for a city characterized by decentralized concentration. This issue will be discussed later on, once the next section has provided some tools to tackle it with.

Transportation Demand, IT and Organizational Change

The previous section was devoted to the relation between transportation demand and urban form. It turned out that the theoretically most energy-efficient urban forms are associated with some difficulties with regard to the balance between jobs and housing. Information technology brings partly new conditions to the analysis of the relation between urban form and accessibility to work. In this section, the effect on the location of work by the development of the information age is discussed.

A number of authors (Amirahmadi and Wallace, 1995; Castells, 1996; Cavalcante, 1994; Engström and Johanson, 1998; Marshall and Richardson, 1996; NUTEK, 1996; Wright and Burns, 1997) have discussed possible changes in future organizations. One feature that the new forms of organization have in common is that their implementation will be simplified through information technology's ability to circumvent spatial needs. When work can be done anywhere it becomes easier to switch more often between activities, and thus to co-ordinate working hours with other activities and circumstances. The increased flexibility of time that may come with information technology is thus not so much an effect of the possibility of doing things simultaneously, as it is an effect of the ability to do things independent of space. And the independence of space is the key to making work accessible without having to travel.

In his three volumes on the information age, Castells has tried to capture the essence of today's society (Castells, 1996; Castells, 1997; Castells, 1998). Castells argues that technology sets a frame for possible developments of society (Castells, 1996). He calls the current mode of development in society 'informational', in order to emphasize that the whole society is influenced by this new technological paradigm (Castells, 1996). Castells emphasizes the importance of flexible organizations with their 'flextimers' and 'networkers'. This will open new opportunities for new forms of work, like the co-ordinated decentralization of small work groups (Castells, 1998).

A number of studies on the extension of telework have been made in Sweden in the last few years (Engström and Johanson, 1998; NUTEK, 1998; SIKA, 1998a; SIKA, 1998b). The studies give quite different pictures of the number and socio-economic background of teleworkers. This is at least in part due to the fact that different definitions of telework are used in different studies. To summarize the studies it seems like about 500,000 people (some 10 percent of the work force) were teleworking at least one day a week in Sweden in 1997. Many of these were working with education and many were highly educated.

Another IT-related type of job, which does not demand a high level of education, is becoming more and more common. This includes service jobs such as ticket ordering, taxi switchboards and people working in insurance and banking companies.

In Sweden there are several examples of such new types of distance-independent jobs that are placed in remote areas where office space may be cheap, accessibility to a motivated work force may be high and the surrounding environment may attract some employees (NUTEK, 1998). These jobs are not telework, as defined in most surveys. However, they are at least as important when issues of work organization, IT and commuting are discussed. Another important factor for these issues is the development of networks for small and medium-sized enterprises (Berg et al., 1996; Cavalcante, 1994; Stjernqvist, 1997).

A number of researchers have analyzed the relation between trip-generating and trip-substituting factors that can be attributed to telework (Andersson and Sylwan, 1997; Brotchie et al., 1996; Engström and Johanson, 1998; Mohtarian and Salomon, 1997; Nilles, 1991; Nilles, 1996; Rapp and Skåmedal, 1996; SIKA, 1998a; SIKA, 1998b; Stockholms stad and Stockholms läns landsting, 1995). The researchers have tried to understand how travel is affected by telework by using trip surveys, models and other analyses. It seems like some improvements with regard to reduced peak traffic may be anticipated, but the effects on total travel demand due to telework are generally expected to be low. Many of these studies take their starting point in how IT will affect transportation. The question in the studies is 'Where are we going?'. This is quite different to the backcasting-oriented perspective that is used here. With this perspective the emphasis is on finding solutions to problems and then discussing how they can be realized.

Above, I have tried to describe how new forms of work are becoming increasingly common. I also mentioned that the main interest in the relation between new forms of work and commuting distances has been focused on telework. But distance work does not seem to give reduced travel. However, a development towards ever-weaker physical connections between the units in an enterprise may, in a long perspective, make a network organization on an individual scale feasible. When the organization is network-oriented rather than space dependent, the members of the network do not have to act in the same physical space. This, together with decentralized organization, may open up new opportunities for a high-access city with low traffic volumes.

Increased Accessibility and Decreased Mobility?

It has been shown above that many researchers find that a decentralized structure, with mixed land-use, could be more energy-efficient than other structures. However, most attempts to build such areas during the 20th century have not been very successful. Obviously mixing homes with workplaces is not a sufficient strategy to achieve low commuting distances. The matching problems must also be solved. With the development of information technology, new solutions to the matching problems may appear. Information technology brings partly new conditions to the analysis of the relation between urban structure and accessibility to work.

This section is concentrated on the discussion of the 'telecommunicators' scenario'. First, the scenario is presented briefly. The actual scenario contains no description of the path of development. Instead this scenario is merely a description of a state, which is a common way of presenting scenarios in backcasting studies. It could be said that the path towards a backcasting scenario begins with the generation of the scenario description. The presentation of the scenario is followed by a discussion of effects, prerequisites and finally driving forces.

This somewhat unusual order of presenting the scenario is perfectly in accordance with the backcasting approach. With that approach, the primary aim is to generate a scenario that fulfills certain goals. Therefore, the scenario generation is followed by an analysis of expected effects. Only if the effects are regarded as desired is the analysis continued by looking at prerequisites and then at driving forces. The idea is that if prerequisites are not achieved, but the scenario is desired, something should be done to fulfill the prerequisites.

The Telecommunicators' Scenario

Figure 16.2 presents the principal location of activities in two different IT-based scenarios. In the figure, telework (figure 16.2a) is defined as a job with two workplaces. For some days or parts of days, work is done at home. For other days/parts of days, work is done at a workplace more like today's common workplaces.

Figure 16.2b illustrates how activities could be located in a society where work organization has developed in line with the thoughts in the previous section. One crucial difference between the IT-Telework scenario and the IT-Telecommunicators' scenario is the number of workplaces for each person.

In the first case, there is both a workplace at home and the main workplace. In the latter, there is only the node workplace.

The IT-Telecommunicators' scenario is a development of ideas presented in a Swedish futures study on transportation (Steen et al., 1999).

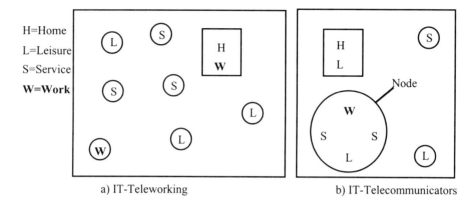

a) IT-Teleworking   b) IT-Telecommunicators

Figure 16.2 Location of activities in two scenarios

Figure 16.3 is another way of presenting the differences between the two possible developments.

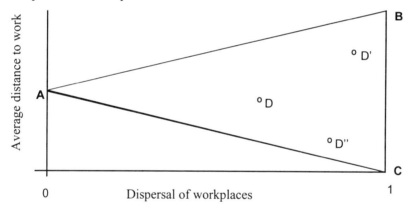

D in the figure denotes a fictive city of today.
D' denotes the IT-Telework scenario.
D'' denotes the IT-Telecommunicators' scenario.

Figure 16.3 The urban triangle (cf Figure 16.1)

In the IT-Telecommunicators' scenario, networkers work in teams organized around individuals connected with telecommunications, whereas their workmates are found at office hotels in the node. Thus, workmates need not be colleagues. Instead of meeting with their colleagues on a daily basis, the networkers *telecommunicate* with each other. This new organizational form facilitates an urban structure organized around a network of nodes for work, telecommunications and public transportation. In such structures, many office and service workers can find suitable places of work at a node located near their home.

The Telecommunicators' scenario is characterized by decentralized concentration with network organizations. The nodes are local sub-centers located around a city nucleus, where networkers can find a workplace at an office hotel. The sub-centers are located at good public-transportation sites, and in rather densely populated areas. This facilitates and stimulates the increased use of non-motorized transportation modes.

Effects

It is hard to quantify the effects of a scenario described as briefly as the one above. The effects would depend for instance on the extent to which the scenario was implemented. Below I will, despite the difficulties, mention some possible effects of the Telecommunicators' scenario and of the informational society.

In large villages and cities, people living near a node could get shorter commuting trips but just as many of them as today. This would encourage non-motorized modes. In sparsely populated areas, the number of commuting trips could be reduced, since the network organization makes it easier to work from home. Altogether, work trips would decrease in volume.

The imbalance between housing and working areas could be reduced, since it becomes easier to change job without changing workplace, and since two-worker households would have the opportunity to live near both workplaces, if at least one of them is a networker.

The demand for workplaces close to housing areas would increase. This would lead to a relative move of workplaces out from the city nucleus, leaving room for more housing in the city. Thus, the mix of functions in the multinuclear city is greater than in most cities today.

The concept of 'workmate' would change its meaning, since friends at one's workplace would normally not work in the same organization. Professional contacts with others in the same network organization would primarily be over telecommunications networks.

The labor market for network organizations would be physically limited only by the supply of office hotels. Such a jump in accessibility could lead to a higher frequency of job changes. As mentioned above, this would not necessarily have to lead to a higher frequency of moving. Moreover, someone who does not like one office hotel can easily change to another, without changing jobs.

It seems like our future society will be very much influenced by information and telecommunication technology. Without basic knowledge about how to handle this technology, many people will in practice become disabled. In this way new social gaps may develop between those with knowledge and those without it. It is possible that technology will become increasingly more user-friendly. But even in this case, in order to learn the codes, technology must be available ('double-clicking' 'icons' to 'open' them is hardly a generic knowledge, at least not yet). If access to technology is high, such things can be learned very early. But there is a risk that the availability of both technology and competent teachers will vary a lot between families and schools, leading to an increased duality in society between good telecommunicators and others.

Prerequisites

The Telecommunicators' scenario could not be fully implemented in a short-term perspective, since a number of prerequisites are not fulfilled. The prerequisites are not independent, but would need to develop in parallel.

One prerequisite is that today's space-dependent work organizations would have to develop in the direction of network organizations. This implies, as discussed above, that individuals belonging to the same work group are not dependent on physical contact with each other.

Moreover, a number of security issues would have to be solved, that is, telecommunications networks would have to be reliable both in terms of function and security. Telecommunications would also need to be much faster and cheaper than today, so that it becomes economically feasible to keep videolinks to other members of the work group open essentially continuously.

Perhaps the most crucial prerequisite however is something which I have called 'the telecommunicating prerequisite'. A widespread implementation of network organizations requires that the ability of workers to telecommunicate is much better than today. This means that the ability of many people to communicate using telecommunications must become just about as good as their ability to communicate face-to-face. Thus, this is not purely a technical question concerning the quality and capacity of communication networks, but is just as much a question of attitudes and learning. School is one important factor in this learning. And the role of games should not be underestimated. With the increased use of computer games from a very early age, the relation to telecommunications may change completely over a generation. Children today may develop an ability to telecommunicate that is much better than what we can imagine today. And some of this new knowledge may spread to older age groups.

There is also a prerequisite regarding the physical planning of cities. An interest among business to introduce network organization as described above will require the availability of attractive, well-equipped office hotels, located near the homes of the anticipated work force.

Driving Forces

Even if all the prerequisites were fulfilled, it is not evident that the Telecommunicators' scenario would be implemented. In order for a change to occur, someone must desire it. Mohtarian and Salomon have presented a number of driving forces for individuals to begin teleworking (Mohtarian and Salomon, 1994). These are expanded below and include driving forces for organizations and society as well.

For many people, working closer to home would imply shorter, healthier and cheaper commuting trips. And the scenario would give increased personal flexibility and presumably a more attractive workplace. A city structure organized around nodes would encourage livelier, more secure surroundings. For environmentally-minded people the Telecommunicators' scenario offers the opportunity of a wider variety of occupations, without requiring long, ecologically harmful, commuting trips.

For organizations, the most important driving forces for network organizations would be increased flexibility and an increased supply of labor. Physical location would become irrelevant in employing people. Moreover, those enterprises that establish the network organization gain an advantage over other enterprises, since their employees may work where they want. Potential losses in identification with the company could be compensated for by the broader contacts that employees would have.

Driving forces in the Telecommunicators' scenario for institutions in society would primarily be the environmental threats. Another energy crisis, or growing evidence of global warming, could imply that travel would have to be reduced drastically. A city where commuting is low is less vulnerable to great changes in the transportation supply. Another driving force in this scenario may be that investments in the transportation infrastructure could be limited. And the node structure may make investments more efficient. Finally, the increased use of non-motorized modes could result in substantial health benefits.

The driving forces that have been mentioned here grow in importance if, for instance, transportation costs rise or attitudes towards the environment or towards the benefits of more attractive housing areas, increase.

Conclusion

Much of the work in the field of urban structures and transportation demand is about urban structures. And much of the work in the field of IT and transportation is either related to Intelligent Transport Systems (ITS) or to teleworking and travel. Neither the research on ITS nor the research on teleworking and travel seems to conclude that any substantial environmental benefits can be anticipated from changes in these fields. If the environmental threat is to be taken seriously, the conclusion based on these results should be that new research angles are needed.

The scenario presented depicts an awareness of the conflict between a society with a low level of commuting and high accessibility to work, but tries to suggest how network organizations could help overcome this conflict. The result is a city with possibly much lower volumes of commuting than before. The potential number of people working in the nodes is considerably higher than the potential number for teleworking, since the concentration of office workers in the nodes becomes a basis for new service business.

In the previous section, a number of prerequisites for the Telecommunicators' scenario were given. It is important to realize that all these must be fulfilled for the scenario to be possible. For example, there is not much point in building a lot of office hotels or telecottages as long as the other prerequisites are not fulfilled. This also means that the Telecommunicators' scenario should not be dismissed just because some previous attempts with telecottages have failed.

The aim of this chapter has been to illustrate how accessibility to the labor market could be kept at a high level, while commuting is reduced. An implementation of the illustration would imply great changes. But the risks that follow from continued environmental degradation and the welfare losses that come with increased congestion are great. Moreover, environmental degradation and congestion are definitely negative, while it is not evident that most people would perceive the restructuring that has been described here as negative. These factors should be taken into consideration in comparing the Telecommunicators' scenario with other scenarios.

Even the most advanced forecasts have a tendency to reinforce trends by affecting expectations, whereas if a greater change is needed, the trends must be broken. This is a reason for complementing forecasts with the use of different types of scenario methods in future studies. Scenario methods usually explore the future from a starting point with a limited number of different assumptions on developments that are expected to be of major importance for the issue at stake. In backcasting, which is a scenario approach, scenarios are developed as independently as possible of contemporary forecasts.

This means that when the scenario is first explored in backcasting, the external constraints are minimized. One advantage of such an approach is that the prospects of finding unconventional solutions are greater. And it is possible that such solutions will be needed in order to break trends that point in undesirable directions. A disadvantage of backcasting can be that too much effort can be spent on generating scenarios that are so extreme that they do not add to the debate, or to the planners' sense of potential opportunities.

Backcasting scenarios are often criticized for making assumptions on behavior changes that are too vague. But one point in producing backcasting scenarios is that they may actually be the starting point for changes in behavior. By presenting new options, they can broaden the perception of what is possible and desirable and thereby, at a later stage, become the initial reason for changes in behavior. In this sense, behavior change comes after scenario generation in backcasting, while it is taken as a starting point in forecasting. In other scenario methods, a number of assumptions regarding behavior change are sometimes used, but then again, these precede the scenario generation.

Evidently, the Telecommunicators' scenario is not the Ultimate Solution. It should be challenged by other scenarios, in a process aimed at broadening the views on what is possible. The Telecommunicators' scenario can hopefully work as inspiration for a continued discussion on how society can develop in a more sustainable direction.

Future research on the feasibility and desirability of the type of scenario that has been described here will be necessary. This will have to include both continued research on attitudes towards different kinds of teleworking, and modeling and other analyses of how different developments affect travel.

Three issues in particular can be identified. One is how total travel volumes change when commuting decreases according to the

Telecommunicators' scenario. The second is how housing patterns change, if workplaces are concentrated in sub-centers. A third issue treats how the ability of people to telecommunicate actually develops, since nothing like the Telecommunicators' scenario can develop unless this ability improves considerably.

Note

1 This chapter is based on a Swedish report from 1998 (Höjer, 1998).

References

Amirahmadi, H. and Wallace, C. (1995), 'Information technology, the organisation of production, and regional development', *Environment and Planning A*, vol. 27, pp. 1745–75.
Andersson, Å.E. and Sylwan, P. (1997), *Framtidens arbete och liv*, Natur och kultur, Stockholm.
Banister, D. (1997), 'Reducing the need to travel', *Environment and planning B: Planning and design*, vol. 24, pp. 437–49.
Berg, A., Johannesson, C. and Kempinsky, P. (1996), *IT-företag i samverkan - nätverk för bättre affärer*, Rapport 10, Teldok, Stockholm.
Brotchie, J.F. (1984), 'Technological Change and Urban Form', *Environment and Planning A*, vol. 16, pp. 583–96.
Brotchie, J.F., Anderson, M., Gipps, P.G. and McNamara, C. (1996), 'Urban Productivity and Sustainability – Impacts of Technological Change', in Y. Hayashi and J. Roy (eds), *Transport, Land-use and the Environment*, Kluwer Academic Publishers, Dordrecht, pp. 81–99.
Brotchie, J., Gipps, P., James, D., McRae, D. and Morris, J. (1999), 'Sustainability of Eastern and Western Cities', in J. Brotchie, P. Newton, P. Hall and J. Dickey (eds) *East West Perspectives on 21st Century Urban Development*, Ashgate, Aldershot, pp. 355–77.
Castells, M. (1996), *The Rise of the Network Society, The Information Age: Economy, Society and Culture*, vol. I, Blackwell, Oxford.
Castells, M. (1997), *The Power of Identity, The Information Age: Economy, Society and Culture*, vol. II, Blackwell, Oxford.
Castells, M. (1998), *End of millenium, The information age: economy, society and culture*, vol. III, Blackwell, Oxford.
Cavalcante, H.S. (1994), *Arbete i nätverk och förändrad näringsstruktur*, Rapport 88, Teldok, Stockholm.
Cervero, R. (1989), 'Jobs-housing balancing and regional mobility', *Journal of the American Planning Association*, vol. Spring, pp. 136–50.
Dreborg, K.H. (1996), 'Essence of backcasting', *Futures*, vol. 28, pp. 813–28.
Engström, M.-G. and Johanson, R. (1998), *Following IT into New Forms of Organisation and Work Methods: Flexibility in Time, Space and Organisation*, KFB report 1998:5, Kommunikationsforskningsberedningen, Stockholm.

Gudmundsson, H. and Höjer, M. (1996), 'Principles of sustainable development and their implications for transport', *Journal of Ecological Economics*, vol. 19, pp. 269–82.

Hayashi, Y. (1996), 'Economic Development and its Influence on the Environment: Urbanisation, Infrastructure and Land Use Planning Systems', in Y. Hayashi and J. Roy (eds), *Transport, Land-Use and the Environment*, Kluwer Academic Publishers, Dordrecht, pp. 3–26.

Höjer, M. (1998), *Ökad tillgänglighet och minskat resande? – en framtidsstudie om bebyggelsestruktur och IT för minskad pendling*, KFB-rapport 1998:40, Kommunikationsforskningsberedningen, Stockholm.

Höjer, M. and Mattsson, L.-G. (forthcoming), 'Determinism and backcasting in futures studies', *Futures*.

Marshall, J.N. and Richardson, R. (1996), 'The impact of telemediated services on corporate structures: the example of branchless retail banking in Britain', *Environment and Planning A*, vol. 28, pp. 1843–58.

Mohtarian, P.L. and Salomon, I. (1994), 'Modeling the choice of telecommuting: setting the context', *Environment and Planning A*, vol. 26, pp. 749–66.

Mohtarian, P.L. and Salomon, I. (1997), 'Emerging Travel Patterns: Do Telecommunications Make a Difference?' Paper presented at the *8th meeting of the International Association of Travel Behavior Research*, Austin, Texas, September 21–25, 1997.

Næss, P. (1996), *Urban Form and Energy Use for Transport – A Nordic Experience*, Doctoral dissertation 1/1996, Norges Tekniska Högskola, Trondheim.

Newman, P. and Kenworthy, J. (1989), *Cities and Automobile Dependence – An International Sourcebook*, Gower, Aldershot.

Nilles, J. (1991), 'Telecommuting and urban sprawl: mitigator or inciter?', *Transportation*, vol. 18, pp. 411–32.

Nilles, J. (1996), 'What does telework really do to us?', *World Transport Policy and Practice*, vol. 2, pp. 15–23.

NUTEK (1996), *Towards Flexible Organisations*, Report B 1996:6, Närings- och teknikutvecklingsverket, Stockholm.

NUTEK (1998), *Arbete på distans – i siffror och exempel*, Rapport R 1998:6, Närings- och teknikutvecklingsverket, Stockholm.

Owens, S. (1992), 'Energy, Environmental Sustainability and Land-use Planning', in M.J. Breheny (ed.), *Sustainable Development and Urban Form*, Pion, London, pp. 88–93.

Rapp, B. and Skåmedal, J. (1996), *Telekommunikationers implikationer på resandet En litteraturgenomgång av arbete på distans och resande – nationellt och internationellt*, KFB-rapport 1992:2, Kommunikationsforskningsberedningen, Stockholm.

Robinson, J.B. (1990), 'Futures under glass: a recipe for people who hate to predict', *Futures*, vol. 22, pp. 820–43.

SIKA (1998a), *IT-utvecklingen och transporterna 2 Redovisning av en kommunikationsundersökning 1997*, SIKA Rapport 1998:4, Statens institut för kommunikationsanalys, Stockholm.

SIKA (1998b), *IT-utvecklingen och transporterna Redovisning av en undersökning om kommunikationsvanor 1996*, SIKA Rapport 1998:1, Statens institut för kommunikationsanalys, Stockholm.

Steen, P., Dreborg, K.-H., Henriksson, G., Hunhammar, S., Höjer, M., Rignér, J. and Åkerman, J. (1999), 'A sustainable transport system for Sweden in 2040', in H. Meersman, E. van de Voorde and W. Winkelmans (eds), *World Transport Research – Selected Proceedings from the 8th World Conference on Transport Research, Antwerp, Belgium, 12-17 July 1998, 3*, Pergamon, Amsterdam.

Stjernqvist, I. (1997), *IT-visioner i verkligheten*, Rapport 111, Teldok, Stockholm.

Stockholms stad and Stockholms läns landsting (1995), *Konsekvenser av en växande IT-pendling – regionala strukturstudier*, Rapport 4, Regionplane- och trafikkontoret, Stockholm.

Wegener, M. (1996), 'Reduction of CO2 emissions of transport by reorganisation of urban activities', in Y. Hayashi and J. Roy (eds), *Transport, Land-use and the Environment*, Kluwer Academic Publishers, Dordrecht, pp. 103–24.

Wright, D.T. and Burns, N.D. (1997), 'Cellular Green-teams in Global Network Organisations', *Production Economics*, vol. 52, pp. 291–303.

17 Visions of Sustainable Urban Communities in Post-Conflict Zones

TIGRAN HASIC

Introduction

In the aftermath of natural and man-made disasters, two major tasks emerge, the repatriation and resettlement of temporarily homeless persons (in the case of natural disasters) or internally displaced persons and refugees (in the case of man-made disasters), and the reconstruction of the basic infrastructure and the economy of the disaster zone. It is important to emphasize that besides the first two groups of displaced persons, there is also a third one – development oustees. They are the result of involuntary population displacement (Cernea, 1996). For the purpose of this article, this third category will not be handled. In standard development literature, the body of research that most closely applies to war-torn societies is the work devoted to how societies recover from natural disasters. Indeed, specialists in this field are now beginning to treat man-made disasters as they do war; and massive refugee flows and other induced population movements as a part of the disaster field. Following natural or man-made disasters, it is essential that lending institutions and donors respond rapidly, and are flexible in their criteria for disbursing aid. In both instances, if they are not sensitively handled and monitored, relief may be diverted to purposes for which it was not intended. It may distort local economies, produce dependency, strengthen the economic power of the already powerful and bring about other negative impacts (Fagen, 1994).

During the four-year war, Bosnia and Herzegovina (Figure 17.1) has suffered the almost complete destruction of its social systems, physical infrastructure, environment and economy. Its territory was riven into ethnic enclaves, with hundreds of thousands of people losing their homes and becoming refugees or internally displaced. In general the urban fabric suffered heavy damage with some areas being completely devastated. In the aftermath of ethnic violence, the country and its people now face the challenge of post-war reconstruction and reconciliation.

Figure 17.1 Map of Bosnia and Herzegovina

Source: The Perry-Castaneda Map Collection, University of Texas, Austin, 1997.

Other countries such as Afghanistan, Lebanon, countries in Central America, Central Africa and in the Horn of Africa have experienced similar devastation (Lake, 1990). From the smoldering fires of a brutal war comes the opportunity for Bosnians to rebuild their society in a way that could put them back on their feet.

In the process they may be creating a model of development that other countries or regions, going through similar changes, could eventually emulate. This area presents a unique chance to employ the concepts and theories of sustainability in a most humanitarian way.

What role can sustainable communities have in the post-conflict reconstruction? The essence of this idea is to look at the dwelling question and promote the introduction of *urban villages*, where the *revitalization of neighborhoods* would be the main focus of sustainable communities. Settlement reconstruction would then be a priority. Urban areas, small towns and suburbs in particular are the focus of (Figure 17.2), but in this context, rural areas also present a challenge.

Figure 17.2   Destruction of Housing and Infrastructure in Bosnia and Herzegovina, Sarajevo

Source: Gilles Peress, 'Uncertain Paths to Peace', 1994.

In contrast to the urban areas and because of the mountainous landscape, rural settlements were spatially dispersed. This influenced the type and spatial distribution of the settlements, as well as their economic activity. Two types of rural settlements were characteristic in Bosnia and Herzegovina: the so-called *fragmented* type of hilly-mountainous settlements with extensive cattle-breeding – highland villages, and the so-called *condensed* type of valley-plains settlements with intensive agriculture, cattle-breeding and fruit-growing – lowland villages. Neither of them were well integrated into the national infrastructure and had only basic local facilities. A particular characteristic of the rural areas was the urbanized larger village, which never fully developed into a urban village because of the general problems of the mountainous landscape and the lack of investments in infrastructure systems. Agriculture, which was the main economic activity for most of these villages, was limited and ineffective.

Following in the aftermath of the ethnic conflict, most of the rural areas sustained horrendous damages and a large number were totally destroyed. The challenge is now to rebuild these communities, offer a better, healthier, safer and sustainable environment to the population that left (refugees, displaced and those that left involuntarily). It remains to be seen whether the societal changes that are required by the concepts of sustainability are so great that stable social groups resist the impetus of change and whether, in contrast, societies that are under stress of instability resulting from a conflict are potentially more receptive to initiatives that introduce sustainable development practices. In other words, this area could presents a unique chance to employ the concepts and theories of sustainability in a most humanitarian way (Hasic and Roberts, 1999).

The key elements that we should consider in this context are community, sustainability and post-conflict reconstruction. Sustainability is defined here as integrating human patterns and natural systems into dwelling habitats which promote stability and placemaking. *Sustainable communities* are collections of individuals that hold several important things in common: their sense of place or locality and their social, religious, and governance systems and derive from both their individual interactions and their surrounding environment the power to adapt to changing conditions and remain intact for multiple generations. Most individuals who belong to communities of this type are loyal and respectful of their historical traditions and derive personal satisfaction and happiness from them. Within this context the theme of this chapter can be seen as a complementary part in the ongoing reconstruction. This is in accordance with the overall plan and effort of the international community to rebuild and prioritize areas for recovery and sustainable growth:, *health, housing, infrastructure systems, agriculture, industry* and *education*.

Communities include things held in common, like government and social structure as well as a common sense of place or location. The main function of the *community* is to mediate between the individual and society, so that people relate to their societies through both geographic and non-geographic substructures of communities. We can pose six questions that are important in a post-conflict context: (1) *what should be the size of the community and how should it be spatially organized,* (2) *what kind of institutional setting should it have,* (3) *how can we achieve community stability,* (4) *what will the social structure look like,* (5) *how can the community residents share common resources* and (6) *how can significant primary and secondary interaction be achieved* (Rubin, 1983).

The questions given above are closely linked to the return of refugees and displaced persons to their home areas, and their integration into everyday life on a sustainable basis. The task is to ensure adequate security, employment opportunities and the availability of housing and infrastructure. Settlement reconstruction is one of the priorities and, as mentioned before, small towns and suburban areas present a particular challenge in that respect.

One of the fundamental keys to the development of a sustainable community will be ethnic healing, and within that reconciliation. Ethnic healing would mean to 'bring upon an end or conclusion to a conflict between people or groups with the strong implication of restoring former amity'. Reconciliation is a part of ethnic healing where opposing communities, after the war traumas, are to be brought into harmony and won over by friendliness to settle their disputes. People should have the will to work through the social trauma of the war, which should be followed by a real implementation of collaboration with the neighbors against whom they have a deep grudge. This is a process which should not be hastened nor forced. Haste could bring even more suffering, personal resentment, mistrust and hate. Complexities are numerous in this respect: distrust between national, ethnic and religious groups and individuals; distrust within the same groups; distrust between those who fled and those who stayed; distrust between those who benefited (profited) from the war and those who lost everything; and distrust from those who suffered and witnessed death, destruction and pain and those who survived without personal losses. This is why ethnic healing means much more than just a sheer step of reconciliation. It is a process that cannot happen over night. In a sensitive situation like this, one should not necessarily regard ethnic communities as something negative (in the short term), but look at how multi-ethnic communities can develop in a long-term perspective. This is an extremely difficult challenge, which is as great as the inertia to change opposed by stable communities.

Towards a Sustainable Economic Recovery

As in the case of the Middle East, with the conclusion of the war and of the impact of regional peace becoming clearer, it is necessary for Bosnia and Herzegovina to determine a medium and long-range development policy. Past and ongoing experiences, like those in Palestine, Cambodia, Lebanon, etc, have to be taken into comparative account. Such consideration must determine the goals and means of developing policies on three levels: the general, the sectoral and the regional (Labaki, 1993). War that has ravaged the territory of Bosnia and Herzegovina has destroyed much of the existing physical infrastructure and disrupted the economic systems that were in place. As a result of this the annual per capita income has fallen from $1,900 prewar, to $500 today. Industrial output in the middle of the 1990s was 5 percent of the prewar 1990 output (World Bank, 1996). The country now faces an enormous challenge in putting the economy back on its feet and subsequently providing for its population. Sustained- donor support for post-conflict reconstruction is essential for Bosnia and Herzegovina in the short term. Eventually, with the consolidation and restructuring of the economy, the country will be able to gradually complement (in the medium-term) and eventually replace donor assistance with its own resources in the long-term. But external support, both technical and economic, will still be necessary in the coming years.

It is extremely difficult, as we have seen from history, to rebuild a country after a prolonged armed conflict, especially a country which is not politically and ethnically cohesive and stable. In addition, the country of Bosnia and Herzegovina holds the legacy of a centrally planned socialist economy, albeit in the years preceding the war. The whole of the former Yugoslavia was slowly starting a transitional journey towards a market economy.

Bosnia and Herzegovina faced three major post-war challenges: *firstly,* implementing the reconstruction and recovery program necessitated by the war damage; *secondly,* developing new governance structures and institutions for economic management; and *thirdly,* managing the transition to market economy (World Bank, 1997). A fresh example of a place that will soon face these challenges – and that will go through similar changes, for all the wrong reasons – is the province of Kosovo in the former Yugoslavia.

The most important challenge for economic recovery (which is a hallmark of all post-conflict zones) is the creation of opportunities for employing the returning refugees, displaced persons and demobilized soldiers (Lake, 1990; World Bank, 1996). The program of reconstruction, which is being financed mostly from abroad, focuses on the reconstruction of housing and infrastructure services partly or totally damaged by war, transportation, the water supply, telecommunications, energy and waste disposal. This is a sine qua non in any post-war, ravaged environment. Only when these aspects are covered and treated on a sustainable basis can production and trade start up again on any significant scale with no threat to economic self-sufficiency and a steady supply of food.

Reviving agriculture is a top priority (along with the revival of small-scale industry in particular) for countries like Bosnia and Herzegovina, where agricultural production was one of the key pillars of its economy and livelihood. It must recover from the war damages and at the same time, adapt to a market economy. The new system will have to rely on private food producers and agro-industries, rather than on state-owned farms and enterprises. Raising farm output and increasing the share of production that is marketed are therefore important objectives for agricultural development. For this to occur, a new generation of competitive, market-oriented, and privately owned agro-industries is needed (Koch, 1998). Experience from countries similarly affected by war shows that economic recovery could proceed quickly if a number of conditions are satisfied. These conditions generally include a core group of factors (Lake, 1990; World Bank, 1997):

- a stable macroeconomic environment conducive to growth and job creation;
- a market-friendly legal and regulatory framework;
- strong institutions and good coordination within the government;
- sufficient donor assistance, official and private, channeled through good organization and coordination mechanisms.

The return of people, or of *drained human capital*, often shadowed by other aspects, is a key prerequisite for any fully sustainable economic recovery. Many similarities can be found in the examples of Lebanon and Bosnia and Herzegovina. As in the case of Lebanon the human component in Bosnia and Herzegovina must be mobilized through a series of measures like fighting the brain drain and effecting its reversal, and implementing policies in the fields of education and scientific and technological research, to raise intellectual, technological and educational levels. This will have to compensate for the decline since 1975 (in the case of Lebanon) and 1992 (in the case of Bosnia and Herzegovina) of skilled workers enacting measures and policies with the goal of bringing about the return of emigrants (Labaki, 1993).

Sustainable Reconstruction Systems

The most important challenge for the post-conflict recovery program is to create employment opportunities. These programs firstly focus on the reconstruction of transportation, telecommunications, the energy supply, and other infrastructure severely damaged by the war, without which it is not possible to restart production and trade on any significant scale. They also focus on the repair of water, sewerage, and health facilities. Financing for such a reconstruction program comes mostly from abroad. Getting such a major reconstruction program started and running smoothly is a task of enormous proportions and complexity. A well-coordinated effort from the country's government and the donor is required to deploy these resources, not only for the effective targeting and efficiency in the use of resources but also for maximizing the impact on the domestic economic recovery. The development and establishment of an institutional structure that clearly defines responsibilities for each of the elements in the program are paramount.

We have already seen signs of such complexities in the reconstruction in Bosnia and Herzegovina (World Bank, 1996). The time period just after the acute emergency situation stabilized is the moment to begin aligning the direction and intent of the long-term reconstruction. The effort will involve a major grass-roots push to educate local populations and emphasize the long-term positive aspects of sustainable economic and human development. This can be initiated through the use of what are called participatory rural appraisal (PRA) techniques (Halloway, 1994) involving the NGO community and mass media campaigns. PRA techniques are approaches and methods which enable local (rural and urban) people to make their own appraisals, analyze and plan, share information, monitor progress and evaluate development actions and programs (Chambers, 1992).

A basic understanding of sustainability concepts by local authorities and populations is a prerequisite for starting any activity; otherwise the whole effort is stillborn. Community participation will be a very important component of the process. The community should be encouraged to become involved in the decision-making process in the project and to influence how resources are used, how choices are to be made, and the role that external agencies take. This type of participation is based on a recognition of the increasing importance of the role which communities take in solving their own problems and relying on their capacity to manage projects which aim to develop their settlements (Arossi et al. 1994, Figure 17.3).

Sustainable systems are the collective mechanisms and relationships that operate together to maintain a sustainable society. In turn, a sustainable society can be perceived as a society that persists over generations, one that is flexible and wise enough not to undermine its environmental or social systems of support.

In order to be socially sustainable the combination of capital, technology and demographics has to be configured to reduce disparities in living standards and meet the needs of the local population including their health and well-being (Keating, 1994).

A sustainable society's material and energy throughputs should be in equilibrium with its consumption rates of renewable and non-renewable resources.

PARTICIPANTS AND THE MOST SIGNIFICANT ORGANIZATIONAL RELATIONS

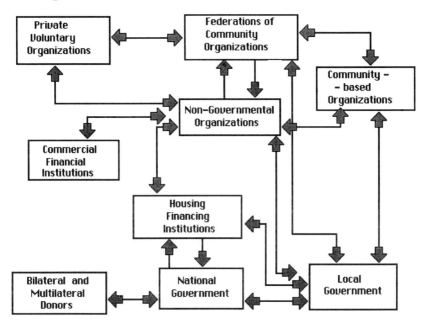

Figure 17.3 Flow Chart of the Participants in the Decision-Making Process

Source: Adapted from Arossi et al. 1994.

When dealing with any system with subjectively defined multiple purposes, it is of crucial importance to understand how to balance the various purposes, and how to periodically check and adjust the equilibrium of the system. While all of us are learners in this arena, what we strive to design in sustainable living are environments, seen as systems, with effective feedback mechanisms and constant monitoring of our goals and our progress toward those goals over time. Above all, the purposes and congruity of our methods and purposes are constant preoccupations in designs for sustainability (Ikerd and Berry, 1997).

All parts comprising the sustainable society, as well as systems invented to study them, must be self-sustaining. Sustainable systems will find their true application, when they have post-conflict zones in mind, in the interrelationship of three systems: agro-industrial ecology, the built environment and natural resource management (see also Figure 17.4).

Precisely those three areas could be the prime focus of sustainable systems linked in a post-conflict zone like Bosnia and Herzegovina (Hasic, 1997).

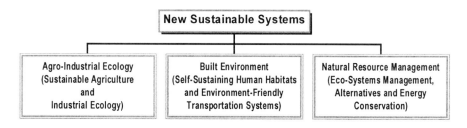

Figure 17.4 Sustainable Systems Chart

A sustainable systems approach will link these areas and give way to the development of sustainable agriculture, something which is needed badly in Bosnia and Herzegovina. This means bringing agricultural technologies and production back to their feet enough to increase yields, while also protecting the environment. This is thus where sustainable technologies will play a crucial role to enable the kind of farming production that will meet the rising demands and needs at economic, environmental and other social costs consistent with rising incomes. This also applies to the development of industrial ecology, which should be developed as a clean and efficient industrial economy, providing an economic base for people and the country, while at the same time maximizing the natural world's ability to recycle materials and minimize waste.

The other key issue of the built environment will encompass the revival of neighborhoods as the foci in which sustainable dwelling is established. Such communities will be the places for the enactment of sustainable systems approach. Sustainable infrastructure will be an integral part of that idea. Accessibility will be about creating places that reduce the need to travel and, in so doing, help to conserve resources, protect the environment and promote social justice. As Cervero says: Have technology, will travel, have sustainable communities, will prosper (1995).

Ecological systems management and energy conservation will play a vital role in this system. Adaptation to the on-ground possibilities and needs of people will be crucial. Solar, wind and water sources of heat energy and the technology that expands this energy while reducing demand hold the key to sustainable energy sources. Reduced energy needs in industrial production, transportation and home heating systems and an array of other energy-saving measures will pave the way to energy sustainability (Patrick and Macoskey, 1997).

All of the above factors are closely tied to the post-conflict zone's initial recovery program. Unsustainable systems, on the other hand, are those that destroy the foundation on which they have based their existence. The concept of sustainability is about regeneration and about designing systems that allow resources to regenerate themselves. Fundamentally, this implies working with nature. In order to be socially sustainable, the combination of capital, technology and population has to be configured so that the material living standard is adequate for everyone, within the constraints of a specific physical setting. A sustainable society's material and energy throughputs should be in equilibrium with its consumption rates of renewable and non-renewable resources. Attention must be paid to pollution emissions versus the assimilative capacity of the environment and economic growth versus non-growth. Van der Ryn and Calthorpe (1986) note that our old patterns of growth are built on isolation from the environment, isolation between activities and ultimately isolation between individuals. They continue by saying that for a city or suburb these qualities of isolation are the same. Buildings ignore climate and place, uses are zoned into separate areas, and individuals are isolated because of the lack of convivial public places. Sustainable patterns, on the other hand, break down separations; buildings respond to the climate rather than overpower it, mixed uses draw activities and people together, and shared spaces reestablish community.

Sustainable Community Patterns

At this moment we might turn to the works of Alexander et al. (1977). The new angle is in the adjustment, adaptation and operationalization of their ideas in post-conflict habitats. They argue for a timeless way of building and says that every society and its individuals will have their own unique and distinct language pattern, which is shared and similar. They continue by saying that the elements of this language are entities called patterns, which describe problems that recur in our environment.

Communities are composed of patterns, patterns that make up a community or design function in a home or building. Alexander et al. (1977) talk about habitable spaces – our dwellings, neighborhoods and social places that create the networks of our existence. These patterns were shattered and destroyed in the aftermath of a man-made conflict. The work of Alexander et al. (1977) can be used to better understand the complexity of the sensitive and vulnerable environments of post-conflict zones. The overriding idea is that hidden patterns can be identified and used, to create sustainable communities, settlements for the 'human use of space'.

In order for the sustainable community to emerge and the neighborhoods within to be resurrected on a sustainable and self-sufficient scale, new and revived spatial target patterns must be implemented. Recognizing the communities as complex organic systems, we can use Alexander's patterns to develop a methodology of town planning, design and implementation, which respects and replicates this complexity. So Alexander et al.'s patterns have to be looked upon as a set of design principles which see the function and the structure of the community as interdependent. Duany and Plater-Zyberk (1992) have set out a set of rules that are very much in line and based on (incorporate) Alexander et al.'s 253 patterns.

They are as follows:

- The master plan.
- The street network.
- The pedestrian network.
- The street section.
- The regulating plan.
- Public building and squares.
- Codes.

Growth management issues such as the balance of jobs and housing, school size and placement, traffic congestion and pollution, affordable housing, equitable distribution of resources, etc. all have a place in the design principles above. What is important is the basic premise that physical environment design can either promote community or divide people and that the basic patterns of interaction between people, buildings, roads and the environment have to be taken into account. So these principles are flexible enough in accommodating program and place and a natural evolution and growth.

If we identify the main problems addressed in the wide and emerging literature on sustainable communities, we can arrive at the following three points: A systems approach is promoted which attempts to deal holistically with spatial, social, economic, political and environmental concerns. We need to adapt a long-term frame and focus, build consensus and foster partnership among major players and stakeholders about community problems and solutions.

In the context of Bosnia and Herzegovina, focus would be the revitalization and transformation of devastated and abandoned towns and suburban areas into sustainable communities designed to be self-reliant on a long-term basis. These communities could offer to their residents sustainable housing, physical infrastructure, economic security, health services and technological innovations. This could enable people (refugees and displaced persons) to return to these areas, relieving the pressures on urban centers. The areas could then provide a better quality of life, a sustainable livelihood for their residents and a better complement to the core urban centers. By reviving the small scale industrial sector and agriculture, new production will meet the rising demands and needs of the population. In combination with other activities a sufficient economic base would be provided for the population.

		Spatial	
T	Group Zoning of	Mixture of Commercial	Transportation
h	Residential Neighbor-	and Cultural Activities	Flow Systems
	hood Areas		
e		**Economic**	
	Ownership of Property	Base for Business	Strong Institutions
	- Property Rights	Growth and Employ-	and Stable Markets
S		ment	
C		**Social**	
	Restoration of Social and	Neighborhood	Ethnic Healing and
O	Cultural Integrity in	Cohesion and Recon-	Well-being
P	Community	ciliation	
		Political	
E	Flexibility of Top-down	Building of Consensus	Social Justice and
	and Bottom-up	and Fostering	Governance
	Approaches	Partnership	
M		**Technological**	
o	New and Better Infra-	Hi-tech Development	Internet Systems
	structure Services and	and Techno Structures	and Innovation
d	Networks		
e		**Environmental**	
	Protecting Human	Reduction of Pollution	Eco-systems
l	Environments and Health	and Natural Hazards	Management

S t r a t e g i c   M a n a g e m e n t

Figure 17.5 The SCOPE Model

In order to structure these questions in a systematic way a model called *Sustainable Communities in Post-Conflict Environments* (SCOPE) could be developed. This model would be linked with the ideas of language patterns mentioned above, and have spatial, economic, social, political and environmental pillars as its foundation (see Figure 17.5).

In developing this model we should answer the following general questions: are all these phases equally important? Are they inter-linked? Should all of them be considered in the context of post-conflict zones? Can we achieve the idea of sustainable communities by only focusing on one phase? Are the structural points of the model applicable to the situation on the ground etc?

The SCOPE Model is a strategic and innovative approach to effectively conceptualize and design policies, programs and projects that efficiently address post-conflict communities. The SCOPE approach is an integrated and inter-disciplinary approach that presents a way to reap the benefits of developing a policy initiative which is economically viable, social and spatially compatible, and politically acceptable while being technologically state-of-the-art and environmentally friendly.

The model offers versatility and flexibility, which are most necessary for it to be applied to varied scenarios and situations. It also offers a comprehensive platform for the development of a sound policy initiative and fosters cross-fertilization and closer interaction within relevant fields to exploit synergies and benefit from complementarities. SCOPE differs from conventional thinking as it is based on the principle that it is not solely economic and political factors that matter in a successful policy initiative. It believes that in a complex arena of human settlements arising from crisis situations, no one aspect by itself can result in the success of an initiative. What is required is an approach that integrates and facilitates cooperation among various relevant fields to deliver effective and successful results. SCOPE attempts to offer this. The expectations and the ambition of such a model are such that its application could become an important part of the framework for the reconstruction of these areas.

Studying Post-Conflict Management Studies

In societies recently recovering from war, people operating at the community or national levels are pressed to deal with reconciliation, development, reintegration and security. Sustained donor support in post-conflict reconstruction is essential for Bosnia and Herzegovina (as well as for Kosovo) in the coming years.

Donors, including the World Bank and UNDP, maintain emergency funding to be used either for natural or man-made disasters. Research has shown, however, that the two situations require different approaches. In the former, there are identifiable communities to rebuild, recognized political authorities in the areas receiving aid, a legal system in place and, usually, a benign attitude on the part of the central government toward the aid-givers. In a number of war-torn societies, few if any of these factors prevail. Moreover, natural disasters are short-lived, even if they occur frequently. The conflicts recently concluded in Central America, the Middle East, Cambodia, Mozambique, and Ethiopia/Eritrea, in contrast, all lasted well over a decade. The task following prolonged war no longer consists solely of reconstructing entities that have been destroyed. It requires creating alternatives to the structures, systems and living patterns that have permanently disappeared (Fagen, 1994; Anderson and Woodrow, 1998).

A stable society resists any impetus to change – as evidenced by the self-defeating obstinace of industrialized countries towards an honest re-evaluation of their consumer and industrial priorities. Even in the light of substantial evidence demonstrating that current socio-economic trends are stressing the planet's life support systems, government and industry basically hold fast to economic policies and programs that are growth-oriented and environmentally unsustainable.

Many communities are finding that conventional approaches to economic development, transportation planning and development of the built environment – efforts that are intended to increase residents' opportunities and quality of life – are in fact creating a variety of negatives: congestion, sprawl, air pollution, overflowing landfills, distributional problems, etc. Sustainable development and the development of sustainable communities are a far-reaching approach to manage these problems (Roseland and Henderson, 1998).

In the reconciliation context, we may ask what new role urban and regional planning should play. A completely new scenario and a different type of challenge now face us. We see population changes involving migrations and resettlement of a huge number of people which in turn bring about changes in the location of economic activities. Planning in the earlier socialist mode has to be fundamentally reshaped so that it now can reverse the negative changes that a man-made catastrophe brings. Changes and advancements are already at our front door in political philosophy, technology, communications, infrastructure, and shifts in the attitudes and behavior of people.

All of this will affect regions and communities and basically alter the requisites for future planning. Planning is needed to assist people and communities in managing change using all the methods and skills that it possesses: urban design, decision tools, quantitative methods, etc. The future is reshaping planning here and now. In Bosnia and Herzegovina the legitimacy of planning also needs to be reestablished.

Somebody said that managing and promoting change in a way that will benefit society is an enormous challenge for urban and regional planning. These challenges have to be accepted to develop a sustainable environment that provides for a better quality of life, new opportunities, equality and new beginnings.

In viewing the situation of the former Yugoslav republics we find a region of mid-level industrialization, geo-physically close to Europe, that has been ravaged by a civil war. By definition, the events in the area have caused extreme disruptions in society and destruction of life support infrastructures. It is precisely this type of tragic situation that may provide an opening for instituting those practices of sustainability that a self-centered West finds so hard to manage.

The move to practicing sustainable rhythms of life requires a certain level of desire to change traditions. Status quo is generally the anti-thesis of change, but in the post-conflict zones of Bosnia and Herzegovina radical change *has been* the status-quo, for all the wrong reasons, since 1992 (Hasic, 1997).

The argument is that, as a result of recent history, the region of former Yugoslavia presents a prime opportunity for demonstrating that societies can work together for a common good. Bosnia and Herzegovina are disaster areas, with an overwhelming need for reconstruction at all levels, physical, environmental and moral. It is an area that is ripe for the enlightened programs that the concepts of sustainable human settlements embody.

Institutionalizing sustainable practices in the region would serve to bring a war-torn society back up off its knees. It would be a constructive capital investment for the West, and it would generate a base of desperately needed operational knowledge about implementing wide-scale sustainable practices.

The exercise outlined here would take 'sustainability' out of the books of theorists and onto the agendas of politicians, NGOs, community groups and professionals, including engineers, teachers, public health officers and regional planners. The knowledge base would not come quickly or cheaply, but it would come, and it would be in the form of valuable 'experience capital' a commodity – that Bosnia and Herzegovina could share with a world that ought to undertake a self-appraisal – and socio-economic change (Hasic and Roberts, 1999).

References

Alexander, C., Ishikawa, S., Silverstein, M., Jacobson, M., Fiksdahl-King, L. and Angel S. (1977), *A Pattern Language – Towns, Buildings, Construction*, Oxford University Press, Oxford.

Anderson, M.B. and Woodrow, J.P. (1998), *Rising from the Ashes: Development Strategies in Times of Disaster*, Lynne Rienner Publishers, Boulder, Colorado.

Arossi, S., Bombarolo, F., Hardoy, J., Mitlin, D., Coscio, P.L. and Satterthwaite, D. (1994), *Funding Community Initiatives*, Earthscan Publications, London.

Cernea, M. (1996), 'Bridging the Research Divide – Studying Refugees and Development Oustees', in T. Allen (ed.), *In Search of Cool Grounds: War, Flight & Homecoming in Northeast Africa*, Africa World Press, Lawrenceville, New Jersey.

Cervero, R. (1995), 'Why Go Anywhere?' in Key Technologies for the 21st Century, *Scientific American*, September, New York.

Chambers, R.R. (1992), *Rural Appraisal: Rapid, Relaxed and Participatory*, IDS Publications Office, Institute of Development Studies, Sussex.

Duany, A. and Plater-Zyberk, E. (1992), *Towns and Town Making Principles,* Rizzoli, New York.

Fagen, P.W. (1994), 'After the Conflict: A Review of Selected Sources on Rebuilding War-Torn Societies', *Journal of Humanitarian Assistance*, War-Torn Societies Project Occasional Paper 1, UNRISD/PSIS, Geneva.

Halloway, L. (1994), *PRA and How it Relates to Disaster Management*, IDS Publications Office, Institute of Development Studies, Brighton.

Hasic, T. (1997), *Locus Amoenus: Towards a New Sustainable Housing – The Case of Post-Conflict Zones*, Royal Institute of Technology, ALV, Stockholm.

Hasic, T. and Roberts, W.A. (1999), 'Opportunities for Sustainable Human Settlements in a Post-Conflict Zone', *Open House International*, vol. 24, No.1. Newcastle Upon Tyne.

Ikerd, J.E. and Berry, W. (1997), *On Sustainable Systems*, North Center Institute for Sustainable Systems, University of Missouri, Columbia, Missouri.

Keating, M. (1994), *The Earth Summit's Agenda for Change – A Plain Language Version of Agenda 21 and Other Rio Agreements*. Centre for our Common Future, Geneva.

Koch, M. (1998), *Reviving Agriculture: A Top Priority for Bosnia and Herzegovina*, World Bank Resident Mission in Bosnia and Herzegovina Publications, World Bank, Washington, D.C.

Labaki, B. (1993), *Development Policy in Lebanon Between Past and Future,* The Beirut Review, Lebanese Center for Policy Studies, Beirut.

Lake, A. (1990), *After the Wars: Reconstruction in Afghanistan, Indochina, Central America, Southern Africa and the Horn of Africa*, New Brunswick Transaction Books, New Jersey.

Patrick L. and Macoskey, R. (1997), *A Quest for Sustainability,* University of Slippery Rock, Pennsylvania.

Roseland, M. and Henderson, H. (1998), *Toward Sustainable Communities. Resources for Citizens and their Governments*, New Society Publishers, Gabriola Island, British Columbia.

Rubin, I. (1983), 'Function and Structure of the Community: Conceptual and Theoretical Analysis', in R.L. Warren and L. Lyon (eds), *New perspectives on the American Community*, pp. 54-61, Dorsey Press, Homewood, Illinois.

Van der Ryn, S. and Calthorpe, P. (1986), *Sustainable Communities – A New Design Synthesis for Cities, Suburbs and Towns*, Sierra Club Books, San Francisco.

World Bank (1996), *A World Bank Country Study. Bosnia and Herzegovina – Toward Economic Recovery*, The World Bank, Washington D.C.

World Bank (1997), *A World Bank Country Study. Bosnia and Herzegovina – From Recovery to Sustainable Growth,* The World Bank, Washington D.C.

Zolberg, A., Suhrke A. and Aguayo, S. (1989), *Escape From Violence – Conflict and the Refugee Crisis in the Developing World,* Oxford University Press, New York.

PART V
REGIONAL EVALUATION OF POLICY PROCESSES

18 Planning for the Preservation of the Cultural Built Heritage

KRISTER OLSSON

Introduction

The physical environment is local in the sense that environmental values are spatially attached to the local community. In particular, cultural and natural tangible and intangible values in the environment are important for local citizens as carriers of meaning and identity. In that sense, the environment has an existential dimension (Werner, 1991). This can be interpreted as a claim, or rather as many different claims, on the common environment. In contrast, there are other claims based on other interests or perspectives, for example, perspectives held by real-estate owners or businesses and public heritage management agencies. The assumption here is that various perspectives include conflicting directions regarding the management of the physical environment.

Thus, local public sector planners (i.e. the municipality) are essential. Their task, according to the planning and building legal framework, is to co-ordinate various public interests, as well as balance public and private interests, in planning in areas like housing, transportation, preservation of heritage, real estate and business development. However, there are no clear guidelines for the municipalities concerning how to weight different public and private interests against each other and how to co-ordinate various public planning objectives.

The specific problem focused on in this chapter is how to weight the preservation of cultural built heritage against other public and private interests. In this chapter, two fundamental questions are discussed.

The first question is what constitutes the cultural built heritage. As society develops further into a post-industrial society, the traditional and nationally homogenous concept of cultural built heritage is challenged (see Beckman, 1998). Because of societal development, the ideal notion of a place-based community, where social relations are tied to particular groups and places, falls apart. We are currently facing a globalized and multi-cultural world, with a vast range of possible social relations and supplies of knowledge and insight. In that sense, the assumption of homogenous societies which share common public interests does not hold anymore (Healey, 1997).

The second question is what the value of preservation is in a short- and a long-term perspective. Those charged with the preservation of the cultural built heritage (i.e. conservators, curators, municipal planners, etc.) face challenges daily in setting priorities among preservation activities and choices of treatment for various individual objects and environments. Central to the setting of priorities are the values of the experts and the tension between those values and values held by society at large, from the individual to the global level.

The assumption is that various public and private actors will provide differing answers to these questions. The purpose of this chapter is to contribute to knowledge about the value systems held by different actors. Furthermore, the aim is to discuss how general knowledge about the value systems held by different actors can be taken into account in planning practice, using economic theory and environmental economics as a starting point.

Planning for Preservation

The development of the built environment is a slow and incremental process. New buildings will be constructed, buildings will be rebuilt to fit new purposes and buildings will be demolished and replaced. Some parts of the built environment will be defined as cultural built heritage and chosen for preservation activities.

In the past older buildings were essential material assets. It was natural to utilize and preserve buildings as long as they were technically useful. As a result of economic growth from the mid 1950s onwards, there was a demand for new commercial, industrial and housing structures, or other urban infrastructure (i.e., transport, utilities, etc.), which affected the need to remove or redesign the existing built environment (Andersson, 1981).

Over the last few decades the interest in preservation has changed from an interest in preserving single monuments to an interest in buildings in a wider physical context (Tschudi-Madsen, 1986). Insensitive and comprehensive rebuilding of cities in the 1950s and 1960s can largely explain the change in attitude (Linn, 1978). This is a shift from an object perspective to an area perspective. However, an area perspective is still usually no more than an object perspective applied to a group of buildings and its close surroundings (Wetterberg, 1992). Hence, the interest in preservation currently includes monuments, other specific objects and well-defined areas.

From this point of view one important task is to discuss what comprises cultural built heritage from local, regional, national and global perspectives. This is especially important in a society where changes are rapid and far reaching at many levels, and where cultural values are regarded as important means for urban regeneration and development (see for example Nyström and Fudge, 1999). In the last decade, the need for new preservation and planning methods has been identified. In a substantial way, the search for new methods has extended outside the scientific field traditionally concerned with the cultural heritage (archaeology, art history, architecture). For example, attempts have been made to employ economic analysis to decision-making concerning the preservation of cultural property (see for instance Coccossis and Nijkamp, 1995; Allison et al., 1996; Hutter and Rizzo, 1997).

Motives for the preservation of the cultural built heritage are often divided into historical motives, aesthetic motives, and social motives (Ross, 1991). The historical motive embraces the idea that it is important to preserve a picture of the lifestyle and society in times past. Aesthetic motives for preservation indicate that the built heritage has an architectural or artistic value. For social reasons it is possible to argue for preservation in the sense that well-known physical surroundings are important to people. There is a notion that such demands are likely to increase in societies that are characterized by rapid social, cultural and economic change. Along with these motives, an economic motive for preservation has surfaced in the last decade as a result of the structural change in trade and industry, whereas culture and cultural values are regarded as important means for firms as well as competing European cities (see for example Bianchini and Parkinsson, 1993).

In Sweden, preservation of the cultural built heritage is traditionally seen as a public sector responsibility. The planning and preservation legal framework implies that the initiative for preservation should be a public matter rather than a private one, although it is stated that management of the cultural heritage is a responsibility shared by everyone. The common method employed by public heritage management agencies is identification and protection of monuments, specific objects and well-defined areas that are especially valuable from a historical perspective (see Backlund, 1998).

From the perspective of public heritage agencies, the management of the cultural built heritage in general is handled by different means of control, i.e. legal regulation, economic incentives (like loans and grants) and information. However, the assumption here is that regulation and direct economic incentives can not likely be the sole solution in future heritage management. The main reason for this is that the economic resources needed for maintaining the heritage in that way will presumably not be covered by the public resources available.

Thus, the planning process is traditionally characterized by a strong public sector and by strict procedural links to the existing regulation system. However, the public sector is no longer dominant in planning, since private initiatives have come to play an increasingly important role in the planning process. Negotiations among various actors, especially between public and private actors, have become an important method to reach mutually acceptable solutions (Cars, 1992). These changes have led to a situation where decision-making becomes informal. Consequently, the approval of development plans is often only a formality that confirms decisions that, in reality, have already been taken. Under these circumstances, legal regulation and loans and grants as well as information appear to be means used in negotiations, rather than having a self-adjusting effect. In specific negotiations, information can play a substantial role in the outcome of the process. However, this might presuppose that the information exchanged between participating partners matches the different value systems that are employed by the partners. Research at the division of Regional Planning (Olsson, 1994; Cars et al., 1996; Snickars, 1997; and Olsson, 1999) have shown that built heritage preservation planning is complex, also in situations where several actors have a mutual interest in preservation as such.

The main concern in the local preservation planning process is the individual object, monument or well-defined area. From the perspective of real-estate owners, this attitude is reasonable. However, one conclusion drawn from the research is that a more comprehensive view on the issues handled in the planning process is beneficial for public as well as private interests.

The value of a certain object or area in the urban landscape is to a substantial degree dependent on the environmental context. Each individual property has an external impact on surrounding properties. This external effect can be negative or positive, and will influence the value of adjacent properties (DiPasquale and Wheaton, 1996). In this way the surroundings, the neighborhood, the district or the city will add and compound the real value of each building or area.

Different actors have differing perceptions of preservation activities, and thus conflicting opinions of how and what to preserve. There often is no clear understanding from the private as well as the public side, about the complex values constituted by the specific buildings, and especially about the cultural values at stake. The preservation interest is often revealed or discovered late in the planning process.

One explanation for this late occurrence is that during the first steps of the process, the actors have very little knowledge about the other actors' demands for preservation or change. In general the actors representing the preservation interests are not heard early in the process simply because other actors do not thoroughly understand or are not aware of the interest in preservation. It is especially apparent that the municipalities in many cases seem to be unsure about how to value the buildings concerned, and consequently act in a contradictory or unclear way. One conclusion drawn from the research is that there is a lack of knowledge about other actors' preferences.

The problems discussed above call for consistently accounting for the complex values that the built environment has or will have in the future, and hence for new and more dynamic approaches in public preservation planning. Consequently, the issue is to find new ways within the municipal planning to assess and assert the short- and long-term value of the preservation of the cultural built heritage. The starting point for assessing preservation values is not merely a question of restricting the preservation issue to tangible monuments, other objects or well-defined conservation areas. Rather the task is to broaden and diversify the planning issue, given the various purposes behind specific preservation activities and different, tangible and intangible, characteristics and qualities in the built environment as a whole.

Two Case Studies

Umeå is the most populated municipality in the northern part of Sweden and the eleventh most populated municipality in Sweden. The population increased from approximately 60,000 in the mid 1960s, when the University of Umeå was established, to approximately 100,000 inhabitants in the late 1990s.[1] The rapidly increasing population has put a great deal of pressure on local comprehensive and structural planning over the years. One of the main tasks has been to provide housing for new citizens. More than fifty percent of the population living in Umeå today were not born in the municipality.

Consequently, one of the most important goals expressed in the comprehensive plan from 1990 as well as from 1998 is to provide increased housing in the city center. At the same time, there is also a general goal to protect and preserve the cultural built heritage. These goals do not necessarily fit together, since most heritage buildings are located in the city center, and on properties with a low exploitation. Hence, these specific properties are of special interest to real-estate developers.

In the 1980s the municipality of Umeå invested extensively in the field of culture, adding in part a new city library and new theater, as a strategy for attracting people to move to or stay in Umeå. However, there is a sense that the local authorities have neglected preservation of the city's cultural built heritage in their cultural strategy. Nevertheless, there has been some listing of specific buildings and certain areas of local importance within the municipal comprehensive planning, although they are spatially limited to the city center.

The empirical findings presented in this chapter are based on studies of two recently completed planning processes concerning specific properties in the municipality of Umeå.[2] The case studies include studies of documents available and a series of interviews with different actors participating in the local planning. The actors interviewed include planners at the municipal planning office, real-estate owners and developers, as well as representatives of public heritage management agencies, i.e. the county board and county museum. The aim of the studies is to broaden and develop knowledge and understanding of how different actors value the cultural built heritage. The case studies are presented in brief in table 18.1, which includes the participating actors, relevant planning issues, which includes listing of buildings and outcome of the process.

Different groups of actors, on the private as well as the public side, participate in the planning process, e.g. real estate owners, developers, and public agencies at the local (i.e. municipality) and regional (i.e. county board, county museum) level. Table 18.2 describes the main interests of the actors involved in the case studies.

One way to characterize the planning process, in both cases, is to note that property owners initiate the planning, with the intention of making changes on their property. The key issue then, is how to allow owners to change their property without spoiling existing cultural values, as defined by heritage experts. Participating actors have different solutions for this issue, because, as shown in table 18.2, they have different objectives for participating in the planning process. However, this does not necessarily mean that the various interests exclude each other. Nevertheless, the owners and developers are arguing only for change, whereas the public heritage management agencies are arguing firstly for preservation, and secondly for how preservation can be combined with new constructions.

Table 18.1 Two case studies in the municipality of Umeå, Sweden

Case study	Räven	Höder
Owner	Construction firm.	Real estate company.
Participating actors	Construction firm, County Museum, Real estate developer, Municipality.	Real estate company, County Board, County Museum, Municipality.
Planning issues	Demolition of late 19th century building and re-development for housing *or* preservation and adjusted exploitation.	Demolition of three late 19th century buildings and re-development for office space *or* preservation and adjusted exploitation.
Listing of buildings	Building listed (proposed for protection) by County Museum 20 years earlier.	Buildings listed (proposed for protection/as monument) by County Board early in the process.
Outcome of the process	Demolition of existing building and redevelopment for housing with much higher exploitation.	Agreement on preservation of external appearance and on new construction.

Table 18.2 The main interests held by actors that participate in the planning process

Actor	Räven	Höder
Real estate owner	Production of new constructions.	New office space for own use and to let.
Real estate developer	Design and sale of new apartments.	–
Public heritage management agencies	Preservation of existing building with external cultural value.	Preservation of existing buildings with external cultural values.
Municipality	New housing possible and desired in the area. Unclear valuation of preservation, because various representatives have different opinions.	Housing, parking and shopping space possible and desired in the area. Unclear valuation of preservation, because various representatives have different opinions.

The main arguments that were used by the actors in Umeå are listed in table 18.3. The table shows that actors in favor of preservation emphasize the benefit of preservation rather than the cost of re-development, whereas actors in favor of change stress the cost of preservation rather than the benefit of re-development. However, this can be understood as the actors in favor of change present arguments that directly target the arguments used by actors in favor of preservation.

Furthermore, as shown in tables 18.2 and 18.3, the preservation interest is oriented firstly towards ensuring the future existence of the buildings concerned because of their historical character, and secondly towards preservation from an aesthetic and social viewpoint. On the other side, the development interest is focused on the future use of the properties concerned.

The municipality has more than one objective in participating in planning, since they have to co-ordinate different public interests (e.g. preservation of the heritage and new housing), as well as co-ordinate public and private interests. Given that, it is not surprising that the municipality appears to be unclear or unsure about how to weight preservation against other interests.

Moreover, it is not surprising that different individuals and departments representing the municipality (e.g. politicians, planners) have different opinions about the value of preservation and the value of change. It seems quite clear that the municipality, as such, is unsure about how to value preservation versus re-development.

The municipality is obviously not prepared to make a decision on its own in this respect. In the case of Höder, a first proposal for a development plan includes, for the property owner, both the possibilities of preserving the buildings as well as demolishing them. In that way the municipality, more or less, leaves the initiative to the private owner to do what ever they please.

The municipality is more concerned with adjusting the owner's redevelopment plans to the overall character of the townscape. This is also true in the case of Räven. However, at the same time, some municipal representatives try to put forward arguments in favor of preservation, although without direct success.

The outcome of the process in the case of Räven is demolition of the existing building and redevelopment for housing with a much higher level of exploitation. In the case of Höder, the outcome includes an informal agreement between the property owner and the municipality on the preservation of the external appearance and on new construction close to the existing buildings. The outcome in this case is a result more attributable firstly, to a recession in the real-estate market and, secondly, to an extensive debate in the local press than to a well thought-out plan by actors involved.

Table 18.3   Arguments used by actors in favor of preservation and in favor of change

Actors in favor of	Arguments
PRESER-VATION	• The age of the building and its genuine appearance.
	• An environmental and pedagogical value since building is located close to street with extensive bus and bicycle traffic.
	• Building can give a historical link for new constructions nearby. (Räven)
	• The last example in Umeå of several buildings from late 19th century facing the whole street in one block.
	• The genuine (original) appearance of typical late 19th century architecture in Umeå.
	• Buildings give the street a pleasant and charming appearance.
	• Buildings associated with personal memories for many citizens in Umeå.
	• The technical standard of buildings is good, hence far-reaching renovation activities not necessary for preservation.
	• Possible to add new constructions to old buildings without loss of cultural values. (Höder)
CHANGE	• Preservation and adjusted new constructions will mean inferior living environment (i.e. inferior apartments and outdoor environment).
	• Financial difficulties to preserve existing buildings.
	• More expensive to rebuild existing building compared with constructing a new building.
	• No constraints for property development regarding preservation given by the municipality previously. (Räven)
	• Necessary to demolish existing buildings in order to develop the property from a functional, technical and economic point of view.
	• The technical standard of the buildings is very bad – preservation in a long-term perspective not possible.
	• New constructions will be designed in a way that reminds people of the local building tradition. (Höder)

Analysis

For some parts of the physical environment, the issue is instead the direction of management rather than a question of whether a specific building or environment should be preserved or replaced. For some heritage buildings, like churches, this has always been the main issue. These buildings and designated areas have been of public interest for a long period of time. They are referred to here as *monuments*. Other parts of the environment have been of interest to preservation in their early years from a business or practical perspective, and hence mainly a concern for a private interest. As time has passed, some buildings or defined areas have come to qualify as monuments, whereas other parts have not. The parts of the environment that have not qualified as monuments are referred to here as the *general urban landscape*. This general urban landscape includes a diverse set of artifacts that are spatially and/or socially linked together. The issue for preservation planning is, therefore, the value of preservation versus re-development considering the urban landscape as a whole including monuments and other artifacts. The question is what constitutes the urban landscape as a cultural heritage.

For the general urban landscape, the planning task is to identify cultural amenities and qualities that characterize the landscape, hence identifying preservation values in a broader sense. The issue, then, is to discuss how preservation, renewal and re-development can be co-ordinated.

It is quite clear from the case studies that various actors value the heritage from the perspective of different value systems, including differing temporal perspectives (see also Alzén, 1996). The municipality is different from other actors, since the municipality is not monolithic; i.e. various representatives within the municipality express different and sometimes contradictory opinions about the direction of planning. This is also underlined by the somewhat contradictory setting of goals regarding different public interests within comprehensive planning. The planning process is further complicated by specific private interests, i.e. interests held by real estate owners and developers.

Since various actors have different interests to guard or values to protect, as well as differing temporal perspectives, conflicts arise in the planning process. However, the comprehensive planning does not seem to have much to offer for balancing these conflicts. The question is whether a compound of traditional motives for preservation, i.e. historical, aesthetic and social motives, expresses the 'complete' or 'true' value of the preservation of the cultural built heritage. Put in another way, the question is whether planning is capable of weighting the values held by all actors affected directly and indirectly. Some actors, representing certain values, might not be prepared to act during the planning process in a way that suits their interest. Furthermore, some actors may not be allowed to take part in the planning process, for instance, future generations.

The traditional motives for preservation are not always easy to identify and to separate from each other in planning practice. Nevertheless, each motive can be associated with different groups of actors or interests. Historical values are the main interest for experts at public heritage management agencies. Aesthetic values are the first concern for architects and city planners. The inhabitants in a city represent a social motive for preservation. Regional planners and politicians may argue for preservation in various ways, but might put forward economic reason as a regional development strategy. Private firms might consider preservation from a business perspective. There is also an obvious conflict between the interest in preservation and the interest in re-development. The interest in re-development is most often based on business interests, whereas a real estate owner finds it more profitable, in full or partly, to demolish existing buildings and rebuild the site.

However, it can be argued that this reasoning is too simple. The social value is to a substantial part connected with historical and aesthetic values. People, i.e. tenants or citizens in a wider group, who represent the social value are in some respect prepared to pay for aesthetic and historical qualities. Furthermore, in that sense, an expression of social motives for preservation is also an economic valuation of the heritage. Consequently, the real estate owner's economic valuation of a property is also partly based on historical and aesthetic amenities, and hence social values. On the other hand, this extended reasoning on the actors' valuation of the heritage is also too limited. The social value is not only a compound of historical and aesthetic values. Valuation of the built environment from a social viewpoint also includes considerations regarding the environment's importance for peoples' well being, irrespective of its historical and aesthetic qualities.

How to Discuss the Value of Preservation: an Economic Perspective

One task for successful future heritage management is the question of finding and approving a new sustainable social and economic use of the urban environment. In other words, it is necessary to stress the question of sustainable use in order to achieve preservation in a long-term perspective. This means that various public heritage agencies must develop strategies in collaboration with other public interests as well as with private interests.

However, this might presuppose that the different value systems that are employed by participating partners match each other in a clear and consistent way.

Economic theory can be a starting point for a further analysis of different actors' spatial, temporal and economic understanding of the cultural built heritage. From an economic perspective, it is reasonable to regard almost all urban outdoor environments as a public good, since it is impossible to prevent someone from enjoying environmental qualities. Economic theory defines public goods as goods that are non-rivaled in consumption; that is, consumption by one individual does not prevent other individuals from consuming them. Furthermore, public goods are characterized by non-excludability; that is, it is not possible to exclude anyone from the benefits of consumption.

It might seem reasonable that public society should be fully responsible for maintaining the cultural built heritage, defined as a public good. For some historical buildings, this has always been the case. However, in most cases the characteristic of public good is a secondary product or external effect of private goods (see also Allison et al., 1996). In that sense, the public good characteristic of the built environment is not always immediately visible. According to this reasoning a real estate owner's spatial, temporal and economic view of the built heritage is one of a private good, and in that way limited to the owner's property, thus being a short-term and a business perspective. By the same reasoning the public actor should to some extent be expected to view the built heritage as a public good, which includes a comprehensive view of the built environment in a long term perspective.

In an economic analysis, only individuals' preferences and valuations count. In that sense, the built heritage expert's view of preservation value should not have more weight than the valuation of the average person. The task of the expert in this perspective is to affect individual understanding of the built heritage (Mohr and Schmidt, 1997). Following this reasoning, knowledge about individual preferences for preservation is critical to planning practice.

With a starting point in environmental economics, it is possible to analyze individual preferences for the preservation of the cultural built heritage. In environmental economics, there are two concerns that are of interest here. First, the task is to identify the different kinds of values represented by a resource or an environment. Secondly, the concern is to identify methods for measuring non-monetary values.[3] The aim is to convert different values into a total value expressed in monetary terms for use in a Cost Benefit Analysis (see for example Turner et al., 1994; Allison et al., 1996; Mohr and Schmidt, 1997; Frey, 1997).

The Total Value consists of several intermediary values, see Figure 18.1. On one side, there is a Use Value, and on the other a Non-Use Value. The Use Value consists of a Direct Use Value and an Indirect Use Value. The first value means that a heritage resource of some kind, for example a building, is used in a direct, economically beneficial way; that is, the building has a market value. The Indirect Use Value embraces indirect use of the heritage, for example recreation. Moreover, there is also an Option Value and an Existence Value. The Option Value is partly a valuation of possibilities to use the heritage in various ways in the future (Option Use Value), and partly a valuation of possibilities for future generations to reveal their valuation of Use and Non-Use Values (Bequest Value). The Existence Value is not linked with actual or potential use, but is a valuation of the existence of the heritage resource based on ethical considerations (Turner et al., 1994).

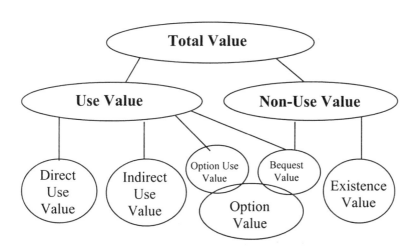

Figure 18.1 Total economic value of a heritage resource

Figure 18.2 shows a taxonomy for the cultural built heritage with respect to rivalry and excludability in consumption of the Direct and Indirect Use Value, Option Value and Existence Value (see also Muren, 1994). Consumption of the Direct Use Value is rival and excludable, hence a private good. It is rival with respect to its market value, and excludable because the value only goes to those with direct access to a certain building. On the other hand, Indirect Use Value, Option Value and Existence Value can be characterized as public goods, since they are non-rival and non-excludable in consumption. It is not possible to charge for consumption of these intermediary values, nor exclude anyone from consumption. This is especially true for consumption of the Existence Value.

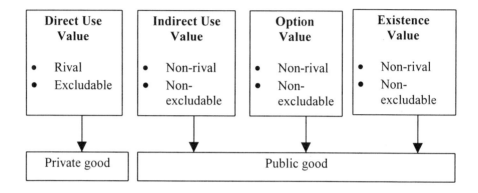

Figure 18.2   Rivalry and excludability in consumption for economic intermediary values concerning the cultural built heritage

The reasoning used above indicates that if a certain building or area is regarded not to have a Direct Use Value, it is mainly a public task to preserve and maintain that building or area. However, in most cases the public good characteristic is a secondary product or external effect of private goods.

It is likely that most (private) actors directly involved in the planning process value the cultural built heritage from their own direct and indirect use or potential use of the buildings concerned. Consequently, an actor who primarily focuses on the Existence Value runs the risk of being placed at the margin in planning, with no real influence on decisions concerning preservation of the cultural built heritage.

Thus, it is critical to find a new sustainable use for deteriorated heritage buildings with a cultural value in order to achieve preservation in a long-term perspective, especially when public resources are scarce. In that sense it is essential for actors involved in preservation to give more attention to the question of potential direct and indirect use of the deteriorated built environment. The ultimate challenge is to turn the question of preservation into a question of creation of sustained cultural value.

Conclusions

One important issue in the management of the cultural built heritage is to develop new methods to evaluate the short- and long-term value of the preservation of the general urban landscape as well as of monuments, other specific objects and well-defined conservation areas. Such an evaluation must take as its starting point the different value systems employed by public and private actors at the national, regional and local levels, including the individual perspective. In conclusion, the public heritage management policy must draw on the actors' incentives for preservation, and hence their implicit or explicit valuation of the built environment as a whole. In other words, knowledge about actors' preferences is critical for preservation planning. Consequently, the potential of information and marketing can be further developed as a means of control.

The valuation scheme according to environmental economics is one possibility for developing municipal preservation planning. However, it is not necessary to convert different values into monetary terms. The scheme can also be a useful tool in planning practice. It has the specific use of providing a foundation for expressing a preservation value in a comprehensive and more precise and clearer way than is done today. Furthermore, it can also lead to a more careful consideration of preferences that different groups of actors have, whether the preferences are explicit or not.

Notes

1   Both figures refer to the current administrative borders of the Municipality of Umeå.
2   The case studies are a part of an ongoing research project at the Department of Infrastructure and Planning, Regional Planning, Royal Institute of Technology, Stockholm, Sweden.
3   Several methods for measuring non-monetary values are available, such as the Contingent Valuation Method, Travel Cost Method and Hedonic Prices. See for example Turner et al. (1994), Mohr and Schmidt (1997), Frey (1997).

References

Allison, G., Ball, S., Cheshire, P., Evans, A. and Stabler, M. (1996), *The Value of Conservation?*, English Heritage, London.
Alzén, A. (1996), *Fabriken som kulturarv*, Brutus Östlings Bokförlag, Symposium, Eslöv, pp. 66–69.

Andersson, H.O. (1981), 'Tätbygdsutveckling och stadsförnyelse', in Statens offentliga utredningar, *Stadsförnyelse – kontinuitet, gemenskap, inflytande*, Liber Förlag, Stockholm, pp. 70–71.

Backlund, A.-C. (1998), *Kommunala kulturmiljöprograms betydelse för bevarande av kulturvärden*, Riksantikvarieämbetet, Stockholm.

Beckman, S. (1998), 'Vad vill staten med kulturarvet?', in A. Alzén and J. Hedrén (eds) *Kulturarvets natur*, Brutus Östlings Bokförlag, Symposion, Eslöv.

Bianchini, F. and Parkinsson, M. (eds) (1993), *Cultural Policy and Urban Regeneration*, Manchester University Press, Manchester.

Cars, G. (1992), *Förhandlingar mellan privata och offentliga aktörer i samhällsbyggandet*, Kungliga Tekniska Högskolan, Stockholm.

Cars G., Olsson, K. and Snickars, F. (1996), *Kulturmiljö på spel*, Riksantikvarieämbetet, Stockholm.

Coccossis, H. and Nijkamp, P. (eds) (1995), *Planning for Our Cultural Heritage*, Avebury, Aldershot.

DiPasquale, D. and Wheaton, W.C. (1996), *Urban Economics and Real Estate Markets*, Prentice Hall, Englewood Cliffs.

Frey, B.S. (1997), 'The Evaluation of Cultural Heritage: Some Critical Issues', in M. Hutter and I. Rizzo (eds) *Economic Perspectives on Cultural Heritage*, Macmillan Press Ltd, London.

Healey, P. (1997), *Collaborative Planning. Shaping Places in Fragmented Societies*, Macmillan Press Ltd, London, pp. 65–66.

Hutter, M. and Rizzo, I. (eds) (1997), *Economic Perspectives on Cultural Heritage*, Macmillan Press Ltd, London.

Linn, B. (1978), *Husen vi äger. En tillgång värd att vårda*, Liber Förlag, Stockholm, p. 17.

Mohr, E. and Schmidt, J. (1997), 'Aspects of Economic Valuation of Cultural Heritage', in N.S. Baer and R. Snethlage. (eds) *Saving Our Architectural Heritage*, John Wiley & Sons, Chichester, pp. 336.

Muren, A. (1994), 'Argument för offentligt stöd till kultur – en genomgång av nationalekonomisk teori', in *Varför kulturstöd? Ekonomisk teori och svensk verklighet*, Finansdepartementets rapport Ds 1994:16, Fritzes, Stockholm.

Nyström, L. and Fudge, C. (eds) (1999), *City and Culture. Cultural Processes and Urban Sustainability*, The Swedish Urban Environment Council, Karlskrona.

Olsson, K. (1994), *Bevara-förnya*, Kungliga Tekniska Högskolan, Stockholm.

Olsson, K. (1999), *Kulturmiljö i teoretiskt perspektiv. Om värden, aktörer och ansvar*, Kungliga Tekniska Högskolan, Stockholm (unpublished).

Ross, M. (1991), *Planning and the Heritage – Policy and Procedures*, E. & F.N. Spon, London.

Snickars, F. (1997), 'How to Assess and Assert the Value of Cultural Heritage in Planning Negotiations', in N.S. Baer and R. Snethlage (eds), *Saving Our Architectural Heritage*, John Wiley & Sons, Chichester.

Tschudi-Madsen, S. (1986), 'Architectural Conservation: The Triumph of an Idea', in Y.R. Isar (ed.), *The Challenge to Our Cultural Heritage. Why Preserve the Past?*, UNESCO, Paris, pp. 145.

Turner, R.K., Pearce, D. and Bateman, L. (1994), *Environmental Economics*, Harvester Wheatsheaf, New York, pp. 111–13.

Werner, K. (1991), *Staden som livsrum*, Byggforskningsrådet, Stockholm.

Wetterberg, O. (1992), *Monument och miljö*, Chalmers Tekniska Högskola, Göteborg.

19 Customer-Based Quality Measures in Swedish Special Transportation Services

STIG KNUTSSON

Introduction

The methodology for estimating rider quality in Special Transport Services (STS) using utility modeling has not been discussed frequently in the literature. In this chapter the model used is based on a basic logit formulation and estimated using the ALOGIT program. An outline of an Index of Rider Quality (IRQ) for Swedish STS is provided as a platform for calculations based on data from the Greater Stockholm area in 1997.

The chapter compares the Swedish values of five key quality attributes. In addition and as a consequence of the findings, a customer profile is presented of low and high willingness to pay for the STS in Greater Stockholm. Finally a cost benefit approach is introduced and examined against the empirical results in a consequence scheme. This is done in the light of some actual effectivization strategies in Swedish STS policy. Transportation connects people and activity in the built environment. Traveling is indispensable in our daily life, even for disabled people. This is why issues of Special Transport Services (STS) are of vital interest in regional planning perspective.

The mode of 'färdtjänst', or transportation service for the disabled, with its 420,000 riders (Socialstyrelsen, 1998) is the main STS travel mode in Sweden and has been planned as an integrated part of the public transport system since 1998. The quality standard of this mode must be compared with the standard of present public transportation as opposed to the common interpretation of the Swedish legislation (SFS 1997:734, SFS 1997:736). In the field of STS many researchers have considered that performance evaluation methods are important and useful elements in the transportation development process. Studies with these elements extend at least as far back as Paaswell (1977). Special transportation textbooks have frequently included chapters on financial and economic measurements of transportation productivity from the producer perspective. It is also common in Sweden to measure STS productivity from the producer side in terms of quantity before quality (Knutsson, 1999).

Social evaluation methods like cross-sector benefit analysis and marginal social benefit analysis are both infrequent and underdeveloped in the international literature (Sutton and McLaughlin, 1991; Lund and Oxley, 1992; Gillingwater et al, 1995; Thatcher et al, 1991). Even though most researchers only deal with the productive apparatus from the production aspect some attention has also been paid to rider quality aspects, and attributes. In the UK Sutton (1990) uses a multinominal logit model in his work estimating travel demand for STS. McKnight et al (1986) provide a rider quality index. McKee (1993) offers an outline of a rider quality model intended to focus on rail vehicles accessible to disabled passengers. In a Swedish context there is no published attempt known to model STS travel demand in terms of rider quality attributes.

In the present chapter we report on a Swedish study in Greater Stockholm for 1998 using rider quality attributes to estimate STS travel demand. To be able to construct the survey questionnaire, standard stated preference techniques were used (Jones, 1989; Pearmain, 1991; Widlert, 1992). For the statistical analysis we employed a logit model (Algers, 1987). To run the estimations, the ALOGIT program (Hauge Consulting Group, 1992) was chosen.

Methods

A sketch of a comprehensive overall rider quality index of Swedish STS (Knutsson, 1998) is used as a platform for the planned stated preference experiments; see also Appendix 1. The index (IRQ) is meant to map the most important parts of rider quality in a Swedish context based on customer utility and well-being in terms of the right to make choices, to act independently, and to maintain dignity and self-esteem.

The index has its roots in quality aspects from a broad spectrum of different transportation contexts:

- a general model of passenger traffic by Woodson (1992);
- a set of strategic goals from Greater Stockholm Public Transportation in Sweden for 1996 (Knutsson, 1998);

- a special transportation rider quality index from the US by McKnight et al (1986);
- a rider index approach especially focusing wheelchair-bound people from the US by McKee (1993);
- an evaluation of the Swedish STS system by the National Board of Health and Welfare (1998).

The current index is meant to be a platform for further research activities in the field. The definitions of the index attributes are still under consideration in an ongoing research project (Knutsson, 1999). Therefore, preliminary attribute definitions are used in the following discussion.

The stated preference (SP) technique has long been a common tool in transportation research (Jones, 1989; Pearmain et al, 1991; Widlert, 1992). SP normally deals with the demand of the average passenger. Here SP design has to be done with an instinctive feeling for the target rider group. But are the planned stated preference experiments a realistic and beneficial strategy in this particular case? Judging from the results of a customer postal questionnaire, the answer has to be yes. Both a focus group and a pilot study were carried out. The pilot study was conducted using a random sample of 100 STS customers. The response rate was 72 percent. Calculations revealed significant t-values for the parameters of price, waiting time in the switchboard, and pick-up time. The other parameters (see also the list below) were not significantly different from zero. No changes were made from the pilot study in the present principal investigation. The SP design itself does not seem to be a widespread reason for non-responses (Knutsson, 1998), not even for the oldest respondents.

With this preparation completed, we designed a customer postal questionnaire in the Greater Stockholm area, in which socio-economic information was collected about the respondent and the household plus information related to STS trips and responses to stated preference experiments. The questionnaire included a set of four choice situations. It was distributed to 2,241 STS pass holders in Stockholm County in late 1997. The response frequency was 65 percent. Based on our outline of the Index of Rider Quality (IRQ) in Appendix 1, the six following key attributes were considered to depict rider quality in STS in a Swedish context (Knutsson, 1998):

- Switchboard waiting time.
- Pick-up time.
- Pre-booking time.

- In-vehicle time.
- Driver behavior.
- Fare.

Switchboard waiting time is the space of time needed to wait on the STS telephone switchboard to be able to book a STS trip while pick-up time is the deviation between the actual and agreed arrival time. Pre-booking time is the internal time before the agreed departure time when prebooking the vehicle is needed, while in-vehicle time is the amount of time spent in the vehicle during transportation.

Driver behavior is defined in this study in two different ways: a) no statement about driver behavior or b) the driver is nice and helpful. Fare is the ticket price for a single STS trip.

Basically three reasons for choosing the attributes above are highlighted. First, the quality standard of STS must be compared with the standard of present public transport in Swedish metropolitan city context. This as a result of the common interpretation of Swedish legislation (SFS, 1997:734; SFS, 1997:736).

Second, the attributes chosen correspond in a favorable way with the established value of time modeling for passenger traffic from the Swedish National Road Administration and the Swedish National Rail Administration (Vägverket and Banverket, 1995). The third reason is to focus attention on the key attributes which successfully depict the day prism of the customer (Hägerstrand, 1970, 1972).

In order to explore the differences of how employment, age, income and other socio-economic variables influence the estimation results, the population was segmented using the following criteria:

- employment status and household income;
- age and gender;
- type of municipality;
- trip purpose and frequency;
- type of mobility obstacle;
- level of confidence in STS.

For the statistical analysis a logit model (Algers et al, 1987) was employed. The utility function was formulated as follows (p10 – p16 are parameters to be estimated):

$$u1 = p10 + p11*FB + p12*VV + p13*HT + p14*RT + p15*P + p16*FBET \qquad (1)$$

The measurement scales for the variables are given in Table 19.1. A method to fix the price of the quality attributes (Algers et al, 1987) is introduced in two steps.

We use the utility function in equation (1) above as a point of departure. A level of 60 minutes of in-vehicle time gives us a contribution to u1 equal to p14 * 60.

Table 19.1 Variables used in the estimations

Attribute	Explanation	Level I	Level II
FB	Pre-booking time	25 min	60 min
VV	Switchboard waiting time	0 min	20 min
HT	Pick-up time	0 min	20 min
RT	In-vehicle time	15 min	35 min
P	Fare	SEK 30	SEK 65
FBET	Driver behavior	No statement	'The driver is nice and helpful'

If the exact fare which contributes to a utility function of 60 minutes in-vehicle time is represented by k we get:

$$p15 * k = p14 * 60 \qquad (2)$$
$$k = p14 * 60/p15 \qquad (3)$$

Here, k is the fare cost that the traveler values as equal to one hour of in-vehicle time. As a consequence, we get a measurement of the value of in-vehicle time. The value can be used as an input in cost-benefit estimations. The attribute driver behavior (FBET) does not have a connection with the value of time in the same way as in-vehicle time. Instead, the transformation equation for this attribute is formulated as follows:

$$FBET = p16/p15 \qquad (4)$$

To run the estimations, the ALOGIT program (Hauge Consulting Group, 1992) was chosen. Based on the segmentations presented above some 30 estimations were made.

Results

The values presented in Table 19.2 below constitute a summary of the main findings. The maximum, minimum, median and mean values are all collected from the different ALOGIT estimations. All estimations in the study are reported in the paper, see Table 19.2. In the table the range of findings is collected in order to demonstrate both the extremes and the mean values of the attributes tested.

Table 19.2 Estimated values of rider quality attributes (SEK)

Attribute	Maximum	Minimum	Median	Mean
Pick-up time	260	96	124	140
Switchboard waiting time	248	65	112	124
In-vehicle time	59	13	20	26
Pre-booking time	55	11	20	25
Driver behavior	5	−28	–	–

The results presented depend on the study design. Therefore, the selected levels of the attributes are very important. The levels of the key attributes chosen seemed realistic from a Greater Stockholm point of view in 1997. Alternative sets of attribute levels will provide an opportunity to evaluate the underlying question: 'How are STS rider quality attributes to be valued from a customer perspective?'

Based on customer preferences, reflected in the SP game choices, the attribute path is clearly divided into two separate factions in Table 19.2. The main problem is the lack of planning opportunities in the rider's daily life.

This is illustrated in the upper part in the table (pick-up time and switchboard waiting time) with its high values. Timetable issues are as important for this group of riders as for non-disabled riders. Note especially the differences in valuation strength between pick-up time and in-vehicle time. The amount of variation in the values for these two attributes highlights the importance of punctuality in departure according to the agreed timetable. Is a pick-up time of 15 minutes acceptable? Public transport buses are delayed from time to time. But the situation is different if someone has to wait in uncertainty for 10 minutes for every single trip and purpose, year after year. This depicts an actual STS performance standard for many riders today (Stockholms läns landsting, 1999). Of course it is crucial that the rider has a fixed daily schedule, at least if the government and local authorities do not appraise travel time for these riders at zero. Up to now this has been the case (Knutsson, 1999).

From a regional planning perspective these facts have to be stressed and expressed in public. In the Greater Stockholm area alone we have more than 80,000 STS riders (Socialstyrelsen, 1998). The STS mode is planned as a vital part of the public transport system. Therefore, the timetable questions are equally important for all riders, disabled or not.

Only a few ALOGIT estimations calculated in the study are significantly separated from one another in a test of the confidence interval at the 95 percent level.

The following differences can be noted:

- employees and students value pick-up time higher than others;
- younger people value switchboard waiting time and pick-up time higher than old people;
- people with a low household income value switchboard waiting time lower than people with a higher household income;
- people with a high household income value pick-up time higher than people with a low household income.

The supporting ALOGIT estimations for the statement above are presented in Table 19.3, where we show the results of the ALOGIT estimations using the full database resulting from the SP games. First, statistical results are given with and without the constant in the ALOGIT estimation.

As can be seen, the differences are small when the two cases are compared. Note also the strong t-values. The parameter of driver behavior is an exceptional case where the parameter chosen seems to reveal a weak point in the design.

Table 19.3 **Comparison of results of the estimations for the total population**

Variable	Constant	No constant
Constant	0.278	–
t-value	6.4	–
Pre-booking time	−0.009	−0.010
t-value	−6.0	−6.8
Switchboard waiting time	−0.059	−0.058
t-value	−20.4	−20.5
Pick-up time	−0.066	−0.066
t-value	−22.7	−22.8
In-vehicle time	−0.009	−0.007
t-value	−3.4	−2.8
PriPrice	−0.032	−0.031
t-value	−19.4	−19.5
Driver behavior	−0.026	0.007
t-value	−0.5	0.1

Table 19.4 **Monetary valuation of STS attributes for total population (SEK)**

Variable	Constant	No constant
Pre-booking time	17	19
Switchboard waiting time	111	111
Pick-up time	126	126
In-vehicle time	18	14
Driver behavior	*	*

* Not significant at the 95 percent level

Table 19.4 shows the fundamental relations between the variables using the full database. Note especially that pick-up time is seven times more valuable to the riders than in-vehicle time.

Table 19.5   Monetary valuation of STS attributes for employment categories (SEK)

Variable	Employed	Others
Pre-booking time	40	13
Switchboard waiting time	193	100
Pick-up time	233	112
In-vehicle time	*	13
Driver behavior	*	*

* Not significant at the 95 percent level

There are frequently timetable restrictions involved in an employment situation. Therefore, as seen from Table 19.5, the waiting time parameters of pick-up time and switchboard waiting time are essential to obtain punctuality. In-vehicle time itself is less important compared with previous attributes. The willingness to pay for exactness in STS supply is high in comparison with the attribute in-vehicle time itself. On the other hand, a person who is unemployed or a senior citizen can spend the time more freely. That person does not depend as strongly on exactness in on time transportation delivery. As a result the parameter values are lower for the category 'others'.

Table 19.6   Monetary valuation of STS attributes age groups 18–64 and 65–84 (SEK)

Variable	18–64	65–84
Pre-booking time	20	12
Switchboard waiting time	121	101
Pick-up time	140	110
In-vehicle time	16	19
Driver behavior	*	*

The target groups for STS are disabled or elderly people. In Table 19.6 the age group of 18–64 years represents the most travelling-disposed of the customers in general terms. As a consequence this group is willing to pay more for STS than the older customer group, senior citizens.

Table 19.7   Monetary valuation of STS attributes for household income (SEK)

Variable	<99	100–299	300–599	>600
Pre-booking time	13	13	42	44
Switchboard waiting time	90	115	191	194
Pick-up time	107	123	257	256
In-vehicle time	20	*	58	59
Driver behavior	*	*	*	*

* Not significant at the 95 percent level

Not surprisingly, Table 19.7 indicates that the households with the highest incomes are willing to pay more than the others (Vägverket and Banverket, 1995) whether they are disabled or not. Again, if we take a look at the relation between in-vehicle time and pick-up time values in Table 19.7, we have a good illustration of the importance of punctuality.

Finally, in Sweden, it is a well-known fact (Socialstyrelsen, 1998) that women comprise the great majority of STS customers. Why women theoretically would be prepared to pay more for switchboard waiting time and for pick-up time is not totally clear. One hypothesis could be that female customers do not have the same alternative access to a private car in their neighborhood as men.

Table 19.8   Monetary valuation of STS attributes for gender groups (SEK)

Variable	Men	Women
Prebooking time	21	14
Switchboard waiting time	109	114
Pick-up time	118	130
In-vehicle time	23	16
Driver behavior	*	*

* Not significant at the 95 percent level

In the following tables we discuss valuation depending on district type, trip purpose and number of one-way trips. In the Greater Stockholm area we find the highest values in general. There is less of conformity in the south and north periphery, and the rest of the county.

In the SP games we had two variations of trip purpose given, namely trips associated with a Saturday party and a chiropody visit. The results show especially that the attribute pick-up time is crucial for social events like a party.

Table 19.9 Monetary valuation by district type in Stockholm County (SEK)

Variable	Greater Stockholm	South and north periphery	Rest of county
Pre-booking time	27	*	20
Switchboard waiting time	120	114	103
Pick-up time	143	114	124
In-vehicle time	20	*	22
Driver behavior	*	*	*

*Not significant at the 95 percent level

Table 19.10 Monetary valuation of travel purpose (SEK)

Variable	Saturday party	Chiropody visit
Pre-booking time	15	18
Switchboard waiting time	111	112
Pick-up time	138	113
In-vehicle time	17	18
Driver behavior	*	5

* Not significant at the 95 percent level

Next, we consider the valuation depending on the number of one-way trips. In short, trip consumption reflects different life styles. It is thus critical to note switchboard waiting time and pick-up time in Table 19.11.

Note especially the difference between men and women in the category of highest travel consumption 201 or more one-way trips.

Full-time working women depend on punctuality and control over the transportation timetable. The attributes switchboard waiting-time and pick-up time are vital.

Table 19.11 Monetary valuation of one-way trips for men and women (SEK)

Variable	Up to 20		21–60		61–200		201 or more	
	M	F	M	F	M	F	M	F
Pre-booking time	29	*	24	*	*	15	29	55
Switchboard waiting time	111	103	116	94	115	109	65	248
Pick-up time	96	116	130	96	102	143	153	260
In-vehicle time	*	*	*	25	51	*	*	*
Driver behavior	*	*	*	*	*	*	*	*

Table 19.12 Monetary valuation of wheelchair-bound riders (SEK)

Variable	Wheelchair-bound rider	Not wheelchair-bound rider
Pre-booking time	24	11
Switchboard waiting time	107	119
Pick-up time	130	120
In-vehicle time	52	17
Driver behavior	*	*

*Not significant at the 95 percent level

People who are wheelchair-bound always have to plan ahead, plan their lives in smallest detail. Therefore, the daily STS pre-booking process and poor punctuality pick-up time can be seen as situations that create friction.

Finally, we turn to the question of confidence in STS. It is logic that poor STS confidence gives the highest values. Again, switchboard waiting time and pick-up time are crucial for the standard of performance. Negative customers are willing to pay more than positive or neutral riders.

Women are in the majority in the customer group. From the perspective of regional planning confidence findings must be noted, if any serious comparison with the public transport system in the area is to be made.

A cost-benefit analysis has been performed using the empirical results in a consequence scheme. This was done in the light of some actual effectivization strategies in the field of Swedish STS. The background is a policy shift that took place related to STS from the social policy area to the transport domicile, supported by the Swedish Special Transport Service Act of 1997 (SFS, 1997:736).

The present situation of the STS reform is a result of the strongly expressed demand for Swedish transport policy effectiveness in terms of governmental cost reduction (SFS, 1997:736).

Table 19.13 Monetary valuation of confidence in STS (SEK)

Variable	Positive		Negative	
	Men	Women	Men	Women
Pre-booking time	19	11	48	55
Switchboard waiting time	104	113	157	187
Pick-up time	117	117	110	179
In-vehicle time	22	*	*	*
Driver behavior	*	*	*	−28

* Not significant at the 95 percent level

As can be seen in Table 19.14 all strategies increase in-vehicle time and most of them are a drawback in terms of driver behavior. The service line mode is a newly adopted public transport mode especially designed to attract older and disabled riders.

One way to do so is to select, develop and educate drivers so that they become more aware of different customer needs. Switchboard waiting time disappears in most of the strategies. This is a positive for the riders. As was pointed out in the introduction, it is common in Sweden as well to measure STS productivity from the producer perspective in terms of quantity before quality (Knutsson, 1999).

From a regional planning perspective this cost-benefit approach can be one of many ways to place STS riders on a more equal footing with other public transport riders.

Table 19.14 Rationalization strategies for travel demand grouped by effect on rider quality and willingness to pay

Strategy	Willingness to pay				
	Pick-up time	Switchboard waiting time	Pre-booking time	In-vehicle time	Driver behavior
Transfer to bus	advantage	advantage	advantage	drawback	drawback
Service line	advantage	advantage	advantage	drawback	advantage
Winding road line	drawback	advantage	advantage	drawback	drawback
Scheduled traffic	drawback	advantage	advantage	drawback	drawback
Adjust departure time	drawback	–	–	drawback	drawback
Allow divergence from desired depart time	drawback	–	–	drawback	drawback

Discussion

This chapter has presented an analysis of a Swedish rider quality index (IRQ) and a methodology for the estimation of rider quality in STS using utility modeling. On the whole, the study has produced a set of Swedish rider quality values distributed over a set of customer groups traditionally used in regional planning and traffic planning. A limitation of the study is the poor result for the parameter of driver behavior. Only two estimations carried out are statistically proven for this variable. As a consequence, the findings in this part need to be more thoroughly examined.

With this shortcoming in mind, a customer profile can be presented of low and high willingness to pay for STS in Stockholm County. The profile is a summary of the results from all estimations; see Table 19.15.

Two quite different personal life conditions are illustrated. In fact the table identifies two very typical rider categories in Swedish STS. On the one hand there is a full-time working rider and on the other hand a retired rider. The differences in valuation depend on whether the rider has to have control over the transportation timetable or not.

Table 19.15 Factor distribution for the willingness to pay for STS

High willingness to pay	Low willingness to pay
Woman	Man
High household income	Low household income
Low confidence in STS	High/neutral confidence in STS
Highest travel consumption	Lowest travel consumption
	Not employed or student
	Purpose of travel: chiropody
	Not wheelchair-bound

STS is the main disabled mode of transportation in Sweden. In a Swedish context there is no published attempt known either to formulate a rider quality index or model STS travel demand in terms of rider quality attributes. From the perspective of regional planning the results of the current study can be seen as tools for policy-relevant transportation system analysis, targeting disabled people.

Furthermore, in this research project Swedish STS rider quality values can easily be compared with up-to-date rider quality values for general riders in passenger traffic in Sweden for the first time. In addition regional planners are given an opportunity to test the findings in a standard cost-benefit approach.

Appendix 1 Outline of an Index of Rider Quality (IRQ) of Swedish STS

Attribute	Measurement
Information	Information access
	Understandable information
	Faultless and complete information
	Unambiguous information
Dignity	Being taken seriously as a traveler
	Confidence with respect to what to do and where to go
	Personal privacy
	Reliability of service
	Day and night-time safety
	Medical emergency capability
	Suitability and motivation of driver
	Courtesy and friendliness
	Familiarity with personal needs
Comfort	Service on weekdays
	Service on weekend
	Punctuality of departure
	Punctuality of arrival
	Freedom from crowding
	Booking
	Follow-up to complaints
	Few travel restrictions
	Prebooking of return
	Smoothness of ride
	Design of vehicle interior
	Number of steps
	Space and seating
	Lift or ramp
	Distance to vehicle
	Driver assistance
	Ease of registering a complaint
	Possibility to choose departure time
Travel time	Reasonable in-vehicle time
	Waiting time away from home
	Switchboard waiting time
	Total trip time
	Delays in vehicle
	Pre-booking time
	Punctuality of pick-up time
Fare	Worth its price compared to public transport
	Fare

References

Algers, S., Colliander, J. and Widlert, S. (1987), *Logitmodellen. Användbarhet och generaliserbarhet*, Rapport R30:1987, Swedish Council for Buildy Research, Stockholm.
Gillingwater, D., Sutton, J., Frye, A. and Banister, D. (1995), 'Community Transport: Policy, Planning, Practice', *Transportation Studies*, vol. 15.
Greater Stockholm Public Transport (1996), *Strategical Plan 1996*, Greater Stockholm Public Transport, Stockholm.
Hauge Consulting Group (1992), ALOGIT Users' Guide, version 3.2: September.
Hägerstrand, T. (1970), *Tidsanvändning och omgivningsstruktur*, in SOU 1970:14, Stockholm.
Hägerstrand, T. (1972), *Om en konsistent, individorienterad samhällsbeskrivning förframtidsstudiebruk*, in SOU 1972:59, Stockholm.
Jones, P. (1989), 'An Overview of Stated Preference Techniques', *P.T.R.C Course Lecture Notes*, Oxford University Transport Studies Unit, Oxford.
Knutsson, S. (1998), *Funktionshindrades värdering av färdtjänst*, TRITA-IP FR 98–43, Department of Regional Planning, Royal Institute of Technology, Stockholm.
Knutsson, S. (1999), Färdtjänstens produktionsmål. *En jämförelse mellan Stockholms län, Göteborgs kommun och Östergötlands län*, KFB-Meddelande 1999:9, Stockholm.
Lund, T. and Oxley, P. (1992), *Cross-Sector Benefits of Accessible Public Transport*, 20th Summer Annual Meeting, University of Manchester, Institute of Science & Technology, England.
McKee, C. (1993), *Rail Vehicles Accessible to Disabled Passengers*, Proceedings of Seminar held at the PTRC European Transport, Highways and Planning 21st Summer Annual Meeting 1993, UMIST, vol. P371.
McKnight, C.E., Pagano, A.M. and Paaswell, R.E. (1986), 'Using Quality to Predict Demand for Special Transportation', *Behavioral Research for Transport Policy*, pp. 423–41, VNU Science Press, Utrecht.
National Board of Health and Welfare (1998), Special Transport Services Statistics 1997.
Paaswell, R.E. (1977), 'Estimation of Demand for Transit Service Among the Transportation Disadvantaged', *Transportation Research Record 660*, pp. 38–49.
Pearmain, D., Swanson, J., Koes, E. and Bradley, M. (1991), *Stated Preference Techniques: A Guide to Practice*, Steer Davies Gleave, Hague Consulting Group 1991, 2nd ed.
SFS 1997:734, Lag om ansvar för viss kollektiv persontrafik (Specialized Public Transport Responsibility Act).
SFS 1997:736, Färdtjänstlagen (Swedish Special Transport Service Act 1997).
Socialstyrelsen (1998) 'Färdtjänst och riksfärdtjänst 1997', *Statistik Socialtjänst*, 1998:3, Stockholm.
Stockholms läns landsting (1999), Årsredovisning för Färdtjänstnämnden 1998, Stockholm.
Sutton, J. (1990), 'Travel Choice and Mobility Handicapped: Some Preliminary Investigations Utilizing a Disaggregated Choice Model', *Transportation Planning and Technology*, vol. 14, p. 229–41.
Sutton, J. and McLaughlin, E. (1991), 'Social Services Transport in Camden', *Traffic Engineering and Control*, vol. 32, No.9.
Thatcher, R.H. and Gaffney, J.K. (1991), *ADA Paratransit Handbook: Implementing the Complementary Paratransit Service Requirements of Americans with the Disabilities Act of 1990*, UMTA, Washington DC.
Widlert, S. (1992), *Stated preferences: ett sätt att skatta värderingar och beteende*, Division of Traffic Planning, Royal Institute of Technology and Transek AB, Stockholm.

Woodson, W.E. (1992), *Human Factors Design Handbook: Information and Guidelines for the Design of Systems, Facilities, Equipment, and Products for Human Use*, McGraw-Hill, 2nd edition, New York.

Vägverket/Banverket (1995), *1994 års tidsvärdestudie, Slutrapport*, Transek, Stockholm.

20 Culture, Jobs and Regional Development – An Empirical Study of Innovation Networks in the Culture Industry in the Stockholm Metropolitan Region

FOLKE SNICKARS

Study Background and Aim

The paper reports results from a research project on the topic of culture, jobs and regional development with the aim to increase the knowledge of the contribution of culture to regional economic, and social, transformation. Three aspects of this process are focal.

The first aspect concerns the role of the cultural sector in regional development at large. Cultural activities are often conceived as being part of the public sector responsibilities, implying that the demand for cultural activity is not large enough for the sector to sustain without support from the public purse. However, if regarded in broad terms, the cultural sector contains both private and public parts. If properly delineated and defined, the sector will indeed have a role to play as an engine also in the creation of economic wealth in a region. Thus, the question of the study is to assess the economic importance of the cultural sector seen as an industry.

The study relates to both the supply of cultural production capacity in a region and the demand for culture, locally and regionally as well as externally. The ambition is also to address the question of the functioning of cultural production and consumption markets with their peculiar segmentations, networks and market-clearing dynamics. The culture industry contains small and medium sized enterprises with a high degree of innovation behavior in their value-creating activities. They are often local and regional firms, involved in various stages of the value-added chain from primary production of cultural and artistic commodities to the final consumption of services, which are often involved in a global, dynamic, and very competitive market. The film and media industries are prime examples of this contemporary global phenomenon, see Vogel (1998) and Pine I, Gilmore and Pine II (1999).

The second aspect covered in the study concerns the role of culture in public policies, public strategies, and public-private partnership for the formulation, and implementation of regional development policy. One question here is whether a region can successfully specialize in cultural production in the same way as some regions have become university centers, centers for car production, or nodes for manufactured-goods distribution.

If this is the case, maybe the cultural sector is a candidate to solve some of the employment problems in metropolitan regions and in declining industrial regions of the Swedish settlement system. Following this line of argument, the question becomes how cultural development should be made an element of a strategy for regional development. The ultimate aim of the study is to further the knowledge necessary to support such possible planning and policy measures from the point of view of different actors involved.

The third aspect of the study concerns the development of the production factors for cultural development. The cultural activities under scrutiny will encompass both cultural services and cultural industries. It is often argued that cultural activity thrives in the creative region where there is a multitude of versatile activity niches and a population which contains subcultures exhibiting a taste for a broad range of established as well as avant-garde cultural activities, see for instance Andersson and Strömquist (1988).

The existence of a skilled labor force having positive attitudes towards the activities of the culture sector is another important production factor. Also, it is often argued that cultural dynamics is associated with special institutional and locational assets, and physical environments. The notion of a cultural environment is a shorthand way of expressing the contribution of both the socioeconomic and the built environment's contribution to the viability of cultural production.

The research in this part of the study aims to further the understanding of the location factors for cultural activity be they stable or dynamic, local or global, institutional or physical.

Infrastructure and Cultural Development

Traditionally, the location of workplaces has been closely related to location factors such as proximity to ports, rivers, natural resources and large input and output markets. Today the situation for many firms is different due to factors as technical change, and the increasing internationalization of the economy. As one of the tangible results of this development we can also observe an increasing degree of mobility among firms. In many industries firms are no longer bound to particular geographical location, instead they seek a production milieu which contains important environmental qualities for the firm. In this perspective a well developed and smoothly functioning infrastructure represents an increasingly important mean of competition. Therefore, the extent and quality of the infrastructure is of strategic significance for individual firms as well as for industrial networks, cities, regions, and nations.

The cultural industry is no exception to this general pattern. The mobile cultural events industry, for instance, will locate its production activity in the most accessible places in a national and international system of cities, see Snickars (2000). Within a region it will strive to locate its production outlets, temporary or permanent, to a selection of the most accessible locations. There is also a tendency that activity environments are sought by the events industry, as well as many other segments of the cultural industry, which exhibit a cultural ambience. This ambience might well be present in modern urban districts and derelict urban environments alike. The crucial point of the argument is that for firms in the cultural sector the cultural infrastructure in the sense sketched is very important for the viability of the production activity.

Rejuvenation of old industrial estates or other production environments in a city or region will often be paralleled with a gentrification process among firms in the cultural sector. Culture activities often tend to seek locations in the city, which are undergoing economic transformation, see Söderlind (2000). One reason for this is simply their weak rent-paying capability. When the industrial estates are reconstructed this has often implied a complete demolition of the old building stock. This strategy of realizing only the locational value of the estate may not be optimal in the new situation with an increased importance of the cultural industries for the economy of the city.

For some of the reasons discussed above, the value of cultural production can be seen as an important part of the social infrastructure of a city. This value is difficult to contain within individual property rights and it is often impossible to create functioning competitive markets for cultural transactions, even in metropolitan regions. This is basically why it is warranted to use the term infrastructure to denote its role. Cultural activities in the city create an open cultural landscape in the city in the same way that agriculture – besides food production – also creates an open cultural landscape in the countryside.

It has long been a well known fact that technical infrastructure is of vital importance as a basis for favorable regional development. Good transport and communication systems as well as well functioning water, sewage and energy systems are basic prerequisites in order for a place or a region to have good development possibilities. Similarly, there is also an extensive and well documented body of knowledge about the significance of proximity to subcontractors and access to qualified support services for firms in the choice of location. There is also evidence about the significance of higher education facilities and commercial services.

During recent years, with the support of research as well as practical experience, new insights have been achieved and knowledge has been developed concerning the significance of cultural and environmental factors in the choice of location. The experiences which have been gained indicate clearly that the latter factors play a very important role in determining the attractiveness of a place. By cultural factors we mean both the different forms of current cultural activities which are offered as well as the heritage and architectural qualities which characterize a place, see for instance Ashworth and Ennen (1996). It is a central aim of the current study to develop the notion of culture as an infrastructure in the form of social capital, which underpins and supports social and economic development of cities and regions.

Cultural Industries in the Stockholm Metropolitan Region

The metropolitan region of Stockholm has essentially a polycentric structure with the City of Stockholm as the strongest player. The rest of the Mälar region can be said to constitute the hinterland of metropolitan Stockholm, see also Figure 20.1. The ample availability of land in Sweden implies that the pressure is not as large on scarce land resources for urban development as in other European metropolitan regions. Lake Mälaren is an environmental asset, and a trade infrastructure, at the same time being the major supplier of drinking water to all the urban settlements in the area. For the moment there is no comprehensive physical plan that controls the future land-use in the region, which houses a number of small and medium-sized urban settlements.

The hinterland of the Stockholm region used to be the core of the Swedish manufacturing industry.

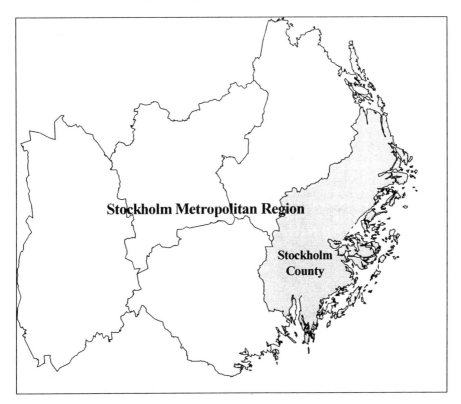

Figure 20.1   The geographical and administrative structure of the Stockholm metropolitan region

The Stockholm metropolitan area is the most service-specialized functional urban region in the western part of Europe with more than three out of four jobs occurring in the private and public service sector, see also Figure 20.2.

Although being one of the largest urban regions in Europe, Barcelona still has a strong concentration of manufacturing activity. It can be noted that the three metropolitan regions have the common trait that they are located away from the core regions in Europe. They are all gateways regions to the south, north and east, respectively, see also Andersson and Andersson (1999).

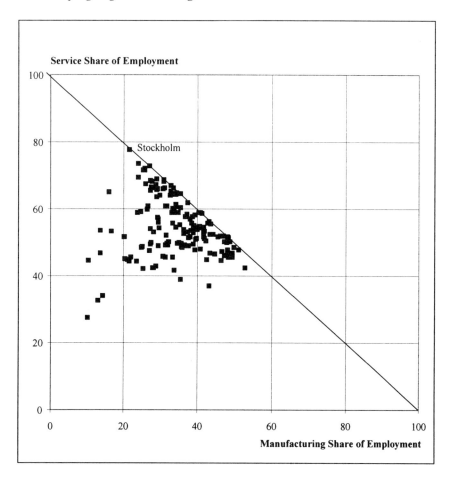

**Figure 20.2   Specialization of the Stockholm metropolitan region
among European functional urban regions in the middle
of the 1990s**

A number of research studies have been performed investigating the role
of local entrepreneurship for regional development. Another branch of
research focuses on the requisites for corporate environments, and cities, of
being innovative and creative. The research on innovations has most often
dealt with the manufacturing sector, having information technology as a
nexus of interest.

The idea here is to test a similar hypothesis for the culture industry. As a
background to this analysis, the current section will provide some
information on the role of the culture industry in the Swedish regions. In

particular, the ambition is to show the peculiar role of the Stockholm metropolitan region in the culture industry.

The only reliable source of information is the detailed employment statistics, which are published yearly for detailed regional and sectoral classifications. This source holds information of the full pattern of employment in the economy both for the private and the public sector. The current registers in principle allow the tracing of the full pattern of employment for all individuals each year based on their tax declarations. Thus, if a person has had several sources of income during a year this can be covered. In the current case we have only used the sum of the employment held by each individual during a year. The culture industry is difficult to define since the industrial classification has not been developed with this sector in mind.

In the presentation of results below we will use the standard international classification system, in which the following sectors form the core, film production firms, film distribution firms, cinemas, radio and TV companies, artists, theatres, news agencies, gambling firms, and other recreation firms. In those analyses that relate to the culture industries in the strict sense gambling firms and other recreational firms have been excluded.

In the broad sense the sector had an employment level of some 25000 jobs in 1997 whereas the amount was 18500 in the strict sense. The City of Stockholm had some 73 percent of the region's jobs in the broad definition of the culture industry and 83 percent in the narrow sense. The total number of jobs in the country in the broad definition was 75000 and 42500 or 56 percent.

Figure 20.3 shows the culture specialization among Swedish municipalities in 1997 in the strict definition of the industry. Some 20 municipalities have a specialization in cultural jobs more than double the national average. A majority of the municipalities in the uppermost segment of the specialization hierarchy are found in the Stockholm metropolitan region with the City of Stockholm occupying the top position. Some 180 of the municipalities have a specialization index of less than half of the national average.

The number of jobs is insignificant in most of these local labor markets. It may be noted that five municipalities have no jobs at all in the culture industry defined in the strict sense. They are all located in the northern and inland part of the country. The figure shows the skewed regional structure of the industry indicating that the culture sector is a specialized service sector, which belongs to the upper segments of the settlement system hierarchy.

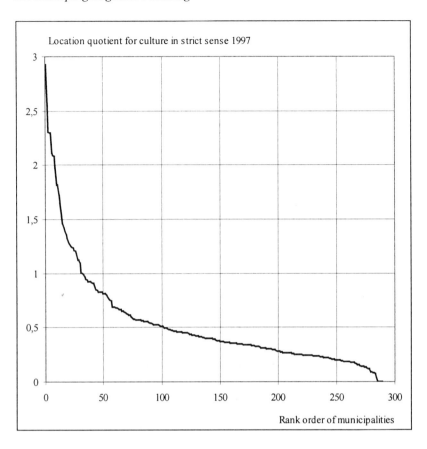

Figure 20.3 Culture specialization in Swedish municipalities 1997 (national average = 1)

Figure 20.4 illustrates the division of labor between the different parts of the Stockholm metropolitan region. It should be noted that we will use the term Stockholm metropolitan region to encompass the whole of the Stockholm region and its economic hinterland disregarding the subdivision into political jurisdictions. In operational terms this means that we have surveyed the industry in both Stockholm County and the four surrounding counties, extending some 200 km in north, west and south directions. When we use the term Stockholm County we refer to the jurisdiction at the county level. It has some 25 municipalities within it. Reference it made to the central municipality in Stockholm County as the City of Stockholm. We will use the term Stockholm region broadly equivalent to Stockholm County.

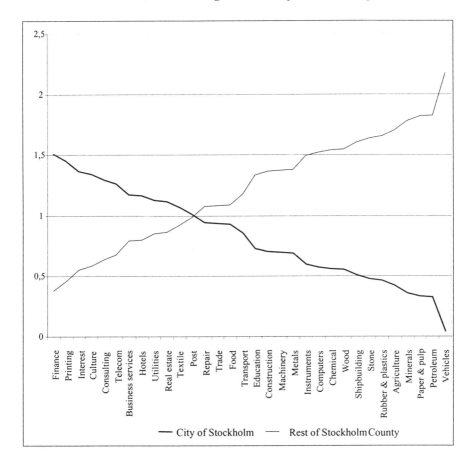

Figure 20.4   Sectoral specialization among municipalities in the Stockholm metropolitan region in 1997 (regional average = 1)

The question raised is whether there is weak or strong intraregional specialization within the metropolitan region and which sectors exhibit the most distinct patterns. In Figure 20.4 a specialization index value of one means that the sector's share of the total employment in the City of Stockholm is the same as the sector's share in the rest of the metropolitan region.

It turns out that only service industries have a specialization index above one in the City of Stockholm with the postal services sector as the limiting one. The highest specialization is in financial activities, printing and publishing, interest-based organizations, and culture industries.

Table 20.1 illustrates what industries are the most clustered ones at the municipal level in Stockholm County. The idea is to investigate whether the culture industry is one of those clustered industries. This does not turn out to be the case, however.

Table 20.1   Location quotients for selected industries in the Stockholm region municipalities 1997

Industry	Municipality	Location quotient
Petroleum	Nynäshamn	81.0
Stone &Clay	Värmdö	42.4
Paper & Pulp	Norrtälje	24.2
Vehicles	Södertälje	22.4
Agriculture	Ekerö	13.0
Shipyards	Sigtuna	12.5
Rubber & Plastics	Nynäshamn	10.9
Chemicals	Södertälje	10.6
Computers	Järfälla	8.5
Machinery	Botkyrka	8.1
Minerals	Norrtälje	8.0
Food	Upplands-Väsby	7.8
Transport	Sigtuna	7.2
Wood	Norrtälje	6.3
Telecommunications	Nynäshamn	6.2

There are in fact 25 industries which have a location quotient relative to the Stockholm region as a whole of five or more. This clustered employment amounts to somewhat less than three percent of the possible industry-municipality combinations in the database. It is evident that the specialized industries are almost exclusively to be found in manufacturing. The transport service specialization of Sigtuna reflects the location of Arlanda airport north of the city center.

The telecommunications specialization of Nynäshamn, in the south, arises from the location of production facilities of the Ericsson corporation in that part of the region.

The municipalities involved are almost exclusively to be found in the periphery of Stockholm County. In fact, the City of Stockholm has no peculiar specialization profile at all when the analysis is performed at this detailed level of aggregation.

Innovation Potentials within the Stockholm Cultural Industry

One central question in this study is the level of innovation activities (product, process, organization) and the variation of these across industries and regions. Such a study can further the understanding of what constitutes the innovation potential of a cluster of firms in the culture industry within a region or across regions. The idea pursued here is to accept the definitions of innovation used in earlier studies, Nutek (1998), Fischer, Revilla Diez and Snickars (2001), and apply these also to the culture industry. The hypothesis is that the culture industry can be regarded as any other service-producing industry both in its support to manufacturing firms in their innovation work and in its internally generated need for innovation.

Another question relates to furthering the empirical understanding of the innovation networks among a set of firms within a metropolitan region. It may be expected that a city or a region will house a number of activities which interact with each other at different geographical scales. Some of those interactions are associated with innovation activities while others are parts of normal business relations. The main dividing line that defines whether interaction is of innovative type concerns the degree of novelty for the actors involved. The innovation cycle is used as a conceptualization of the different steps that any new activity embraces both for the user and the actors working with the user to supply new products or processes. The question then is in which sectoral and regional networks, and in what stages of the innovation cycle, the external firm networks become most important. A related question concerns the strength of the innovation networks between firms of different type, and the role of R&D institutions in the region and elsewhere this context.

An empirical study has been performed of the innovation potential and innovation networks in the Stockholm metropolitan region (sometimes called the Mälar region). The study is one component of an international study where the European regions of Vienna and Barcelona are compared to Stockholm, see Fischer, Revilla Diez and Snickars (2001). In earlier phases of the Germany-based international research program within which this study has been performed comparisons have been made of the innovation traits of a number of German and French regions. The current study has corresponding ones for old industrial regions and core regions of Europe. The three regions selected here belong to the economic periphery of Europe at the same time having strategic roles in their part of Europe.

The study of the regional innovation system in the Stockholm metropolitan region has involved all firms in manufacturing and business services with at least 10 employees in 1996. Furthermore, similar questions have been asked about innovation behavior of all R&D institutions in the extended Stockholm region. Thus, it is possible to compare how firms belonging to the manufacturing sector, the business services sector, and the R&D sector look upon their roles in relation to other actors in the regional production system.

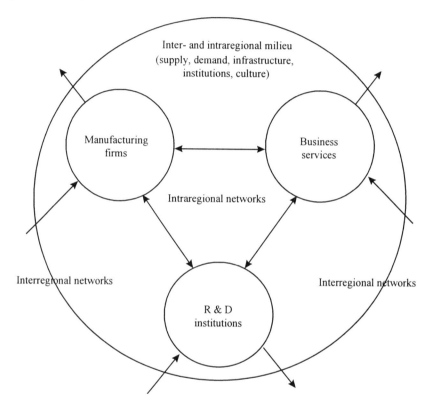

Figure 20.5   An intraregional milieu for innovation generation and innovation diffusion and its internal and external networks

Figure 20.5 provides a principle illustration of the conceptual framework of the innovation study. The study regards the innovation activities in a regional context to be placed within an intraregional and interregional milieu consisting of other firms, suppliers, customers, competitors, and R&D actors. The environment also comprises the institutional setup in the form of legal and administrative frameworks as well as physical infrastructures.

The framework is further developed in Fischer, Revilla Diez and Snickars (2001).

The sample of manufacturing firms includes some 450 establishments belonging to manufacturing firms (27 percent of the total number in the region), some 350 establishments within business services (26 percent) and some 175 R&D establishments (52 percent).

The response rate has been set to allow statistical representativeness at a macro level but not to accommodate detailed analyses for subgroups of sectors and subregions. The collection of data from the R&D sector is among others a trait of the study for which it stands out from earlier work in the field.

Table 20.2   Composition of subsectors among business services including a definition of the culture and media sector

Business service industries surveyed	
IT firms	**Marketing and consulting firms**
Software consulting	Banks
Computer firms	Financial leasing firms
Software product firms	Other financial firms
Computer service firms	Attorneys at law
Data base hosts	Patenting firms
Other IT firms	Accounting firms
	Marketing firms
Culture and media firms	Corporate consulting
Film production firms	Architect offices
Film distribution firms	Technical analysis firms
Cinemas	Public relation firms
Radio and TV companies	Advertising firms
Artists	Home marketing firms
Theatres	Other marketing firms
News agencies	
Gambling firms	
Other recreation firms	

In the Stockholm study that is reported here, a special role has been given to culture in the regional innovation systems in two principal regards. Firstly, the culture and media industries, as well as the finance and banking sectors, have been included among the business service sector, see also the list of subsectors from which answers have been received in the survey in Table 20.2. The table can be seen to contain an operational definition of the composition of the culture and media industry used in the survey. Secondly, all firms and institutions have been asked to assess their contacts with culture and media industries, and to state the role of cultural activities and cultural environments as location factors and carriers of locational value to the innovation activities. The table reveals that the culture industry comprises film and media firms, artists and theatres, news agencies, as well as gambling and recreational firms. The main dividing line within the sector is between entertainment and classical culture. Internationally both parts are seen as important elements of the sector which is often termed the entertainment industry or the experience industry, see also Vogel (1998), Pine et al (1999) and Wolf (1999).

Table 20.3 shows the composition of the business services sector in the Stockholm metropolitan region while The table compares the structure of the cultural industry to the other firms in the business service sector. It is seen that the IT firms employed about the same number of persons as the culture and media industry in 1997 while the marketing and consulting firms make up the same employment share of the sector as a whole as those two sectors together. The whole business service sector in strongly concentrated to the Stockholm metropolitan region which a share more than double the one for the employment as a whole. Some 57 percent of the marketing and consulting firms in the country were found in the Stockholm metropolitan region measured in terms of employment in 1997.

Table 20.3   Composition of the business services sector in the Stockholm region 1997

Sectors and basic indicators	Number of jobs	Sector share (%)	Share of Sweden (%)	Share in Stockholm County (%)
IT firms	25200	3	46	85
Marketing and consulting firms	74600	9	57	82
Culture and media firms	25200	3	33	79
All business services	125000	15	48	82
All jobs	826000	100	22	66

The corresponding numbers for the IT industry and the culture and media industry were 46 percent an one third, respectively.

The other important observation is that the sectors in question are also concentrated to the central parts of the Stockholm metropolitan region. Four out of five jobs in the sector are found in Stockholm County with a clear domination of the City of Stockholm. The concentration is highest for the IT firms.

Earlier studies at the national level have clearly indicated the connection between education, R&D and innovation, see for instance Nutek (1998) for the case of Sweden. Table 20.4 shows that the education level is clearly lower for the average culture and media firm than for business service firms on average.

Still, as many as one out of four employees in the culture industry had a university education in 1997. The education level is clearly highest in the IT firms. There are no significant differences between the central part of the Stockholm metropolitan region and the hinterland.

Table 20.4   Share of workforce in selected service industries in the Stockholm region with university education in 1997 (percent)

Location of firm	IT firms	Marketing and consulting firms	Culture and media firms	Business service firms
Stockholm County	42	33	25	35
Rest of region	33	40	24	37
Stockholm metro-politan region	40	35	25	36

Culture has the same level of innovation intensity as the average business service firm, see also Table 20.5. The sample size is too small for any stricter conclusion to be drawn.

However, the empirical evidence shows that more than one third of the firms in the business service sector invest at least five percent of their production cost in innovation-related activities. The interesting thing about the table is that IT firms on average tend to have a more concentrated structure as regards the focus on innovations.

Table 20.5   **Firms with innovation share of total production costs more than five percent (percent of responses)**

Firms	Share of firms (%)
IT firms	27
Marketing and consulting firms	38
Culture and media firms	36
All business services	31

The culture industry has a lower share of firms participating in innovation activities than the rest of the firms in the sample as seen from Figure 20.6. The figure illustrates the share of firms in the survey that have stated that they are engaged in three different forms of innovations.

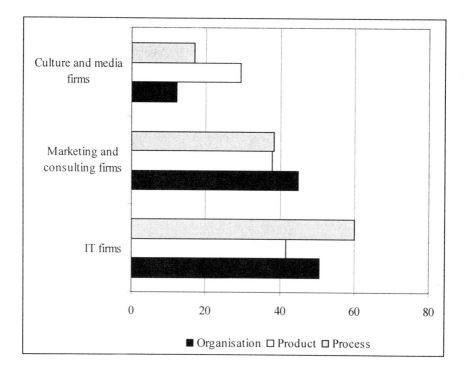

Figure 20.6   **Share of firms participation in various forms of innovation activities (percent)**

Product innovation is more common as a development activity than organization, market or process innovation. The pattern for the culture industry differs from that of the other business service firms in this respect. The marketing and consulting firms state that they perform somewhat more organizational innovations than the others while the IT firms are more often engaged in process innovations.

None of these results deviate from what one might intuitively expect. It is noteworthy that the culture and media firms do engage themselves less in innovation activities than the rest of the firms.

Some of the reasons for this might be that innovation is a less common concept used among these firms to focus on transformation processes. They see these activities more often in terms of creative and shaping processes.

Innovation Networks within the Stockholm Culture Industry

The culture industry is a networking industry as most other parts of the business service sector. The networks do not only relate to innovation processes but also to ordinary business relations. If, for instance, an IT consultancy firms sells computer systems to a company they will circumscribe these activities with a series of service offers. The general tendency is for the service firms to become more involved in networking for these, and other related, reasons.

Figure 20.7 is intended to give a picture of the role of the three broad macro sectors as partners in innovation work with the business service sector. The pattern of cooperation is similar among all categories of business service firms as regards contacts with R&D institutions.

The cooperation pattern is very similar for the culture and media firms and the marketing and consulting firms. IT firms are more intensive in networking, which is in line with that sector's role as a provider of communication opportunities.

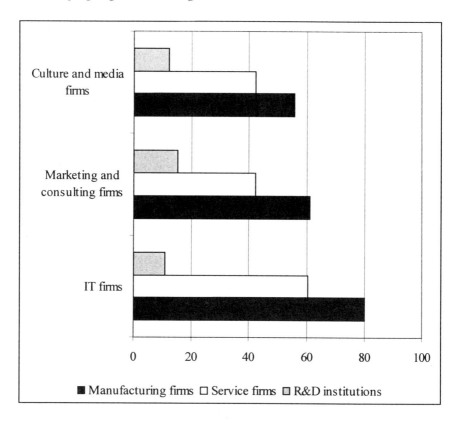

Figure 20.7   Share of firms in the business services sector involved in innovation cooperation by character of customer (percent)

The cooperation in networks of innovation is concentrated to different stages of the innovation cycle. The definition into stages follows the research literature on innovations in manufacturing, Fischer, Revilla Diez and Snickars (2001).

The first three phases of the cycle belong to the non-competitive stage whereas the other three involve competition between firms. Figure 20.8 shows the networking of firms in the business service sector in different stages of the innovation cycle.

We see from the figure that networking is most intensive in the early stages of the cycle. The patterns are somewhat different for IT firms than for the marketing and consulting firms, and the culture and media firms. IT firms seem to stay involved in later stages of the cycle, following the clients well into the competitive stage of the innovation cycle. This is again a reflection of the crucial role played by IT in innovation activities at large in the Stockholm metropolitan region.

Even though the pattern is not quite clear one can draw the tentative conclusion that firms in the culture industry are as involved in innovation activities with clients in the first stages of the cycle. The involvement tends to decline faster for those firms than for other business service firms in the region.

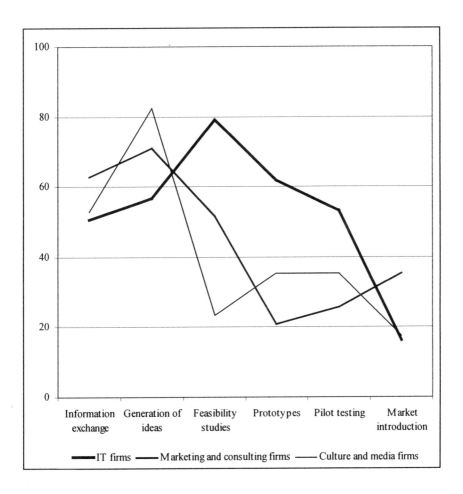

Figure 20.8 Firms in the business services sector involved in innovation cooperation by character of activity in different stages of the innovation cycle (percent)

Table 20.6   Hindrances to innovation activities in the business services sector in the Stockholm region (share of respondents agreeing to statement)

	IT firms	Marketing and consulting firms	Culture and media firms	All business service firms
Lack of capital	53	41	58	50
Risk assessment difficult	58	18	59	41
Lack of skilled labor	69	57	59	52
Result implementation difficult	44	34	41	39
Cooperation with firms difficult	21	21	20	21
Cooperation with R&D institutions difficult	18	9	12	13

The firms in the business service sector in the Stockholm metropolitan region have been asked to state the major hindrances they see towards innovation activities that they would like to pursue. For the average firm in the sector the lack of skilled labor in the primary bottleneck with the IT firms giving that a higher score than the rest.

It is interesting to note that the second most important hindrance is the lack of capital. Here it seems that the culture and media firms feel larger difficulties than the others. Culture and media firms mainly lack capital. It might also be noted that relatively few firms state that cooperation with other firms, or with R&D institutions, is a major hindrance for their innovation activities.

At least for the R&D institutions this result is partly a reflection of the fact that the contacts with R&D institutions are less prevalent in the first place.

Figure 20.9 shows that culture firms are more customer-related than average in their use of earlier contacts for current innovation work. The figure contains the summary results of responses to the question which background factors have been most important for the current innovation activities of the firm. It is seen that the pattern is similar across the three segments of the business service sector.

Around one third of the firms state that they are using networks created during studies or research while around one fourth of them state that contacts generated with earlier employers is important. Some 35 percent of the firms say that they have generated the innovation ideas together with their current network of customers.

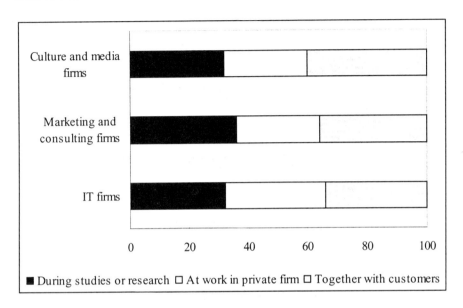

Figure 20.9 Background factors for the initiation of innovation cooperation in different firms in the business services sector (percent)

For the culture and media firms one can broadly say that the firms out of five state that the background for current innovation activities are networks that have stayed on from earlier education, research or customer contacts while two firms out of five say that the generate the ideas primarily with their current customers. The policy observation is that the role of the personal history of the employees seems to be larger that one would expect.

This picture is complemented by the information contained in Figure 20.10 where we list some factors which the firms have seen as positive components for the current innovation cooperation. The first observation is that spatial proximity is regarded as a less important factor for the network creation than the other ones.

Even if the spatial factor is not so important it seems that face-to-face contacts are. Such contacts can of course be upheld even at longer distances, for instance, in conjunction with conferences, fairs and exhibitions, and most importantly in the direct contacts with customers.

The firms also mention that a similar sectoral knowledge and equal qualifications are important factors for the emergence of innovation cooperation. The latter factor has a relation to the result presented above that contacts established earlier in the career are important.

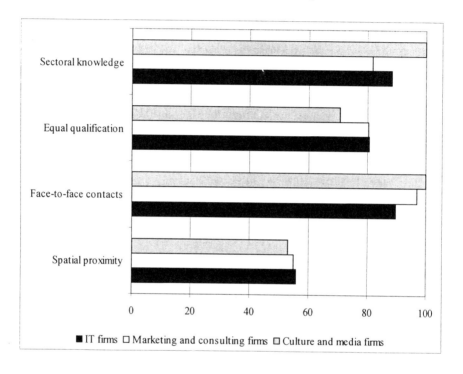

Figure 20.10 Positive factors for the establishment of innovation cooperation in different subsectors of business services (percent)

When comparing across the subsectors of the business service industry it seems that the patterns are relatively similar. It may be noted that the sectoral knowledge is assessed to be somewhat more important for culture and media firms that for the others. Also, the respondents in that subsector tend to place somewhat less emphasis with the importance of equal qualifications. On the other hand they judge face-to-face contacts to be more important than the other firms.

The picture that emerges from this analysis is that the flow of information is a positive factor for the chance that innovation cooperation will emerge. Spatial proximity as such is not regarded as a crucial factor.

On the other hand contacts between persons seems to carry more weight.

Figure 20.11 illustrates that the networks of culture firms are more Stockholm-oriented than the business services average. Two out of three contacts in innovation work are taken with firms in the Stockholm metropolitan area. The share of contacts in other countries varies somewhat between subsectors and is largest for the culture and media firms. Those firms have much fewer contact partners in the rest of Sweden than the other firms. The results are of course partly a reflection of the location of the supply of partners. Bigger regions house more potential partners than smaller regions. The result that the IT industry is more locally oriented than the other firms is somewhat surprising at first sight. It is a reflection of the high market demand for services provided by those firms in their home market.

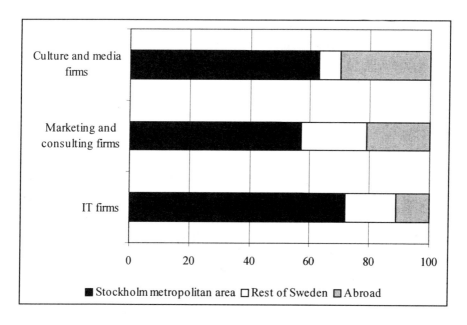

Figure 20.11 Share of innovation partners in different subregions for various components of the business services sector (percent)

Figure 20.12 indicates that the culture and media firms have approximately the same number of innovation partners as IT firms whereas the marketing and consulting firms have a somewhat broader network of partners. The average IT or culture and media firm will on average be involved in innovation work with eight partners, with somewhat less than half of them in the Stockholm metropolitan region.

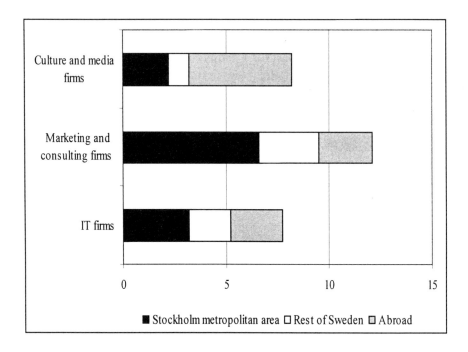

Figure 20.12 Average number of partners involved in innovation activities by subsector of business services

The marketing and consulting firms, on the other hand, have on average 12 partners of which six are located in the Stockholm metropolitan area. Even if one can suspect that the business service firms have had some difficulty in clearly defining what contact partners they have for their innovation work from the contacts they have with firms involving so-called normal business relations, the results indicate a network-oriented business service industry in the Stockholm metropolitan region.

The number of innovation partners will need to be reasonable for there to come out a large enough flow of marketable products since the success rate will normally be relatively low.

Culture as Infrastructure for Innovation Activities in the Stockholm Region

The metropolitan innovation potential is only partly determined by factors internal to the firms and institutions involved in the innovation activity. One of the external factors is hypothesized to be the nature of the innovation networks, and other networks, to which to firm or institution belongs. According to this argument the networks transfer positive externalities thus increasing the innovation potential, which in the longer run lead to enhanced economic growth through an increased frequency of innovation. The theory applies both to the manufacturing sector, which has traditionally been seen as the major carrier of innovation potential and to the service industries of the new economy, which are nowadays seen as major carriers of economic growth potential. The theory of national innovation systems considers mainly sector-specific factors as important in this context. The innovation potential then lies within a cluster of economic activity, which includes the firms, the labor they use, and the institutional structure in which they operate. Institutions differ across nations, and so does the competence given to labor through the educational system.

The approach of metropolitan innovation systems argues that regional factors are necessary to explain the differences in the innovation potential among economic sectors. The economic development occurs in space, and the metropolitan regions are major actors in the economic development game. The metropolitan regions differ in their capacity to act as incubators for innovation, see for instance Capello (2000). These differences have been measured in the survey using a number of environmental indicators. One particular type of indicator has been formed by asking the respondents to grade the qualities of the region according to a set of predetermined environmental factors. The factors are intended to measure the quality of supply factors in the metropolitan environment relating to capital, labor, manufacturing networks, manufacturing producer service networks, R&D networks, other innovation networks, infrastructure factors, and factors relating to public sector activities in the promotion of industrial development.

Figure 20.13 provides a summary of the results of this analysis focussing on the differences and similarities of firms and R&D institutions. The question addressed is how the different actors perceive one another as producers of positive externalities, how highly they value the quality of the urban infrastructure in the metropolitan region, both hard and soft, and how they assess the performance of the public sector in various respects. The intention is to provide guidance in the selection of policy to boost the potential of the region in serving as an efficient environment for innovation. The figure does not show how highly the respondents value the factors relative to one another but how they rank the performance of the Stockholm metropolitan region as an environment for innovation in the selected aspects (a five-degree scale has been used).

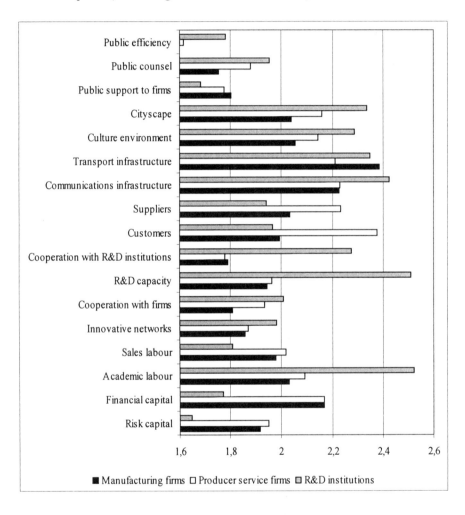

Figure 20.13   Ranking of the quality of a set of environmental factors in the Stockholm metropolitan region for innovation work in manufacturing firms, producer service firms and R&D institutions (average grading using a five-degree scale)

The most distinguishing feature of the results presented in Figure 20.13 is that industry and universities perceive the quality of the environmental factors quite differently. For the R&D institutions the most highly valued assets of the metropolitan region are factors related to the supply of academic competence and the functioning of academic networks. They value the hard and soft infrastructure factors in the region higher than the manufacturing respondents. They are somewhat more positive to the activities performed by public agencies in the promotion of university-industry linkages.

The second distinguishing feature of the results is that the average grading is not higher than in the order of two in the five-degree scale. This indicates that the respondents have not seen a reason to praise the Stockholm region as an innovative environment to the extent that one would maybe anticipate. Of course, the grading is relative and depends on expectations. It is warranted to interpret the result to indicate that the respondents feel that the region is not performing up to its full potential. A benchmark for that would have been to see the average being raised from around two to at least the middle of the five-degree scale. It should be noted that the fact that the scale is relative and refers directly to expectations means that it is difficult to compare the results with other regions in Europe.

The third distinguishing feature of the results is that the producer services firm's grade the environmental factors more positively in several important dimensions than the manufacturing firms. Since the manufacturing firms are more prevalent outside of the core of the metropolitan region this might be seen as an indication that the supply quality is not a well developed in the periphery as in the core. For the producer service firms both the supply of customers and providers of intermediary inputs are highly graded. Apparently, the Stockholm metropolitan region provides amply opportunity for them to find new customers, and choose appropriate suppliers of intermediate products.

It is a fourth distinguishing feature of the results that all respondents give high grades to both the hard and the soft infrastructure factors. The variations are realistic with due notice taken of the differences between the respondents. The cultural factors are seen as well developed as the transport and communications ones. One might also notice that the respondents have given relatively low grades to the institutional infrastructure factors as innovative networks, and R&D capacity. One explanation might be that firms and institutions see these factors mainly as sectoral ones, operated and influenced mainly by national innovation actors rather than being a part of the metropolitan environment. Again, the results here show that there is a rather distinct barrier between industry and university. Firms do not grade the quality of the contacts with the universities at all as highly as the contacts with customers and suppliers.

The fifth and final distinguishing feature of the results in Figure 20.11 is the low rating of public activities relating to innovation from the point of view of both industry and university. It might be noted that the manufacturing firms have the least good to say about the supply of public counsel, public support to firms, and public efficiency. This could be interpreted as a signal that the activities of the public sector are too national in character. Firms in the metropolitan region might not have enough experience from cooperating with public agencies so that the assessment is based on more general expectations.

The results of the comparison of the valuation of environmental factors are important in that they further emphasize the results of other parts of the survey pointing at the lack of knowledge about the other actors in the metropolitan region. The result that one actor, for instance the R&D institutions see their contacts in a different way than the firms with which they cooperate is also clear from responses to questions on cooperation in different stages of the innovation cycle. It is evident also from responses to questions concerning hindrances to cooperation between university and industry.

Maybe one of the main contributions from a study as the current one then is to point at these differences in anticipations and expectations. It is as if the actors in the region are not fully aware of the qualities that their cooperation activities have given to the region as an infrastructure system and incubator for urban innovation, see also Capello (2000).

Concluding Remarks

The study reported here has a distinctly empirical orientation. The main thrust of the analysis has been to test the hypothesis that the culture industry firms are, in a broad sense, as innovative as the average business service firm. Of course, the analysis is limited by the fact that the sample of firms in the survey is relatively small. Therefore, the analysis has not at all dealt with the differences and similarities between firms within the culture industry. Also, the study is explorative in the sense that we have not performed any formal hypothesis testing. Neither have we penetrated deeply into the causal links between the activities of the firms in the culture industry and the role that culture plays as a location factor and soft infrastructure for the Stockholm metropolitan economy at large. The study should be seen as an initial explorative attempt to further the understanding of the structure of the culture industry in the region as regards a factor that is often seen as being of central importance for the economic development in the region, viz the innovation potential and innovation networks.

We may summarize the results of the study in a few conclusions, which are set at a level where it is reasonable to assert that they hold for the culture industry as such and not only for the sample we have happened to gather in the survey.

The picture that emerges is that the culture and media industry has reasonably similar characteristics as other business service firms, which is a result that might be somewhat surprising in view of the relatively low level of attention that innovation work in these firms has in public policy:

- the innovation-intensive firms in the culture and media industry spend at least as much on innovation as the other business service firms;
- culture and media firms have a higher share of product innovations than the rest of the business service sector;
- culture and media firms cooperate with other firms and R&D institutions in the same fashion a other business service firms;
- about two out of five of the innovation activities of the culture and media industry arise from contacts with customers while the remaining share has the origin in earlier contact networks;
- the culture industry uses approximately the same number of partners in their innovation work as the IT industry;
- the innovation networks of the culture industry extend beyond regional and national borders to a higher extent than the average business service firm.

Cultural activities, and the built urban environment – the cityscape – of the Stockholm metropolitan region are stable infrastructure factors across manufacturing firms, business service firms, and research institutions in their innovation work. Culture functions as a soft infrastructure as is valued as highly in the region as the classical hard infrastructure factors as transport and communication supply. This is a result of the study which is definitely worth conveying as an input to policy-makers in the Stockholm region. The likelihood is high that the conclusions also hold for other regions in the country.

References

Andersson, Å.E. and Strömquist, U. (1988), *The future of the C-society*, Prisma, Stockholm.
Ashworth, G. and Ennen, E. (1996), 'Art as Marketing Instrument: The development Function of the Groningen Museum', *Paper presented at the 36ᵗʰ European Congress of the Regional Science Association International*, Zürich.
Bennett, T. (2001), 'Cultural Policy – History and Theory', in F. Snickars (ed.), *Culture, society and market*, Bank of Sweden Tricentennary Fund and National Swedish Council for Cultural Development, Stockholm.
Bianchini, F. (1993), 'Remaking European Cities: The Role of Cultural Policies', in F. Bianchini and M. Parkinson (eds), *Cultural Policy and Urban Regeneration. The West European Experience*, Manchester University Press, Manchester.
Dahlrot, E., Snickars, F. and Söderlind, J. (2001), *Culture as Infrastructure*, National Swedish Council for Cultural Development, Stockholm.
Fischer, M., Revilla Diez, J. and Snickars, F. (2001), *Metropolitan Innovation Systems – Theory and Evidence from Three Metropolitan Regions in Europe*, Springer Verlag, Heidelberg.
Frey, B. (2001), 'Cultural Economics – History and Theory', in F. Snickars (ed.), *Culture, society and market*, Bank of Sweden Tricentennary Fund and National Swedish Council for Cultural Development, Stockholm.
Gnad, F. (1998), 'Business, Location and Networks of Selected Companies in Culture Industries in the Region of Stockholm', *Working Paper, Department of Infrastructure and Planning, Royal Institute of Technology, Stockholm*.
Greffé, X. (1999), *L'emploi Culturel a L'âge du Numérique*, Anthropos, Paris.
Kunzmann, K. (2000), 'Culture industries in Europe – An introduction', in Ministry for Economics and Business, Technology and Transport (ed.), Culture industries in Europe – Regional development concepts for private-sector cultural production and services, *Proceedings from the European Congress of Experts held under the German Presidency of the European Union, Zeche Zollverein*, Essen, Germany.
Löfvenberg, M. (2001), 'Catalysing Culture', in F. Snickars, B. Olerup and L.O. Persson, (eds), *Reshaping Regional Planning*, Ashgate, Aldershot.
Ministry for Economics and Business, Technology and Transport (ed.) (2000), Culture industries in Europe – Regional development concepts for private-sector cultural production and services. *Proceedings from the European Congress of Experts held under the German Presidency of the European Union, Zeche Zollverein*, Essen, Germany.
Nutek (1998), *The Swedish National Innovation System – A Quantitative Study*, Report B1998:9, National Swedish Agency for Industrial and Technical Development, Stockholm.
Olsson, K. (2001), 'Planning for the Preservation of the Cultural Built Heritage', in F. Snickars, B. Olerup and L-O Persson (eds), *Reshaping Regional Plannning*, Ashgate, Aldershot.
Pine I, J., Gilmore, J. and Pine II, J. (1999), *The Experience Economy*, Harward Business School Press, Cambridge, Massachusetts.
Rader Olsson, A. (1999), 'The Impacts of Culture on Regional Development – Sponsor Value of Investment in Stockholm as Culture Capital of Europe 1998', *Working Paper, Department of Infrastructure and Planning*, Royal Institute of Technology, Stockholm.

Salinger, E. (1999), 'Forecasting International Tourist Flows – Stockholm as the Culture Capital of Europe 1998', *Master of Science Thesis, Department of Infrastructure and Planning*, Royal Institute of Technology, Stockholm.

Snickars, F. (2000), 'Some Consequences of the Project Cultural Capital of Europe 1998 for the Development of the Stockholm region', *Working Paper*, Department of Infrastructure and Planning, Royal Institute of Technology, Stockholm.

Snickars, F. (ed.) (2001), 'Culture, Society and Market', *Proceedings from international seminar held in Sigtuna. Bank of Sweden Tricentennary Fund and National Swedish Council for Cultural Development*, Stockholm.

Snickars, F., Olerup, B. and Persson, L.O. (eds) (2002), *Reshaping Regional Planning*, Ashgate, Aldershot.

Söderlind, J. (2000), 'Culture as Soft City Infrastructure', in Ministry for Economics and Business, Technology and Transport (ed.), Culture industries in Europe – Regional development concepts for private-sector cultural production and services. *Proceedings from the European Congress of Experts held under the German Presidency of the European Union*, Zeche Zollverein, Essen, Germany.

Vogel, H. (1998), *Entertainment Industry Economics*, Cambridge University Press, Cambridge.

Wolf, M. (1999), *Entertainment Economy: How Mega Media Forces are Transforming our Lives*, Times Books, New York.

Wynne, D. (1998), 'Planning for Cultural Quarters', *Working Paper*, Department of Sociology, Manchester Metropolitan University, Manchester.